ALSO BY MILOVAN DJILAS

Fall of the New Class

A History of Communism's Self-Destruction

EDITED BY DR. VASILIJE KALEZIĆ
TRANSLATED FROM THE SERBO-CROATIAN AND
WITH AN INTRODUCTION BY JOHN LOUD

ALFRED A. KNOPF NEW YORK 1998

MILOVAN DJILAS

FALL
OF
THE
NEW
CLASS

Portions of this book have been re-translated from Milovan Djilas's earlier works,
including *Land Without Justice, Anatomy of a Moral,*
Conversations with Stalin, Wartime, Tito, and *Rise and Fall.*

Library of Congress Cataloguing-in-Publication Data
Djilas, Milovan, 1911–1995.
Fall of the new class: a history of communism's self-destruction /
by Milovan Djilas; edited by Vasilije Kalezić. — 1st ed.
p.   cm.
Includes index.
ISBN 0-679-43325-2 (alk. paper)
1. Communism—History—20th cenury.   I. Kalezić, Vasilije.
II. Title.
HX40.D59   1998
335.4'09'04—dc21   97-49420   CIP

Manufactured in the United States of America
First Edition

CONTENTS

INTRODUCTION

This is a book about the loss of illusions.

Milovan Djilas was once infatuated with Stalin, but in the course of his actual encounters with the man (1944–1948) he became thoroughly disillusioned. This led directly to a loss of faith in the Soviet systems as such, then to disillusionment with his own Party in Yugoslavia. Djilas was expelled from its Central Committee early in 1954, turned in his Party card a few months later, and by the end of 1956 had landed in prison for daring to openly criticize the Red Army's suppression of the revolt in Hungary. That he should have become disenchanted with Tito is hardly surprising; yet Djilas, a man who did not stand still, also ended up rejecting communism as such, finding fault with the driving force behind it: the thirst for equality under law.

That was where he had started: the Montenegro of his childhood was a land without justice, meaning a land without a legal system for all. The thirst for social equality, as he explains in his first chapter, seemed to point to a society without divisions, a classless society. Now in retrospect, he charts the course taken. First, he had risen almost to the very top, to a point where he could do something about eradicating ancient class divisions, where society and man himself could be "perfected." But from those heights he saw that such a society probably could not be achieved after all, and began agitating for democratization within his own Party. Swiftly then, Djilas "fell": starting at the bottom again, he rethought his old ideals and concluded that any faith in perfection was a delusion, a false idea.

His expulsion from the Central Committee was the trigger. Indeed, it is specifically this that has always been termed his "fall": a fall from power. Djilas had been one of the four principal authorities in Yugoslavia during the nine years covered in the last volume of his memoirs, *Rise and Fall*. This book he himself titled *Vlast*, "power," or "the powers that be," the authorities; it dealt with his years in power, from 1945 to 1954. But the trajectory it traced suggested to the publisher of its English-language edition another, perhaps more evocative (and more marketable) title, and so it appears here as *Rise and Fall*. Djilas had risen to the heights of political power only to be expelled from that little Eden. And it was the "new class," essentially, of Communist bureaucrats that toppled and then ostracized him. He was not put to death but did suffer "political death," as Tito himself expressed it.

At this point Djilas still had forty years to live. During his first four decades, he had been by turns a revolutionary agitator, a revolutionary fighter, and a revolutionary politician. In the latter capacity he had done much journalistic editing and speech-making, of course, but writing of more permanent value was limited to the political essays published at the very end of his "political life," in 1953–54. All his major writing lay ahead. As one of Tito's three top administrators, Djilas had in effect laid the groundwork for his later, post-1954 renown as communism's first dissident of stature. Though his own literary bent and interests lay in fiction, as fate would have it he became famous primarily for his political thought. In the words of his close friend Matija Bećković at the 1995 graveside service held at his birthplace in Montenegro, "a great writer has died who had the ill luck to also be a politician." The books that brought Djilas fame were not fiction at all.

Most important was his ground-breaking analysis of Communist systems as they actually functioned, chiefly in the USSR, but throughout Eastern Europe as well: *The New Class* (1957). He may not actually have coined this phrase himself, but he was responsible for giving it wide currency, and the book's basic thesis—that communism really produced a class society—has ever since been identified with Djilas's name. Several books of memoirs followed: blow-by-blow accounts of Stalin and Stalin's words (*Encounters with Stalin*, 1962, translated as *Conversations with Stalin*), and then four whole volumes covering longer stretches in his life, detailed reminiscences of his boyhood, his career as a committed Communist, and the years up to his final release from prison at the very end of 1966—*Land Without Justice, Memoir of a Revolutionary, Wartime,* and *Rise and Fall.*

Djilas fell, but Djilas survived. He outlived Tito and his other enemies. He lived to write both fiction *and* nonfiction. He has the last word. Perhaps what he did best was a kind of fictionalized memoir, as illustrated at various key points in *Fall of the New Class.* In the first chapter, there are the four "what I learned from this experience" passages, dealing with his dawning disillusionment with Soviet communism and Stalin in particular. These are sharply set off from the surrounding material. (Throughout this introductory chapter, in fact, which Djilas wrote *after* the bulk of the book as a kind of overarching survey of his evolution as a thinker, he has pointed up many a sign of latent disaffection.)

The second major expression of this kind occurs in the seventh chapter: "The Closed Circle of the Privileged," another piece of semifiction. That essay, originally published on January 1, 1954, was the kind of attack on the "new class," focusing in this case on its women, that finally undid its author later that same month; for Tito, Djilas's erstwhile friend and "father-figure," it was the last straw. But in *our* hindsight, it was the piece of writing that released Djilas for his new life to come, his four decades of life as a world-class dissident. As he remarked at the end of his life, the nascent outlines of *The New Class* can be discerned in this essay.

The word "dissident" was borrowed by Serbians from Russian specifically to be applied to Djilas. His tenth chapter in the present work, which mainly concerns writers who were dissenters, includes himself as one of them in yet a third stretch of semifiction. "Of Prisons and the Sea" is a wistful, regretful look back at the time when he developed into a hardened Communist and, as such, learned not to speak up for others. He recalls here the relatively short period spent in Ada Ciganlija, a detention center for political prisoners on an island in the Sava River, before two and a half years in the penitentiary at Sremska Mitrovica. (Mitrovica was Djilas's *first,* prewar imprisonment.) Water provided the symbolic linkage between the long-ago and the here-and-now.

The present work was the last full-length manuscript under Djilas's own control. (To a subsequent book [1994] about a Bosnian intellectual figure, Adil Zulfikarpašić, he contributed only as an interlocutor.) Most of *Fall of the New Class* appears to be a compilation, a selection from previously published work. The principle of selection—what and why—has to interest us. For this is how Djilas saw himself at the end of his life, and how he wished to be seen in history. Hindsight, we know, tends to be selective. In the second chapter of this book (the beginning of his charted course), Djilas retells the incident of his strange vision of Christ, in 1943, while trying to sleep in the forest at night and under enormous stress. Today this account can be seen as marking the beginning of his future disenchantment with "classlessness."

As Djilas grew disillusioned with the Communist elite in his country, he wrote a "conte à clef" that depicted communism's privileged—and closed—circle, its denizens hungry for power, grasping at privileges, and in every way becoming a repulsive, pitiable repetition of all such "new classes" in history. This essay had been translated earlier as "Anatomy of a Moral." It leads directly to the next chapter (VIII), "The New Class," where communism's essence is defined as power: first the seizure of power, then the preservation of it.

Shedding the sharpest light on the subject is Chapter Ten's last section, concerning Gorbachev and the diehard Communists he raised to power. This is a newspaper clipping, published in Belgrade, "Gorbachev's Palace-Party Putsch." As he walked down the ramp off the plane that brought him back to Moscow safe and sound from his summer vacation, Gorbachev was heard to mutter that despite all, "the idea [of a classless society] was noble." To the contrary, it is ignoble, Djilas retorts in his *final* chapter (11), "The End in Grief and Shame." Society is inherently unperfectible and deeply flawed. Its evils cannot be eradicated—although man, in full awareness of this, is obliged to fight them nonetheless.

When Djilas was in power, he clearly didn't like Ivo Andrić, the future Nobel laureate, as opposed to Miroslav Krleža, whom he had once fought. But paradoxically he ends up taking Andrić's position: "For Andrić," he wrote in *Rise and Fall,* "to live meant to exist in more or less continuous pain and tragedy . . . he regarded history as a chain of error and evils, which culture only mitigates." In Andrić's native Bosnia, cutting off heads for public exposure was "normal," the writer once remarked in Djilas's hearing. He had discussed Bosnia, "land of hatred," in a semifictional story of his own (*Letter from the Year 1920,* published in 1945), which resembles Djilas's own best writing. There, Andrić's fictional protagonist discoursed on the seething hatred that pervaded the region and if "that volcano" ever did erupt—watch out. The volcano, of course, has erupted. In his last pages, Djilas too sees only "ethnic" hatred in the future for Eastern Europe, where antagonistic groups are forced to live cheek by jowl.

Djilas regarded the transfer of knowledge to others as as much an act of creation as fiction itself. And although that act of creation was painful, he took a grim pleasure in it. He speaks in this book's first chapter, for instance, of walking the streets at night thinking through his forthcoming work on communism, his "New Class": "Creation is the joy of suffering conscious of itself."

Serbs characteristically think of themselves as martyrs, as the world's victims. And they wouldn't have it any other way. The Serbs are close in spirit to the Byzantine world and its values. All know the epic story of Tsar Lazar and his dream on the eve of Kosovo: You can have victory on the battlefield tomorrow—or you can have death, and therefore spiritual survival, a spot in heaven. Spurious or not, a concoction of the Church or not (true oral epic is more concerned with the mythic than with any imitation of Christ), the fact that this story is known to every Serb says something about their otherworldliness. They are proud of their defeat by Murad, proud of having been trampled for 500 years. Pride in defeat: is this not Milovan Djilas too? He, too, was first and foremost a Serb. Djilas, too, was defeated. But he rose above his defeat. Not for five centuries, of course, but for at least forty-one years. His message is: "We cannot eradicate evil, evil is real, a palpable presence. Man and society are *un*perfectible. But love your struggle, your conscious, despairing struggle." It is a profoundly, characteristically Serbian as well as human message. "Grief and shame" there may well be, but this is not the end. The story goes on.

ACKNOWLEDGMENT

I learned my first lessons in the translation of Milovan Djilas from Drenka Willen, my editor at Harcourt Brace Jovanovich. It was she who wrote in the margin of an early draft of my translation of Djilas's memoir *Vlast,* "You already used this word two pages ago," and again, where I had translated the original's simple verb "to be" as "were," she had remonstrated, "Use 'embarked upon.'" In short, don't be loath to strike out freely in paraphrase; don't be a slave to the text. These were lessons learned and applied.

WORDS AS WORDS, STYLE AS STYLE

As with any language, some words in Serbian create peculiar difficulties for the translator. *Vlast,* "power," the original title of Djilas's *Rise and Fall* (a title that rides on Gibbon and one that was only later bestowed on the book, by its publisher, William Jovanovich), often recurs in the original text of the present work. *Vlast* means both power in general and power in particular (not horsepower). On the first page of Chapter Two, to choose one instance, the author wrote (in literal translation): "radical decisions were already announced by the creation of new power," meaning the communist regime that replaced the royal one of King Peter. The word here combines the idea of control with those who were exercising control, the rulers, the "new class." Here I had recourse to "power structure" (a jargon term of our own). Elsewhere I have often used "the authorities," "the powers that be," or some more extensive paraphrase in lieu of just plain "power." The term comes up so frequently in Djilas as to suggest an obsession with the concept of "power," even apart from what he says about communism and Communists.

Two troublesome terms that very often crop up in Djilas (perhaps reflecting his Hegelian heritage), as if on purpose to obfuscate the thought, are *saznanje,* "realization," and *svest,* "consciousness," which combine philosophical and psychological implications. The author usually intends something like "the sum total of my experience translated into conscious knowledge." It is difficult to render these terms in ways that carry the full meaning to us. I have often thought to paraphrase, translating not only as "realization" or "understanding," but at times as "the ripening of my conscious awareness."

Some words that look like an English counterpart must be spelled out: *forma,* as used by Djilas, does not mean simply "form" but "political structure," and often occurs where English would say "pattern."

In Chapter Ten, the word that would normally be rendered as "dissidence" became "dissent" because the English words "dissidents" and "dissidence" are homonyms.

The word "vila," meaning a large house in a residential area (and thus cognate to the Italian and our own word "villa"), naturally occurs often in any book on the mode of life of the "new class." This is how the elite referred to their residences in Belgrade. It was carried over by

Djilas to the Russian situation, and earlier translations always refer, for instance, to Stalin's "villa" outside Moscow. The word is not used in Russian, however, and even looks absurd. In this translation it is always rendered "dacha" in any Russian context, as that is how Russians refer to their own shelters (even garden houses) or residences outside cities, humble or not, elite or not.

Paragraphing generally follows the original, but I have split up some particularly lengthy ones and run together a good many two-liners. There were many ellipses within and between paragraphs, probably indicating the start and finish of omitted material. Djilas also employed more dashes in place of stops than is customary today in non-epistolary English prose. These may sometimes have been deliberate, to impart a certain breathlessness or immediacy to his narration. In this translation the dashes are usually replaced by periods, or colons, or some subordinating conjunction.

I have not hesitated to break up sentences as well. Djilas habitually wrote extremely long sentences, with many parenthetical afterthoughts (placed between dashes), as if he were giving a speech. His written prose therefore cries out for at least some degree of cleaning up. In dealing with these long sentences, I have tried to turn this writer's very journalistic prose into plain written English, and to that extent have rewritten him. The concluding paragraphs of sections 6-8-9-10 in the first chapter, however, "what I learned from . . . ," each consist of one very long run-on sentence, and these I have indented to make them stand out from the surrounding text. (Indents are not used in the original.) Given that extended sentences are a feature of the author's writing generally, here they notably represent a deliberate attempt to convey a stream of consciousness in which the meaning is free to wander off on its own. (Particularly the last in the sequence.) If these, along with the semifictional story told in "The Closed Circle of the Privileged," are viewed stylistically together with the author's works of fiction, we see here an experiment in fusing fiction with memoir. The purpose of the experiment (if such it be) is to mark stages of doubt, like the vision of Christ taken from the author's *Wartime.*

The typewritten manuscript is speckled with emendations and marginal additions written in by hand. I have drawn attention in my notes to those that seemed important.

Another marked characteristic of Djilas was that he liked to dot every i, to cross every blessed t, even when his meaning was clear—probably a legacy from his years as an official, a bureaucrat, a "functionary." One regularly occurring Serbian word is *odnosno*, "meaning," "that is," "in other words." This has been glossed over in various ways and sometimes simply forgotten about. As I tracked the existing translations in English of Djilas's many books, the silent omission of this stylistic tic became obvious. Other translators or editors have done the author a great service in virtually rewriting him so that he "reads well" (or tolerably well) in English.

MATERIALS PREVIOUSLY PUBLISHED

I have made my own translation, treating every chapter as fresh material but checking against previous work wherever an "original" could be detected. *Vlast* has already been printed (London, 1983), as has this book too: *Pad nove klase: povest o samorazaranju komunizma* (Belgrade, 1994). The author himself refers to the Serbian publication of his *Conversations with Stalin* (Belgrade: Kniževne novine, 1990). Chapter notes give details. In most cases the present text tracks the earlier one (or its translation) sequentially but seldom quotes verbatim.

Judging from what he chose to leave *in,* one would suppose Djilas is building a case for his latent disaffection from Communism, once Communism came to power—disaffection from the "new class." Take, for example, his lengthy description of Tito being congratulated by all his cronies ("Djido"—Djilas's pet name—was there too behind the stage at AVNOJ), coupled with the routinized applause (see pp. 34–35 in this book; also *Wartime,* pp. 361–62).

In Chapter 10, all the subchapters had been published in the media in the original. (The last one in the series, "The Kremlin's Palace-Party Putsch," is presented not even in typed form but as a photocopy of a newspaper article.) The final words (in the hand of the author) are "End of August 1991." One can read faintly through the blackout that this was actually August 12–24. Judging from the subject matter, the series as a whole dates back to the waning days of Gorbachev in late 1991, while the earliest in the series seems to have been written in the 1960s. Each subchapter concludes with a dateline that has been carefully inked out.

Fall of the New Class

1 THE DEVELOPMENT OF MY POLITICAL THINKING

I decided to trace the course of my political thinking to its final outcome only out of a conviction that this would help the reader better understand the book to come. For me, thought and reflection have always closely accompanied active participation in the political events through which I have lived, and it is this intimate relationship that mainly drives my discussion. However, I will try not to discuss events as such except as they accompany or encompass speculative thought. This is a book about the effort exerted by a certain way of thinking to first grasp a given reality and then to reject it. Originally that reality was the "bourgeois," non-Communist one, which I thought of as evil and wicked simply because it had given birth to me, even if through no fault of my own. Then I tried to comprehend the Communist reality. For its sake I fought like a zealot, never suspecting that this Communist reality would turn out quite the opposite of all I ever wanted or believed in.

Whether one accepts such realities as given or exchanges them for others, it is hopeless to expect that they will conform to one's own desires and efforts. Man once born becomes what he will become, striving to make reality adapt to him or himself to it. I chose communism because reality, not suiting my temper, was not Communist. I may not have been born a Communist but I was predestined to become one by my own nature: impatient of wrong, mindful of the poor, undeterred by violence, believing in the natural equality of all persons—in short, I craved absolute freedom and believed that the path to this final goal was realistic.

The reader may find it hard to credit, but I felt myself to be a Communist even at the age of seven or eight. This was perhaps because my poor, downtrodden fellow villagers and renegades would tease me or (the main reason) because I aspired to be outstanding. That sense of being a Communist stayed with me through all ebbs and flows up to the moment I matriculated as a university student in Belgrade in 1929.

For I was not driven to communism by material circumstance, nor by some intellectual family birthright, nor especially by national tradition. All else remaining equal, if the times had been other than they were, so too would I have been different. It was not I who found communism but communism me, as a convenient medium. I was pliant material for its purposes.

Add to personal inclination the sturdy, martial legacy of Montenegro and our national tradition of heroic song and the epic, and the path pointing to revolutionary answers, if not smooth and straight, nevertheless could be regarded as an honorable path for me personally and one that also offered hope for the needy and disenfranchised.

There is in each of us a Communist spirit: hunger for fair dealing and social equality. This is a hunger that is felt more or less strongly, as the case may be. Such a spirit need only encounter ideas and movements worthy of it. After passing through the crucible of actual politics, the hopes of its true believers, and the battle for political power, the spirit is transformed. Something of the sort happens with other elementary feelings and political movements. Man is a social animal (Aristotle's *zoon politikon*) and so at the mercy of his own, idealized victories, whatever their moral outcome.

This spirit of communism (if such it can be called) I discovered within myself. I found it in literary classics (especially the Russian ones); I found it in good friendships; and I found it in the repudiation of political conditions. From puberty onward I had cherished a dawning impulse to create literature. Little by little this impulse became engaged by my thirst for a better world, a more righteous world. Art and politics, while not identical, are each creative in their effects: The one turns the horizon into something magic, the other brings about bliss through pain. For this reason I was not drawn to socialist realism.[1] (True, at one time I had to defend it as a part of doctrine.) A work of art as I saw it was either a work of art or not, regardless of its theme or the writer's political stance.

As a student I was not industrious. I did write, however, and so far as the short story form was concerned, I wrote copiously. At the same time I was a social malcontent. I was a Communist who had nothing to do with Communists. The existing regime in Yugoslavia, a dictatorship, had in any event put the Communists to rout and demoralized them. Besides, I knew nothing of Communist teaching save what I had heard about martyrdom and an idealistic movement. It was like some new religion, all the more attractive for being brutally persecuted.

The existing government itself set up the conditions for revolt by students when single-party elections were held in the autumn of 1931. The most rebellious flocked together in kindred groups. As one of the instigators, I found myself among the leftists. Supporters of the proscribed urban parties included educated, cultivated young people; those who were the most militant joined the rural parties. We leftists, though, Communists judging from all we had heard about communism, were by definition the most active in preparing and leading demonstrations on the eve of these elections. To our surprise, the regime was relatively gracious toward "its own" young people and I too, after going into hiding followed by a short prison term, was set free under the presumed surveillance of an informer.

Our groups purged themselves of the unreliable and the wavering and gradually consolidated their strength. We ran across brochures explaining the Marxist viewpoint, brochures that intoxicated us for all their superficial, popularizing tone. We thirsted for the narcotic of truth, new and final truth, truth that had been blocked at one blow by the dictatorship. True, government censorship provided some respite to leftist periodicals. In their Aesopian language these propagated such themes as a "scientific outlook on the world" and "the modern scientific perspective."

There can be no disputing the fact that a consistently revolutionary, Communist organization at the University of Belgrade dates from this time. It was never successfully broken up by the police and it spread its influence over the majority of the students. It was the strongest organization in Yugoslavia and contributed to the revolution a significant number of leaders.

The Party's so-called rightist faction was the first to get wind of us, slipping us illicit brochures that were hard to find and trying to make us, who were already organized, organize. Only in the autumn of 1932 did we establish contact with the actual, official Party, though in Belgrade, as elsewhere, there existed hardly more than some kind of agency for the Communist Party.

It was we who carried out the first demonstrations against the dictatorship. It was we who rallied and defined who we were without benefit of Party affiliation: Communists without a Party, Communists without theory. Prior to the royal dictatorship a semilegal Communist Party had idly slumbered. Now, a shattered political life was giving rise to young forces prepared to suffer and ready for relentless struggle. These were ready to hand, ideal material for that victorious and insistent variant of communism called Stalinism.

From the very start I found myself caught in a dilemma: Was I a writer, or was I a revolutionary? The first drew me with compelling power. To the second I surrendered myself as one surrenders to duty and (I think) to pride and the special vanity of wanting not to lag behind one's flock. I was responsible for toughening them. If I were to back off now, could they read it otherwise than as the coward's way out? The path of literature was simply more comfortable and less dangerous. To this very day the dilemma remains: I would be happier writing stories on themes long dreamed about than to be composing this book. But that would mean to cut and run from the critique of Communist ideology and practice that I myself set in motion many years ago, when I first put aside my beloved literary dreams and often exposed myself and those nearest me to unforeseen difficulties.

In thrall to literature, only half-baked ideologically, bonded to my girl by an unconsummated love, I was arrested in the spring of 1933, tortured, and sentenced to three years at hard labor. That experience brought about my early, half-conscious disappointment in the workers. Workers under torture proved to be more spineless than intellectuals! Both theory and my own way of thinking had held, to the contrary, that laborers were paragons of toughness and consistency, especially by comparison with "confused little intellectual types."

When the prison gates closed for good behind anyone sentenced for political reasons, when Siberia opened its arms, there would ensue much weeping and wailing. You were parting company forever with everything and everybody—except, of course, your own miserable, not to say bitter, life in the flesh. But there was no choice, no turning back. Only the poor in spirit tried to turn back. Only traitors to an idea and to themselves. Either you endured in pride or you lost your identity in shame. Obsessed with masochist heroism as I was, I had no second thoughts about choosing to endure. Even so, I cherished the hope that time and circumstance would favor my writing fiction, prison or no prison. Such wishful thinking had to be choked off and smothered from the very first. In a Communist collective any free time was taken up by studying Marxism and by Party debates. We possessed the basic Marxist texts, we had literate, well-drilled teachers. In such surroundings, lacking any newspapers, relying on mere scraps of whispered information gleaned from the monthly visits of family and friends, my understanding of Marxist theory grew purified and refined. This process of purification went on without interruption. It became part of my dream life. Only the topics changed.

The Stalinist brand of Leninism had now come to dominate the Yugoslav Party. And it was here at hard labor that Stalinism could be seen at its most rigid, most uncompromising. It would be oversimplified and somehow off the mark to think that personality got lost in that seething, ideological cauldron of revolutionaries. To remain obdurate before authority, to display one's loyalty to the collective, to be a zealous student wholeheartedly eager to deepen one's grasp of doctrine— these were qualities that bore witness precisely to the personal, to the individual. Stalin's authority was beyond question, but it was the authority of a political leader, not that of the incarnation of an idea and a movement. Yugoslav Stalinists were such only by political orientation, something that could most clearly be seen under hard-labor conditions. They were not Stalinists by nature or because they had been intellectually emasculated. Leninism, and Stalinism in particular, were chiefly understood in their revolutionary aspect; their power-grasping, tyrannical side was not perceived. Theory was a living, spiritual weapon of revolution, not gelded or petrified dogma. Debates were very often fiery but they were free, although they took place, of course, within the framework of the Party line and the general assumptions of Marx and Lenin. For though Stalinism is indivisible, it is not uniform. National variations exist. As theory, Stalinism is neither original nor homogeneous. It is a only a gathering of theories. That, plus a well-defined and consistently totalitarian practice.

Prison put the finishing touches on my Marxist education. What with the prison authorities on the one hand and my demands on my own self on the other, my nerves were in a constant jangle. I was overwrought.

Preoccupied with group study, sharing everything with my collective, from little lumps of sugar and thin slices of bacon or soap to the occasional, smuggled cigarette, I became tempered as a Communist. I learned quickly and easily and became a teacher in my turn. Communist "science" (as it was called) was simple and involved little of the mystery that ordinarily veiled its crude outlines behind Hegel's complex style and explication. Marxist teaching and Leninist doctrine merged with the legacy of epic poetry and my personal devotion to the ideals of brotherhood and equality. Moreover, I conceived of communism as absolute freedom. The Communist movement and the daily work of a Communist may not have been to everyone's liking, and under certain circumstances they were unavoidably harsh, but I understood them to be the "scientifically revealed" path to freedom. Nor were the sparks of my fantasy life in literature quite extinguished there, either. More than once, dreams sadly flickered to life as I first composed, then memorized, literary motifs. Even in prison I tried to impart a literary touch whenever I argued and to whatever I said, to add a dash of my personal style and language as it existed off the podium.

True, true believer in communism! Endlessly fretting over your failures! Ever in the throes of adapting practice to an ideal!

After emerging from hard labor in 1936 I thought I would be returning to literature, for I was to edit an illegal journal for the Party and so would have made my influence felt on its cultural and political work in the legal domain. But Satan sleepeth not! Hardly had I taken up my duties when the police penetrated Party organizations in Belgrade and northern Serbia, breaking up all assemblies and arresting a considerable number of members. Only the university organization held on.

Since I was by now well known among Communists and had the look of a convict, the remnants of the Party and the media under its influence turned to me. At first, most of the work and responsibility fell to my lot. From dawn till late at night I was busy with the work of the Party, until I would literally collapse from fatigue. Nor did things get any easier for me when the organization came back to life once more and stood on its own two legs. In 1937–38 Tito[2] arrived from Moscow to head the Party, and along with others I was taken by him into the innermost circle of leadership (the Politburo), a move soon to be confirmed by the Comintern. Of the yearning for literary creation there remained only restless dreams. But impact I did have—as, often, I was supposed to have—on the leftist cultural and antifascist movement. I was at once the editor and the only writer for an illegal journal, *Komunist*. At last the theory I had mastered at hard labor could be put into effect and made to fit reality. I was all the more reliable for being an intellectual well drilled (as they said) in Marxism, and all the more zealous for having outlived thereby, all unawares, my enforced literary sterility.

It was a time when the Party was finally becoming "Bolshevized" in the Yugoslav way (or more exactly, Stalinized). Taking little thought in advance and without the slightest hesitation, the Party was incorporating a kind of revolutionary brotherhood and unsparing self-criticism. If I was not the first in this regard, I was surely among the first: the true believer, molding himself into a Communist missionary. Thus we Yugoslav Communists, not even daring to think what we were about, were unwittingly outpacing our model, the Russian Bolsheviks. It was all in tune with my puritanical leanings and played up to my militancy. At some later time a final decision could be made with regard to literary work, with its characteristically long and tormented period of reflection and meditation.

In the midst of my fiery ascent to the heights of Bolshevism I came into conflict with a renowned leftist and man of letters, Miroslav Krleža.[3] Krleža after World War I had been a Party member. At the time of savage harassment of Communists when the Party was being demolished, he withdrew from active participation in its life. Never, though, did he cut his ties with the Party entirely, no more than he ceased to subject all existing institutions, especially European militarism, to his own poetic brand of criticism. In the meantime the Soviet Union had evolved from Leninism to Stalinism and the Yugoslav Party had arrived at a watershed. The "Krleža" generation of leaders, which had grown out of the left Social Democrats, to the extent it had not been neutralized or destroyed by the Soviet purges, had been replaced by a new, younger generation, tempered in struggle with the royal dictatorship and steeled in Stalinist doctrine. Krleža, knowing them as he did, could not accept the new leaders with their simplistic, uncompromising views and hot-tempered ways. He was also deeply shocked by the Soviet purges of the 1930s, where ruthless bloodshed was steeped in slander. Partly by indirect hints, partly in the form of literary criticism, he mounted an attack on the Party and its policies. And since he enjoyed (with good reason) enormous prestige both in literary and in non-Communist urban circles, his criticisms had a devastating impact.

This was especially true among the left intellectuals in Croatia. Schism threatened. There was vacillation within an illegal Party that had managed finally to consolidate itself through pain and sacrifice in the midst of a war in Europe (1940) and on the verge of a likely invasion by Nazis and Fascists. I took the initiative to part with Krleža clearly and with energy, and to subject his positions to a critique. This found favor with the leadership, including Tito. (Tito was still in Moscow when the confrontation began.) Krleža's views were suppressed and repudiated, and even though I still valued him highly as a writer, it spelled my coming of age as a revolutionary as well as the maturation of the Party as a revolutionary movement. True believers thus confirmed their "belief." Although Krleža was right to think that one's artistic work should be independent of any political party, when I look back now I still think that his political views, even with no prospects of being taken up in the Party core, did sow doubts and hesitation among sympathizers, both at the center and throughout the periphery, at a time when the coming military occupation was to bestow upon us the leading role as the most consistent, most organized, anti-Fascist revolutionary force.

Each revolution is special and shuns all preconceived schemes. No revolution's course can be predicted, even by its protagonists. The Yugoslav revolution too had its unique features and unforeseen contingencies, to unravel which there is no space here. It is important simply to say that our revolution was an inextricable tangle of rebellion against an occupying force combined with a civil war, a *war within a war* waged against a conquering enemy. All Communist opponents, even those who took a principled stand against the invaders or who had personal reasons for being opposed to them, aligned themselves one way or another with the occupation forces. As a result, the course of war impelled the Western allies (Great Britain) to accept as allies the Communists, Communists being the strongest fighting force on their side.

Before the civil war ever flared up, at the very start, I judged that what was at issue was an anti-Fascist revolution whose whole idea was that all opponents of fascism, whether foreign or homegrown, must coalesce into a militant partnership. The Party leadership, however, meaning Tito and Edward Kardelj, in line with prevailing policy and conforming to Moscow's relations with the West, criticized my formulation. They maintained that what was at issue in Yugoslavia was not revolution but a national liberation struggle. Tito and the other leaders thought that any allusion to revolution, even an anti-Fascist one, was limiting and off-putting. I myself saw no great difference, though to me the term "national liberation" as such lacked clarity.

Many years later, following the Soviet confrontation in 1948 and when the rights we had won in our struggle deserved the spotlight, an idea took hold, mainly on the basis of my pronouncements, that it was indeed a revolution we had produced within the war, a Yugoslav revolution. And yet out of that disagreement with the leaders, meaningless now but for my memory of it, I drew self-confidence and learned a moral lesson. This was to be disciplined and to subscribe in good faith to the views of the majority but at the same time, deep inside, not to yield to pragmatic, everyday, political "generalizations." To have a mind of one's own and think for oneself while at the same time doing what has to be done.

Yet war and revolution not only left indelible imprints on my thinking and on me as a writer but also indirectly and gradually, just because they were indelible, essentially stamped the way I formulated them.

At first the civil war, treacherously and unexpectedly insinuating itself into the struggle against the occupation forces, caused me to lose heart. Evil was a necessity, evil was inescapable, but this was evil beyond any other. I used to imagine revolution and civil war as a process of lining up the troops in two classes, bourgeois and proletarian; I had imagined them as making war in the cities, fighting for the great urban centers; but this war, this revolution, had degenerated into a village bloodletting among predominantly working people, often even between neighbors and close relatives. Periodically it assumed such cruel forms that the fight against the occupying power blurred over and receded into the background. My imagined ideological confrontation, like my ideological motivation, grew pale and twisted. What kind of ideology was this, what kind of Marxism that, instead of taking up arms against the bourgeoisie and the exploiters, fought the little people of the villages and towns, the petty employees and peasants? And what kind of Serbs and nationalists were they who accepted weapons from the occupier, fed in his mess halls, and collaborated in his military operations?

I myself was implicated in this double-edged war, and among the most responsible, at that. There was a strict mandate to carry out the Party line, the Party's decisions. They were all the more mandatory in that I agreed with this line and had even helped make the decisions. Man may be the creator of his own history, but man is also history's victim. Nonetheless, alongside my own belligerence and inseparable from it, an inexplicable, boundless sadness could seize hold of me, especially when I found myself alone after witnessing fearful events. Was this the way things had to be? Could they not be otherwise? A vague awareness would come over me that our own peoples, the peoples of Yugoslavia, primarily Serbs and Croats, had stumbled into a great and irreversible disaster. In time, with my estrangement from communism and Communists, this awareness would take firm and unbending shape:

> *no greater misery* can befall a people than civil war, the kind of war in which no one side is ever guilty—or rather all sides alike are guilty, and to emerge the victor means little or nothing so far as history is concerned, only misery being the winner, misery that so far as I am aware not a single people has ever avoided, and it may not only be simply the product of some specific, unsolved and unsolvable, political relationship but instead arises out of mankind's sleep-drugged, potential nature, or is the outcome of those who extravagantly want change—often with reason— vying with those who grip fast to a given reality and obstinately, stupidly, with all their might and main thwart change.[4]

For nearly six months without letup a German-Italian offensive had been under way in an effort to destroy the heaviest concentrations of Partisan troops around our Supreme Staff. The culminating battle arrived and I found myself the senior man politically, my only companions the gravely wounded and units that were encircled. At dawn on June 13, 1943, we attacked a network of SS bunkers and ramparts amid a hail of machine-gun and artillery fire. Units that just that morning had been well bloodied, some left with only a third of their complement, were now nearly cut in half. Commanders and commissars alike were mowed down in the act of making hopeless assaults; non-Communist patriots fell too. The renowned rebel commander Sava Kovačević was killed. We leaders, along with a group of fighters from the splintered units, withdrew into a craggy, wooded ravine.

During the night I awoke. All around me, in the soft light of the moon filtering through the thick treetops, slept our soldiers. Then between the tree trunks and branches appeared the countenance of Christ. As the night wore on, whether before or after that unexpected vision I can't say, I kept fitfully reflecting on this vision, asking myself: *What force drives men to exterminate each other?* Obviously it could not be just ideology—particularly the Nazi one, simplistic and antihuman. Yet national discipline, even German national discipline, also was inadequate to explain this sheer destructiveness. What was it that drove Heidelberg professors and the descendants of Hanseatic patricians to flounder about in the wilds of Montenegro and Bosnia for the purpose of taking the lives of herdsmen and students, for the purpose of dispatching the wounded and the unlucky wherever they lay hidden, and for the purpose of killing off Jews the length and breadth of Europe? If such slaughter could not be explained by Nazi ideology, was it on the other hand really our own ideology that drove us Communists to hurl our own people into death, to drag our own men and women into our own deadly whirlwind? Even if our own people were in fact dying for their mother's breast, for their human and ethnic identity? No, it was not just ideology, *neither ours nor theirs*, it was *some inexplicable force* that ideology, politics, and the nation sensed to be lurking within peoples and ethnic groups, that was indeed found where it was suspected of being, and that was then used for "exalted purposes." That *something* is a basic quality. Only the inspiration of art can articulate this essential something, somehow, *in its own way;* only the mystical ecstasies of the believer, only the insights of the philosopher.[5]

But meditations such as these, or rather such presentiments, such self-questioning, were overshadowed by new military problems, by assignments that could not be postponed, and by more important obligations. Above all I was slated to go to Moscow in the spring of 1944 as part of a military mission, when I could at long last realize my dream of meeting the living incarnation of an idea—Stalin.[6]

There will be much to say about Stalin later in this book. Here I would only point up what had an impact on my intellectual development.

In the Kremlin I approached Stalin in an ecstasy of idolatry that had first taken root during my years at hard labor and had later been whipped into a passion during the "Bolshevization," or Stalinization, era of my Party. For all that, I was still capable of forming a healthy impression of Stalin even when we first met, though this impression was as yet raw and undigested. I was especially rational at our second encounter on the night of the fifth and sixth of June, in his dacha outside Moscow.

What especially stood out with Stalin and captivated a listener was the absence of trite phrases, of clichés. Even when he showed his true colors as a demagogue and trickster, Stalin did so in such a crisp and weighty, confidence-inspiring manner that he bewitched not only his conversational partner but himself as well. Or if he wanted the person talking with him to think he was being led by the nose, then that too was exactly the way it was and what Stalin really wanted. He got right to the heart of a matter with lightning speed and in such a way that little or nothing was left to discuss and resolve. Stalin was decisive. Even at those moments when, like any human being, he might have been mistaken or uninformed, he acted decisively and scarcely hesitated. Such raw, naked realism made Stalin the true representative of both the problems and the answers to them that were vital for his country, as for his political power, and vital for his people—as he, of course, understood these and wanted them to appear. To Stalin, not only the world of politics but also the world in general was a world of enemies, real or potential. If you wanted to survive as your own master, you dared not trust a soul. Everyone but yourself was either a crook or a knave. You had to battle it out, you dared not rely on anyone's strength but your own. Take no action ahead of time, but also don't delay. Be master of time and man. Only thus is history made. Such is true history. To Stalin, Machiavelli's prince would have been a blushing acolyte.

Here, then, is what I learned in the Soviet Union from Stalin and from Soviet conditions, such as I understood them to be:

we Yugoslav Communists, being undeviating internationalists, were tied to the Soviet Union and had to remain so and yet . . . and yet we had to solve our problems of national policy all by ourselves, for they, too—Stalin and the other Soviet leaders—they, too, were before all else turned inward and preoccupied with their own country, of that there could be no doubt, the reasons for it being probably enemy encirclement, long isolation, and, more specifically, Russian backwardness, while we on the other hand were relatively developed, some parts of Yugoslavia being close to the level of Western Europe, added to which our socialism was somewhat different, but we dared not lean on the West for support unless it be in our safe and secure interest, for the West was anti-Communist and our enemies' friend, through whom they hoped to perpetuate their influence and safeguard interests that had broken the back of our national struggle for liberation.

Such was the insight I carried back with me from my first stay in the Soviet Union. My colleagues had come to the same understanding independently. As for my second visit, in 1945, in the capacity of an unrepentant penitent before Stalin (owing to my having "insulted" the Red Army)—it left me harboring doubts. From my third visit, at the beginning of 1948 I returned a faultfinder, disappointed with nearly everything in the "first land of socialism," while yet remaining insufficiently critical toward the idea of communism, as such, and its embodiment in Stalin. I still cherished the delusion that *they*, the Soviets, had not yet put everything well into practice, whereas He, now an old man, was inadequately informed. To attain to a full understanding, to have the courage to embark on the path of final criticism, one has to live long enough to grasp that one's own political reality (I being among its creators) is a lie, a delusion, a dead end. To shake oneself loose from an ideal, to emancipate oneself from a faith, is always a painful and slow process, more painful and slower than choosing to serve that ideal in the first place.[7]

Victory takes a very different shape from the way it is expected or foreseen.

Thus I, too, was taken by surprise at the ending of war. I had anticipated hardships and what we called national renewal and reconstruction. I had imagined that victory, which is to say the war's end, would confer freedom on everyone alike, liberating Communists and lifting the restraints of Party affiliation. A brotherhood of Communists, though begun already in wartime by the Party and military hierarchies and by the cults of Stalin and Tito, would readily spread to all Yugoslavia's citizens. For me, freedom did not consist of this or that political structure but instead meant freeing up a whole way of life. Freedom would begin by abolishing exploitative, capitalist property and class ownership and would continue by destroying capitalist representatives and lackeys. In short, freedom meant empowering working people. I had imagined myself as finally set free from Party responsibilities and everyday political work. I would be a free writer, a writer who was a Communist.

It all turned out otherwise. The exact opposite. The debasement and betrayal of an idea and of oneself began first with the Communists, and (it could be said with equanimity) only with them. As for their hangers-on, it must be remembered that Communists held absolute power. There ensued the looting of villas and riches, including personal property, and finally the fabrication of charges against many proprietors—that is, charges of collaboration with the enemy. Still more drastic action was taken against the owners of factories, banks, workshops, trade establishments, and large estates. Not that I was against punishing collaborators: They were being meted out the same measures the length and breadth of Europe. No mercy was shown them there, either, by victorious anti-Fascism. Nor, naturally, was I opposed to nationalizing big property. For Communists, being in power presupposed socialization of the capitalist mode of production. It was the very basis of power, and the only way to construct a classless society.

And yet the thought plagued me of having to devise false, shameful reasons for reaching this end. Justice and truth, no matter how savage, should be unmarred and unclouded for every person. In those days the absolute power that victory had brought Tito was transforming his personality into a cult right alongside the cult of Stalin. I had always inwardly protested all cults, particularly the ones within the Communist movement, if only because I considered that they were at variance with basic Communist teaching and Communist friendship, and that they signified undeniably and surely the transformation of a revolutionary movement into a power-grasping, bureaucratic one. The new state more and more resembled an absolutist police state in its capacity to throw off the habit of trite phrasemaking. Without terror and a monopoly over Party and state, Tito could never have been anything more than a distinguished revolutionary leader. Maintaining that semblance, he subjugated Party and state to his absolutist rule while at the same time getting rid of revolutionaries by fair means or foul. Here we had a little Stalin, one who was a bit more temperate, one who operated in a small, nonimperialist country.

Such political power first arose and flourished under conditions of revolutionary war. But it consolidated into limitless terror only out of fear for its own survival and its standing in the outside world, and out of fear for a loss of influence within the country. A conquered and armed enemy was now replaced by a hypothetical, potential, political enemy—the remnants of fascism and reaction.

This was the most barren and painful period in my life, especially in my intellectual life. To the extent that Party and state obligations permitted, I withdrew into solitude. But those obligations consisted of meeting people and reading endless papers and projects, exasperating tasks. It was as if everything had been said in advance, all decisions made. Theoretical speculation was now, under better circumstances, reduced to monotonously belaboring the trivialities and generalizations already voiced by the founders of Marxism-Leninism, while practice was largely reduced to imitating Soviet experience. Light and life had become enclosed by a crust of dogma or by trumped-up claims of hostility. I found myself psychologically and mentally disoriented, disengaged. I was not willing or able to abandon myself to such victor's perquisites as come with total power, nor had I the knowledge or skill to set such power to rights, even within my own self. Besides, in secret I was always grieving for my two fallen brothers, my slain sister, my murdered father. Little by little we all were turning willy-nilly into imitators of a foreign power, politically, turning into courtiers and clerks for our own ambitious master.

What do I now conclude about that time lost?

> victory won by blood in a civil war is more destructive and poisonous for the victors than for the vanquished because defeat ennobles some at least of the conquered, lifting them out of their wretched adversity, while the victors, almost without exception awash in the spoils of war, lapse into spiritual decay and so no one, least of all a man of thought, ought to take much joy in victories like these and this is all the more true since it is wishful, stupid thinking to believe that your enemy and compatriot has been annihilated merely because he has been beaten, for just like you, the winner, he too is a product of the same vital spirit, the same tradition, the same national attainments, he emerges from the same national community, and the time will come when he will rise again, if only as a plaintiff in the court of history and unerring justice.

Where this path might have taken me I do not know, nor how I might have extricated myself, but I would have had to remove myself somehow from a bureaucratic reality that had gone stale and where I myself was disintegrating had there not intervened an underground dialogue in the top ranks involving critical, questioning observations and disagreement with the Soviet government.

On the history of that confrontation much has been written. Soviet attempts to treat Yugoslavia as a vassal state, its colonial domain, were beyond dispute but have been given too much attention. The confrontation actually began—how else under communism?—in Soviet attempts to assist their military and political intelligence organs in imposing control over our leading Party and state organs, meaning the established power structure. A similar train of events took place when they browbeat the conquered lands of Eastern Europe. Here, they began by bickering and squabbling with the Yugoslav political police and by trying to gain power over the media, which I was in charge of.

To back up even further, when it all began at the end of 1944 I was witness to this confrontation at first hand. The Soviet leadership, now grown conservative, tried to keep a young, revolutionary Yugoslav force from developing independently and thereby from broadening its own influence and contributing to the theory and practice of Soviet socialism. My remarks to that effect, however, were subdued and indirect, buried in the tightest circle of leadership. This circle had already closed ranks around Tito in the prewar period of illegal struggle, and our ensuing sacrifices, our suffering, the exploits of both Party and people as they made war against the Nazi and Fascist occupiers and their quislings and supporters, had only further toughened and hardened the leaders.

Within that circle we used to debate deep into the night, trying to find answers, leafing through the Marxist classics to penetrate the meaning of what we viewed as Soviet deviation, trying to understand the metamorphosis of the Soviet Union into an imperialistic power. How? How come? Who? It was a case of fresh, consistent dogmatism against ossified, utilitarian dogma.

No matter how preoccupied we were dogmatically with finding a more honest path than the Soviet one, however, we were at the same time firmly and pragmatically loyal to defending our country and its revolutionary heritage. Dogmatism, once a real path is found, can be and certainly is extremely pragmatic and effective. But in the course of distancing ourselves from particular delusions about the Soviet model and what it had to teach us, we would feel as if the plated helmets protecting us were instead bursting inside our very heads.

Although the Yugoslav Party was already well advanced in bureaucratization, the flame of an ideal still burned brightly for most of its leaders, a patriotic, revolutionary ecstasy. And as for the people—they caught their collective breath with enthusiasm when the confrontation broke into the open.

We knew beforehand that at the end of June 1948 the so-called Information Bureau of the Communist parties of Eastern Europe plus Italy and France had been summoned to meet in Bucharest. It was the Soviet re-creation of a mini-Comintern, to which we, too, belonged up to that point. But taking our cue from preliminary letters addressed by the Soviet Central Committee to the other Party members concerning the sins and errors of the Yugoslav Central Committee, it was not hard to figure out that there, in Bucharest, the Yugoslav Party and Yugoslavia itself would be anathematized as anti-Communist and treasonous. So Tito called a plenary session of the Central Committee and I, waking in the middle of the night (as I recall), wrote out for the Yugoslav media a point-by-point rebuttal of the bill of indictment. The next day, June 28, our Central Committee adopted this text with minor changes as its public reply.

It was with our rift with the Soviet Union and Stalin that my own independence and self-sufficiency began. This was a process at first intellectual, then emotional and private, slow to mature but perfectly sure. My growing independence would have come to light more rapidly had I been able to part company with the collective leadership; had I not been obliged to function within this circle. Otherwise, in the heated atmosphere then prevailing, I would have been arrested and proclaimed a pro-Soviet traitor, a deserter to the cause at the most critical and dramatic juncture for Party, for country, and for the socialist ideal. As if the sluices had opened, all my suppressed, critical ideas began to gush forth unbridled, aimed, of course, at the Soviet system and Stalinist methods but also indirectly, silently, reflective of Yugoslav realities. For there can be no question that the Yugoslav and Soviet realities were essentially alike, if not identical. Neither Tito nor some of the other top leaders were happy with these newfangled Djilasisms, at least at the beginning. But they were in no position to take issue with my ideas, mirroring as these did the state of mind and the thinking of many in the Party's highest ranks and directed against the grotesque, deadly enemies of our Party, our country, and our people. I was convinced at the time that my ideas were still largely antidogmatic, or represented a rejuvenated dogmatism. Even dogma can be creative. Once it has become ritualized, the faith of officials can be shattered by a dogma still more persuasive, more logical, by a faith still more redemptive.

No sooner, though, had we introduced democratic measures (relatively so, by comparison with the Soviet Union and the East European countries); no sooner did we reject the notion of imposing our own brand of Stalinism and endorse the ideas of democratic socialism; no sooner had we begun to overcome the inertia of an inherited, petrified way of thinking and fossilized forms of governance, all a mixture of Yugoslav and Soviet experience—than we noticed that the current had started to flow in the opposite direction, toward conservatism. It often happened that just to show Moscow we had not betrayed the Communist idea in adopting a new course, in practice we adopted punitive forms such as collectivizing villages and persecuting Stalin's followers, outrivaling in perfidy Moscow's own methods of double-dealing and retaliation.

That Stalin was in the wrong was plainly to be seen from the beginning, though such a view did not pass beyond the narrowest circle of leaders. By the fall of 1948 I dared to declare, with Tito's grudging consent, that "this time Comrade Stalin is not in the right." But in proportion as Soviet pressures spread and grew stronger, taking even such silly forms as "trying to convince," to that same degree our own perceptions grew keener and we began pushing back. At a UN session in 1949, in the name of the Yugoslav delegation, I delivered a critical report on Soviet behavior toward our country.

However, to rest our case simply on repudiating Stalin was not a smart thing to do and would be unconvincing. In my own reflections, and partly, too, in internal discussions with certain top-ranking colleagues, Lenin's name would regularly emerge. For Stalin had merely "perfected" the Leninist system.

A group of us turned finally to Marx as a source of explanation and a road sign. Even I plunged into diligent study of Marx. But I could find no explanation for Soviet socialism's conversion to state capitalism. (It was I who formulated this term, which was then taken up by the Party until I was expelled from its Central Committee at the beginning of 1954, on the eve of my government's reconciliation with the USSR.) Accurate or not, my term "state capitalism"—one that gained currency in the West, though at the time I was only vaguely aware of this— served the Yugoslav Party as a pointed weapon, even the major one, with which to criticize the Soviet system and to set ourselves apart from it ideologically.

But if after rereading Marx I could arrive at no explanation for the Soviet deviation from the path of socialism, I did come up with the concept of self-management. Others later elaborated and applied it with a broad brush, in wholesale fashion and dictatorially, throughout Yugoslavia. Self-management was a utopia as well, but one that cushioned the Lenin-Stalinist dictatorship of the proletariat, the totalitarian power of a Party bureaucracy.

Finally, I turned to the classical and European philosophers, though with no intention of myself becoming a philosopher. What I discovered was that final truths were not to be found in Marx, and that Marx had taken many of his own truths from German and European classical philosophy. At the time I could not completely rid myself of the notion that Marx was a "scientist" and a first-rate economist and philosopher. For that to happen, years of meditation were required, years mostly spent behind prison bars.

Here in substance is what I learned from the experience of having confronted the Soviet Union:

> If national policy, even that of a great and mighty people, wishes to play a creative role, it inescapably must stand alone spiritually, intellectually and programmatically, must be in character when it collaborates with others, distinctive and original even when it unwillingly bends the knee before them, for though no one's ideas and ideologies are uniquely one's own, if and where they do exist they must raise their own voices and spring from their own roots, yes, yes, they must emerge from their very own fountainheads and if this be not so then such ideas and ideologies and indeed the whole national policy is but a naked imitation and either it must change or the ideas and ideologies must be replaced and the same holds true for the individual, if he wishes to be creative, and I was capable of being creative to the end, in fact had to create in order to become a whole being, free and unrestricted in thought and deed throughout all hesitancies and twistings and turnings, but this I came to recognize only when I found myself alone, alone with my wife Štefaniya[8] and our son, for it was only then that I discovered how self-sufficiency and solitude are intertwined, or to state it differently I was on the way to becoming my own man and alone but this was something that did not come to pass all of a sudden, only gradually, at intervals, something I became fully aware of only after parting company with Stalin and the Soviet system, with all the disgrace and risk that action brought down upon my head, and only after parting company

with the companions whose business, whose thoughts—whose bread—I had shared for years, all so as to finally become what I am, to belong to a spiritual world of my own, hounded and cursed by those very comrades with whom I had shared all I had ever owned up to then, all that I was, all I believed in, exposed to risk, risk both unpredictable and fatal, risking even that which I had no right to risk—my family, my wife and children, a son and daughter: without sacrifice and damnation, mild or harsh depending on the circumstances, no one at bottom is or can be even tolerably independent and creative in a human world where nothing is so odious as authentic independence and creativity.[9]

The parting of the ways occurred gradually and almost unnoticeably, even to me. In my criticism of the Soviet Union there was much that bore, if only indirectly, on the Yugoslav political and economic system. I was aware of this but kept it out of sight, a fact that was noticed by certain comrades who favored greater democracy as long as the power structure and their own slots within it were not threatened thereby. Partly for this reason, but more because the ruling circle was rendered powerless by its own inflamed anti-Sovietism, my criticism was tolerated by our sovereign "strong arms" and by Tito. They suppressed their frowns and merely gave me comradely rebukes.

Within Yugoslavia I freely offered opinions on sundry topics in sundry directions. There was too much of it. Nor did it behoove a responsible official in a normal political and bureaucratic system to offer such opinions.

This situation steadily intensified up to the very moment of Stalin's death. Quite soon thereafter criticism so caustic, criticism that was growing ever more pointed, began to disturb the ideologists of what was termed Tito's Marxism, who had hitherto lain low and held their tongues. In July 1953 the Central Committee, at Tito's initiative, put a stop to our modest liberalization and announced that criticism of the bureaucracy and of totalitarian structures was to be toned down. To me, it was an unambiguous signal to cease and desist, to change my way of working, or, in other words, to suppress the evidence and choke off its free expression. More, I was entrusted with the highly visible position of president of the Yugoslav Federal Parliament.

But I was hardly a devotee of titles. The glitter of high politics turned me off, and at that point, familiar as I was with the origin and essence

THE DEVELOPMENT OF MY POLITICAL THINKING

of these things, titles even disgusted me. I could be only a leader or a common soldier—leader on a path of my own, soldier like others on that same path.

I simply was not able to "cease and desist." I was being carried along by ideas and ideals that were more freedom-loving than Marxist. Something stronger than my still wobbly willpower and my still unripened thoughts. Something that did not permit me to halt, even with the prospect before me of ostracism, humiliation, and prison, of my young wife's suffering and that of my newborn son, my daughter. Something that did not shrink from death itself. What that something was is unclear to this day: Man is in thrall to his work, to his creative work, to the extent that it is his own and that he believes it to be original.

That something which was stronger than I would perhaps not have come into the open, or at least not to such a degree, had concrete political circumstances not dictated a turning point, a watershed: We could move toward democracy or turn back into totalitarianism and the cult of the leader. We were faced with a choice, not one involving policy but inner consistency: Either rot in sly pretense, awaiting the leader's demise, or affirm our conviction, our own new faith, one that was all our own. Be true to our own selves.

I resolved to proceed with my criticism. Mild and confined to generalities, it was in line with my striving for a gradual democratization. The Communist order in Yugoslavia was very close to my heart, after all. But the clarity and concreteness of my criticism left no doubt that above all it was directed at the Yugoslav Party. In one narrative text the nascent contours of my future book *The New Class* are noticeably present.

I had no thought at that point of organizing a factional group within the Party. Indeed, this would have been beyond my power, even though in the top ranks there were comrades who shared my views. I was aware of the fate of factions in Communist parties, especially Stalinist ones. But I also knew and had seen for myself the futility of all attempts to "Bolshevize" communism. The sole possible path was criticism. Communism can only change itself from within by using its own resources in the form of ideas.

I wrote a series of articles for the Party newspaper *Borba,* articles that would continue to be published for some time since the themes I had sketched and the ideas I was forging were still incomplete. But in January 1954 a plenary session of the Central Committee was convened to consider "the case of Comrade Djilas," a session that ended with the first verdict on me and my work.

At the session my "erroneous conceptions" failed to serve as the basis of any discussion, such as might have been expected from a Party that had long proclaimed itself to be a departure from Stalinism. We might have escaped domination by the Soviet state, but from the point of view of ideology and the basic features of the system any such escape was a delusion, a mistaken idea, real only to the extent needed by Tito and the bureaucratic circle around him.

Halfheartedly and unconvincingly, I "acknowledged" my "errors"— an unexpected thing for me to do. To this day I cannot explain it other than by my loyalty to communism and the fact that I was simply unable to part company without shamefully stumbling. Such is the lot of all true believers before they detach themselves from their faith for good.

At that plenary session of slander, lies, and threats, all substantive arguments came down to my being excluded from the Central Committee. The verdict was initially pronounced by Tito, followed by Kardelj's theoretical-bureaucratic explication (Kardelj[10] was informally number two in the Party). The two of them were joined by others who expressed their opposition to a "revisionist," a "flag-bearer of Counter-revolution," a "fractionalist," a "Bernsteinist"[11] under the influence of British Labourites, and so on and on. Total ostracism began at once, automatically, and two months later I handed in my Party membership card.

In itself the Plenum would not have meant anything decisive for me, but the way in which it was conducted—fabrication of guilt, humiliation, groundless ferreting out of "Djilasites"—did touch me deeply. Even here, in my own Party, the leaders and fellow fighters with whom I had worked closely for nearly two decades differed from Stalinists only in having one ear cocked to the outer world and in having in some cases become soft ideologically. They were incapable of resorting to the most savage methods of maintaining what was essentially dictatorial power. Incapable of clipping the wings of any and all criticism of the system. Incapable of settling accounts with innocent and well-intentioned faultfinders. And they were not up to doing these things more ruthlessly inside the Party than outside it. In other words, the problem lay not with this or that leader, but with communism as such: From communism there is no exit, and for this reason a critical judgment, if it is to be really honest, *has to find fault with the very idea itself.*

I set to work on cherished literary projects, writing my memoirs and clearing the way for a literary study of the great Montenegrin poet Njegoš,[12] and along with these preparing a critique of communism.

The idea of *The New Class* was finally thought through and shaped into a book in closest conjunction with a new and merciless attack on me: The Central Committee forbade the printing of my literary description of my childhood, *Land Without Justice*,[13] though there was not a thing in it that might in any way have been construed as censure of communism or of the Communist order in Yugoslavia. I understood this prohibition to be setting a price: Either knuckle under in shame, or spiritual death will ensue for you.[14] Instead of fostering irresolution this only made me resolved to fight on wherever I could, using any honest means. That is, I would publish abroad. I now had a keen grasp of how matters stood. This was the way it had to be because communism, once in power, "evolved" into a monopolistic ideology and Communists themselves into a closed and privileged social layer, a new class of its own kind. "Sparks live in the rock; blows only find them there," in the words of Njegoš.[15]

Critics have taken note that *The New Class,* in structure and manner of argument, remained to a certain extent Marxist. And this was no coincidence. A Marxist approach appeared to be the most authentic and convincing way to tell how Communists create not a classless society but the reverse—*their own class society.*

The work would not have been published but for the courage of my wife, Štefaniya, who entrusted it to the American newswoman Catherine Clark while I was in prison. (I had been sent to prison for a statement to the Associated Press and an article in *The New Leader,* in both of which I was critical of the Yugoslav government's stand on the Hungarian uprising of 1956.) Sending the manuscript to the United States evoked hesitation and painful second thoughts for the purist that I was. To publish abroad a work opposed to ideas that had been until so recently my own? Surely, for the bigoted consciousness of a Communist this would be plain proof of mercenary betrayal.

Writing *The New Class* came easy for me: I had first lived through and then recovered from injustice and disgrace, while the gist of the book had gradually been ripening to maturity within. But in my sleepless wanderings about the nightmarish, unpeopled expanse of Belgrade (as it appeared to me), I shilly-shallied and wobbled, imagining at times that I was going mad, looking for topics and retorts, finding them, constructing them. All is of value once created—created of obstinate, convoluted meditation and brought to completion as a personal drama. Creation is the joy of suffering conscious of itself.

Imprisonment followed. I went to prison for defending the Hungarian uprising, I was kept there for coming out with *The New Class* while being punished, and I went back to prison for *Conversations with Stalin* while on probation: prison for thirteen years, of which I served nine. On the last day of December 1966 I was let out of prison and, to the accompaniment of threats and interference, continued energetically to find fault in the foreign media with specific Communist countries and with specific, sometimes current, instances of behavior and viewpoint on the part of the Communist governments. Open publication in Yugoslavia was permitted me only in 1989.

In prison I worked intensively on writing fiction, and during my second term, between 1962 and 1966, I thought through *The Unperfect Society,* writing it down upon my release.

"Jail is a strange house," goes the Serbian song.[16] What is so for everyone is especially so for the prisoner of conscience, the person who resists morally—the person under discussion here. For him, the issue is whether his personality will break or whether he will master himself. The oscillation between these alternatives either breaks the will or strengthens it, daily and hourly. Nights are filled with nightmares, mornings with crazed confusion. Savage, irrational thirst for life is followed by a tranquilizing faith and pride. At the victorious conclusion— if victorious it can be called, for anyone—you leave yourself out of history, particularly your own history. You deny life, turn your back on any life beyond your own ideas, your own beliefs, your own inner world. History vanishes. There remains only the person. Personal ambition, personal plans—all are superseded. Weaknesses and errors in overcoming history, overcoming life, overcoming oneself, are neither denied nor justified. There is no system without fault, no perfect world. Perfection, to the degree it exists at all, is only to be found in our "unperfect" selves.[17]

Such would have been the message at the end of this book, to the extent that it is not spelled out in what follows.

2

THE YUGOSLAV REVOLUTION
AND
THE SOVIET UNION

JAJCE 1943[1]

The Central Committee met several times to prepare for the second session of AVNOJ.* Most important decisions, like the convening of AVNOJ itself, were made in October. Some were adopted at a meeting of Politburo members. But if memory serves, the crucial meeting occurred at the end of October, when it was decided that the country would have a federative structure, that there would be a provisional government, and that the king,[2] together with his government, would be forbidden to return. That meeting was held on a sunny afternoon in front of Tito's tiny quarters next to the entrance to an underground shrine. Differences arose over whether the government should be permanent or provisional, also over whether to depose the king straight out or simply forbid his return. We all, though, agreed with Tito in choosing to take a fairly moderate, transitional course. Kardelj and I shared Tito's point of view exactly, while it was the indigenous Serbs who were more radically disposed: Žujović,[3] Pijade,[4] and judging by his silence, Ranković[5] too.

By the time we met, the chief reasons that had been advanced in favor of moderation had to do with the Allies, above all the British and

---

*Antifašističko veće narodnog oslobođenja Jugoslavije (Anti-Fascist Council for the National Liberation of Yugoslavia).

the Soviets: How acceptable would such a course be for them? Our thinking was that we had to make it easy for the British to distance themselves from the king and the government-in-exile, and on the other hand that we ought not to complicate and impede Soviet relations with Britain. In view of our ideological dependence on Moscow, this was the major consideration. But domestic reasons existed as well: The broad masses, the Serbian peasantry in particular, were not yet sufficiently radicalized to do without having a monarch; monarchs were traditional. Creating a new power structure itself signified extreme measures. Taking our time over its precise forms harmonized with what we thought of as the backward consciousness of the masses. It also accommodated our need for legitimacy: Mobilization had to be legally valid, and we had to be recognized internationally.

Like considerations underlay our judgment that in the end we would decide what to do with the king and the monarchy in postwar elections. The Western Allies had adopted the Atlantic Charter, and this had a clause about free choice of government, meaning the form taken by a power structure. To forbid the king's return met our understanding of this clause, for at that point we had no doubt of the final fate of the monarchy. There was no ambiguity concerning an election carried out by our own established authorities on the ruins of the old power structure, the old order. The course of moderation, as we called it, a course of transition, was prompted by our wanting to make it easier for the people as a whole to ease us into power. But our goal was inexorable, and it was to legitimize ourselves and to make sure that the new power structure that would arise would belong to us.

The name "National Committee for the People's Liberation of Yugoslavia" was also confirmed at that meeting, with one eye on the reaction of the Allies. Such a term as "National Committee" was aptly chosen. Kardelj recalled the French having employed it, and that struck a responsive chord with Tito. So the term was adopted alongside our own word "people." With us, everything had to be "the people's" this and that, and there was no getting around it.

At this crucial meeting someone observed that the "Russkies" would not understand (meaning "approve") all our decisions, especially the ones concerning the king and the king's government. After the meeting concluded or perhaps a day or two later, Tito remarked—I remember that Kardelj, Ranković, and I were present—that the "Russkies" need not be informed of all our decisions, because they would not grasp their import and would oppose them, thereby nullifying the whole proceeding. What he conveyed to Dimitrov,[6] which is to say the Soviet regime, was that a provisional government would be formed. And this he did relatively late, only on November 26, three days before the session of AVNOJ, without mentioning the fact that we were depriving the royal government of legitimacy and were prohibiting the king's return to his country. The new power structure began by cleanly breaking off with the old one and thus by "betraying" its spiritual fathers.

Tito hurried the meeting into session. Over and above what has been said, he calculated that the royal government and the king might be able to take advantage of the conference of foreign ministers in Moscow and return to Yugoslavia, even though it was not clear where they could establish residence without becoming either allies of the Germans or captives of the Partisans. Undoubtedly the session would have been convened before this had the delegates from Montenegro and Slovenia been able to get there earlier.

Up to that time the Party had taken the stand that Bosnia and Hercegovina should have autonomous status but not be republics. The assumption was "autonomy under Serbia." But war had made Bosnia an arena where Ustashi[7] and Chetniks[8] settled accounts; had turned it into a wellspring of Partisans and a place of asylum for them. Autonomy under either Serbia or Croatia would only have led to more bickering and would have deprived the Muslims of all individuality. Furthermore, the Bosnian leadership, like every political power that grows out of rebellion, insisted on "its own" state, as later on "its own" hereditary access to the sea. In any case, republican status for Bosnia and Hercegovina was not decided at that time, nor in the session of AVNOJ, but afterward. Where and when, I do not exactly recall. It happened at a meeting that took place while we were on the march, after withdrawing from Jajce at the beginning of January 1944. Ranković told us the Bosnian leadership was proposing a republic, Tito went along with this idea, and the others followed suit as though it were acceptable by definition.

Delegates to the second session of AVNOJ were picked in various ways: from the republic parliaments; from the local power structures; or else they could be nominated from the center. All, though, no matter how they got there, were "vetted." Party gatherings tried to include well-known figures who were not Partisans, to include patriots (as they were called), but patriots who would not argue with our aims or methods. The majority of these people later became Party members, but some of them were members already, in secret. The Central Committee nominated from military units the delegates representing Serbia.

Kardelj undertook to draw up the greater part of AVNOJ's coming decisions. Here he was helped by Pijade, in whom the future "parliament" found its man just as Pijade found in the parliament his own self. One could say that Pijade's lively and imaginative intelligence came to the fore in a practicable way only with AVNOJ and the parliament that followed. My own part in AVNOJ's second session hardly went beyond stylistic corrections of Kardelj's texts, aside from making propaganda out of them, and there were no great possibilities of that.

The precipitous strengthening of our position and our role led the British to welcome a military mission from us. Considering that the British tended to dump compromised royal governments, this mission had quite a broad political significance besides military. The Partisan troops were thereby formally acknowledged to be the sole opposition force battling Germany. Laying the groundwork for recognizing the rebel authorities was a more important objective than immediate military assistance.

At first Vlatko Velebit, who had already mastered English, was slated to be head of the mission. But at about the same time, Lola Ribar had proposed taking on new duties, relinquishing his position as secretary of the Communist Youth League. He now felt too old for this kind of work, and broader possibilities were appearing on his horizon. Ribar first brought this up in a conversation with Ranković and myself, following which the two of us persuaded Tito and Kardelj. Ribar, too, knew English. So it was he who was appointed head of mission. Velebit took it in stride, not being a self-important person; moreover, Ribar was a Central Committee member.

The mission was to take off on November 27 from Glamočko Polje in a Dornier 17. That happened to be two days before the second session of AVNOJ; there was no direct connection. The aircraft had been flown into our territory by some Home Guard (i.e., Croatian) aviators, who had deserted. But just as the mission's participants were bundling onto the plane, a Storch reconnaissance aircraft flew overhead and commenced bombing and strafing the area. Ribar, who happened to jump out as a bomb exploded, was fatally wounded in the head and two other places, a few meters from the plane. Two British officers and a Partisan also were killed, plus a pilot in the machine-gun turret, but Velebit managed to pull himself out of the plane's tail, which was now on fire. Ribar's body was charred by the heat. It seemed quite unlikely that the Germans knew of the mission's flight, as then the attack would have been carried out by faster and better-armed aircraft. Most probably, the Storch was reconnoitering to see where the airplane might have taken refuge, and happened to find it just when the mission was embarking. Five minutes later and their plane along with the mission would already have been airborne and the Storch powerless, if not itself prey to our own aircraft.

Ribar was killed in the morning, and we in Jajce knew of it that same day around noon. Central Committee members, the personnel of the Supreme Staff, rebels in Jajce, all were overcome by frustration and sorrow the moment word of his death began to spread. And spread it did at once, although horror and disbelief quelled any open talk. Ribar was the youngest and the first to be snatched away of the group that had become friends around the person of Tito, the first to be eliminated from the revolutionary youth leadership, at a moment that we all were preparing for and felt to be historic. Also, just as happens in classic drama, the historic event became interwoven with personal tragedy. On the same day that Lola Ribar lost his life, his father, Dr. Ivan Ribar, president of AVNOJ, arrived from Slovenia fresh with new impressions and in a mood to talk about the upcoming session. Just a month before, his younger son, the painter Jurica, had been killed in Montenegro, and Lola Ribar had known of it. By agreement with him, the elder Ribar was not told of this, it being left for Lola to do so at an opportune moment. Now he too was dead, and there was neither any reason nor any possibility of hiding from the father the death of his only children.* And strangely enough, the fact that the Ribars belonged to a propertied, bourgeois milieu had the effect of deepening the tragedy for us Communist leaders. Life and history had played a game with them. In 1920 old Ribar had been president of the Constituent Assembly that had approved the ban on the Communist Party, and now his sons had fallen for the sake of the Communist idea while

---

*Dr. Ribar's wife had three other children from her first marriage, who grew up in her second home. She too was shot by the Germans.

he presided over the very gathering that was legalizing power for the Communists.

That same day toward evening, at a meeting in Tito's quarters, along with other immediate issues the question arose of how to let Dr. Ribar know of the death of his sons. Kardelj said it would be most appropriate if Tito were to do so. The rest of us agreed, and Tito replied, as if mustering up the courage to say something decisive, "All right, I'll tell him."

As soon as the meeting was over, Tito invited Ribar to come see him, in order to inform him of Lola's death that morning. The old man responded, "Does Jurica know? Has he been told? He'll take it hard." Tito took Ribar by the arm: "Jurica died too, a month ago, in Montenegro. . . ."

Dr. Ribar stayed with Tito rather a long time. Supper was not formally served, people eating what and where they could. No one expressly extended condolences to Ribar—our dejection and speechlessness were eloquent enough, both for us and for him. Perhaps of those in the circle around Tito it was I who took the young man's death hardest of all, though during the war we had not been as close as we had been earlier. Lola Ribar often returned to me in memory, especially when I was in prison, now stepping up close, now standing off to one side, but never passing judgment on my break with the Party. He was in tune now with my frame of mind and with the Lola who dwelled within. His father, too, felt the special closeness between Lola and me, after the war often turning to me for unofficial needs such as his memoirs, or small matters having to do with his stepdaughters.

Again it is late in the afternoon—I think this was the next day, November 28—and Kardelj at a meeting with Tito has told us that the Slovenian delegation proposed to make Tito a marshal. Tito, turning crimson, has stood up as though wanting to think things over while pacing: "Isn't this far too much? And won't the Russkies take offense?" We had rejected out of hand the idea that the "Russkies" were so thin-skinned. "Why, we can have our own marshals!" As for the magnitude of the honor for Tito, it had not even been brought up. If anyone deserved such an honor it was he, and the troops and the Communist movement both now had a new supreme authority "in the Soviet style," providing a counterweight to the traditional monarchic one.

By November 28 the majority of delegates were assembled. Acquainting them with our proposed decisions was a process that began unfolding the next morning, in the shelter beside the central power station. At any one time, members of the Central Committee could be seen next to Tito, so that comments by the delegates could be worked out jointly with him and among themselves. Kardelj was the most enterprising person in these discussions. There were not many comments, and those there were were extremely terse. Most of the delegates were for declaring a republic on the spot and had to be dissuaded from being overly hasty, especially those who had belonged to the former urban parties. At one moment Kardelj, standing next to Tito and carried away by the flow of consultation with the delegations, whispered to me: "A revolution is being proclaimed!" I made no reply. I shared with him and the others faith in the significance of the session, but its decisions—indeed, the session itself—I felt to be a legitimizing of already created relationships and not a watershed. General Koča Popović had his own way of interpreting the process of coming to an agreement with groups of delegates: "Well sure, it's in corridors that politics is carried out."

And indeed, at the session itself, which took place on the evening of November 29 in the Sokol Club, there were no differences whatever, no real debates. Close attention strained for the opportunity to explode in applause. Loud exclamations responded to slogans. Rhythmic, uproarious enthusiasm would only slacken off to pause for a moment in delight. The delirious uproar was intensified and sometimes initiated by the young people, by the staff officers, and by the officials from various organizations, all of whom were lining the sides of the cramped hall.

Only Tito's speech, though interrupted by applause over and over again, inaugurated an atmosphere that was reasonable, that one could work in. He read more fluently than usual, with the unemphatic self-assurance natural to him. In his bearing, and especially his voice, one could sense dignity, even tragedy. And his speech had a striking effect: Reading it, I had thought it somewhat dry, but in delivery it was precisely this dryness that gave it purchase in bringing together a war on two fronts with a civil war whose horrors no one could even imagine, warfare whose end was barely in sight.

As a delegate I sat off to the side to the right, but still in front of the stage. And although I followed the procedure of the session, especially Tito's speech, Lola Ribar's death was never very far from my thoughts, Lola, sealed up already in his tin casket and set down on the floor of the little chapel in Jajce. I could not take my eyes off his father sitting in the chair, a man whose slowness and composure I read as stoniness and torpor. All the delegates, I thought, behaved and felt the same way, at least those who were closer to the leadership and to the Ribars— though no one mentioned them.

And yet it was during that stretch of the session where Tito was proclaimed a marshal, precisely then, when our unanimity was the most stormy, most intoxicating, that I forgot about the Ribar family. This, even though all knew about the proclamation beforehand and were "attuned" to such unanimity in themselves. I too expressed the collective transports, I too was carried away in ecstasy, but not for a moment did I drown in it. Always I stayed fully conscious and alert. It was even the case that I grew colder and more collected the more frenzied and stormy grew the general consensus. And yet, I diligently applauded, and with enthusiasm. Later, such prolonged hand-clapping would often be prompted, with me as with others, by fears lest someone think me against the Party and Tito. But all the while that evening I kept asking myself in perplexity how Tito's being named marshal might alter the relationships on the Central Committee and in the government to come. Up to that moment he had treated the members of the Central Committee as "my cherished associates." Our sense of collegiality and personal dignity were not altered. Tito's hot temper in discussions appeared unimportant. And no major or essential differences existed among us anyway. Yes, the army, the political system, the new Yugoslavia now coming into being, all were advanced by adding to Tito's standing and nourishing his function. Even before this he had been playing the leading role, and his resourcefulness and initiative had been put to the test. But to what political structures, what kind of relationships, would this lead? Especially when the bearer of the highest title was predisposed toward personal power in any case? And when the title of marshal was being introduced in such a way that only he would be granted it?

Following Tito's election, the chair withdrew behind the stage curtains. Only the new coat of arms remained above the stage. It was not yet a coat of arms, but everyone knew that it would become so. It had been drawn by Djordje Kun, who based it a little on the Soviet coat of arms, a little on his own ideas, and a little on suggestions coming from Central Committee members. That emblem, augmented later by Pijade, did become the state coat of arms. And as for the date of this congress—November 29, 1943—it became Yugoslavia's state holiday.

Behind the curtains, congratulations were now in full swing. And with the arrival of Ranković and myself and other officials, eager devotion turned into an impassioned fervor, all the more unrestrained because it was being performed in a tight setting. We embraced and kissed Tito, first we Communist leaders and after us the non-Party patriots. They had no way out. The rapture was transferred to Tito. It grew and transformed itself into intoxication. We Communists, not standing on ceremony, went on hugging and kissing Tito while the "patriots" looked on with incomprehension or astonishment. Himself caught up in this joyous, mad maelstrom of congratulation, Tito bestowed a reply on every person there. Our eyes glistened, our breasts swelled, sweat broke out on our flushed faces, to the point that our hearts nearly burst and each of us was close to a breakdown.

I too was drowning in the drunken frenzy. But at the same time I knew that my destiny was now being set. That by surrendering myself to the general rapture I was of my own free will attaching myself to Tito as my personal liege, my lord and master, notwithstanding my thirst for a world without lords, notwithstanding my own integrity, my self-respect. It is laughable to hear anyone today telling tall tales to the effect that Communists, or some of them at least, did not want Tito as leader. An idea, a party, a power structure, all find a fitting leader, and in them that leader discovers himself, his creativity. It is surely true that Tito not only was glad to accept the leadership but also insisted on it. His popularity, though, or the popularizing of his personality and role, became routinized. It became a regular part of the job for Party officials and for the Party apparatus, work that could be counted on. It was the Party that took the lead when, for example, in Montenegro it might be said that "from the arrival of Comrade Tito to head the Party" there had been a complete turnaround. During the war, though, Tito became popular among the people at large and in the lower echelons of the Party, before ever it took up the task of popularizing him. Imitation of the Soviets played a certain role, though not the decisive one. What was basic was the need of an ideological movement and an insurgent populace for an "infallible leader" and a "caring guardian." We leaders observed that by popularizing Tito, the Communist movement as a whole was strengthened and so was his immediate entourage. Then it took on the nature of an assignment, or at least an obligatory ritual. All of us from the top Party echelon were aware of the situation. We were attached to our leader, each in his own way inspired by his position and his firm leadership within the Party. Kardelj had been linked with Tito since the time when they schooled themselves and others in Moscow in 1934–35. True, Kardelj regarded himself as the better theoretician, and if by theory one meant fitting new realities into old "truths," then superior he undoubtedly was. But Tito as a personality and a leader was so overpowering that in the 1950s (when differences began to appear among us) we had the strong impression that Kardelj was even physically afraid of Tito. As for Ranković, he was unconditionally loyal to Tito. Sentimentally, worshipfully loyal. And I? It is this very point that I have been addressing. In me alone the betrayed ideal would rebel every once in a while. I was the one conscious of my own unworthy role. If so heretical an observation as this ever crossed someone's mind—I was that person more often than not—the other two men would set him straight and talk him out of it. Other leaders found themselves in the still more hopeless, invidious position of having to envy Kardelj, Ranković, or me our special closeness to Tito.

The delirium of congratulating Tito behind the curtains went on for a long time, perhaps twenty, even thirty minutes. Until someone reminded us that the session was supposed to resume.

We returned to our seats exhausted and, down inside, perhaps ashamed. At least that is how I felt. All resolutions were adopted enthusiastically, with stormy consensus. A new government and a new, yet to be confirmed, chief of state had been arranged for. It had been done with forethought and method. And now it was proclaimed aloud in the hope of final happiness and freedom.

The next day we assembled at the grave to see off Lola Ribar in his casket. The weather was cool and gloomy. We had decided that Pijade would speak, that as the oldest Communist he should be the one to bid adieu to the leader of youth. The man was shaken, his voice shrill, his thoughts scattered as never before. However, he was well-read and he dredged up some Frenchman's unforgettable phrase: Revolutionaries are but dead men on leave of absence. . . . Old Ribar liked to talk, and this occasion was no exception. But he could utter only stale phrases: Our struggle is hard, our struggle seeks victims, nothing can stop our struggle. Those shabby platitudes, as if they were being snatched on the fly, lacked continuity and smoothness. Ribar choked in a hoarse, dark voice. At the end it burst out of him, as out of any father: "Farewell, Lola, farewell, my sons! . . ."

Lola was borne away to a secret spot so that the enemy could not desecrate his body.

Like many, I was in tears. But life went on, and the din of war was more insistent than ever.[9]

I ENCOUNTER THE LEADER OF
THE LAND OF DREAMS

By the beginning of March 1944 it had already been decided that we would dispatch our own military mission to the Soviet Union. Next it was determined that I would be part of the delegation, Ranković informing me that such was the "Old Man's" thinking, meaning Tito. These tidings vaulted me into a state of secret rapture and pride: I was to venture forth into the land of my Slavic roots and cosmic faith, I was leaving for Russia, land of hope, going to the Soviet Union. And both my Party and an army created in the course of struggle with the Nazi monster would be represented by me.

Formally, the decision was made later, on March 16, as the remaining members of the mission had to be chosen and assembled. Tito had approved the selection of me because I was but one step down from him as the Party head and because I knew Russian well and could explain to the Soviet leaders what was characteristic of us and what we needed.

Actually the mission had another chief, General Velimir Terzić. I was its real head only to the extent that I was a member of the Politburo and the Supreme Staff. Terzić and I worked well together, all the more so because he was a cooperative person.

The mission included people who had no place there, strictly speaking, but who bestowed on it a broader, more representative character. For example, the physicist Pavle Savić, in recognition of his painstaking work encrypting and safeguarding a radio station over the course of the war, and Antun Avgustinčić,[10] the well-known sculptor and vice president of AVNOJ. It occurred to someone that we ought to bring Stalin a present. But we had nothing worth giving to a personage who was the object of adoration. In such a predicament we decided that what Stalin would feel important was not the value of our contribution but its expression of love. As soon as word got round that gifts were to be provided for Stalin, they began to pour out of the desolated villages—gifts mostly left over from bridal outfits. Then women officials of the AFZ* made a selection of the prettiest towels, handbags, and stockings; they also chose the plainest peasant shoes. Such an expression of the people's love, however, would have been unthinkable without a martial gift. So we got hold of a rifle of the "Partisan" type. It took a lot of time to track one down, even though such weapons had been turned out by the thousands in Užice in 1941.

Tito charged the mission with obtaining Soviet recognition of the National Committee as Yugoslavia's legitimate government; with securing the help of the UN Relief and Rehabilitation Administration (UNRRA); and finally with obtaining military assistance. We were also asked to seek a loan from the Soviet government in the amount of $200,000 to cover the expenses of the trip. Nor was the matter of medals and orders overlooked, I undertaking to sketch how Tito's marshal's uniform would be decorated.

Tito reminded me to inquire of Dimitrov, or rather Stalin if I could get through to him, whether there were any comments to be made concerning our work. This directive was formal and deliberate; it laid emphasis on our ties to Moscow. Everyone in the leadership echelon, after all, felt that the Yugoslav Party alone had passed the test of war. The Soviets knew this. Our people knew it. Tito had the best reason of all to know it. On another note, I was warned not to get involved in émigré squabbles, and especially not in the Yugoslav émigrés' resentment of the Soviet "services." Tito emphasized that one had to watch out for female office workers. There were all kinds of such people. Not spelled out was that this was less a matter of morality than of the special nature of the Yugoslav Party and the integrity of Yugoslav Communists. Later on, women did indeed play an important role in Soviet intelligence, demoralizing Yugoslav Communists and causing their estrangement from the leadership.

Tito and I did not speak of what to answer the Soviets should they mention our negotiations with the Germans, something that was hardly likely in view of our relationships, warm with the one and bloody with the other. He would have known that I would stick to our official version: We were just negotiating an exchange of the wounded. With Ranković, though, the matter did come up, perhaps

---

Antifašistički front žena (Anti-Fascist Women's Front).

at Tito's initiative. Smiling slightly, I replied that exchanging the wounded was the only thing I could be sure about. My colleague gave a mischievous grin.

The Supreme Staff archives were part of our baggage. These the mission safeguarded from British intelligence officers with such atavistic watchfulness that they were bound to attract unusual attention. I took along Dedijer's[11] wartime diary as well, a work that had earned the right to special care.

At the beginning of April a British plane left Petrovački Field at night with the mission on board. I was overcome with joy at the thought of seeing the Soviet Union but was at the same time sad at leaving my friends behind and a homeland racked by sufferings and losses. My country seemed as if cloaked in mourning garb from which only the mountain peaks, still covered in snow, poked out.*

I had always imagined Russian terrain as something pastel-colored and limitless, but at this season of the year it was gray with a hard horizon. Moscow appeared rust-colored, and was practically without any tall buildings. The welcome ceremony for us at the airfield was markedly restrained, presumably so that the Soviets' Western allies would not see unduly lavish treatment accorded to any foreign mission, even one coming from a Communist state.

We were accommodated at the Central Club of the Red Army, surrounded by comforts that even in peacetime could only be dreamed of. But then we waited. And we waited. Far too long, considering what we were asking for. We waited to be admitted by someone—anyone—of the top rank, if not Molotov[12] or Stalin himself. No one could do a thing about it. Everyone with whom we came in contact, including such well-known Communists as Dimitrov, Gottwald,[13] and Manuilsky,[14] accepted the Kremlin's closed doors as a given. It was almost a higher legality.

The structure of the Soviet movement was hardly unfamiliar to me and I knew rather a lot about it, while the Communist Party of Yugoslavia, in whose formation I had long participated and which had begun as an embryonic power structure, in the course of the war had become transformed into something similar to the Soviet apparat. It

---

*The curious reader is directed to my book *Conversations with Stalin* (*Književne novine*, 1990), where I describe in greater detail both this and my two later trips to the Soviet Union.

crossed my mind that they were eavesdropping on me and checking me out, but this did not bother me because we were sincerely enchanted by the Soviet Union and Stalin. I was only bothered by the apathy, if not outright rudeness, with which the Soviet top rank approached issues of substance that they ought to have felt as pertaining to them as well as us. We were all Communists, affected alike by such issues.

We were not left alone by any means, however, and had plenty to do. The Soviet service departments organized receptions and meetings even for the mission's youngest members. We could always go to the theaters, including the first-class ones, and higher officials could get prime seats there by using connections. The center of our gatherings was the Pan-Slavic Committee, created during the war and installed in fine quarters, probably the former house of a rich merchant. But neither its leadership nor its opinions conferred any great standing on this committee. It owed its prominence and dynamism to the Soviet government, as all knew who had any dealings with it. Pan-Slavism[15] as an idea was out of date and put one in mind of Tsarist imperialism. Under Stalin what was appearance and what was essence had shifted meaning, not to mention any given project. Even at that time it was felt that the Pan-Slavic Committee was an "anti-German" facade for Soviet patronage of the Slavic peoples living outside the USSR. To Communists, therefore, particularly those who came out of the "Slavic sea," Pan-Slavism was an acceptable Stalinist cover, for the very reason that it offered them the prospect of coming to power.

The Soviets fitted our reality into their own external needs and prestige interests, as did their propaganda. For them, our reality could only change with a change in the attitude of the top echelon—Stalin and the Soviet government. The peoples of Yugoslavia and Yugoslav Communists never won any Soviet acknowledgment that they had carried out a revolution.

The Comintern had in fact been disbanded, but that did not include the Soviet Central Committee's "foreign affairs" section. Dimitrov, in the utmost secrecy, administered a subdivision of the Central Committee responsible for links with foreign parties, and this group gathered information and made recommendations to the Soviet leadership.

I had written two articles for the Soviet press, one for *Pravda* about the uprising in Yugoslavia and one for *Novoye Vremya* about Tito. Problems arose with the editors over certain of my expressions, especially those that referred to Tito. Some of the time I could not understand what they were talking about; in other instances I pretended not to understand. This went on till one editor, in even more desperate straits than I, muttered that among them only Stalin could be written about like that. With all the artlessness I could muster, I retorted, "But you know, it's the same thing—Stalin and Tito are both Communists. However, if you regard this as so important . . ." And I set to work correcting what I had written. In the USSR, to praise anyone but Stalin was not to be tolerated, especially where Communists were concerned. I already knew this, but it was worth checking to see whether our sacrifices had made any difference to them.

In the Soviet Union one mounted to bliss by gradual degrees, starting at the bottom. And so it was with General Terzić and me, in the way we reached Stalin. We had no idea whether or when we would be received. It was around five o'clock one afternoon. I had finished giving a lecture at the Pan-Slavic Committee and was just starting to take questions when someone whispered to me to stop because I had important business that could not be put off. Confusion ensued, but it was short-lived, as if everyone were used to the unlooked-for. A colonel from State Security informed us—naturally, after the auto had started off—that we were going to be received by Stalin. The thought of our poor little gifts crossed my mind, but State Security, unerring and trusty, had considerately brought them along in the car from the dacha on Moscow's outskirts where we were now staying. All of a sudden I turned quite empty and cold. Stalin was the incarnation of an idea,[16] the idea of a humanity that might be wretched today but tomorrow would be happy. As never before, I sensed how fortuitous was this coming encounter between Stalin and an insignificant creature like me, and yet at the same moment I was puffed up with pride that this had happened to me before anyone else and that it was I who would be in a position to give an account of it to other people. All the misunderstandings vanished, all the disagreements, all that was bad about the USSR so far as we could know what was bad—all vanished before the inconceivable, earthshaking grandeur of what now had to happen, what indeed already was going on inside me.

Without complicated procedures or long delays we were led to a room in the Kremlin that Stalin, walking out of his study, was entering at the same moment we came in from the secretary's office. Already standing there were Molotov and Zhukov,[17] the general from State Security who was responsible for foreign military missions. Shaking hands with Stalin, I gave him my last name, to which there was no reply. Terzić, though, clicking his heels, barked out his whole title along with his first and last names. To which the reply was "Stalin." Which everyone thought a trifle amusing. Did Stalin need to introduce himself?

Stalin was in marshal's uniform, but there was nothing of the warrior in his appearance. Even that stateliness was lacking to which photographs and newsreels had accustomed us. He was small of stature and poorly proportioned: trunk too short, arms too long. And he had a face that was pockmarked and sallow except for high color on the cheekbones. His teeth were black and irregular, his mustache and hair in disarray. But he did have a well-shaped, patriarchal head with watchful, wary, yellow eyes, lively and roguish. His brow was less firm than in his pictures and bore the strain of uninterrupted work.

Such a Stalin took me by surprise, a surprise both agreeable and pitying. Here was a man who ought to appear to the world powerful and strong but who was instead feeble and depleted, wasted away for the sake of all us Communists, for the sake of an idea. In conversation, though, the impression of exhaustion was at once erased. Stalin was incessantly in motion. He fussed over his pipe, fingered his blue pencil, passed readily from topic to topic. He was a bundle of nerves. Not a word, not a look, got by him.

And he had a sense of humor, humor both coarse and sudden. This was not unexpected. Of all Stalin's qualities it took me the least by surprise, probably because I had heard such stories about him and had read his own writings. It was just now that upper-echelon Moscow was circulating his quip when told that Simonov's[18] collection of love lyrics had been given a huge printing: "Two copies would be enough, one for her, the other for him."

No sooner were we seated, with me citing our enthusiasm over what we were seeing in the Soviet Union, than Stalin retorted, "We're not in the least enthusiastic, though we're doing all we can to improve things in Russia." Later on as well he used the word "Russia" two or three times instead of "Soviet Union." I gathered that this was how he underscored the role of Russia and the Russian people at that time, a time of war. Maybe that was his real thinking as well. Now I might add that by then Stalin, with experience, had made up his mind that what one undertook to do was more important than the justification for doing it.

Turning to Molotov, he mentioned the matter of recognizing the National Committee: "Couldn't we contrive to fool the English into recognizing Tito, who is the one man fighting the Germans?" Molotov gave a complacent smile. "No, that is impossible. They're quite aware of what is going on in Yugoslavia." But with regard to material assistance Stalin was more generous than we had been seeking. He himself kept finding ways. He gave approval for an air base to be established on Italian soil that would supply our troops, commenting, "Let's give it a try, we'll see what kind of position the Western Allies take and how far they'll go in helping Tito." And he flew into a rage when I mentioned payment: "You insult me! You're the ones shedding your blood! I'm only the one paying for the weapons! I'm no salesman, we're not doing deals! You're fighting for the selfsame thing as we are, we're obligated to share what we have with you."

Stalin looked over our humble gifts quickly. I thought I saw in his face compassion for our poverty. Or maybe the gifts reminded him of his Georgia.

The unreality of that hour-long visit was now carried over to the outdoors, as we were driven off into the bright dusk of the northern sky. Reality became robbed of all meaning. Or rather, it looked more beautiful: The light was better, more could be seen. And the city, darkened by war, seemed to be agog with anticipation: "Rations" would be bigger, there would be more *salyuts*.* The Moscow I harbored deep within was relaxed and gladdened.

Just before we returned to Yugoslavia I had one more talk with Stalin, unofficial and secret. This one was more interesting and even more meaningful. Again I had no forewarning that it would happen, let alone knowledge that I would get to see Stalin once more. Our talk took place on the night of June 5, on the eve of the Allied landing in Normandy.

A car simply picked me up in the evening around ten and took me to the Kremlin to see Molotov. Here I was casually informed that he and I would be having supper at Stalin's. And next we were being whisked away to Stalin's dacha outside Moscow.

Along the way Molotov, without appearing the least agitated, took an interest in the dangers that could have ensued from the German paratroop descent on our Supreme Headquarters which had taken

---

*Payok (паёк) (supplies), *salyut* (салют) (fireworks), on the occasion of the liberation of significant places.

place on May 25, 1944. Our mission enjoyed lively contacts with Soviet intelligence, and their service had stayed in touch with the Soviet mission in Yugoslavia. Duty officers briefed us daily on the course of the struggle after the German airborne assault in Drvar, and consulted with us over what kind of help to offer. Molotov was able to obtain from me a clearer picture than what the dispatches from Yugoslavia were merely sketching.

Stalin's surprisingly small dacha on the outskirts of Moscow was located in a grove of young firs. No sooner did we come in via the small entrance hall than he appeared in a simple blouse buttoned up to the chin. Such a Stalin was still smaller and still more unofficial. He led us into his cramped study, paneled in bare wood. He would put questions to himself and to us, would answer them without waiting for a reply. The man had a passionate, many-faceted nature, but he was just as capable of reining himself in as of losing his temper. He could become tight-lipped and silent out of passion. And this quality of passion was transmitted rapidly but inconspicuously to all around him.

Somehow I managed to assure him that "our troops won't die of hunger." And again, "I go along with Molotov that Soviet pilots are no cowards and only the great distances involved keep them from rendering effective assistance."

I also agreed with Stalin that in view of the growing complexity of our political tasks Tito and the leadership ought to be installed in a headquarters that offered safety and permanence. The Soviet mission was in any case already taking action along those lines, for at their insistence Tito removed to Italy with part of the leadership on the night of June 3 and from there to the Yugoslav island of Vis. When I was with him, however, Stalin was not yet thoroughly informed and only knew that Tito had for the time being gone to Italy.

He attached great importance to our not letting the red stars we wore frighten the English. However, I insisted that we could not get along without them, having fought so long under these stars. Stalin stuck to his opinion but held no grudge, as if dealing with a fidgety child.

He kept pacing back and forth while Molotov and I stood quietly by. But then, half sitting on the desk, he resumed, now in a worried tone, now sarcastically: "You might suppose that we, being allies of the English, have forgotten who they are and who Churchill is. For them, there's nothing more delectable than leading their allies by the nose. In the First World War they were always deceiving Russians and the

French. And Churchill? Churchill is the kind of man who if you're not watching will sneak a kopeck right out of your pocket! Yes, a kopeck right out of your pocket! Right out of your pocket, by God! Roosevelt, now, he isn't like that, he sticks his hand in only for bigger change. But Churchill? Churchill goes for the kopecks. Yes, and those English would have killed General Sikorski[19] had it not been for Tito. What would they care about sacrificing two or three men to get Tito? They've no mercy on their own people. And this business about Sikorski, it isn't just me talking, it's what Beneš[20] told me. They got Sikorski onto the plane and then neatly shot it down, no proof, no witness." In the course of our meal Stalin kept repeating these warnings and I later relayed them to Tito and the leadership. So they did play a role in his clandestine flight from Vis to territory held by the Soviets on the night of September 18, 1944.

He then took up the matter of the royal commissioner Šubašić,[21] and what our relations should be with this man. As distinct from earlier royal spokesmen, Šubašić had promised to come to terms with Tito and to recognize the National Liberation Army. "Don't refuse to speak with Šubašić," insisted Stalin, "don't refuse under any circumstances. Don't launch an attack against him right away without our seeing what he wants. Talk with him. You can't gain recognition all at once, you have to find a way of getting to that point. With Šubašić you must be on speaking terms to see if you can reach an understanding somehow." I let Tito know how insistent Stalin was on this point but he already had adopted a similar stand, and the signal from Stalin only reinforced his willingness to negotiate with the man.

I asked Stalin if he had anything to say about the positions we took and our work in general, but his rejoinder, almost as if he were taken aback, was, "No, I haven't, and after all, you yourselves know best what's to be done there."

Passing through the corridor to the dining room, Stalin stopped before a map of the world and, gesturing to the Soviet Union all colored in red, he heaped a little more abuse on the British and Americans: "They'll never be reconciled to letting a large space like this stay red—never. Never!"

My glance rested on the space just to the west of Stalingrad that was circled in blue pencil, and I had the impression that he liked seeing me pause there, though he did not utter a word. Then I, probably associating the enormous German breakthrough with the fateful Battle of

Stalingrad, remarked that "without industrialization the Soviet Union would not have been able to hold out, could not have conducted such a war." Stalin interjected that it was precisely over that issue that "we squabbled with Trotsky[22] and Bukharin."[23]

In the dining room there stood waiting for us two or three high officials, but, except for Molotov, no one from the Politburo. Everyone served himself from the warmed silver dishes lined up on the front end of the table. Everyone sat where he wanted at the lower end, only Stalin's seat (which was not at the head of the table) being fixed. Everyone enjoyed his food, but only the drink, with the frequent toasting usual among Russians, caused any excitement. There were no waiters. People ate and talked at the same time for a period of five or six hours, right up to dawn. Stalin's colleagues were obviously used to such suppers. To a significant degree it was here that Soviet policy got made, those most closely concerned being in attendance. Stalin ate with relish, but he was no glutton. The quantities of food he took in, however, would have been huge even for a heavyset man. He drank moderately and was slow and cautious, unlike Molotov and, especially, Beria.[24]

Conversation revolved mainly around "Slavic" topics. Now it was whether the Albanians had any Slavic roots, now it was how much Serbian resembled Russian, now it was the sins of Tsarism toward the South Slavs. There were anecdotes. I told two or three. Stalin guffawed outright while Molotov laughed quietly up his sleeve. Stalin praised Dimitrov as more intelligent than Manuilsky. About disbanding the Comintern, he said: "Those people, the Westerners, are so low that they've never so much as mentioned this to us. The situation with the Comintern was becoming more and more unnatural. The very existence of a general Communist forum is wrong in circumstances when Communist parties have to find their own national languages and to struggle under conditions arising from within their own communities. There's something abnormal about it."

An officer brought in a dispatch. I had the impression that it had not just then arrived but had been ordered up for me to read. What Šubašić had done and said at the U.S. State Department was reported in detail. He had emphasized that it was not possible for the Yugoslavs to be against the Soviet Union, since the Slavic and pro-Russian tradition was extremely strong among them. "He's saying it to scare the Americans!" remarked Stalin. "But what's he scaring them for? Yes, he's scaring them! But why? Why?" And for my benefit he threw in, "They steal our dispatches, but we steal theirs, too."

The second dispatch really had just come in. In it Churchill announced that the invasion of France would commence the next day. Stalin began to scoff: "Oh, sure, there'll be a landing—if there's no fog! Always up to now there's been something to get in their way. I doubt it'll take place tomorrow, either. They might stumble across some Germans! Suppose they do stumble across some Germans? It's quite possible there won't be any landing and all there will be, just like all there ever has been, is promises."

Stammering, Molotov tried to show that a landing would take place. Stalin really had no doubts of this and only felt like jeering at his allies.

He gave me to take to Tito a beautiful saber, gift of the Supreme Soviet.

Long tendrils of fog were lifting at dawn out of the grove of firs surrounding the dacha. Stalin and Molotov, both of them tired and anxious, saw me off in front.[25] I was filled with wonder at the infinity of raw willpower belonging to the Soviet leadership. And with horror at the infinity of treachery and evil surrounding Russia, surrounding my own land. And my conclusion was this: The smart ones, the mighty ones, survive. But we little folk alongside them have to follow our own path and do things our own way.

3

FIRST SIGNS
OF
FALLING OUT

After setting Belgrade free we were welcomed to Valjevo[1] two days later, on October 22, 1944, and at that
moment, late at night, we naturally thought of the
hospitality being extended to us in terms of the welcome the Serbian generals had enjoyed after return-
ing from the Salonika expedition following World War I. We too were
lodged in a respectable city house. We too were given a room set apart,
and so as not to wake us up, people walked around on tiptoe. And when
we finally did get up, there were preserves for breakfast, and plum
brandy, and we were waited upon.

But we lost no time in proceeding by train to Arandjelovac[2] the next
day. That very afternoon, with an escort, I continued on by jeep, arriving in Belgrade before dark. Everywhere there were scenes like Valjevo.
Groups of peasant women in motley headscarves and soldiers' caps,
wearing country shoes with pointed toes, were being escorted into
headquarters buildings by heads of households and soldiers from the
Salonika front. Squads of high school students and apprentices
patiently stood in front of the central offices, awaiting orders. Teams of
animals hauled food. Swine and cows were being herded through the
streets. All for the troops. In the outlying districts the very walls cried
out with our thick-painted slogans, scrawled in bigger, bolder letters
than ever before.

So that Tito could move in, the staff of Dapčević's[3] corps had already left the villa at Rumunska 15 that had belonged to the German economic minister for Serbia, Neuhausen. I spent the night in temporary lodgings on Andre Nikolić Street. At once I found myself bombarded on every side by tales told in detail of the violent behavior of Soviet troops. Revolvers and watches were being stripped from our officers; there were robberies, rapes. Dapčević too was taken aback. Perhaps what stunned him the most was the insulting behavior of Soviet noncoms who were acting like "liberators," even though it was we who, in the battle for Belgrade, had lost three thousand men to their one thousand. When I retired late at night I could not fall asleep for dwelling on these outrageous acts. I was troubled by notions concerning "Soviets," notions derived from propaganda and my own wishful thinking. There had been so much to admire, to remember: young people meeting in the stadium, at the very moment when Belgrade was being fought over; newspapers being printed on the first press we captured; carpets being spread out before the Soviet tanks; townsmen charging with bare hands; the steady onslaught of Soviet troops, the defiant rush of our own fighters. And yet all these memories faded in the face of my chagrin, my suspicion that the Red Army was not what we had thought it was, not what it was supposed to be. I had seen a leaflet that was being handed out to Soviet troops by their commanding officers as they entered Yugoslavia: it was just a notice, shallow and bureaucratic, to the effect that Yugoslavia was an allied country inhabited by patriots who had risen up against the Germans.

The next day I went to the Majestic Hotel, headquarters of the National Committee and of higher officials and members of AVNOJ. People there were telling many a story and at the same time they were eating well. I was informed by Vladislav Ribnikar[4] that the newspaper *Politika* might print any day but that he was not sure whether our own paper, *Borba,* ought not to have priority. It was, after all, the Party organ. My feeling, however, was that *Politika* should not be held up, that it was an important paper, in its own way just as important as *Borba.*

After lunch I dropped in at staff headquarters on Andre Nikolić Street. The comrades were busy, so I sat down in the hall. Suddenly the stairs creaked beneath the tread of a heavyset Soviet general with coarse features. I reckoned this to be Belgrade's emancipator, Zhdanov.[5] He was a gruff man, it was said. I resolved not to get up for him.

Zhdanov, jaw jutting and muscles clenched, came to a halt: "Why don't you salute me?" Yanking myself out of my armchair, I retorted, in Russian: "And what about you? Aren't you going to acknowledge the rank of one of your allies?" The man turned on his heel in a blaze of anger and stalked out. I was in a state of exasperation when Dapčević and some staff personnel appeared from upstairs and calmed me down. But they were not at all unhappy at what had happened.

Upon Tito's return from Moscow, his first act was to establish a Guards unit on November 1. I remember remarking to Ranković that such a revival of royal forms pleased me not one whit, to which he replied, "It has to be so, it's the tradition." And a powerful detachment of soldiers was indeed created, one that was under Tito's direct personal command, one that bore the same name as our kings had bestowed. Possibly Moscow inspired all this, but we carried it out in our own way. Finally, along with Tito there came a Soviet general to organize his security.

Tito too was displeased with the behavior of the Soviet troops, nor did he like their commanders' response to our warnings, a response that was either caustic or indifferent.

Beneath the surface, matters were seething. There began to emerge newer, ever more horrific particulars. From the city committee we heard that on Čukarica Street, in the Belgrade suburbs, Soviet soldiers had raped and cut open a woman, a pharmacist; that as many as five thousand citizens had come running to her defense. The conduct of Soviet troops had assumed fundamental importance to our hopes of achieving influence and stabilizing our position. We were witnessing the rapid collapse of any illusions about the Red Army, and thereby the collapse of any illusions about Communists. As yet undeveloped organizationally, we were trying to take action in an unstable milieu that was hostile and to some extent out of control.

The pot had boiled over and no end was in sight when our Politburo decided to have a talk with the chief of the Soviet mission, General Korneyev. Tito took the view that to be more authoritative all four members should attend (of the original group, two had been killed and one was absent), plus the two most prominent commanders, Peko Dapčević and Koča Popović.[6]

Korneyev must have realized right away that something was afoot, and something unpleasant at that. He at once assumed a stiff, defensive posture. Scarcely had he heard Tito out when he snapped back that these were isolated cases and we were overreacting. We exchanged looks. Tito, restraining himself, tried to explain further while Korneyev kept interrupting him ever more testily. In the end I blurted out, "The problem is that this is being used by our enemies. They compare the offenses committed by Red Army soldiers to the behavior of English officers, who never engage in such provocations." At that, Korneyev turned red and stood up: "I protest in the sharpest terms this insult to the Red Army, equating it like this with the armies of capitalist countries!"

For all practical purposes, our talk with Korneyev ended right there. Nevertheless, the Soviet commanders began issuing orders, and the provocations diminished. Also, the Soviets were redeployed in Hungary, an enemy country that had never put them on a pedestal and where there was no need to abide by the correct relations observed between allies.

Korneyev had no sooner left the room than Kardelj muttered reproachfully, "You needn't have said that." And Ranković: "It really was uncomfortable." Tito did not take me to task, but his face did betray uneasiness. Only Dapčević seemed pleased.

It never crossed the minds of any of these comrades to let an incident involving respect for the Soviets alter their behavior toward me; there was no thought of reducing my role. Indeed, I was assigned by the Politburo to speak at the celebration of the October Revolution in the recently restored National Theater. Soviet agents, however, mostly returnees from the USSR, began spreading rumors that I was a Trotskyite. The source of this first attempt to discredit a member of the Central Committee was uncovered by Ranković. As for the agents themselves, after striking their blow at one of the bulwarks of our Party, a man whose past history and views were well known, they breathed not a word. In actual fact I was the only one to put up with the lack of understanding and belittling of me on the part of these "new," idealized Soviet people.

At the beginning of 1945 a delegation from the National Committee headed by Andrija Hebrang[7] left for Moscow. It included Arso Jovanović,[8] chief of the general staff, and my wife, Mitra.[9] The delegation went to seek economic, military, and other assistance, but both the group as a whole and individual members of it were subjected to complaints about the state of affairs in Yugoslavia and insinuations against particular leaders. Such charges were more often than not half true.

They were mainly leveled against Tito, to the effect that he cared more about royal palace repairs than about the front line, that he had little understanding of military affairs and even less of economic questions, that he thrust his own personality forward too much. At the same time, Hebrang was writing reports one after another to the Soviet leadership. This he did not conceal, nor would we have taken it as any great sin had such activity not undermined our own leadership.

The final, "tragic" moment in the delegation's demoralization was played out by Stalin himself. A banquet was staged at the Kremlin. Molotov and Stalin each assumed his own part, the one stoking the fire, the other falling into fits of tragic pathos. Ostensibly no hands were raised against Tito, the Yugoslav Army instead being the object of attack together with its commanding officers and myself. Stalin was in tears as he spoke of my "attack" on the Red Army, "an army that marched for a thousand kilometers across devastated countryside, an army that for you did not spare its blood, an army that was attacked by none other than Djilas! Djilas, whom I welcomed like a brother! Does Djilas, himself a writer, know what human suffering is? The human heart? Can he really not understand the soldier who after wading through blood and fire and death now, at the end, fools around with some woman or swipes some little object?" At every turn Stalin would drink a toast, crack a joke, feed the fires, weep, and kiss my wife, "because you're a Serb," all the while jeering that "I'll give you a kiss even if the Yugoslavs and Djilas accuse me of raping you!"

Jovanović defended our army—and wept, while Hebrang reproached him for crossing Stalin. Even Mitra burst into tears. "How can you help crying," she later said to me upon returning to Belgrade, "when you see Stalin in tears?"

My wife's story disquieted and even astonished me. But not to the extent that I failed to see in it all an attempt to weaken Tito and Tito's associates, if not to replace them. Mitra soon ceased to be depressed, and meanwhile my other leading comrades were familiarized with the dramatic supper at Stalin's.

Even in Belgrade, Soviet intelligence was the source of peculiar comments "for which no grounds existed."

Recruitment by Soviet intelligence had already been carried out in the upper reaches of our organizations, sensitive positions occupied by trusted Party people. The Soviets justified such actions by saying, "Yes, we're on good terms at the moment, your leadership is certainly loyal to the Soviet Union. But we have to guard our flanks, having had some bad experiences with Trotskyites and other enemies and with foreign agents within the Party." Naturally, nonideological methods were employed in this effort, including the seduction of women, the planting of Soviet actresses, "gifts," and the like. For instance, an attempt was made to recruit the Central Committee's cipher clerk, a woman. Very upset, she rushed in to see Ranković: Why did we need more "protection" over and above what our Central Committee itself was privy to? In such cases Ranković would call in the head of Soviet intelligence, a Colonel Timofeyev, and methodically lay the facts before him. The man would blush and promise over and over, "That won't happen anymore! It's zeal on our part, we're overeager." Tito would react angrily to these recruitment efforts: "What! So we have to 'keep this from happening,' do we! But aren't we Communists too? Once someone plants a spy on you, next thing you know it's off with your head. This demoralizes our people, kills their confidence in the leadership."10

As a way, now deliberate, of counteracting these Soviet "misunderstandings," our side began to emphasize the role of Tito, particularly in propaganda. Anytime we were at issue it would always be recalled that he was our leader along with Stalin. Tito was thus magnified. Tito grew out of our need for autonomy and a special status; he was not simply the product of our internal impulses to be authoritarian.

Finally, on March 7, 1945, there was hatched the Tito-Šubašić government. After Jajce the British and Soviets had exerted pressure on King Peter to accept the proposed regency. I was brought into the government as minister for Montenegro. (Later I became minister without portfolio.) Only occasionally did I have any assigned tasks in this government, and in reality it was a sinecure, a title with pay. My real work continued to be on the Central Committee, right up to the moment I fell from power in January 1954.

The struggle with Soviet representatives swirled around this government, too. It first was over Milan Grol,11 leader of the Democratic Party, and whether we should make him vice-president. Grol had impressed Tito and Kardelj with his reasonableness and sophistication, and so they brought him into the government without consulting the Soviets. The latter took this to mean that the English had penetrated us, although it could not be said of Grol that he was anybody's tool. He represented only his own views and those of his foreign friends.

Accordingly, when Kardelj and I edited the government's charter, the three Allies—the USSR, Great Britain, and the United States—were referred to as equal partners rather than the USSR being singled out for special recognition. This was taken as yet another "proof" that we had turned to the West.

Finally, on the occasion of a dinner arranged by Tito for the newly arrived ambassadors of the three major powers, an Englishman and not a Russian was seated in the place of honor. Actually, Tito was proceeding by protocol, for the Briton was doyen of the diplomatic corps. But within his own narrow circle Tito regretted it: "You just never know what these Russians want."

With our arrival in Belgrade my headaches began, to this moment incurable and inexplicable. But even had there been no such physical problems, if headaches didn't exist, they'd have to be invented (to borrow the phrase). For no reason in particular—simply from the fact of having power and abundance—I started at that time to grow emotionally estranged from Mitra, and we would have fights. We would argue for days on end, then be silent for weeks, also on end. It was a period when many people were severing the ties of their wartime and Party loves. Maybe this was the very reason I did not break off with her just then. Or maybe my time had not yet come. I was still not my own man. Within me, ideas and emotions had not yet parted ways.

The Soviets, of course, hastened to underscore their dominance in Yugoslavia by means of a mutual-aid treaty with the newly formed government. Šubašić, as minister of foreign affairs, showed off his importance in this way, even though everything had been worked out in advance behind his back. At first glance the pact was senseless: an alliance against a Germany on the point of collapse, involving countries that had been waging war against it for almost four years. But such was the form, by now hackneyed, through which the Soviets first established and then consolidated their precedence.

At the head of the delegation was Tito, without whom it would have lacked the necessary representative character. Besides Šubašić it included two economic ministers. Plus me, not so much because Tito wanted to have along someone close to him as that by direct contact the "insult" I had bestowed on the Red Army might be smoothed over. I was told by Tito himself, now with an enigmatic but friendly smile, three or four days before departure that I too had to go to Moscow.

The delegation set out on a Soviet aircraft on April 5. Tito felt so ill that he kept throwing up. As for me, the closer we got to Moscow under a somber, impenetrable sky and over a dark, ravished land the more bitterly lonely I felt. It was a feeling I already knew. For months in Belgrade an atmosphere had been forming about me not unlike the aura surrounding a great sinner who is finding that redemption comes hard. There was something painful and insubstantial in the space swaying about me—in my own faith. Only in Tito did I sense support, and he had kept silent throughout the affair, though never modifying his attitude toward me of cordial protectiveness.

He was taken off to a dacha by himself, the rest of us being billeted in the venerable Metropol Hotel. There, problematic Katyushas and Natashas offered their services over the telephone to us ministers. I never asked Šubašić whether such seductive snares had been thrown his way, for I was ashamed, as a Communist, of such methods being employed by the homeland of socialism.

The treaty was signed on April 11 in the Kremlin, Stalin and the waiter all the while offering toasts and draining glasses to Yugoslav-Soviet friendship. This was the only so-called charming episode.

Stalin sat directly across from me in a sulk; not a word did he address to me. After supper there were toasts and the unavoidable films and he gave me a flabby handshake, again without a word. I for my part felt calmer, whether on account of the tolerable atmosphere or because of my own growing toughness—even sitting opposite Stalin.

At lunch in the Kremlin Palace Stalin warmed up to me, at least to the extent that his inscrutable expression took me in. It was at that meal that Stalin—and only he had the authority to do so—broke the false, stiff atmosphere. We were in the habit of addressing the Soviets as "Comrade" except at banquets and receptions, where because Šubašić or Westerners were present we used the term "Mister" [*gospodin*]. Stalin, raising his glass, addressed Tito as "Comrade" [*drug*], adding that he was not about to call him a *gospodin*.

Stalin was in a mood to jest. He leaned over the table, he threw into confusion the senile, half-blind President Kalinin,[12] he tittered loudly. But neither there nor anywhere else did he make fun of himself. Divinity remains divinity only if it behaves like divinity. The adoration of Stalin and Stalin's dominance could be felt in that circle more fully and immediately than during the suppers at his dacha.

I was also taken to one of those suppers, which pleased me even though I suspected that Stalin and I were going to have it out over my "insult" to the Red Army. The Soviet side was represented by Stalin, Molotov, Malenkov,[13] Beria, Bulganin,[14] and General Antonov. On our side were Tito and the three of us Communist ministers. Šubašić was absent; he did not even know that we were dining at Stalin's. A supper had been dreamed up separately for him, which he bragged about the next day.

Tito was seated to Stalin's right, I across from them to Molotov's right. Face to face with Stalin, I found that my self-assurance was whetted and refined.

Only after the toasts and gibes had warmed our spirits and the conversation had acquired a comradely immediacy did Stalin "remember" to liquidate his quarrel with me. This he did half-playfully, pouring me a glass of vodka and calling on me to drink to the Red Army. In the first moment, no doubt owing to too intense a concentration, I did not grasp what Stalin had in mind. Strong drink gave me headaches, and so as not to spoil the company, I was drinking beer. But to refuse a glass offered me by Stalin was impossible, and I was about to drink it to his health. "No, no," insisted Stalin, laughing like an inquisitor. And then it dawned on me what he intended. "I mean to the Red Army. What, don't you want to drink to the Red Army?"

I drained my glass at a gulp. It was as if I were making a confession, and I felt no guilt as I drank it off but rather felt joy, for I was "confessing" to Stalin.

Briefly, I sketched the reasons and the meaning of my remarks about the Red Army. All this was obviously long familiar to Stalin. In the Soviet indignation over my "attack" the dominating factor was Great Power sensitivity; truth and good intentions were secondary considerations. Stalin interrupted my explanation: "Yes. You have, of course, read Dostoyevsky. Have you seen how complex a creature man is, the human psyche? Well, imagine the man who has fought from Stalingrad to Belgrade—thousands of kilometers across his own devastated land, stepping across his fallen comrades, his nearest and dearest! How can such a man react normally? And what's so awful in his messing around with a woman after horrors like that? You imagined the Red Army as an ideal. But it is not ideal, nor can it be, even if there were not a certain number of criminals within its ranks—we opened the jails and shoved everyone into the ranks. No, not even the Red Army is ideal.

What's important is that it beat the Germans—and it's doing a good job of that, and everything else is secondary."15

Here ended the argument over the Red Army's conduct. Or so we thought. It was then that my primary impression of Stalin took shape: an excellent, still lively memory, and a power of imagination that was vibrant but concrete. Now I would add to this by saying that Stalin seemed to possess a unique and spontaneous power to penetrate to the essence of people. Facing him I felt completely exposed, and glad of it. One could never guess from his behavior that in the war he had lost his son Yasha. Even we had no inkling of this. Stalin had grieved for his son for two or three days, then accepted the death as a "necessity" and gone on as though nothing had happened.

He would tease Tito with a kind of mirthful malice that most often took the form of flattering the Bulgarian army at the expense of the Yugoslav: "The Bulgarians had their weaknesses, their army harbored enemies, then they shot a couple of dozen and now everything's all right. But your Yugoslav soldiers—why, they're still guerrillas, unfit for serious fighting in a face-off! One German regiment last winter routed a division—that was your division! One regiment—a whole division!" By praising the Bulgarian troops Stalin had nothing more in mind than goading us Yugoslavs. The Soviet leadership, like the Tsarist before it, was simply fonder of Bulgarians.

Next Stalin proposed drinking to the Yugoslav army, adding, "But they'll put up a good fight, even on level ground!"

Tito held himself in. Whenever Stalin launched some witticism at our expense, Tito would glance at me with a smile and I would give him a look of sympathy in return. But when Stalin said that the Bulgarian troops were better than ours, Tito lost patience and exclaimed that our army would soon show that it had eliminated its weaknesses.

It seemed as though Stalin and Tito held a grudge against each other. Without openly offending our leader, Stalin kept carping at the state of affairs in Yugoslavia. Tito related to Stalin as to the senior man, but he did not grovel. And he even rebuffed the slights directed at Yugoslavia.

Tito emphasized that socialism today was advancing in a different manner than in the past. Stalin caught him up: "Today socialism is possible even under the English monarchy. Revolution is no longer needed everywhere. Not long ago I received a delegation of British Labourites and we were talking over precisely this point. Yes, there's much that's new. Yes, even with an English king, socialism is possible."

Yugoslavia essentially had a Soviet power structure, I put in, inasmuch as the Communist Party held the key positions and there were no other genuine parties, let alone opposition ones. "No, you do not have a Soviet power structure," retorted Stalin, "you've got some sort of a cross between de Gaulle's France and the Soviet Union."

Inwardly I did not agree with this appraisal of Stalin's, all the more since he seemed unaware of the essential nature of the changes in Yugoslavia, or simply refused to acknowledge them.

Stalin had no patience for monologues, even his own, but he did take the lead. Only Tito and Molotov shared in the conversation, I very little, the rest practically not at all. About the ongoing war, Stalin said: "This war is not as in the past, instead whoever takes territory imposes his own system there. Everyone installs his own system to the farthest point reached by his army."

Giving the reasons for his "Pan-Slavic" policy, he explained that "if the Slavs remain unified, if they stand together, no one in the future will lift a finger against them." And to someone's observation that it would take the Germans fifty years to recover, if not longer, Stalin shot back, "No, they will recover, and very fast at that. . . . In twenty years, or fifteen, they'll be back on their feet again. And that's why Slavic unity is important. . . ."

Once, hitching up his pants, he exclaimed: "We'll be over and done with the war very soon. And in fifteen or twenty years we'll recover. And then we'll go at it again."

In response to a remark made by Molotov he said that the Soviet leaders respected Churchill as a farsighted man and a dangerous adversary.

On our way back Tito, who likewise could not tolerate large quantities of alcohol, said, "I don't know what the devil makes these Russians drink so much, it's simply some sort of decadence." Yet I could not but reflect that the issues in dispute had now been settled, though not from comradeship and cordiality but for reasons of state, political reasons.

We also had dinner with Dimitrov in his dacha outside of Moscow. Tito and he exchanged Comintern reminiscences; Bulgarian-Yugoslav unification came in for some discussion; and some excellent Soviet performers entertained us ad nauseam. Otherwise it was pleasant and a little melancholy, for one could sense resignation in Dimitrov on account of being detained in Moscow, whereas all the émigrés had long since gotten back to Bulgaria and were dividing up the most important positions.

The Soviet people in charge, thinking ahead to their admission to the United Nations, had by that point set up a commissariat of foreign affairs in Ukraine and in Byelorussia. Those commissars had no infrastructure at their disposal, nor for that matter did they have any foreign policy. Newly established, they had not yet succeeded in defining themselves beyond a mere formality. We were supposed to visit Ukraine on the return trip, the initiative for this probably coming out of Kiev, which was quite likely since Nikita Khrushchev was the prime mover down there.

Khrushchev; the minister for foreign affairs, Manuilsky; and various Ukrainian dignitaries welcomed us cordially because they regarded our arrival as a great state achievement of their very own. It was less formal than in Moscow. There were no hesitations and tensions, things had a lively immediacy. To us, even the Ukrainian speech intonation seemed closer.

The Ukrainian top echelon was dominated by Khrushchev, and this was due not just to his function but also to his personality. He pulled all the strings, and these were even more within his reach than they were with Stalin. People did not bow down before Khrushchev in awe, however. With Stalin, no connection with the public at large could be observed except in the abstract sense of ideology. Stalin was preoccupied with an ultimate goal, not at all with people and their daily lives, or minimally. Khrushchev insisted on everything's being *narodni,* springing from the people. Even the general's uniform he wore at the time was comfortable and loose-fitting. He himself, of course, was folksy, at least in speech and conduct. But his thinking, his way of thinking, was a mixture of Marxism taken straight out of the Party schools and an inherited peasant practicality. He also possessed a good and lively memory, and a sense of humor, humor that was sly and a little crude. He seemed to hold grudges: Despite all Manuilsky's entreaties and reproaches, he refused to let a singer who had entertained the Germans perform in the opera. But this vengefulness was never visible, and even when it was directed at the singer it took the form of an "infantile," dogmatic grudge, not reprisal. Khrushchev was very talkative and looked closely at every detail. One could argue with him without putting relations under a strain. He was in fact a "popular democrat," an authoritarian without formality and self-puffery. Plump yet nimble, he ate well and drank well, like a man of the people who had unexpectedly struck it rich. As distinct from Stalin, for whom ideas were tools, Khrushchev readily appealed to ideas to justify practical turnabouts.

Not until April 20 did we take off for home. Ukraine, with its impoverished, half-Russified public life, lost itself in faceless, vain expectations. Doubts about the official representations of Soviet reality burned themselves into my consciousness.

4   DIFFERENCES WITH MOSCOW

It is very hard—impossible, I think—to date precisely
the onset of Yugoslavia's confrontation with the Soviet
Union and to list the causes of that conflict. Differences arose during the war. But that was also a time
of extremely close association with the Soviets, to the
point of identifying with them. And afterwards our intimacy only grew
in enthusiasm and sense of purpose. Problems might arise and prolif-
erate, only to dissipate, but the essence of our relationship remained
what it was right down to the beginning of 1948. On the eve of war the
Yugoslav Party had felt "Bolshevized," conscious of being one of the
Comintern's most loyal partners—most loyal, that is, to the "bastion of
socialism," Moscow. During the war, joint action with the Soviets had
the force of immutable custom: We lived it. The war's end brought
altered circumstances and a change in tactics, but we had the same
leaders and the same orientation. Our Yugoslav Party remained the
most pugnacious, the most doctrinaire, and the most pro-Soviet. In the
Western press they called us "Satellite Number One." I got sick of this
label and raised my voice against it. We really did not feel ourselves to
be a satellite (which only confirmed our delusions), and we were not
one in the sense that the Soviet Union controlled our regime and had
the power to reduce us to a vassal state. So the roots of the confrontation lay in our sense of being an independent power. And it was our
revolution that spawned such an awareness. To the extent that we

consolidated our authority and realized what lay within the realm of possibility, confrontation with a tyrannical hegemony became inevitable.

It was our two intelligence agencies and the two propaganda services that were first at odds. Friction can be expected between countries over questions of authority and sensibility. But in our case, two states where democracy was utterly absent and ideology reigned, discord appeared initially in these two areas. It was the Soviet side, however, that took the initiative and exhibited the greater impatience and maladroitness.

No sooner did they arrive on our liberated territory than the Soviet military missions began to forge links with our administrative personnel. This may have been customary among the great powers, but it was incomprehensible to us. Unacceptable. We, after all, were open toward Moscow. We identified ourselves with the Soviets in philosophy and goals. They would hint at dangers from the West, especially from the direction of England. They were, they said, "taking lively precautions" for the unity of our Party, appealing to their painful experience with Trotskyites and other such double-agent deviationists. They would relax and enjoy the pan-Slavic, pro-Russian toasts offered by fellow travelers from the bourgeois parties. And they were courteous and tolerant with the Western missions. But Communists were almost the only people they would cultivate. Nor would they cringe with aversion if someone's Party past could not stand up to close inspection.

Failing to grasp that we Yugoslavs had registered a new and enriched perception of revolution, the Soviets were dismissive. They explained away the dilemmas of Yugoslav Communists in the service of Soviet intelligence as a "unique form of nationalism" and as "ideological immaturity." We, though, dug in our heels and drew nourishment from such enriching change, for all that we remained consistently Leninist and loyal to the Soviet Union.

That is why the schemes of Soviet agents were always miscarrying and bringing humiliation down upon their heads when they dealt with Communists. In Agitprop the friction began early, as if in tandem with the friction that had sprung up between the two intelligence agencies. At first it was not as irritating.

Our propaganda resembled Soviet propaganda and in every respect supported the Soviet Union. But there was a striking distinction in tone: Ours was fresher and more militant. Such a superficial, to all appearances unessential, distinction concealed tensions of a different sort that pulled in contrary directions and of whose existence we were at first unaware. The Soviets had long since become accustomed to ideological clichés and bureaucratic limitations and they expected change to come from the top down, whereas our own leaders, fresh from the fire, administered directly and their limitations arose mainly from ideological conviction. The biggest and most meaningful revolution of our era was now mired in its own bureaucratic, caste structures, and unlike the earlier, "bourgeois" revolutions had grown thereby less tolerant and more aggressive. But a second revolution, Yugoslavia's, which was small, weak, and ideologically dependent, was now freeing itself to work out its own living forms, to pursue its own course.

Not for one moment did our propaganda lose its independence, either organizationally or politically. Believing as we did that we all belonged to the same universal, socialist community, we elected to publicize Soviet positions and to publish Soviet materials. But they could not force anything on us. Our editors and propaganda apparatus were part of a chain of command leading up to the Central Committee. More exactly, they were closely linked with the center for political propaganda, Agitprop, which was under my direction. Anything Soviet that might be disproportionate or clashed with our own manner and tone, of course came up for discussion. But there was no anti-Soviet intent.

It was around Tito that the Soviet-Yugoslav confrontation first began to crystallize. This was not only due to his dominant, central role but also owing to the distinguishing traits of Yugoslav communism, imperious and authoritarian. Which were essentially those of Soviet communism as well.

Identical as these may have been in essence, they were not traits we had mechanically taken over from "Leninism" and the Soviet Party. Rather, Soviet experience provided the handiest and most expedient mold for the spiritual properties common to every Communist movement, including the Yugoslav. An ideology that fuses a worldview with political action (a philosophy that interprets the world only to the degree it changes that world) unavoidably generates despots and oligarchies. Even during the war, our raising of Tito to the level of Stalin had provoked muffled resentment among the Soviets. But they knew no way out of this trap of their own making. Tito too was a Communist, and they found it convenient to strengthen communism in Yugoslavia by glorifying him. We accorded Stalin primacy on the stage of world history, but in Yugoslavia Tito was his equal.

In the first official attack on Tito, Soviet envy was held in check, however. Or else we who were closest to him noticed nothing because Stalin, naturally, while not standing alone, could not be compared to anyone. Or compared only to Lenin.

The attack was triggered by Tito's speech in Ljubljana on May 27, 1945. Carried away by victory but feeling bitter toward the Western Allies for having forced our troops out of Trieste, an action the Soviets had gone along with for reasons of their own, Tito said outright what the Party leadership had been saying in private and with wonder when it came to our relations with the USSR but what bourgeois leaders took for granted in Great Power politics, and unavoidable:

> It has been said that this was a just war and we have regarded it as such. But we also seek a just conclusion. Our goal is that every man be the master in his own house. We are not going to pay the balance on others' accounts, we are not going to serve as pocket money in anyone's currency exchange, we are not going to allow ourselves to become entangled in political spheres of interest. Why should it be held against our peoples that they want to be completely independent? And why should that autonomy be restricted, or the subject of dispute? We will not be dependent on anyone ever again, regardless of what has been written, regardless of what has been said—and much has been written and what is written is ugly and unjust, what is written is insulting and unworthy of our allies. [Here Tito had in mind the Western press, which was saying that Yugoslavia had fallen into the Soviet sphere and was a satellite of the USSR.] Today's Yugoslavia is not an object to be sold or bargained for.*

This speech of Tito's, though not it alone, served Moscow as reason to lodge a protest. Our government itself was not made privy to the protest, actually, but was bypassed in favor of the topmost circle of Central Committee members. Stalin, we know, did not act in haste, but neither did he dawdle, and the letter had already arrived by the beginning of June 1945, in the form of official instructions to Ambassador Sadchikov to be handed to Kardelj. This was before any rumors of Soviet

---

*Quoted from *Borba,* May 28, 1945.

collusion at our expense with "imperialists," before any thought of the similarity between Soviet behavior as a major power and that of the Western imperialists. Their note revealed that they were offended and angry at being lumped together with the Western imperialist powers. It contained the threat of public disavowal:

> We regard the speech by Comrade Tito as an unfriendly attack on the Soviet Union and Comrade Kardelj's attempts to explain it as unsatisfactory. That is how our readers understand Comrade Tito's speech; it cannot be taken otherwise. Tell Comrade Tito that if he should mount such an attack one more time on the Soviet Union, we will be compelled to answer him in the press and to disavow him.*

In one way or another the incident was smoothed over. Tito offered explanations to Ambassador Sadchikov, the Soviets made a tactical withdrawal, and there emerged more important problems in common. Yugoslavia's internal situation at that juncture, when the bourgeois democratic leaders Grol and Šubašić had passed over to the opposition, did not play into Soviet hands for purposes of sowing division among Communists by mounting public attacks on Tito. The Soviets would not reveal their hegemonistic intentions. But we at the top certainly were prompted by this episode to popularize Tito still more systematically as our leader.

Tensions and frictions carried over to other areas, especially economic. The sharpest differences had to do with the jointly owned companies the Soviets were establishing all over Eastern Europe. These companies were regarded with mixed feelings by our leadership. It did not escape us that they would serve Moscow as a tool for perpetuating its political dominance. In this regard Moscow had no different aims than all other victors. On the other hand, we felt that she was justified because of the weakness of socialism: Prewar economic relations might well be restored in those countries. We saw no such weaknesses and dangers in our own case, and so our negotiations with the Soviets at once got down to hard bargaining, which made for tension and disagreement. This in turn led us to compare Soviet claims with

---

*Quoted from S. Kržavac and D. Marković, *Informbiro—šta je to* (The Cominform—What It Is), Belgrade, 1976, p. 95.

exploitation by Western companies before the war, exploitation that for all its shameless injustice had been far more lenient by comparison. Appeals to socialism's "weakness" now began to lose credibility as a justification for the tributary position of the East European countries. Among those countries, some were allies of our own. All without exception were intensely conscious of their nationhood and sensitive to their status as separate peoples. As we played host to their representatives and paid them return visits we could see the resentment among their leaders over the joint companies. Our independent and sometimes overconfident bearing must have been painfully conspicuous.

We had not thought through our ambiguous position. No leader was against joint companies, but also no one was willing simply for that reason to give up our sovereign rights and forgo a mutual, just profit. None, that is, but Hebrang and Žujović, for whom sovereignty and independence in relations between socialist countries were "purely bourgeois prejudices." Once I happened to be with Tito on business when Velebit, then assistant minister for foreign affairs, warned him that the agreement with the Soviet government regarding a joint air transport company was in violation of state sovereignty, since it provided for Soviet crews at our airports. Tito flew into a rage: "That can't be! Sovereignty has to be preserved!" But his proposed solution was not well considered: "It's got to be explained to the Russians! The agreement has to be accepted, but sovereignty must remain in our hands."

Above all, we were the victims of propaganda about the development and economic might of the Soviet Union. For us, industrialization was not merely a vital necessity, the vindication of our sacrifices and wartime destruction, but also the very premise of the classless society to come. Socialism meant not merely a better life but the brotherhood and equality of persons and peoples as well. And that the Soviet Union would help us industrialize seemed most natural, most logical. It was a country with the same ideals and with an already highly developed industrial base. Our excessive demands on the USSR were often born of these delusions and self-deceptions. But the Soviet representatives not only were unable to meet our unreal, sometimes megalomaniacal, "planned" requirements, they did not even deliver the equipment contracted for the joint companies.

We were then also buying weapons from the Soviet Union. It was only in 1948, after the confrontation had broken out, that we discovered the Soviets had sold us used, repainted field pieces for their dollar value. Our commissions took note of it when the equipment was received but did not sound the alarm, thinking that that's the way things had to be done. And few cared a hoot about cost. Our sending students to the USSR was similar. The sending was easy enough and we began feeling the pinch only when it came to footing the bill—at the official, "real," ruble-to-dollar exchange rate.

Negotiations over joint companies either progressed not at all or progressed only sluggishly in secondary branches of the economy. But for that very reason, tension was less noticeable and our attention was distracted by domestic stress and strain over the "bourgeois" opposition, or the Catholic Church, or relations with the West, especially the United States. As for the Soviets, in their hurry to consolidate their position in Eastern Europe they were being cautious with Washington. Finally, when Kardelj visited Stalin in March 1947 in connection with a Big Four conference of foreign ministers in Moscow over a treaty for Austria, Stalin "reasoned" as follows:

> How would it be if we didn't set up any joint companies at all? . . . Clearly, this isn't a good form of collaboration with an ally and such a friendly country as Yugoslavia. It would always end up in discord and disagreement, the other country's own independence would suffer and friendly relations would be spoiled. Such companies are appropriate for satellites.*

Stalin's way of "reasoning"—classifying the socialist countries as either satellites or independents—seemed curious to us as first. He often surprised non-Soviet Communists by reacting and thinking "unidealistically," a style more associated with the power politics of autocrats. But we adjusted to it and even grew to accept this, as if we were not the objects of discussion. We ourselves had tasted power and thought in a "power-political" way. Not yet had we seen through Stalin's seduction of us. He was "reasoning" precisely in our own "power-political" way, knowing that we now found power to be sweet.

Tito left for Moscow on May 27, 1946, at the head of a delegation that included nearly all our most trustworthy comrades. At stake was

---

*Vladimir Dedijer, *J. B. Tito, prilozi za biografiju* (J. B. Tito: Contributions Toward a Biography). Belgrade: Kultura, 1953, p. 465.

nothing less than our industrialization and rearmament with the Soviet Union's help. The visit to Moscow lasted longer than was usual for a state delegation. But the delegation returned very happy with the promises made and quite overcome by Stalin's wit and personality at a dinner he gave that departed from protocol.

On the issue of joint companies, Stalin was reticent. After Tito spoke up for them, however, as a way of promoting Yugoslav economic development, Stalin and Molotov went along, as a way of generating a mutual profit. I have mentioned that once they had been negotiated, these companies led to nothing but bickering and misgivings. Other economic agreements with the Soviets came to the same dead end, though it must be said that we, too, did not fulfill our obligations.

Even then Stalin took a lively interest in Albania. We saw that he was well informed—better, perhaps, than our own leaders, despite our proximity to the country and our extensive ties. His interest in personalities and currents in the Albanian leadership displayed a knowledge of detail.

Our exchange about Albania was no accident. I would hazard the guess that the idea of subjugating Yugoslavia had already taken shape in Stalin's mind. In early 1948 our friction with the Soviets over Albania would serve him as the most convenient and plausible pretext for attacking us. His dangling Albania before us was a snare, but one woven of actual relationships, entwined in the designs that our top leaders undoubtedly harbored on that country.

We, though, were still in thrall to ideology, to our revolutionary idealism, despite our unbridled craving for power, despite our unfounded pretensions to being a great state. Stalin knew this better than anyone. Such had been the course taken by the Russian Revolution. The Albanian card was only one ploy, albeit the most sensitive, in a strategy of inflaming our egos and leading us down a path of his choice.

During the dinner at Stalin's dacha he dispensed opinions, mainly negative, about the leaders of the European parties: Thorez[1] didn't know how to bite, La Pasionaria[2] couldn't collect her thoughts and hadn't any eyes in her head either, Togliatti[3] was a professor who could write a good theoretical article but couldn't lead people toward a well-defined goal, Pieck[4] was a senile old man who was only up to tapping you on the shoulder.[5]

On the other hand, after first declaring that "Tito must look out for himself . . . because I won't live long and Europe needs him. Yes,

Europe needs Tito!,," Stalin did not neglect to take Tito by the arms and make him stand up three times over. This European mission that Stalin had in mind for Tito never made any sense to me, either at the time or later. And yet our leading comrades, telling and retelling these scenes from Stalin's dinner, would succumb to ecstasy, reason suspended, eyes shining, smiles distracted. Even Tito would glow with pride in "humble" silence and self-restraint. Their rapture was perhaps best embodied in the behavior of Ranković, who, urged by Stalin, drained one glass of pepper vodka after another, though he had never cared for hard liquor. "I would have taken poison had Stalin offered it," he later said.

Another dinner, this one including the Bulgarian leaders Dimitrov, Kolarov,[6] and Kostov,[7] gave Stalin and his cronies an opportunity to reopen unhealed wounds and stir up fresh competition between Bulgaria and Yugoslavia. Stalin made an obvious point of showing that he valued Tito more than Dimitrov, Beria observed for all to hear that Kolarov had lost his intellectual grasp forty years earlier, and when a bottle of Bulgarian wine was opened, Stalin declared that the wine was Yugoslav: "The Bulgarians looted it from them during the war."

Our delegation was granted exceptional consideration in being allowed to stand honor guard over Kalinin's bier during his funeral, and Tito was singled out by Stalin at the burial ceremony by being called upon to take a place among the members of the Soviet Politburo.

What did Stalin want? Why did he do all this? There is no one clear answer, I think, nor can there be. Certainly he himself was enthusiastic about Tito and the Yugoslavs, but at the same time he was misleading them. Stalin's mind worked in many directions, up to the point where, realities having come into focus, he found the way that best promoted his own agenda, that agenda being to strengthen his power. In Tito he saw not only the leader and master of a new Yugoslavia but also an independent, gifted politician—an exceptional collaborator or an incomparable antagonist. Or perhaps all of the above at one and the same time, a man for all seasons.[8]

Our confrontation with the Soviet Union was conceived in anger over questions of influence and prestige in the so-called people's democracies of Eastern Europe, and was inseparably linked to Soviet pressure and provocation. A young and still unbureaucratized revolution in a small and undeveloped country eager to assert its claims had a falling out with a Great Power now stabilized and conscious of its historic, imperial role. That is how it began, at least. And if our highly idealistic aspirations toward those countries at the beginning harbored impulses toward some sort of possibly ideological hegemony, does not politics by definition unwittingly carry such seeds? The Soviets, on the other hand, aspired consciously toward hegemony. They knew what they were doing and only cloaked their actions in a codified, ossified ideology.[9]

Everyday business relations and the prospect of negotiations told Stalin that economic relationships between the Soviet Union and Eastern Europe were no different from those with Western countries. If anything they brought less satisfaction, burdened as they were with ideological obligations and pitfalls. But at the same time we had to generate and nourish relations with the East—such was the situation, grounded in ideological ties and identities. Our leaders, tormented, found themselves in a dilemma.

It is possible that we would have long continued to find ourselves stuck in economic culs-de-sac had not our economic disagreements with the Soviet Union become entangled with ideological, political differences and discord. Self-confident after achieving a revolution on our own, we Yugoslav leaders could not, would not obey in silence. Starting from the inner circle, disputes and resentments spread outward, gradually maturing into conscious criticism.

And this did not lend itself to concealment, even had the leadership insisted on it. Among the leaders themselves and all around them were comrades who took every criticism of, and especially every hint of independence from, the Soviet Union as a retreat from ideology and even a betrayal of the revolution and their own revolutionary past— their revolutionary essence. Confrontation thus became unavoidable, even though no one was completely conscious of the form it might take or suspected its magnitude. No one sought a pretext, no one intentionally struck a spark. Both the one and the other materialized out of the relations between states—political relations.

The occasion arose, the spark was struck, when Yugoslav and Soviet policy toward Albania came into conflict. The founding of the Comintern and the establishment of its headquarters in Belgrade smoothed over and smothered for a time our mutual intolerance and impatience over Albania. But no sooner had the honeymoon of ideological internationalism run its course than our stifled and opposed ambitions emerged once more, with unforeseen violence.

Increasingly nervous, Tito pressed for unification with Albania. Within his narrow circle he neither would nor could conceal his fear that the Russians would get the jump on us and "grab" that small country. Thus unification, instead of being founded on mutual goodwill, looked more and more like an invasion by Yugoslavia. For no good reason except the pretext of danger to Albania from a "Greek reaction" and from "imperialists" holed up in Greece, Tito ordered that two fully equipped divisions make ready to be dispatched to Albania.

It was a question of preparations only. But the issue was not discussed by the Politburo or within Tito's narrow circle of Kardelj, Ranković, and myself. I would add, though—take my word for it—that my conscience was not easy. Bringing Albania to heel was inconsistent with our teaching about voluntary mergers and the self-determination of peoples. True, this would not be the first case of reality correcting theory, but it was a new and very drastic case—our own case—of such correction. On the other hand, it was not pleasant to think of Moscow's gaining the upper hand in Albania and thereby encircling Yugoslavia, preventing unification of the two countries. I knew I could find no support for my reflections, that I was all alone with my doubts. Above all, I had the feeling that the maneuver would not succeed. Tito was tense, our actions seemed hasty, and the times were not propitious. There was a civil war in Greece, and we were being accused in the United Nations of intervening in it. It was a time of intense, feverish endeavors by Tito and the government to draw close to the people's democracies and consolidate our special influence on them, independent of the Soviet Union.

At the end of December 1947 we received a cable from Moscow saying that Stalin wanted me or another Central Committee member to pay a visit to reconcile the policies of our two governments toward Albania. Since I was abreast of Yugoslav-Albanian relations, including the Soviets' tactless and irresponsible scheming in Tirana, I received no special instructions. A delegation from the Yugoslav Army joined me, including Koča Popović, chief of the General Staff and the head of our military industry, and Mijalko Todorović,[10] who wanted to discuss armaments and the development of industry. Svetozar Vukmanović-Tempo,[11] head of the army's political administration, also came along to familiarize himself with the Red Army's experience in political work.

We set off by train on or about January 8, buoyant and full of hope but convinced that Yugoslavia must solve its problems in its own way and rely on its own resources. In Moscow, hardly hours after we arrived, we were recounting the news from home to our ambassador, Vladimir Popović, and wondering what our prospects might be with the Soviet government, when all of a sudden the phone rang. It was the Ministry of Foreign Affairs, calling to say that if I was not too worn out, Stalin wanted to see me. What could have drained me on a trip of several days in a comfortable parlor car, spent in reading and idle chatter? And even if I had been completely exhausted I would have rushed off at Stalin's beck and call. I was the object of envious looks from all, and Popović and Todorović begged me not to forget the reasons why they had come.

Yet in all my joy at the imminent encounter with Stalin there was a certain sobriety and wariness. All through the night I spent with Stalin and his closest collaborators I was haunted by the duplicity in Yugoslav-Soviet relations.

At nine o'clock I was driven to Stalin's office in the Kremlin. Stalin, Molotov, and Zhdanov[12] were already there, the latter because he was responsible for relations with foreign Communist parties. Once the greetings and the usual inquiries about health were over, Stalin sat down at the table and turned to the matter at hand, Albania: "Members of the Albanian Central Committee are killing themselves on your account! That's very unpleasant, very unpleasant. . . ."[13]

I agreed it was unpleasant and started to explain—that by opposing rapprochement between Albania and Yugoslavia, Nako Spiru[14] had isolated himself in his own Central Committee. But before I could finish, Stalin unexpectedly broke in: "We have no special interest in Albania," he said. "We agree with Yugoslavia's swallowing Albania." Here he put the fingertips of his right hand to his lips and made a motion as if swallowing.

I must have looked surprised, but I made an effort to interpret Stalin's words in the spirit of his extraordinary, drastic sense of humor. I tried again: "It's not a matter of swallowing, it's a matter of unification." "But that is swallowing," interjected Molotov.

Stalin caught up the phrase, again with his fingertips bunched. "Yes, yes, swallowing! But we agree—you ought to swallow Albania, and the sooner the better."

Apart from this the atmosphere was cordial enough, and the way Molotov delivered that line about swallowing was amiable, even funny.

Stalin's gestures and approval roused my suspicion that something was amiss in our Albanian policy, that unification was not proceeding voluntarily, any more than the Soviet Union's annexation of the Baltic countries. But Stalin brought me back to business: "What about Hoxha?[15] What is he like in your opinion?" I avoided a clear, direct answer. Stalin then expressed precisely the opinion about Hoxha prevailing among Yugoslav leaders: "He's a *petit bourgeois,* isn't he, inclined to nationalism? Yes, that's what we think too. Xoxe[16] seems to be the most solid man there."

I concurred. Then, bringing the conversation about Albania to a close, Stalin said: "There are no differences between us. But you must personally write Tito a cable about this in the name of the Soviet government and submit it to me by tomorrow."

Not sure I had understood Stalin's unusual instructions—me write a cable in the name of the Soviet government?—I asked him what this meant and he said it again, distinctly. At that moment I was flattered by Stalin's confidence in me, but in framing my words the next day I avoided saying anything that could be used against Tito and the Yugoslav government. The cable was delivered that very day by our ambassador to the Kremlin. But it was never used, probably because it contained nothing that Stalin's evil cunning could turn to advantage. I stated simply that he had received me and that the Soviet government agreed with our Albanian policy.

With the main topic out of the way the conversation turned to nonessential matters such as the location of Cominform headquarters, Tito's health, and the like. Choosing the right moment, I brought up the question of equipment for our troops and our arms industry, noting that we were running into problems with the Soviet representatives because of "military secrets." At this, Stalin rose from his chair. "We have no military secrets where you're concerned! You're a friendly socialist country." He then went back to his desk, got Bulganin on the phone, and gave him a brief order: "The Yugoslavs are here, the Yugoslav delegation—they should be heard out at once. . . ."

Our talk in the Kremlin had lasted scarcely half an hour and then the four of us—Stalin, Molotov, Zhdanov, and I—were driven to Stalin's dacha for dinner. Malenkov, Beria, and Voznesensky[17] also were there. But while we were waiting in the hall for the other guests to arrive,

Zhdanov and I lingered over a map of the world and were joined by Stalin. He was clearly pleased at my noticing his blue pencil mark encircling Stalingrad. He began looking for Königsberg and remembered that it was to be renamed Kaliningrad. He also came upon some German place names around Leningrad that dated back to the time of Catherine the Great. "Change those names!" he ordered Zhdanov. "It's senseless for those places to bear German names today!" Zhdanov pulled out a memo pad and made a note of it.

The dinner began with someone—Stalin himself, I think—proposing that each of us guess how many degrees below zero it was outside and be penalized by being made to drink as many shot glasses of vodka as the number of degrees he guessed wrong. No drinker, I was happy to miss by one degree. Beria was off by three, remarking that he had done it on purpose. That little game of degrees of coldness matched by glasses of vodka put a heretical thought into my head: "Just look at these people on whom the fate of the world hangs, look at their senseless, worthless way of life." My "heresy" was made all the stronger by Stalin's poor physical condition. In the three years since I had last seen him, he had grown flabby and old. He had always eaten a lot, but now he was positively gluttonous, as if afraid of having his food snatched away from under his nose. He did drink less, and with more caution. It was as if his energy and power were of no use to anyone now that the war had ended. He was just as vulgar as ever, though, and just as suspicious— even more so—whenever anybody disagreed with him.

Stalin led the conversation. Now and again others could begin a new subject, but as a rule one topic had to be exhausted before another could be initiated. Usually it was Stalin who introduced topics, according to some bizarre order that alternated current events and complex problems with anecdotes. He made no attempt to hide his admiration for the atomic bomb. "A powerful thing!" he exclaimed two or three times.

When the conversation turned to Germany, Stalin concluded: "The West will make West Germany their own kind of state, and we will turn East Germany into a state of our own." This seemed logical and comprehensible to me. What I could never understand were the statements by Stalin and other Soviet leaders in June 1946, uttered in conversations with the Yugoslav and Bulgarian delegations, that "all Germany must be ours." Such notions were simply unrealistic.

We sat at one end of a long table; at the other end there were heated silver serving dishes. Stalin did not sit at the head, instead that was Beria's place, on Stalin's right, with the rest of us lined up on the other side, facing Stalin. On my left, next to Beria, sat the uncommunicative Molotov; on my right was Zhdanov, followed by Bulganin and Voznesensky. Zhdanov started talking about Finland, about its punctual deliveries of war reparations and their high quality. "We made a mistake in not occupying her," he concluded. "Everything would have been all set up if we had." To which Stalin added, "Yes, that was a mistake. We were too concerned about the Americans. They wouldn't have lifted a finger." "Ah, Finland!" observed Molotov. "There's a peanut."

Zhdanov then turned to me. "Do you have an opera house in Yugoslavia?" Astonished, I replied, "In Yugoslavia, operas are presented in nine theaters." But I was thinking at the same time how little they knew about us and how little interest they took in our life.

Zhdanov was the only one not to drink alcohol, but orangeade. He told me he had heart disease, adding in self-derision, "I could die at any moment, but I could also live a very long time."

Malenkov and Voznesensky were for the most part silent. At one point Stalin spoke of the necessity of increasing pay for teachers, and Voznesensky agreed. Then Stalin asked whether, in the just-adopted five-year plan, more resources could not be made available for the Volga-Don Canal, and Voznesensky agreed again.

I raised two theoretical questions I was anxious to know Stalin's thoughts on. The first concerned the distinction between "people" and "nation." In Marxist literature nothing clearly defined the difference and Stalin, the author of a book titled *Marxism and the Nationality Question,* written prior to World War I, was considered the greatest expert on the nationality issue. As I put my question Molotov interrupted, "People and nation are the same thing."

But Stalin did not agree. "No, nonsense! They're different things! You already know what a nation is, a nation is the product of capitalism with given characteristics, all classes belong to it, whereas a people—a people consists of the working persons of a given nation, working persons with the same language, culture, and customs."

When I praised his *Marxism and the Nationality Question* as an exceptional work, still of current interest, Stalin retorted, "That was Ilyich's [Lenin's] view. Ilyich also edited the book."

My second question was about Dostoyevsky. From early youth I had looked on him as the greatest writer of modern times and had never been able to come to terms with his neglect in the Soviet Union, even though I was opposed to his political ideas. Stalin had a simple explanation for this as well: "He's a bad influence on youth, so we don't publish him. Still, a great writer!"

As for Gorky,[18] Stalin did not agree with me that *The Life of Klim Samgin* was Gorky's most important work, both in its method and in the depth of its portrayal of the Russian Revolution. "No, his best things are those he wrote earlier," said Stalin, "*The Town of Okurov,* his stories, his novel *Foma Gordeev.* And as far as the depiction goes of the Russian Revolution in *Klim Samgin,* there's very little revolution there. . . ."

Stalin also singled out two contemporary Soviet writers, one a woman. Zhdanov retold his remark apropos of Simonov's book of love poems: "They should have published only two copies—one for her and one for him," at which Stalin smiled to himself while the others guffawed. Then Zhdanov said with a sneer that Leningrad officials had interpreted his criticism of Zoshchenko[19] to mean that the writer's ration card should be withheld, and that Moscow then had to tell them not to do it.

"On our Central Committee there are no Jews!" Stalin broke in, with a provocative laugh. "You are an anti-Semite; you too, Djilas, you too are an anti-Semite!"

I realized that Stalin was trying to goad me into declaring my stand concerning Jews. I smiled and said nothing. I have never been anti-Semitic, but I had no desire to contradict Stalin's anti-Semitism. And he quickly dropped the subject.

The evening did not pass without vulgarity, Beria's. After they prevailed on me to taste the *pertsovka*—vodka infused with strong pepper—Beria explained with a leer, and in the crudest of terms, that it had a bad effect on the sex glands. Stalin watched me intently with suppressed amusement, but kept himself from laughing out loud because of my sour expression.

But quite apart from this, there was some ill-defined tension in the air during the entire six-hour dinner. I had a foreboding that they were on the point of criticizing Tito and the Yugoslav Central Committee. Within myself I felt growing a vague resistance and began to measure my every word most carefully. To consolidate my position beforehand, once or twice I mentioned Tito and our Central Committee. Thus not even Stalin's injection of a personal element—why had I not responded to his invitation in 1946 to visit him on the Black Sea?—changed anything, either in my conduct or in that vague something that was in the air but left unsaid by them.

The dinner was concluded by Stalin's raising a toast to Lenin: "Let us drink to the memory of Vladimir Ilyich, our leader, our teacher— our all!" We stood, plunged in thought, and drank to this deity. The expression on Stalin's face was earnest and solemn but also somber.

While we were still standing, Stalin turned on a phonograph and tried to dance, moving his upraised arms to the rhythm of the music. He soon gave up, however, with a resigned "Age has crept up on me. Now I too am an old man."

His entourage flattered and reassured him. He then put on a record where the intricate flights of a coloratura were accompanied by the yowling and barking of dogs. Stalin laughed hard. Too hard. So did the others. But not I. Noticing my discomfort and that I could not understand their way of having fun, he stopped the record and said as if apologizing: "No, but anyhow it's well thought-out, devilishly well thought-out. . . ." On that note the evening at Stalin's came to an end.

We had to wait no more than a day or two before being called to the General Staff headquarters to present our requests. The meeting was chaired by Bulganin, who sat surrounded by high-ranking specialists, including the chief of the General Staff, Marshal Vasilyevsky.[20] First I set forth our needs in broad terms, leaving the details to be filled in by Popović and Todorović. Our desires seemed excessive to me, especially in regard to building up our military industry and our navy. We had talked about it on the train to Moscow, but since this had all been closely worked out with Tito in Belgrade, we left it as it was. The Soviet officers asked searching questions and made notes but remained non-committal.[21]

Still, things appeared to be moving off dead center, and even more so when Popović and Todorović held meetings over the next few days with military specialists. Then some ten days later it all ground to a halt, with Soviet officials giving us to understand that "complications had arisen" and that we had to wait. We suspected, of course, that the complications were between Belgrade and Moscow.

We started killing time by visiting museums and theaters, taking long walks, holding long conversations. These only served to deepen our criticism of Soviet patterns, Soviet reality—criticism that some of us were unable to hide, including delegation members. It had not yet assumed the proportions of outright rejection and would have been understandable, if not acceptable, if directed at any normal law-abiding nation. No doubt a meeting that we had with high-ranking Yugoslav officers, mostly generals who were going to school in the Soviet Union, contributed to the poisoning of our relations with the Soviet government. We informed them about conditions back home but also warned them not to take Soviet Army experience blindly as a model but to make an effort at coordinating it with our own practical knowledge and circumstances.

There were also some careless overstatements about the stodgy conventionalism and rigidity of the Soviet army, of the sort that are hard to avoid when partners begin to diverge in their outlook. A certain resistance to our suggestions could be detected in individual officers. In sum, I left with a painful impression, not only of the influence of Soviet doctrines and resistance to the intentions of our Central Committee, but also of the active presence of Soviet intelligence among the ranks of our people who were being schooled in the Soviet Union.

So as not to waste time, Koča Popović decided to return to Yugoslavia. I would have gone back with him had I not received a wire notifying us of Kardelj's and Bakarić's[22] imminent arrival and directing me to join them to help straighten out the "complications" that had arisen with the Soviet government. Tito had been included in the invitation, but mistrust had taken such firm root by now that the Yugoslav leadership begged off on grounds that he was not feeling well. Representatives of Bulgaria were invited simultaneously, and the Soviets made sure we knew that Bulgaria was sending its top people.

Kardelj and Bakarić arrived on February 8 to a cold and perfunctory welcome. They were put up in a dacha near Moscow, and since there was room for me there (if a desire to eavesdrop was not the real reason), I was moved over to their place from the hotel that same day.

That night, while Kardelj's wife was sleeping and he was lying next to her, I sat down on the bed by him (reckoning that there was no bugging apparatus in the bedroom) and as softly as I could whispered my impressions of this stay in Moscow and of my contacts with the Soviet leaders. It came down to the conclusion that we could not count on any serious help, for Moscow was carrying out a policy of subordinating Yugoslavia to the level of other East European countries.

Kardelj told me that the direct cause of his coming, and of the dispute with Moscow, was the agreement between the Yugoslav and Albanian governments to send two Yugoslav divisions into Albania, which the Kremlin opposed. Not only were our reasons not accepted—that the two divisions were to protect Albania from Greek "monarcho-Fascists"—but also, in his cable, Molotov threatened a public breach.

"Whatever possessed you to send two divisions at this time?" I asked Kardelj. "And why all this feverish involvement in Albania?" With resignation in his voice, Kardelj replied, "Well, the Old Man is doing the pushing. You know, yourself. . . ."

The next day Kardelj, Bakarić and I took a walk in the park, whose paths had been swept clean. There I reported more fully to them, and the three of us gave our relations with the Soviet Union a thorough airing. Our long walk that frosty day caused our Soviet escorts astonishment, even resentment, because we had done our talking outside and not in the dacha. One of them asked us later why music was always being played in the living room, to which I replied that we loved music, especially Kardelj—which was not entirely inaccurate.

On the evening of February 10 the three of us were picked up and driven to Stalin's office in the Kremlin. In the little anteroom occupied by his secretary, Poskrebishchev, we waited fifteen minutes for the Bulgarians to appear—Dimitrov, Kolarov, and Kostov—and then were ushered into Stalin's office. The exchange of greetings was cold and brief. Stalin sat down at the head of the table. To his right were Molotov, Zhdanov, Malenkov, Suslov,[23] and Zorin.[24] To his left, Kolarov, Dimitrov, and Kostov, followed by Kardelj, myself, and Bakarić.[25]

Molotov briefly presented the disagreements between the Yugoslav and Bulgarian governments and Moscow. He cited examples: Bulgaria had signed a treaty of unification with Yugoslavia without the knowledge of the Soviet government and before the signing of a peace treaty with Moscow. In Bucharest, Dimitrov had made a statement about establishing East European federations, to include Greece. Such acts were not permissible, Molotov emphasized, from the point of view of either Party or state.

Stalin turned to Dimitrov. "Comrade Dimitrov gets too carried away at press conferences. For example, the Poles have been visiting here. I ask them, What do you think of Dimitrov's statement? Pretty clever, they say. But I say it's not at all clever. Then they reply that they too think it's not very clever—if that's the thinking of the Soviet government. For they thought Dimitrov had issued that statement with the knowledge and concurrence of the Soviet government, and so they approved of it. Dimitrov later tried to amend his statement through the Bulgarian telegraph agency, but he didn't help matters one bit. What's more, he cited how Austria-Hungary had in its day stood in the way of a customs union between Bulgaria and Serbia, which naturally prompts the conclusion: The Germans were in the way earlier, now it's the Russians. There! That's what's going on!"

Molotov picked up the line of thought at this point, accusing the Bulgarians of moving toward federation with Romania without consulting the Soviet government. Dimitrov tried to smooth things over, claiming that he had spoken only in general terms about federation. Stalin interrupted him: "No, you were talking about a customs union, on coordinating economic plans. . . ." Molotov followed up: ". . . And what is a customs union and a coordination of economic plans but the creation of a single state?"

The purpose of this meeting was by now painfully obvious: The people's democracies were not to develop their own relationships without Moscow's approval. Dimitrov's initiative and Yugoslavia's obstinacy were not merely heresy but a direct challenge to the sacred rights of the Soviet Union.

Dimitrov kept trying to justify and explain, and Stalin kept interrupting him. Stalin's colorful wit turned into malicious vulgarity and his narrow factionalism into intolerance. But he never lost a sense of actual relationships: Even while upbraiding and fulminating against the Bulgarians in the knowledge that they were "softies" and more manageable, Stalin was taking open aim at the Yugoslavs.

"We learn about your doings from the papers!" Stalin would shout in answer to Dimitrov's excuses. "You babble away like women on two sides of the street, saying whatever crosses your mind, and then the reporters grab hold of it."

Dimitrov continued, obliquely, justifying his position on the customs union with Romania: "Bulgaria is in such economic difficulties that without closer collaboration with other countries, it cannot develop. As far as my statement at the press conference goes, I got carried away, true."

Here, Stalin broke in again: "You wanted to shine with originality. It was completely wrong, for such a federation is inconceivable. What are the historic ties between Bulgaria and Romania? None at all! We need hardly speak of, say, Hungary or Poland."

When Dimitrov protested that there were no differences between Bulgaria's foreign policy and that of the Soviet Union, Stalin roughly retorted: "There are serious differences. Why hide it? It was Lenin's practice to recognize errors and remove them as soon as possible."

"True, we have made errors," Dimitrov obediently took him up. "But through errors we are learning our way in foreign politics."

"Learning!" scoffed Stalin. "You've been in politics for fifty years and you talk about learning! About correcting your errors! Your trouble is not errors but a stand different from ours."

Dimitrov's ears were burning, red blotches had appeared on his face, and he looked so dejected and hangdog that I couldn't help wondering: Is this the same man who defied Göring and fascism at the Leipzig trial?

Stalin went on: "A customs union, a federation between Bulgaria and Romania—that's nonsense. But a federation of Yugoslavia, Bulgaria, and Albania is another matter. Here there are historic and other ties. That is the federation that should be created, and the sooner the better. Yes, the sooner the better—right away, tomorrow if possible. Yes, tomorrow. If possible. Agree on it at once."

Someone mentioned—I think it was Kardelj, because Bakarić and I sat silent throughout the proceedings—that a Yugoslav-Albanian federation was already in process.

Stalin broke in with an emphatic, "No. First a federation between Bulgaria and Yugoslavia, and then both with Albania. We think that a federation ought to be formed between Romania and Hungary, and also Poland and Czechoslovakia. . . ."

Stalin did not carry his idea to the end. Judging by indications from top Soviet circles, the leaders were toying with the idea of reorganizing the Soviet Union by joining Poland and Czechoslovakia to Byelorussia, Romania and Bulgaria to the Ukraine, and the Balkan countries to Russia. A grandiose, insane, federal-imperial conception.

Just as it seemed that the dispute over a Bulgarian-Romanian treaty had been settled, old Kolarov revived it. "I cannot see where Comrade Dimitrov erred. We sent a draft treaty with Romania to the Soviet government in advance and your government made no comment regarding the customs union, only regarding the definition of an aggressor."

Stalin turned to Molotov, asking if this was the case. "Well, yes," was the ill-tempered reply. With angry resignation Stalin said, "We too make stupid mistakes."

Dimitrov latched on to this detail. "This was precisely the reason for my statement. The draft had been sent to Moscow. I didn't think you could have had anything against it."

But Stalin was not easily moved by facts. "Nonsense! You rushed headlong like a Komsomol youth. You wanted to astound the world, as if you were still secretary of the Comintern. You and the Yugoslavs don't let anyone know what you're doing, but we find out all about it on the street. You present us with a fait accompli!"

Kostov, who administered Bulgaria's economy and probably had come prepared to raise economic problems, broke in with, "It's hard to be a small and undeveloped country. . . . I would like to raise some economic questions. . . ."

But Stalin cut him short and directed him to the ministries concerned. "Here we're discussing foreign policy disagreements among the three governments and Parties."

Finally Kardelj was recognized. He turned red, pulled his head down between his shoulders, and in his excitement paused where there was no reason to pause. His point was that the Soviet government had been provided with advance copies of the agreements between Bulgaria and Yugoslavia and that the Soviets had requested only one minor change: replacement of "for all time" with "twenty years." "Except for that objection, which we took care of," said Kardelj, "there was no disagreement."

Stalin kept glancing at Molotov, who lowered his head in confirmation of Kardelj's statement. He interrupted Kardelj as angrily as he had interrupted Dimitrov, but not as offensively. "Nonsense! There are differences, and serious differences at that. What about Albania? You didn't consult us at all about sending troops to Albania."

Kardelj: "There was the assent of the Albanian government."

Stalin: "It could lead to serious international complications. Albania is an independent state. What are you thinking of? Excuse or no excuse, the fact is that you did not consult us about sending troops into Albania."

Kardelj went on making excuses that none of this was final, that he could not recall a single foreign issue on which the Yugoslav government had not consulted with Moscow.

"That's not so!" shouted Stalin. "In general, you don't consult. With you it's no mistake, it's your standing procedure, yes, procedure!"

And so Kardelj never managed to present his case. Molotov held a piece of paper in front of him and read a passage from the Yugoslav-Bulgarian agreement: that the two countries would "work in the spirit of the United Nations and support any initiative designed to maintain peace and prevent hotbeds of aggression." "What's that mean?" he asked pointedly.

Dimitrov explained that it meant solidarity with the United Nations in the struggle against aggression, but Stalin interrupted him. "No, that's preventive war. The commonest Komsomol stunt! A tawdry phrase, which only brings grist to the enemy mill."

Molotov returned to the Bulgarian-Romanian customs union, underscoring that this was the beginning of a merger between the two states. Stalin interrupted by remarking that customs unions are generally unrealistic. This eased the tension somewhat, and Kardelj observed that some customs unions have in fact worked out.

"For example?" asked Stalin, disinclined to make any concessions.

"Well, take Benelux," Kardelj replied cautiously. "Belgium, Holland, and Luxembourg."

Stalin: "No, not Holland. Only Belgium and Luxembourg. It's nothing. It's trivial."

Kardelj: "No, Holland is part of it."

Stalin, stubbornly, sarcastically: "No, not Holland!"

He looked inquiringly at Molotov, Zorin, and the rest. It occurred to me to explain that the "ne" in the acronym Benelux refers to the initial syllable for Holland (the Netherlands), but since no one spoke up I didn't either. And so that's how we left it—there is no Holland in Benelux.

Stalin returned to the coordination of economic plans between Bulgaria and Romania. "That's ridiculous! Instead of collaborating you'd soon be quarreling. Unification of Bulgaria and Yugoslavia is another matter entirely—there we have affinities, aspirations of long standing."

Kardelj began to say that at the Lake Bled meeting it was decided to work gradually toward a federation of Bulgaria and Yugoslavia, but Stalin broke in with a categorical, "No! Right away! Tomorrow if possible! First Bulgaria and Yugoslavia should be united, and later Albania should join them."

Next Stalin passed to the uprising in Greece. "It has to wind down!" (He used a word that literally means "to roll up.") "Do you believe," he said, turning to Kardelj, "in the success of their rebellion?"

Kardelj: "If foreign intervention doesn't escalate, and if our Greek comrades don't commit big military and political blunders."

Stalin, bitingly: "If, if! No. They have no prospects of success at all. Do you think that Britain and the United States—the United States, strongest country in the world—will permit their arteries of communication in the Mediterranean to be severed? Rubbish! And we don't have a navy. The Greek uprising must be wound down, and as soon as possible."

Someone mentioned the recent successes of the Chinese Communists. But Stalin remained adamant. "Yes, our Chinese comrades have succeeded, but the situation in Greece is entirely different. Greece is on a vital line of communications for the Western powers. The United States is directly involved here—strongest country in the world. China is a different case, relations in the Far East are different. True, we too can make mistakes. Take the case of the war with Japan. When it was over we invited our Chinese comrades here to discuss how they might reach a modus vivendi with Jiang Gaishek [Chiang Kai-shek]. They agreed with us, but when they got home they did things their own way: gathered their forces and struck. It turned out that they were right and we were not. But the rebellion in Greece is a different matter. No hesitation here—it must be laid to rest."

What prompted Stalin to oppose the uprising in Greece? Probably he was reluctant to see still another Communist state created in the Balkans before those already established had been brought into line. Even more did he shy away from international complications before the Soviet Union had recovered from war losses and destruction. He was just as anxious to avoid conflict with the West, particularly the United States, over China, and probably wary of creating a revolutionary power that, with its innovations, its sheer size and autonomy, could become a successful, invincible competitor.

The discussion slacked off, and Dimitrov raised the issue of economic relations with the USSR. But Stalin did not give an inch. "We'll talk about that with a unified Bulgarian-Yugoslav government." And to Kostov's remark that the treaty on technical assistance was unsuitable for Bulgaria, Stalin curtly replied, "Send Molotov a note" *(zapisochku)*.

Kardelj asked what position should be taken concerning Italy's demand that Somalia be placed under its trusteeship. Yugoslavia was not in favor of this. But Stalin took the opposite viewpoint and asked Molotov if a reply to that effect had been sent. He explained his motivation: "Once upon a time rulers, unable to reach an agreement on division of the spoils, would give disputed territory to the weakest feudal vassal so as to be able to snatch it back at the right moment."

At the end of the meeting Stalin covered himself by invoking Lenin and Leninism: "We, Lenin's disciples, we too disagreed with Lenin himself many times and even quarreled over some things. But then we would talk everything over, fix our positions, and go on."

The meeting had lasted about two hours, but this time Stalin did not invite us home for dinner, which made me feel sad and empty. My attitude toward him was still sentimental and worshipful. I also had been hoping that over a feast the tensions might dissipate, disagreements be clarified if not smoothed out. Outside, in the car, I began to express my bitterness over the meeting to Kardelj and Bakarić, but Kardelj dejectedly signaled me to stop. I took this as a sign that we saw eye to eye, as indeed we did in all things at the time of those Moscow tribulations. Each of us reacted emotionally in his own way.

Although Kardelj did later confirm that we were in agreement, a year or two before he died he alleged that as we emerged from the Kremlin I had said: "Now we really have to unite with Bulgaria." That I said this is quite possible. But that he answered, "Now is precisely when we ought not to do it," is incorrect, a reply construed in retrospect to fit the context of the situation as it evolved. For we had agreed with the Bulgarians, there in the Kremlin, in Stalin's anteroom, to meet the very next day for preliminary discussions on future unification.

And, indeed, the two delegations did gather for lunch, in the dacha outside Moscow which had been at the disposal of Dimitrov since his days as secretary of the Comintern. Without going into the details of federation, we agreed to revive contacts between Belgrade and Sofia on this question. Nor when we returned did anyone, including Tito, raise any objections to our federating with Bulgaria and Albania. But our enthusiasm had noticeably waned now that Stalin's orders had replaced the romantic goodwill of earlier times.

At that lunch we and the Bulgarians were closer than we had ever been—the closeness of the oppressed and the tyrannized. It was then that Dimitrov told us in confidence that the Soviet Union had an atomic bomb, one that was better than the American device. Without a doubt he felt as we did. Talking to us in front of the dacha he said, as if in passing, "Criticism of my statements is not at issue here; something else is. . . ."

That evening or the next one, Kardelj was pulled out of a theater to sign an understanding with Molotov, in accordance with Stalin's directive from the Kremlin meeting—an agreement to consult in matters of foreign policy. And since the accord was presented without explanation, the signing was done without ceremony. But Kardelj signed in the wrong spot. The error was discovered, and the next day he had to do it again.

Three days later, at dawn, we were taken to Vnukovo Airport and, without ceremony or protocol, bundled onto a plane for Belgrade. We were tired and little disposed to talk. And homesick.

5 CONFRONTATION WITH MOSCOW

Back in Belgrade the leadership accepted Stalin's orders with little appetite, but also little argument. Relations with Moscow, however, far from simmering down, grew daily more strained. New Soviet measures, new pressures, followed on and were pursued so high-handedly that they provoked sober-minded resistance rather than confusion or panic. Our sojourn in the Soviet Union together with our joint meeting in the Kremlin with the Bulgarian delegation and Stalin not only furnished a seedbed of anti-Soviet stories, it also set in motion a call to arms. We continued to hew to our pro-Soviet line with feverish determination, especially in propaganda, rejoicing over the February coup d'état in Czechoslovakia, "unmasking" Greece's "provocations" toward Albania, waxing indignant along with Moscow over the Western powers' "illegal" decisions concerning Germany. But on February 12 (as noted by the French newspaper *Le Figaro*) in Romania, Tito's pictures were being taken down, while in Tirana on February 12, in connection with Red Army Day, the Soviet chargé d'affaires, Gagarinov, accepted a toast to Tito's health only insofar, he said, as Tito's work strengthened the worldwide democratic front. And in the most drastic step of all, the Soviet government refused to broaden and extend our trade agreement, even though Mikoyan[1] had promised to do so when Crnobrnya[2] and I met with him in Moscow, and even though 50 percent of our foreign trade was conducted with Eastern Europe,

predominantly with the Soviet Union. Scarcely ten days after returning from Moscow we in Tito's closest circle had become more guarded
about uniting with Bulgaria and Albania. Not that we had shaken off
this time-hallowed ideal of Balkan socialists and democrats, but we
were subordinating it now to political considerations.

I headed a delegation that departed by car for Budapest on March 13
to celebrate the 1848 Hungarian Revolution. A day or two before, I had
had a talk with Tito. From agency news reports we knew that the
Soviet delegation would be led by Marshal Voroshilov.[3] So Tito said,
"You know, if Voroshilov wants to talk with you, go ahead and talk. It
could be useful. But don't humiliate yourself."

I gave a speech at the official session of the Hungarian parliament.
Marx and Engels had harshly criticized the Croatian and Serbian intervention against the Hungarian revolution.[4] With that in mind, and trying to ingratiate myself with contemporary Hungary, I mounted an
extremely sharp attack, one-sided and unhistorical, on the interven-
tionists of that day. At the same time, however, I emphasized that "freedom and progress are not only linked with them [that is, with the
peoples of Yugoslavia] but, if I may say so, are identical with their survival as peoples. . . ." This assertion flew in the face of an assumption
on the part of both Marx and Engels that the condition of "slavery"
(meaning backwardness) among all our peoples would inevitably dissolve and disappear on its own. Now I was making this disappearance
contingent upon our own well-being in Yugoslavia.

But more important, and probably most conspicuous, was the fact
that I was the only one *not* to mention Russia as Hungary's liberator,
not even in my concluding slogans: "Long live the democratic and independent republic of Hungary! Long live friendship and collaboration
between the new Yugoslavia and the new Hungary!"

The Hungarian Communist leaders treated me with a suppressed
but unmistakable coldness, all the more noticeable because up to now
they had been strikingly ingratiating toward our leadership. Obviously
they had been apprised of the deterioration in our relations with
Moscow and just as obviously had come to a decision. I therefore
assumed a pose of official reserve toward them all—toward all, in fact,
but my escort, a simple, warmhearted veteran of the Spanish Civil War
whose name I have unfortunately forgotten.

The Hungarian Party and government attached great significance to
commemorating 1848, no doubt in an effort to present themselves as

heirs to the patriots and democrats of those glorious, unforgettable days. But they held themselves back—more so, I thought then, than necessary. The crushing of the Hungarian Revolution by Tsarist Russia was passed over in silence, while the Soviet Union's liberating, fraternal role was strongly emphasized. Hence the celebration glittered more than it convinced. The citadel of Buda, the city's most conspicuous and beautiful landmark, witnessed the unveiling of a monument, not to the year 1848, not to the Hungarian Commune of 1919, not even to the slain Hungarian revolutionaries, but to the Red Army. At the ceremony I found myself standing next to Rákosi,[5] who asked how I liked the sculpture. I could not resist replying: "Oh, it's good, but why couldn't you have raised a monument to Hungarian revolutionaries? Your history is so full of revolutions and revolutionaries!" Obviously embarrassed, Rákosi replied, "Yes, yes, we'll raise one to them, too."

Up to that point not one of the Soviet representatives had approached me unless protocol dictated it. With Voroshilov I had exchanged a word or two, but if he noticed me at all he did not remember me, let alone ask me to call on him. He was the center of attention, self-satisfied, awkwardly pompous, aglitter with medals, purveyor of a forced, condescending amiability. It was said that as president of the Allied Control Commission he hadn't known what to do, that all the work was done by others, but that he was careful to take faultless long strides as he walked.

As the celebration was winding down I gave up hoping that Voroshilov would call me over. My feelings were hurt. I felt the bitterness but also the pride of the small who long to be understood by the great—the great who have no idea that the small are feeling put down. Then in the midst of all the commotion a Soviet colonel walked up to me. I had seen him somewhere before but knew nothing about him. He began a conversation in which the name of Voroshilov quickly came up. I uttered a few conventional phrases about the marshal's brilliant appearance and dignified bearing. "I know the marshal would like to talk with you," he said. "He's simple and warm—surely he'll receive you."

"All the marshal has to do," I replied, "is to say he wants to see me."

"He's so busy," said the colonel. "All these receptions and duties. But he'll find time for you, I'm sure. Just ask to see him."

"I'd be happy to call on him at his request."

"Just ask. I'm sure he'll see you."

"It goes without saying that I'll accede to the wishes of Comrade Voroshilov."

On this note my talk with the colonel came to an end. Voroshilov did not express a desire to see me, nor did I ask. To tell the truth, I did not expect any results from a conversation with the marshal. His mind was not exactly flexible, and also I doubted that he had any real grasp of the subject at hand, since he had in fact long been on the outside of political life. His reputation, too, must have been in decline among the Soviet leaders, in view of his lack of resourcefulness during the war and of his being sidelined with secondary, representational duties. Between the two of us, I am convinced, no conversation could have been reasoned or well-intentioned. We would simply have ended up bickering and disagreeing.

No sooner had I returned to Belgrade—perhaps two days later—than Tito on March 19 or 20 called a meeting with Kardelj, Ranković, and me (there may have been someone else, I don't remember) to inform us that the Soviet government was recalling its military instructors. The news that they were also pulling out their economic experts reached us, if I recall, while the meeting was in progress. Tito had prepared a reply in the government's name. It was then that he observed, as if noting something very important: "It would be better to shift the whole business over to the sphere of international relations. Relations between Parties aren't all that's at issue here."

Tito's reply to the Soviet government was mild and unprovocative, but at the same time firm and searching. He insisted on true reasons by rejecting Moscow's contention that we were unfriendly and "distrustful" toward the Soviet specialists and that we "dogged" their every step. We accepted his reply without comment.

The days passed in a state of suspense. While waiting for the Soviets to respond to Tito's letter, we polemicized with "the imperialists" over Trieste and issues of peace and were savagely attacked in the Western press for allegedly massing our troops against Italy and for interfering in the civil war in Greece.

The response was not slow in coming, and obviously had been prepared in advance. Essentially it was not a response to Tito's letter, though it formally opened by addressing him. It bore the date March 27, a date seared in our memory for being the anniversary of the royal Yugoslav government's overthrow for acceding to the Tripartite Pact in 1941. Purely accidental as I think this was, and insignificant as it surely was, like a monster out of myth, the coincidence spurred us on to resist. The letter bore Molotov's and Stalin's signatures, in that order. Why Molotov first and not second, as hierarchy and Molotov's own intrinsic importance should have dictated, was never explained. We interpreted it to mean not that Stalin was "hesitating" or "leaning our way" but rather that he wanted to remain somewhat in the background. And to what purpose? To blame Molotov if the undertaking failed? Or to ascribe a secondary importance to it in the Communist movement? Or—what was most likely—to nourish the delusion that he was not so deeply committed that someday he could not "pardon" us? Be that as it may, neither then nor later did Stalin mount a public attack on Tito or Yugoslavia. The man died without publicly uttering a word against his most successful adversaries.

After the Soviet ambassador, Lavrentiev, presented the response, Tito phoned Kardelj; Ranković; the economic minister, Kidrič;[6] and me. We set off for Zagreb the same evening by train. We were given the letter to study, along with a draft of Tito's reply. The four of us spent two or three hours reading it and dining in a separate room.

This letter from the Soviet leaders disturbed but did not stun us.

It cast the blame for our worsened relations on the Yugoslav leaders, pointing to the absence of inner-Party democracy and the irregular work and composition of the Central Committee. "Understandably, we cannot view such an organization as Marxist-Leninist, as Bolshevik," the letter emphasized. It was addressed to "Comrade Tito and the other members of the Central Committee." But although it still spared Tito and Kardelj in the sense that they were not singled out by name for criticism, Moscow did not neglect to warn us that "the political career of Trotsky is quite instructive." Only "dubious" Marxists like "Djilas, Kidrič, Ranković, Vukmanović, and others" were named directly. It was clear to all, though, and Tito first and foremost, that the criticism was aimed also at him and Kardelj. For when I suggested that if need be the four of us mentioned by name could resign, Tito retorted caustically and decisively: "No way! I know what they want: to break up our Central Committee. First you, then me!"

Tito's reply we accepted without demur, with the exception of its conclusion. I noted that it would only make Moscow angry to insist on independence and the equality of the "people's democracies" with the Soviet Union, for that would be tantamount to challenging the latter's dominance, its "leading role." All three of the others, Kardelj, Ranković, and Kidrič, agreed with me. Tito went along with us without further argument: though a little nervous and impatient, he had now grasped the fact that he could not do battle alone with Stalin and the Soviet apparatus. Overnight, so to speak, he had grown "more collective," more open to correction.

At that meeting it was decided to call a plenum of the Central Committee for April 12.

The Central Committee convened in plenary session on the appointed day, before noon, in the library of the Old Palace at Dedinje.* After a brief introduction by Tito the letter from the Soviet leaders was read aloud, followed by the reply he had drafted. Tito then spoke for nearly an hour, stating in essence that the Soviet leaders were taking advantage of so-called ideological differences to put pressure on our country. He called on us to keep our heads in the discussion and insisted that each member make his statement individually. He also said that a transcript of the meeting would be sent to the Soviet Central Committee if it were asked for. They never did, nor did it occur to anyone to send it.

Next, Kardelj summarized the experience and achievements of our Party. With a burst of feeling he concluded that "It would be contemptible of us to concede that these were wrong."

Other speakers rose in turn. To a man they were angry and ready to fight, and I among them, outraged by the lies and hostility of it all.

After the majority had thus spoken out, Sreten Žujović, pale and nervous, spoke up. His declaration against our Politburo and in favor of Moscow had been anticipated. From a multitude of small details and observations it had long been known that he entertained a pro-Soviet point of view. We had been struck by his habitual tête-à-têtes with Hebrang, who was openly dissatisfied with his own position and with the Politburo's orientation toward independent development. We had been struck too by Žujović's extraordinary closeness to the Soviet ambassador and by Hebrang's all-too-frequent sessions with the UNRRA chief for Yugoslavia, another Soviet official, which were unofficial and intimate. All this had seemed innocent enough until our differences with the Soviet government erupted into open conflict.

---

*Remarks by the various speakers are quoted for the most part as they appear in Vladimir Dedijer, *J. B. Tito, prilozi za biografiju* (Belgrade: Kultura, 1953). I made my own notes at the meeting, but they are not in my possession; they may be in the Central Committee archives.

Even though disagreement had been anticipated from that quarter, Žujović's words provoked such angry, impatient interruptions that he was unable to finish properly what he had to say. Our "revolutionary conscience" was appealed to, then we were implored to stick close to the Soviet Union and be doubly receptive to the slightest criticism by Stalin. The Soviet leaders' lies and unjust accusations—the gist of their letter—were passed over in silence.

I was sitting one or two seats to the left of Tito. No sooner did Žujović begin his appeals to "Come to your senses!" than Tito jumped up and began pacing to and fro. "Treason!" he hissed. "Treason to the people, the state, the Party!" Although our conflict with Moscow involved preserving our own power and "our" state, especially where Tito was concerned, it cannot be disputed that he as a patriot, no less than the rest of us, was genuinely angry. This feeling sprang from his characteristic tendency to internalize events so that he took them personally, and on the other hand to externalize his personal situation so as to view it as a problem for the Party and the state.

Tito repeated the word "treason" many times over, then just as quickly sat down, kicking aside his briefcase. But now I in my turn jumped up, tears of pain and anger filling my eyes. "Crni," I shouted (our nickname for Sreten), "you've known me for ten years—do you really think of me as a Trotskyite?" The answer was evasive: "I don't think that, but, you know, some of your latest statements about the Soviet Union . . ."

There was an uproar of shouts and heckling. "Show your colors!" "Don't beat around the bush!" "What are you covering up?" "Be honest!"

Žujović grew confused. "Answer, Crni," Tito interrupted him. "Are we heading toward capitalism? Are our Party principles being watered down in the People's Front? Are there foreign spies in our government?"

Following Tito, Vladimir ("Vlado") Popović took the floor: "What Žujović is saying is neither honorable nor Communist. Our policy toward the Soviet Union—this I know as ambassador to Moscow—has been correct, has been Communist. Stalin himself conceded that the joint-ownership companies are not a good thing." In those days I used to see Vlado Popović rather often. I had known him since 1937, before he left for Spain, but it was during my latest stay in Moscow that we had drawn close together as "companions in misfortune." Now we would take walks around Dedinje[7] till late at night, exploring Soviet policy toward Yugoslavia and concluding that its roots lay deep in the

undemocratic, dictatorial structure of the Bolshevik Party and therefore the Soviet state. Vlado's insights and understanding, gained from
his years in the USSR, were crucial to our judgments. He would tell of
seeing political prisoners in Siberia, for example, in chains and at hard
labor, being whipped by their guards. "There's no mercy there, no
human care and consideration," he would tell me. Kardelj, Kidrič, and
I also engaged in extensive discussions and speculations. Ranković did
not join in much when the talk was theoretical, but his detailed reports
were invaluable on the meddling, intrigue, and recruiting of the Soviet
intelligence services.

   Amid all the bitterness and fury of the plenum, Moša Pijade rose to
speak. He began by saying that what surprised him most of all was the
shallow literary standard exhibited by the Molotov-Stalin letter. This
was greeted by a burst of laughter.

   The session recessed around two o'clock for lunch, which was
served in the palace. When it resumed, Tito took the floor. He spoke
with more composure, steadiness, and firmness, while not in the least
repressing his own anger. He blamed Žujović for assuming the right to
love the Soviet Union more than anyone else, including Tito. He
accused him of wanting to break up the Party and the leadership—a
leadership that had worked together in harmony for eleven years,
through the harshest trials, and that was bonded in blood with the people. At this point, rising from his seat, Tito cried out: "Our revolution
does not devour its children! We honor the children of our revolution!"
It was an outcry that caused excitement and carried conviction. Tito
could hardly have realized that at the very moment he was distancing
himself thus from the Russian Revolution, which had insatiably wolfed
down its children, the Yugoslav revolution was in its turn waiting to
devour its own children. He further declared that our sacrifices and our
war were also contributions to world socialism. They were not contributions that came about by being attached to the USSR and falling
under its yoke, they were ones that arose from equal collaboration as
brothers and from independent development within the framework of
that collaboration.

   Žujović then denied that he had reported to the Soviet ambassador
about the Politburo session of March 1. "Comrades," he went on, "in the
event of an attack from the West, can Yugoslavia defend itself alone?"

   He was essentially parroting the generally accepted Soviet premise
that the people's democracies stood no chance of survival unless they

subordinated themselves to Moscow. But, awash in moral revulsion as we were, overwhelmed as we were by a conviction that we were contributing to socialism, we were quite unconcerned about exposing ourselves to some alleged danger from "imperialism" by breaking away from Moscow. Still, Kardelj replied in measured tones to Žujović: "An attack from the West is not in the cards. And even if it were, we wouldn't be the only target."

We did not have long to wait for these delusions, or hopes, to be dashed. As early as April 16 Judin, of the Cominform, handed Tito a letter from the Hungarian Central Committee. The Hungarians expressed their solidarity with the "criticism" contained in the Molotov-Stalin letter. This meant, first, that the Soviets were pressuring and mobilizing other Communist Parties against us before settling outstanding issues with our leadership and, second, that these other Parties (in the case at hand, the Hungarian) were swallowing Soviet "criticism" of our Party without giving us a hearing. The Hungarian letter infuriated our top ranks, as was evident in Tito's reply. For years the Hungarian leaders had been courting us while at the same time we had bent every effort to forget the bestialities committed by Hungarian soldiers and Fascists on Yugoslav soil during the war. It was a policy that had not always been popular, but we had pursued it in the name of friendship and cooperation. Now it was as if the Hungarians were ignoring our efforts.

The Politburo had no illusions that other Communist parties would fail to support the Soviet leaders. There was, however, a moment when it seemed that our Bulgarian "brethren" might show us some sympathy—if not open, then disguised—particularly since we all still favored unification, and for the Bulgarians any weakening of our position vis-à-vis Moscow meant outright subjection.

On April 19 a Bulgarian delegation headed by Dimitrov was passing through Belgrade on its way to Prague. At the Topčider station it was to be greeted by our minister of foreign affairs, Stanoje Simić. As a member of both the government and the Central Committee, I was to invite our Bulgarian comrades to stop off in Belgrade on their way back for a talk about unification.

It was a damp, overcast afternoon. While Simić was looking for his Bulgarian counterpart, I spotted Dimitrov at a window and boarded his car. He was waiting for me in the corridor. Squeezing my hand in both of his, he said emotionally, "Be steadfast, steadfast!"

Passing it off lightly, I replied, "With us Yugoslavs the danger is in being too steadfast, not too little."

Dimitrov went on, with warmth and excitement: "You must stand fast. The rest will follow."

I conveyed our invitation that they stop over for two or three days on the way back from Prague to discuss further collaboration, including the unification of our two countries. At that point Dimitrov's wife, Rose, emerged from their compartment. She was a plump redhead, a friendly and unassuming German woman from the Sudetenland whom Dimitrov had met in Moscow when she was an emigrée. She, too, said with emotion, "Oh, we've been so afraid for you lately!"

This encounter with Dimitrov and his wife went on for only two or three minutes, when the rest of the Bulgarian delegation appeared. I recognized Vlko Chervenkov[8] and Dobrij Terpeshev; there was also someone else from the Bulgarian leadership.

We gathered in the parlor car. The good-natured, open Terpeshev, who through a liking for Serbs had come to love all Yugoslavs, at once began asking after Tito and the rest of the Yugoslav leaders, Chervenkov meanwhile sulking in silence. Someone asked what was new. From Dimitrov's earlier comments in the corridor it was clear that the Bulgarian Central Committee was familiar with the Soviet letter, so I said there was nothing important except a letter from Molotov and Stalin consisting of a string of inaccuracies, which we had not accepted. At that Chervenkov said irritably that criticism from our Soviet comrades had better be accepted, upon which Dimitrov, his expression now downcast, added, "Since the Central Committee of the Soviet Communist Party says so, there must be some truth to it."

So ended the conversation. Dimitrov had let it be known that he dared not take issue with the argument that our differences with Moscow had come at a time when the imperialists were stirring up war hysteria and preparing for aggression.

The encouragement offered by Dimitrov and his wife came as bracing news to Tito and my Politburo comrades, given the atmosphere of anger and doubt. Their rejoicing was short-lived, however. A day or two later we received a letter, signed by Chervenkov, which not only supported the criticism of the Molotov-Stalin letter but even took the initiative of boastfully extending it. Our ambassador in Prague, Stilinović, was immediately directed to inform the Bulgarian delegation that in view of their unfounded support of the Soviet letter they needn't bother to stay over in Belgrade. And so it turned out: On their return trip the Bulgarians were met as protocol required, but without the presence of a single member of the Central Committee.

It was not long before a second letter, dated May 4, arrived from the Soviet Central Committee. This one was nearly thirty pages long. Time and care had been taken in its preparation, that was obvious. It breathed new life into old disputes; rounded out criticism of Yugoslav Party policy; threw into the mix intrigues among our leaders; quibbled over the number of Central Committee members and the regularity of our meetings; defended Hebrang and Žujović; and flattered other Parties. Tito and Kardelj were named at the end as the sinners-in-chief. In its style and composition could be felt the hand of Stalin. Clearly, the letter was intended to provide the political basis for judging the Yugoslav leadership and bringing our Party into line, all the more because it insisted on a thorough airing of the Soviet-Yugoslav dispute at a session of the Cominform. Lies and half truths abounded, though the letter contained some truths as well. The former gave grounds for our resistance, and whatever was true had by now forfeited any significance.

On May 9 another plenum of the Central Committee was convened to reply to this latest letter. The occasion held little drama, in spite of the document's wide-ranging, more thoroughgoing nature. A brief reply, one that I think had been written by Tito, was accepted. Again we rejected the charges, the latest letter having "convinced us of the futility of all our attempts to show, even with the support of facts, that the charges against us are based on false information."

Far more significant and crucial, we avoided Moscow's "international fishhook" by refusing to submit the dispute to the Cominform. "We are not running away from criticism on questions of principle, but in this matter we feel so unequal that we cannot agree to have it now decided before the Cominform. Nine Parties have already received your first letter without our prior knowledge and have taken their stand in resolutions. To dispose of the matter, we want to prove by our deeds the injustice of the charges against us, to prove that we are tenaciously building socialism and remaining true to the Soviet Union, true to the teachings of Marx, Engels, Lenin, and Stalin. The future will show, as the past already has shown, that we shall carry out what we have promised you."

Once pro-Soviet Party officials had observed with what fury the majority was resisting Soviet pressures and charges, and above all once they had felt the threat of persecution and arrest—the arrests of Hebrang and Žujović were quite instructive—overnight they became two-faced, began to conceal where they stood, to alter their behavior. Deeper practical reasons also existed for hypocrisy. By making false and untruthful arguments with ulterior motives, the Soviet leaders inflamed their adherents and contributed to their ambiguous attitudes. This was all the more true because only continued membership in the Party, churned up as it was, whipped up against "betrayers" as it was, offered any prospect for continued activity along the lines laid out by Moscow, if not for an actual turnabout in policy.

Moshetov, the Soviet representative responsible for Yugoslav affairs on the Central Committee, arrived in Belgrade on May 19. He brought a message from that committee signed by Mikhail Suslov enjoining us to participate in the coming meeting of the Cominform. Other Soviet representatives insisted that Tito must attend in person, and they spread rumors that Stalin would be there too.

But the very next day our Central Committee affirmed our refusal to attend, as directed by the plenum of May 9 which had been convened to consider the Molotov-Stalin letter of May 4.

At some point came Stalin's own intervention in, or more precisely his protest at, the arrest of Hebrang and Žujović. He accused our Central Committee of intent to murder them, which—Oh, heretical thought!—would have been quite in the spirit of Stalinist, Soviet methods, and demanded—no more, no less—the presence of Soviet investigators at the inquiry into their conduct. Pijade and others versed in Serbian history recalled that when Archduke Franz Ferdinand was assassinated in Sarajevo in 1914, Austria-Hungary had made the same demand on Serbia. It was precisely this demand, they said, that the Serbian government had rejected, thus giving the Austrians a pretext to declare war on Serbia, which in turn led to the First World War. I drafted a brief reply, approved by the Politburo, to this Soviet demand. The reply read, in part: ". . . The very thought of our leaders being described as 'criminal murderers' is bitterly rejected. . . . The Central Committee of the Communist Party of Yugoslavia considers out of the question any participation in the investigation of Hebrang and Žujović by the Central Committee of the Soviet Communist Party (Bolsheviks)."

The Soviet leaders, having set their apparatus in motion on an international scale, reacted quickly. In their letter of May 22 they had already confirmed that the Cominform would convene "to discuss the state of affairs in the Yugoslav Communist Party," paying no attention to our repudiation and directly contradicting the original spirit of voluntary participation and equal rights. Ostensibly bowing to a request from the Czech and Hungarian comrades, Moscow's Central Committee now agreed to postpone the session until the second half of June.

In late May or early June a Polish Party representative called on me. I have forgotten his name, but it may have been Filkenshtein, a member of the Cominform's editorial board, forty years old, distinctly blond, with an intellectual look and steady bearing. I had made his acquaintance earlier. Emphasizing that Moscow did not know about it, he brought a message from Gomulka[9] that urged us to attend the Cominform meeting for the sake of avoiding open confrontation. Relations would then have a chance to simmer down gradually. Gomulka was prepared to come to Belgrade along with Jakub Berman,[10] to talk matters over in detail—provided, of course, that we agreed to the meeting. I promised to inform the Central Committee quickly and gave him an appointment one or two days later. I did inform Tito and my closest comrades; the Pole did come at the appointed time; and as our position had not changed and we still would not attend—but would welcome a visit by Gomulka—the Polish offer came to nothing. I believe Gomulka really was working without the knowledge of the Soviet leaders, but cannot exclude the possibility that had his offer been accepted he would have informed them of his trip to Belgrade.

The official invitation from the Cominform came in a telegram on June 19. Tito again told the Soviet representatives that we declined to participate.

On June 20 the expanded Politburo met in the Brdo Palace, near Kranj.[11] Most of the agenda concerned the Fifth Party Congress and economic issues. At the morning session Tito presented the Cominform's invitation. There was no discussion. We unanimously confirmed the position taken earlier. But then Blagoje Nešković,[12] secretary of the Serbian Central Committee, hesitantly took the floor with a proposal for renewed discussion: Perhaps our case would be stronger, he said, both within the Party and in the world Communist movement, if we were to go to the Cominform meeting and state our position. No one agreed with him.

After lunch we took a walk around the pond. I found myself next to Tito, consulting him on some subject or other. The conversation touched on possible Soviet intervention. In bitter exaltation Tito exclaimed, "To die on one's own soil! At least a memory remains!" I remember that cry, not only because I agreed with him but also because it gave me the courage to go on.

We knew that the Cominform was in session in Bucharest, discussing relations between our Central Committee and that of the Soviet Union. Leading comrades in Tanjug, the press agency, had been advised to follow the reports coming out of Eastern Europe and to keep me closely informed. For this reason I did not leave Belgrade.

Around 3:30 on June 28, when I had just awakened from an afternoon nap, Tanjug called to say that at 3:00 p.m. Radio Prague had begun announcing a Cominform resolution against the Communist Party of Yugoslavia. I went immediately to the Central Committee offices, where secretaries Dragica Weinberger and Slavica Fran were typing up the text as it was received from Tanjug in bits and pieces and sending it on to the Politburo members. The resolution was announced by the rest of the East European countries only the next day.

In the late afternoon the Politburo met at Tito's. We decided to call a plenary meeting of the Central Committee the next day to deal with the resolution.

The resolution contained nothing new, and still less anything surprising that had not been in the earlier Soviet letters. But its promulgation on the anniversary of the tragic battle in 1389 at Kosovo, which had inaugurated five centuries of Turkish rule over the Serbian people, cut into the minds and hearts of all of us Serbs. Though we were neither religious nor mystical, it was not difficult for us to notice this coincidence in dates between ancient disasters and living, Soviet, threats and attacks. We observed the coincidence, in fact, with a certain relish.

I fell asleep as usual around 11:00 but suddenly woke up close to 1:00, trembling with anxiety, my mind beset by the Cominform resolution. I knew that we would have to respond, although that question had not come up the evening before, when the Politburo met at Tito's. Without a second thought, driven by cold, measured rage and irrepressible conviction, I locked myself in my study and wrote an answer that could serve as a draft for the next day's Central Committee session and, better yet, as a release for Tanjug. I was sure that tomorrow the Soviet and East European radio stations would begin blasting out the news, to say nothing of the West, and a statement from Tanjug would be a must. The announcement from Radio Prague was at my fingertips, but I scarcely glanced at it. Point by point, the Cominform's charges emerged from my memory as I wrote. Almost feverish, I nevertheless wrote deliberately, composing and compressing my formulations. Dawn crept up on me. Without going back to bed I looked through the newspapers and had a cup of coffee. Even as it was, work was piling up at the Central Committee, and what I had concocted through the night had to be edited and typed.[13]

The Central Committee meeting began in the afternoon, in a calm, almost subdued atmosphere. The confrontation was now public, there was a rift that could not be healed, and no end was in sight. Tito, in contrast to his manner at the previous night's meeting, was nervous and flustered.

After the resolution had been read and briefly discussed—interrupted more than discussed—it was decided at Tito's suggestion to prepare a response. Writing a resolution and disseminating it would take time, all the more as there was no text at hand to serve as a basis. I offered the one I had composed overnight. There were no interruptions. Everyone listened, solemnly attentive. Everyone, that is, but Tito, who stood up and paced nervously, as one who is pondering intensively and carefully. When I finished he exclaimed, "Very good! I think that can serve as a basis . . . ," and at once proposed a committee to edit the reply. The extent of Tito's mistrust, of his nervous, groundless suspicion, could be seen in his choice of committee members, the men closest to himself: Kardelj, Ranković, and me.

The Central Committee accepted our proposed reply in toto. Disagreement arose only over whether to publish the Cominform resolution along with it. Tito was opposed, though not adamantly so; I was adamantly in favor. Kardelj unequivocally supported me, as did the majority. So the next day, June 30, both documents were published together. Since the other East European countries did not publicize either our reply or our polemics, this publication became a powerful argument in our favor later, when we were settling scores with domestic and foreign opposition.

The Cominform resolution was recognized at once throughout the world as an event of paramount significance for the further development of communism. No one in the West had foreseen such a conflict, largely because Yugoslavia was characterized there as Satellite Number One. In terms of the behind-the-scenes relationship between Yugoslavia and the U S S R this was quite unfounded, but on the other hand it was well founded if one took the view that Yugoslavs were ideologically intractable, hard-line revolutionaries. Failure to foresee the conflict seems all the more puzzling, given the public differences aired in the press and in the speeches of state officials. There was one exception: A high-ranking officer of the U.S. embassy in Belgrade had predicted the confrontation in a report he had made. But Washington thought the whole notion stupid and preposterous.

In retrospect, I am astonished by the West's erroneous predictions about the outcome of the confrontation, not only such predictions as were available to everyone through the media but also those emanating from diplomatic sources, which in lesser measure were available to the Yugoslav government. To the best of my knowledge, everyone concurred that the Yugoslav regime would soon fall. Most observers thought a pro-Soviet team—not monarchists—would seize power.

True, the dispute had the immediate consequence of aggravating international relationships. There were threats. There were provocations. Albania led the way, when only two or three days after the resolution that country began to break its agreements with us and jeopardize our relations. But by and large the argument stayed where it was, on the level of ideology, and not a single Party—not even the Soviet one—was ideologically prepared for armed intervention against yesterday's acclaimed, revolutionary Yugoslavia. Besides, the neighboring Communist countries were militarily inferior to us. We ourselves were poorly armed, but their own armies were inadequately organized and plagued by low morale.

We conjectured at the time and even took for granted what is widely known today, chiefly from the speeches of Khrushchev at the Twentieth Party Congress: that Stalin mistakenly thought a complete change in Yugoslavia would be brought about from within, by "sound forces" inside the Party. In other words, as he expressed it to Khrushchev, all he had to do was move his little finger and Tito would come tumbling down.

So we did after all stand fast, in Dimitrov's words. And our self-assurance was bolstered by Party morale and especially by the popular mood.

It cannot be disputed that resistance on all important levels and in all crucial institutions was stiff. This we had foreseen. But our adversaries in the Party—only there did we have significant opposition—were bewildered from the start by being told of changes in a history that was still very much alive to them; the Cominform resolution was absurd on its face. Our courage and determination drove these people to cover up and dissemble. Slander and lies had not been unknown before this time to the Yugoslav Party, any more than to other political parties, but in the Soviet attack clearly more was at issue. Here was an assault against our foundations, one that was directed at the very currents of history recently lived through by the new Yugoslav state and the peoples of our country. At issue was the independence of the nation and the autonomy of its internal development. The truth of this, the reality of it, forced Stalin's supporters in Yugoslavia to be two-faced, even those who were enthralled by internationalism and devoted to the Soviet Union as "the bulwark of world socialism." They had to cover up their true intentions with shopworn phrases.

This happened all the sooner and all the more easily because the Soviet letters and the Cominform resolution, in both substance and style, legitimized hypocrisy and slander in the struggle against Yugoslavia, and thereby in the Communist movement as such. I do not mean to say that such methods were alien to the movement in earlier times—least of all were they unknown to Soviet communism. I believe them to be latent in every totalitarian consciousness and especially a totalitarian movement. But now, in the attack on Yugoslavia, such methods had burst the confines of a single Party and transcended the movement as a whole to slander a victorious revolution. And by attempting to trample the Yugoslav state, such methods threatened to hold in bondage all the states of Eastern Europe. That was why the Soviet and Cominform lies and calumnies seemed so monstrous, so shocking—and so unacceptable.

None of this posed a dilemma for anyone not a Communist. The ordinary Yugoslav citizen understood the whole dispute to be natural and altogether understandable, the threat of Soviet intervention notwithstanding. Pressure and military force exerted by the great against the small has for centuries been the rule rather than the exception, especially in the Balkans.

Among the broad, non-Party masses, therefore, our confrontation led neither to confusion nor hesitation. Rather, it was instinctively taken to be one of those turning points that set the nation's life on a new, more authentic, healthier course. Such a popular presentiment did not quite materialize, but neither was it quite betrayed. Even with all its inconsistencies and burdens, Yugoslavia was beginning to forge ahead on its own.

Everything was still in flux and ideologically confused. But the top leaders and the people were now earnestly resolved to defend their country and their integrity. That is how matters stood with us on the eve of the Fifth Party Congress.

This congress, which began on July 21, displayed the customary unanimity, enthusiastic but a little forced. The choice of delegates had been determined by the Central Committee, with the regional committees sharing in organization and control. Even so, there were some adherents of the Cominform who did not dare to come out openly, and still others who had not yet decided where they stood.

So for all the show of unanimity there were nuances in the delegates' speeches. Everyone was still for the Soviet Union and Stalin, but there were differences in how they addressed the main issues. The inner circle took note of these but did not yet deem them sufficient cause for settling accounts. Particularly with respect to ideology, the leaders themselves had not shifted very far except on the question of independence and the truth about the Yugoslav revolution—that is to say, issues of power and their own integrity.

Generally speaking, the broader membership was still infatuated with the Soviet Union and Stalin, but the top leadership was unclear as to how far the Soviet government and its vassal states would carry their attacks and even less clear about what social causes or reasons of state impelled them. As late as September 29, 1949, Kardelj, speaking as minister of foreign affairs at a U.N. session, supported the Soviet Union without ever mentioning the Cominform attacks. He was not prompted simply by tactical reasons having to do with the "backward consciousness" of the Party rank and file. The leadership itself was slow to catch up with Moscow's intentions.

The congress was held in the Guardhouse—a complex of barracks in Topčider.[14] The trial of Draža Mihailović[15] had been held in that very hall two years before. The delegates were served lunch under tents on the lawn. There was no other hall large enough in Belgrade at the time, but the site had also been chosen for security reasons.

Historians will assess the Fifth Congress according to their own understanding and views, but for us in the leadership it meant above all the final attainment of legitimacy. We were now independent of the Soviet Union and international Communist assemblies. No one wasted much time over the resolutions adopted by the congress, over its Statute or its Program, other than to formulate and adopt them.

To the very end of the Fifth Congress we avoided "cracking the whip," even over those who had openly come out for the Soviet Union and the Cominform. We set great store by the congress's influence, hoping that practical experience and the simple truth would help people see the light. It was obvious that the congress strengthened Tito's reputation, his own personal authority and role, and that of his closest associates as well. This was true of the power of the Politburo and particularly true of the Central Committee Secretariat, whose members had now achieved a legitimacy hitherto bestowed on them by the Comintern through its emissary, Tito.

For our adversaries, however—the Soviet leadership, the leadership of the various other Communist Parties, and the pro-Soviet Communists in Yugoslavia—the congress had a different meaning. It brought change to their lives. These opponents, of course, "understood" the congress in their own way: extortion and deception by a "Tito clique." One direct consequence was an intensification of the campaign of pressure and provocation, both from within and from without. Another was conspiracy and emigration by the pro-Soviet Communists.16

CRITICISM
OF THE
SOVIET SYSTEM

I have mentioned the constant irresolution that afflicted me from the very beginning of my active life: Should I be a writer or a politician? When I did in the end become a public figure this vacillation, my impulse to write creatively, did not wane but on the contrary grew stronger. With the end of the war I was morbid with restlessness and a fear of lying fallow, fear that I would miss my true inner calling if instead of getting back to literature I let mundane political life suck me into its vortex.

And I had in fact resolved to put an end to this irresolution—would it be duty or love, politics or literature?—when over our Party suddenly loomed the unforeseen, fateful threat of the Soviet Union and Stalin. This threat, indeed, hung over the country itself, inasmuch as the Party exercised a monopoly over all social life. But if our ideological kinship with Moscow had blinded us to the dangers lurking in devotion, still less did we suspect the energies that might be released by confrontation. For my own part, I experienced the confrontation as a challenge and an inspiration, the culmination of our revolution. I was certainly not alone in this, but I doubt whether anyone in the top circle experienced it with quite the same pivotal, cathartic intensity as I did.

Both instinctively and consciously I understood that my time had come, that I must answer my calling, complete my own integration. It is no accident that even now I look back on that period of my political and intellectual activity as the most fruitful, the boldest and most decisive of times for me.

My day-to-day work in the Secretariat of the Politburo and in Agitprop stimulated rather than hampered my journalistic activity. Most important—important for a proper appraisal of the period, the Party, and my own work—I set forth on theoretical grounds not only the distinctive features of our experience but also the true nature of the Soviet system, which inevitably drove it to attack us. The real rift with Moscow first began with these public statements of mine, only to be further deepened by them. My own temperament played merely a secondary role; intellectual restlessness and moral revulsion at Soviet behavior were the crucial factors. I was driven in this direction by some irresistible force, some inner backlash of resistance to lies. It was a character trait that would later show up with far greater intensity in my clash with Tito and in my critical recognition of what communism is.

Soon after the Fifth Congress I came to think of that meeting as a hollow enterprise, for all its strong and spontaneous manifestation of unity. We had failed to probe the essential questions, failed to put enough distance between the Soviets and ourselves in ideology and experience. It dawned on me that in trying to prove our oneness with Stalin and the Stalinists and to show how true we were to them, we were walking into a trap. For if all that were true, why then were we not obeying them? Why all the argument? At bottom, I now realize, I was groping for national and revolutionary uniqueness and sensing its vague beginnings, as opposed to the borrowed legacy of ideological identity with Moscow.

But on this score confusion reigned in the Party, even in its topmost echelon. Thus, for example, the Serbian Academy formally met to mark the October Revolution. The newspapers were celebrating "great Stalin's" sixty-ninth birthday. I, on the other hand, was just then completing an article called "On Injustice and False Accusations," which was published in *Borba* on October 2–4, 1948. I took great care in its writing but was moved by inspiration as well, and it was typed by Štefica Štefanija-Barić, my temporary secretary, toward whom I was now drawn by feelings that went beyond Party comradeship.

In that article the claim was first advanced—cautiously, still surrounded by veneration, but nonetheless clearly—that Stalin was in the wrong. Here it was finally said openly and unambiguously that Yugoslavia had undergone a national revolution that justified our resistance to falsehood and injustice. Sensing its importance, I submitted the piece to Tito. After he had red-penciled my criticisms of Stalin I went to see him and persuaded him to let them stand as written. It was surprisingly easy. I argued that everyone knew Stalin was behind all this and that the Party membership was only confused by our silence. "Good," agreed Tito. "Let it stand. We've spared Stalin long enough."

Crossing swords with Stalin and affirming the Yugoslav revolution in one and the same article were intimately connected, and sent me into raptures. The very act of undermining the cult of Stalin confirmed the essence of our revolution. Up to this point the imprecise Comintern and Titoist phrase "war of national liberation" had been used in Yugoslavia to designate the revolution. I had never been convinced that this term accurately conveyed our revolutionary process—revolution through national war. Today, too, I believe that a term pointing up not only the national but also the revolutionary character of our uprising would have served better as a rallying cry and call to arms. The premise of my article—that what was at issue in our country was revolution—met with unanimous acceptance and soon was endorsed by Tito as well. At the same time, widespread questioning of Stalin's infallibility deepened and "legitimized" doubts about the Soviet Union's "pure" brand of socialism. This was the starting point for criticism of the Soviet system, although it developed at a slower pace than awareness of our revolutionary past.

I continued along this line, sometimes with unexpected results. Invited to speak at the plenum of the Central Committee of Montenegro in January 1949, I stressed that bureaucratic deviations and retreats from socialism must be sought in our own selves and in the system we championed. I noticed that some in the audience looked dumbfounded, but others seemed enraptured, as if their intimations of a higher truth had at last been confirmed.

But that was only one side of the confrontation with Moscow, the revolutionary-democratic side. Concurrently and even more dominant, something like a "re-Stalinization" occurred—harsh administrative measures for the economy, a strengthening of the Party and political police apparatus.

The press for what were tactical reasons supported and popularized the USSR and growled at the Western alliance, but by the beginning of February the Second Plenum of the Central Committee was prescribing "greater boldness and a faster pace in setting up collective farms."

The year 1949 was decisive, especially the summer. It brought a change not in our conscious, ideological separation but in our relationship as a state with the USSR and its East European vassals. One after another the top officials throughout Eastern Europe were arrested and put through show trials: Kochi Xoxe, Traicho Kostov, Laszlo Rajk.[1] Nor were they alone. We ourselves were presented as the chief culprit, the evil genius, the diversionist spy center taken over from the Gestapo by the CIA and all the other imperialist intelligence services.

Then came the collapse of the Greek uprising. In my judgment, it was Stalin's greatest service. The Soviet and East European governments violated their treaties with Yugoslavia and imposed an economic blockade. That summer, in a separate development, relations with Moscow further deteriorated because of our alleged persecution of "Soviet citizens," Russian émigrés. Along our borders, incidents multiplied and Soviet and pro-Soviet troops carried out threatening maneuvers. The revolution in China achieved its decisive victory, but for all our secret wishes and cautious hopes, the new Chinese leadership sided with Moscow against Yugoslavia.

Tito and the leadership undertook extensive measures against attack. These included preparations for both guerrilla and conventional warfare, planned dismantling of factories, building up the domestic armaments industry, etc. Our leadership was aware that real danger threatened and did all that could be done to ward it off. Reinforced troop movements were taking place just across our borders—Soviet troops in Hungary, Bulgarian troops in Bulgaria. Then it was that Tito declared unambiguously that Yugoslavia would defend itself if attacked.

We took a great interest in the Eastern European trials, but up to the case of Rajk we failed to react adequately with a well-thought-out and militant position.

When the Greek uprising disintegrated it was we who got the blame, even though it was we and we alone who had continued aiding the insurgents right to the end, the last day, so to speak. Moscow, acting through its agents and retainers, first replaced Markos Vafiadis,[2] its commander, and then forced the rebels to abandon their guerrilla tactics for fortifications and entrenched lines, something that was most welcome to the technically and organizationally superior enemy. It should not be forgotten that in February 1948 Stalin had all but ordered the Bulgarian delegates and us to "wind things down" in Greece, in accordance with his agreements on postwar spheres of influence with the Western Great Powers.

And precisely because we knew all that and had heard it with our own ears, the fact that now it was we who were getting the blame for the collapse of the Greek uprising made us angry. With bitterness we now realized that the Soviet Union was a Great Power "just like all the rest."

Encumbering ourselves ideologically, we were slow to set ourselves well apart from the Soviet Union and its so-called socialism. Kardelj, Bakarić, Kidrič, Milentije Popović, and I were the people who saw this most clearly, each in his own way. Tito still fought shy of, was even opposed to, settling ideological accounts with Moscow. Kardelj and I, before leaving for the U.N. session in New York in 1949, tried to persuade him that we had to begin making a deeper ideological critique of the Soviet system lest our resistance become incomprehensible and lead to confusion and chaos in the Party. "We'd find it hard to fight them to the end," he replied. "They know all the right quotations." "Yes, but we can quote a thing or two ourselves," I responded. Tito gave in and later helped square accounts with the Soviet system in his simple, succinct way.

Trying to grasp why the Soviet leaders were behaving as they were toward us and toward other Communist Parties and Communist countries, neither I nor the other Party theoreticians could be satisfied with what we called "vulgar, bourgeois" explanations: that it all sprang from Russia's backwardness and the totalitarian nature of the Soviet system.[3]

Soviet threats and provocations, the senseless accusations against the Yugoslav leadership, and the deriding and boycotting of everything Yugoslav only strengthened and quickened our leadership's political and ideological activity. Our feverish, heretical tension did not hamper us but stimulated the search for new ways, new discoveries. All the turmoil within us, together with the unpredictable and deadly dangers without, could not fail to renew that closeness and warmth among us top leaders that the war's passing had diluted. We grew more direct, more open and selfless than we had ever been—more even than when we were building a revolutionary Party before the war, more even than during the most frightful wartime combat.

A process of silent reckoning set in. Each of us had received a set of "alien" experiences, our own yet not our own, that now were held up to scrutiny. Indeed, the confrontation with the Soviet Union raged inside us. Everyone rediscovered his own powers, his self-discipline, his delusions. Willing or not, aware or not, we now won the right to be more our own selves than before and to display all the powers at our command against the disasters and betrayals looming over the people and the country, over the leadership as a whole, and over each separate leader as an individual.

By virtue of such "individualization," which removed the inhibitions from free expression, we leaders became more collective and democratic. Tito's role both increased and diminished—increased as the fulcrum of opposition, diminished as the expression of omnipotence, omniscience, and infallibility. Little by little, autocracy was giving way to oligarchy.

The most significant and decisive event in that seething summer of 1949, just when we were searching our souls and making our readjustments, was the Soviet note of August 18. Brutal and unambiguous, it waved a menacing stick at us as "Fascist bullies. . . ." It was prompted by our expelling the Tsarist Russian émigrés who had taken Soviet citizenship. No sooner did the conflict with Moscow break out than those émigrés, newly baked Soviet citizens, were transformed into an elaborate propaganda and intelligence network, one that had a relatively broad base, numbering some twenty thousand. These people formed a compact and cohesive mass that reminded one of the German pro-Hitler *Volksdeutsche.* Openly and firmly, they linked up with the Soviet embassy.

I felt we had to respond to the Soviet note, if not officially through the government, then quasi-officially through Tanjug. So I put together a reply and took it for approval to Kardelj, then our minister for foreign affairs. He liked it and accepted it as the official note, almost without change. It was characteristic of relations with the Soviet government; characteristic, too, of our resolve; and in abbreviated form here it is:

> The government of the Federal People's Republic of Yugoslavia [FNRJ] has no intention of getting into a dispute with the government of the USSR over the character of the regime in Yugoslavia. However, the government of the FNRJ considers it its duty to point out that the Federal People's Republic of Yugoslavia is an independent and sovereign state and that its

peoples and its government are under no circumstances willing to let anyone interfere in their internal affairs. Further, the government of the FNRJ wishes to point out that up till now no external pressure has ever had any influence on its domestic policy, nor will it in the future. As regards foreign policy the government of the FNRJ likewise deems it necessary to declare that it carries out this policy in accordance with its country's independence and sovereignty; in accordance with progressive principles of peace and cooperation between peoples and states on the basis of equality and mutual respect for sovereignty; and in accordance with international treaties and obligations which have been and remain a public act on the part of the government of the FNRJ. The peoples of the FNRJ are unwilling under any circumstances to renounce these principles in response to outside pressure.

It goes without saying that the note urged the Soviet government to take back its citizens, former White Guards.[4] Also sought was the return of our own children and war orphans. In 1945 these children had been shipped off to the USSR, to be educated in the Suvorov[5] military schools, where instruction begins in childhood. They never returned, nor was it ever established, so far as I know, who had sent them there in the first place.

Not long afterward Kidrič and I found ourselves discussing this exchange of notes in Kardelj's office. We were tense and apprehensive but determined. "The Russians wouldn't have sent such a note if they were not in collusion with the Americans," said Kidrič. "What else should imperialists be doing but coming to an agreement of some kind at the expense of the little fellows? Greece to the Americans, Yugoslavia to the Russians. It's entirely likely." I thought so, too, without expressing it as categorically. Kardelj was more cautious, but neither did he entirely exclude the possibility of a Soviet-American agreement at our expense: "It's hard to imagine happening today, and yet . . ." Our ideas, certainly, were premature and unsupported. But even now I wouldn't have put it past Moscow to make a deal—anything to choke off the Yugoslav heresy. They failed, though, to find a partner. The United States was sufficiently strong and sufficiently anti-Soviet, while Yugoslavia was in a key strategic position.

But relief was in sight. On September 3, Secretary of State Dean Acheson[6] of the United States and Deputy Foreign Secretary Hector McNeil[7] of Great Britain put Moscow on notice that an attack on Yugoslavia would have serious consequences. Our press published the Acheson-McNeil declaration without commentary but in a conspicuous spot. We were still wary of being stung by Soviet propaganda with regard to our being supported by "Western imperialists," but we had to acknowledge the importance of such support, which may have been crucial.

It must have been my ideological activism that led Kardelj to propose that I be included in our U.N. delegation. A secondary reason was that he preferred not to be the only leader to engage Moscow in polemics in New York—a strategy that had been decided on after open threats, innumerable border provocations, and an economic blockade. Though I had no experience, God knows, in diplomacy, I was pleased to know that I would be speaking out against Moscow in the world parliament.

Despite all my intellectual intensity, both on shipboard and in New York, I was torn by a wild sense of desolation. I had decided to separate from Mitra but had not yet gotten up the courage to unite with Štefica. Before leaving I had quarreled with her—what about, I don't really know, unless it was that on that long and responsible journey I would be feeling still lonelier and more self-sacrificial. I remember distinctly the endless blue-gray expanse of the ocean, which, in my mind, merged with the hurt and grieved expression in Štefica's eyes.

America's standard of living and technology did not impress me, probably because human and social relations were to me far more important. Such priorities went back to my childhood, before Marxism came to dominate my consciousness. But America did strongly influence the direction of my thoughts, and not mine alone, I am sure. Something must be wrong with our Marxist teachings, I thought, if a country so well developed and with so large a proletariat not only was not socialist but its proletariat was actually antisocialist.

In mid-November I gave a speech to the U.N. political committee that was entirely taken up with Soviet pressures and attacks. Since Soviet delegates, especially Andrei Vyshinsky,[8] made generous use of quotations from literature and examples from history, it occurred to me— not without malice, to be sure—to read them the fantasies uttered by Nozdryov, the irrepressible liar in Gogol's *Dead Souls*.[9] With a wicked grin Kardelj went along with my plan. The result was laughter among the delegates and sour looks from the Soviets. Vyshinsky cast a glance at me of the most delicious, murderous hatred that all but said aloud, "Just wait till we get our paws on you. . . ."

We may have been ignored by the press but not by the diplomatic corps. So many invitations to receptions and meetings came our way that we could barely handle them. At the opening of the General Assembly, when our delegates had already taken their seats, Ernest Bevin,[10] the British foreign secretary, came up and warmly gripped Kardelj by the hand. He held on for a long time, giving photographers time to record the scene and the Soviet representatives time to get a good look. Like Bevin, Kardelj smiled warmly. I had the impression that he was not too comfortable with such a sudden, excessively cordial encounter but that he was aware of its importance. Though we certainly had had enough of the Soviet leaders and their criticisms, we were still anxious not to be perceived as abetting capitalism and imperialism.

The press may have remained indifferent to the Soviet-Yugoslav dispute, but at the United Nations this conflict took center stage, especially after we were put up for membership on the Security Council. Kardelj had raised the idea back in Belgrade, Tito agreeing with it at once. There now commenced a bitter backstage struggle whose climax came after the first vote. The Soviet delegation did everything to block our election, from public accusations about charter violations and our breaking a "gentlemen's agreement," to surreptitious blackmail and threats. Our people, though, were backed by the United States and through the latter (then dominant at the United Nations) got the support of Latin America as well, which with its large number of votes tipped the scale in our favor. We realized that this was a victory on a world scale, not just for our little country but for a great principle as well. I wrote an article about it in New York that was immediately published in Yugoslavia.

I wanted to return home by plane but Kardelj would have none of it. We sailed on the *Île de France;* it was not big and pompous like the *Queen Elizabeth,* but cozier and less formal.

I did not find Mitra at home. Taking our daughter Vukica with her and those things she considered essential, she had moved to a smaller town house. I went over to Ranković's place with little presents for his wife, Slavka, and their children. There I found Štefica, probably at Slavka's invitation. The visit over, I was going to drive her to her apartment on Vojvoda Dobrnjac Street but stopped first at my own town house to present her with a little ring I had bought for her in New York. Štefica was delighted. All this time I had been thinking of her, and now was the turning point in our relations. I no longer found strange the thought of marrying her, although we left it unsaid.[11]

Toward the end of December, soon after our return from the United States, a Third Plenum was held, the main topic being education. I believe that many—in fact, a majority in the Party and not just myself—viewed this plenum as a significant milestone, if not the decisive one, along the road to finding our own way and departing from Soviet ideology and methods. In my paper I posed the issue thus: "The problem is therefore not so much what kind of person we wish to create as what method will ensure our producing this person." In the adopted resolutions, which I also drafted, Marxism was no longer to be a special, separate subject of study by itself. We insisted that instruction be truly scholarly, especially on the topic of Marxism. Russian no longer took priority, but there was now to be freedom of choice between that tongue and other foreign languages (English, German, French). Schoolteachers were no longer to be pro-Soviet, and we strove instead for the freedom of teachers to change their opinions, etc. It would be grotesquely inaccurate for any one person to claim credit for the success of that plenum. Such a democratic paper would have been beyond my powers to deliver had not Kardelj and, later, Tito, given me their support. Nor would such "heretical" thoughts ever have so much as crossed my mind had it not been for fierce Soviet pressures, ever fiercer, ever more terrible, to say nothing of the many passionate, sobering, creative discussions among the Party leadership and within the milieu where I operated. My merit, for what it was worth, lay only in comprehending and formulating the ideas simmering around me.[12]

One need only glance at the election speeches of Tito, Pijade, Kidrič, and others at the beginning of 1950 to realize that our prevailing tendency, varying naturally from one official to the next, was to discard Soviet structures and methods and reinvestigate our own. Otherwise my election speech to our students on March 18 would have been inconceivable. Given the audience, I made it as learned and complex as possible, proposing that in the Soviet Union the state's monopoly of production had turned into a monopoly of society and that we, our Party, were the Hegelian antithesis of the Soviet system.

Democratization was neither simple nor easy, nor did it enjoy courageous or unanimous support. Even the watershed of the Third Plenum had its bureaucratic and Stalinist side: "We must strive earnestly," said the economic resolutions, "to consolidate the existing collective farms."

By the beginning of 1950 theoretical thinking among our top people had not merely abandoned Stalin but was quickly working its way even further back, from Lenin to Marx. We often paused to reflect on the Leninist type of Party. It had been more than the source of victory, it also had provided a way of moving on after power had been seized. We firmly accepted Marx's theory of the withering away of the state to the degree that we broke away from Stalinism, but realized that such "withering away" required a change in the role of the Party. In the domain of Party problems, however, we made the slowest of starts and the least progress. We kept running up against a thick bulwark of fossilized officials, against a solid layer of bureaucracy that was now quite consolidated.

Not for the first time I began working my way through *Das Kapital*, intent on finding the source of truth, namely, the "heterodoxy and errors" of Stalin and, following him, of Lenin as well. My "social" interest in the economy merged with my study of Marx. As I thought things through, no small role was played by keen discussions with Kidrič and Kardelj, not to speak of the hopeless, bureaucratic ruts our economy found itself in.

While I perused those passages in the second volume of *Das Kapital* dealing with a future "association of primary producers" as a form of the transition to communism, it occurred to me that our whole economic mechanism might be simplified by leaving administration to those who worked in the various enterprises, the state only securing for itself the tax. One rainy day in late spring while we sat talking in a car in front of my villa I voiced this thought to Kardelj and Kidrič. Both thought it premature. But at the same time trade union officials meeting with Kardelj proposed, among other things, discontinuing the workers' councils, which had long existed as anemic, purely advisory structures. He on the contrary urged that the councils be strengthened. Then one day Kidrič phoned me: "You know, that idea of yours—now might be the moment to introduce it." At this point Kardelj was linking my idea to the workers' councils. In the ensuing discussion on self-management it was he who was to play the crucial role, both creative and practical. We believed that at last we had discovered the definitive road leading to the withering away of the state and therefore to a classless society. When we presented this in the National Assembly's Hall of Ministers, Tito was at first opposed: "Our workers aren't mature enough yet." But Kardelj and I would not give in, since work on the legal structure had already begun. Tito, after pacing around for a bit, then exclaimed excitedly, "But this is Marxist—factories to the workers!" Tito generally kept out of discussions of theory because he was preoccupied with other matters, was elevated in rank, and not given to theorizing anyway.

Yugoslavia was setting out on a new and unpredictable path toward democracy. Or so it seemed to most people and certainly to most people in the top ranks. Many were our illusions and self-deceptions. These are inevitable in any attempt to idealize one's own practice, particularly revolutionary practice. The Party bureaucracy, pressed from within and without and at the mercy of currents in the top ranks, took cover in ideological anonymity. But it remained tough, pigheaded, and stupid whenever it found its material and social privileges being encroached upon. That is how matters stood until the death of Tito, and after him, too, right up to the fall of Communist Yugoslavia.

I myself was neither silent nor willing to be silenced. At the same time as Pijade was attacking Ćopić,[13] my article titled "Contemporary Themes" came out. It called the Soviet system state capitalism and concluded that the contradiction between us and the Soviet Union was essentially greater than that between the Soviet Union and the capitalist West, meaning the United States. This thesis about state capitalism in the USSR was then taken up by the leadership, including Kardelj and Tito, only to be dropped overnight after my removal in 1954 and the reconciliation with Khrushchev.

The year 1951 saw the climax, and in many respects the winding down, of our confrontation with the Soviet Union.

Besides Ranković I, too, spoke at the Fourth Plenum on "Certain Questions of Party Theoretical Work." Criticizing the Soviet Union for making theory the monopoly not of a Party forum but of a single person (Stalin was still alive then), I pointed out that we, too, tended to monopolize theory. Without doubt my conclusion was overly optimistic, a reflection more of hope than of the real state of affairs:

> . . . Our Central Committee and our Party are struggling against every form of monopoly. In the domain of opinion, not only is monopoly harmful to the progress of human thought but at the

same time it represents the beginning and then the closing phase of the struggle by reactionary forces to create that other monopoly—a monopoly over material and social life—which consists of arrogating to oneself other people and the fruits of their labor. Without a monopoly over ideology, that other monopoly and its reactionary and despotic domination cannot be firmly established nor long sustained.

But this was not simply an expression of my own hopes. A Plenum resolution on questions of theory also was in the spirit of my claims. This resolution confirmed that Party cell approval of public statements was not obligatory unless a Politburo directive was anticipated. It was at this point that the Tito cult really began to subside. No one disputed his services or leadership, but there was a falling off in the idolization of him as a person.

STALIN GOES IN CIRCLES*

It needs to be said first of all that the leading Soviet theoreticians did not sleep with a clear conscience over the confrontation with socialist Yugoslavia. It gnawed at the roots of their own system; it poisoned the awareness of all who subscribed to Moscow's views; it laid bare the essence of the USSR's social structure and the whole substance of its foreign policy. Furthermore, the theoretical positions of Yugoslav Marxists found an echo in the Soviet Union itself. Otherwise how can it be explained that Soviet theoreticians, the major ones included, Stalin personally, felt that they had to respond somehow to our new positions? Why should they have addressed nearly identical issues? Their answers, it hardly need be said, were quite different, but it is a fact (a comic fact) that they were forced to steal from us, their most hated opponents. They of course had no intention of borrowing our theoretical postulates. Indeed, their every effort was bent on falsifying Marxism and socialism still further in order to extricate

---

*Apropos of Stalin's article "Economic Problems of Socialism in the USSR" (*Bolshevik* 18, October 1, 1952). This article is essentially a collection of responses to questions posed by Soviet theoreticians. Above all it contains observations on a textbook dealing with political economy.

themselves, at whatever cost, from the corrosive influence of Yugoslav socialism and Yugoslav social thought.

Here are some examples:

1. At the 5th Congress of the Yugoslav Communist Party in the summer of 1948 Kardelj, thinking chiefly of Yugoslavia, postulated that a people's democracy was a separate and distinct form of the dictatorship of the proletariat. This was an idea soon to be repeated by Dimitrov at a congress of the Bulgarian Party. Then, in 1949, the same idea was attributed to Stalin as a "new discovery" by the journal *Bolshevik,* even though Stalin never spoke publicly on the subject. Later it gained currency in all the East European countries as well as in the USSR itself. This was also, of course, a way of justifying the dictatorship of the bureaucracy, a way of legitimizing oversight and bureaucratic privilege, on the pretext of threats arising from private capitalism. First and foremost, it was a way of fostering subjugation to the Soviet Union.

2. At one point it was much in fashion among us to talk about the state's withering away. By this was meant chiefly the state's role in the economy but also its role in society generally. The law on workers' councils reflected the fashion, as did Tito's speech before the National Assembly on June 26, 1950. There he criticized as antisocialist Stalin's theory of the state. Soon thereafter Stalin (whose subject was linguistics, but this was quite beside the point) felt obliged to take a detour and defend his theory of the state. He alleged that owing to defense needs, the state could neither wither away nor become democratized under socialism. Yugoslav reality (and theory followed suit) indicated just the opposite—that the state, in its economic and social role, could grow weaker while its defensive powers grew stronger. Actually, following Yugoslavia's lead, Stalin was responding here to a question that was beginning to be put in the USSR and elsewhere: Why have we ("they") not yet seen the long-promised withering away of the state? And how did Stalin reply? Again, by falsifying Marxism, again by putting the USSR's "socialist reality" in a false light.

3. So it went, too, in the domain of art and the idea that intellectual conflict is a precondition of democratic development. Take the Moscow "Resolution" on the need for dramatic conflict in art, art that reflects the struggle for socialism: Did it not bear an uncanny resemblance to our arguments? As if lifted directly from our Yugoslav newspapers and periodicals? But we saw that in reality this resolution took issue with those forces in Soviet society that were precisely socialist and democratic,

took issue with antibureaucratic forces—not with their opposites. The first playwright to depict a Soviet manager in more or less accurate colors had quite a bad time of it, for he was stigmatized as retrograde because he touched on truths "untypical of our" (i.e., their) managerial reality! Once again we saw reaction to the same issue, but driven by backroom aims and impulses that were the opposite of socialist.

4. In the work under discussion and without being open and explicit but no less unmistakably, Stalin repudiated his 1939 positions. These had been among the leitmotifs of "Soviet" state propaganda. They claimed in effect that the building of a Communist society had already begun with the Soviet Russians. However, for four years we Yugoslavs had maintained that there could be no talk of starting to build communism in the USSR. We also took the position that the USSR had not yet emerged from socialism's state-capitalist foyer, was even permanently lodged in the vestibule, and that the true social meaning of the counter-revolution that had been carried out in Russia lay precisely in this. The combination of Soviet reality and Yugoslav criticism of it may have driven Stalin to be much more modest, but he was no more realistic or sincere than ever when it came to a transition by the USSR to communism. And again, falsification and mystification! Here he was prattling about "the basic preconditions for the preparation of the transition to communism." Most complicated, most roundabout. But clear enough— if only this were a question (to pick up on Stalin) not of the transition itself but of "carrying out the preconditions for such a transition." And that hardly guaranteed that any such transition will actually commence. Under Stalin's "wise leadership" this issue had been smothered for close to fifteen years. Leadership had "wisely" led systematic political thought in the USSR (and not only there) down the garden path, at the end of which all such thought had been strangled to death. Now, "leadership" was finally compelled to admit the deception.* In reality, carrying out such preconditions was only meant to put the finishing touches on the monstrous edifice of state capitalism, meant to camouflage its completion. The end product, though, whether finished or not finished,

---

*According to Stalin, those basic preconditions that were supposed to lay the foundation for a transition to communism but were not yet realized, were the following: "securing the growth of all social production with first priority being given to growth in producers goods"; and "raising collective farm ownership to the level of general national ownership" (i.e., state ownership).

could never come to pass. For all that it once was proclaimed by Stalin, no final transition to communism ever happened. Nor could it happen simply because someone had willed it or predicted it, even Stalin.

5. Even the latest Stalinist "discovery," the latest "contribution of genius" to the treasury of Marxism-Leninism and socialism, giving rise to these present lines, was in reality a more or less shallow and vulgarized copy of various Yugoslav hypotheses. But again, as we shall see, with a completely different aim in mind than the Yugoslav.

Stalin first claims that even under socialism men cannot change economic laws. They operate, he says, independently of the will of man. Man can accelerate developments only to the degree that he has understood these laws and to the degree that they have come to serve him as social instruments. But this was no more nor less than the Yugoslav position, stated previously by Kardelj and Kidrič in their articles, and in particular at the conference of propagandists held in June 1950. The Yugoslavs had not regarded this as any sort of "discovery" at the time, and even Stalin "modestly" declared his position to be nothing new. And yet when the idea was advanced by our Yugoslav theoreticians it was naturally branded as worthless by backers of the Cominform. Many of our own comrades, good, respectable people, wagged their heads in doubt. Right up to the publication of this work by Stalin in the USSR it had been maintained that the five-year plan was the Soviet government's plan and hence the fundamental law of socialist development, of a socialist economy. But it was only a legal document, after all. No wonder that Stalin, expounding all this, got confused and muddled. Trying as always to don Marxist and socialist garments, he was unable to conceal the essential thing, which was that all these Soviet categories are capitalist by nature, for the system itself is one of state capitalism. It stood to reason that Marxist and socialist garments could not possibly fit well. Earlier, a special economic analysis of Stalin's postulates would have been needed to reveal the whole meaning of his economic theories, which was state capitalism, in all the depth of their falsehood. But as if on purpose his propositions stood revealed in this, his last piece of writing.

Stalin further claims that the categories of merchandise, money, and value are valid in the transitional period as well. (True, in another guise.) Almost word for word, this closely tracks us Yugoslavs, though it is understood in distorted form and, once again, has another end in view than we have in mind.

Matters stood the same way with many of Stalin's other, secondary, postulates.

But no Yugoslav vaccine could have set life in motion in the East, or for that matter anywhere else, were not objective reality such as to impose a solution. The socialized forces of production and the social character of the processes of production sought different social relations. Therein lay the point. Even Stalin had to respond, or try to respond, to these "unfriendly," "un-Marxist," and "unsocialist," "anti-Soviet" questions. And that is why one should not focus only on the stupidity and childishness of what was written in the USSR, but should be aware of muffled but progressive forces in society, of an unwavering tendency to harmonize the forces of production with production relations. To put it more simply, primary producers had first to be broken of the habit of acquiring the fruits of their labor.

It is worth taking the trouble to dwell on certain of Stalin's points.

We know that the theory of harmonious development between the forces of production and production relations in the USSR originated with Stalin.* Yugoslav theoreticians had been trying to refute this idea, and on the whole they succeeded in doing so. Stalin too then backed away from it. He had been cautious, and, moreover, his object was not to modify the theory but to preserve it, for the sake of "developing" existing relations more precisely along the same lines and on the same social basis. He said the following:

> I cannot take the words "complete harmony" in an absolute sense. We dare not understand them as meaning that under socialism there is no lag in productive relations behind growth in the forces of production. The forces of production are the moving forces behind production, the most revolutionary of all forces. Even under socialism they are in advance of production relations, without a doubt. Only after a certain time has passed do production relations undergo a transformation in harmony with the forces of production.
>
> In this case how should the words "complete harmony" be understood? They should be understood to mean that under socialism conflict does not normally arise between production

---

*See the chapter "On Historical and Dialectical Materialism" in Stalin's *History of the Communist Party.*

relations and the forces of production; that society has the means of aligning retarded production relations with the forces of production in good time. Socialist society can do this because it harbors no lingering classes capable of organized resistance. Even under socialism of course there will be internal forces that lag behind and do not comprehend the need for change in production relations. But again it will not be hard to subdue them. It won't come to blows.*

Even Stalin, then, has been compelled today to deny "complete harmony"! But in saying that, we are far from saying half of what should be said. Harmony, complete or incomplete as might be, does not and cannot exist between the forces of production and production relations.[15] This does not apply only to the transitional period but also to communism itself. For it would have meant nothing more nor less than complete stagnation. It would have signified that society as such would "wither away." But wherein lay disharmony in the transitional period? Nationalization of the basic means of production had already been carried out. The bourgeoisie was crushed, for the most part. Disharmony did indeed exist, and could only exist, between the socialized forces of production and bureaucratic production relations. These relationships in reality were a relic of the class struggle. And they could be resolved only through that class struggle. On the other hand, conflict did exist between socialism and the illegal, unlawful conspiracies of the overthrown bourgeoisie. That, too, was disharmony. And as for when socialism would see one or the other as the more dangerous element— the bureaucratic or the bourgeois, or both at the same time—it depended on the concrete struggle.

We could not expect Stalin to perceive this simple, brutal truth. For it was above all he who, throughout his work, identified state ownership with social ownership, the state's monopolistic role in the economy with the role of the primary producers themselves.† Moreover, he saw the further development of socialism in the USSR as lying only in the gradual abandonment of the difference between his "social" (i.e.,

---

*Quoted from *Tass,* October 2, 1952.

†"The owner of the means of production is the state," he explicitly acknowledges in one spot, while elsewhere speaking of this or that property as social, thus identifying it with state property. For Stalin, socialist producers are the state (as consistently socialist) plus the collective farms (as an inconsistent, or lower form).

state) ownership and group, collective ownership; in the gradual transformation of this group ownership into "social" (i.e., state) ownership. If the truth be told, Stalin disclosed two facts, two certitudes, about his own theories and "Soviet" reality. First, he was a consistent theorist of state capitalism (in the name of Marxism, of course, under the guise of that and socialism). He was the consistent instrument of ever greater domination by the privileged bureaucracy in the USSR and the countries under its control. He continued to develop only state capitalist theory, and that ever more openly. Second, the collective farms were only a phase in the further development of state capitalism and the despotism of the bureaucracy. It may have been only the first step, but it was a decisive one.

Proceeding from this position—abolishing the distinction between "social" (i.e., state) ownership in industry and collective ownership in agriculture—Stalin next approached the problem of abolishing the categories of commodities and value. If it were not for that distinction, he said, there would not be any commodity turnover nor, accordingly, would any of the above categories exist in the USSR. Central authority alone would carry out the allocation of goods. Here we saw the usual stupidities. But still we had to dwell on them, even though it was already clear enough that Stalin was wrong, wrong again on two counts: Ownership relations may change, but the categories of commodities and value must and will remain what they are until all humankind is equalized, leveled in some way. The two categories of commodities and value may change, may take on new shapes, new contents. Society may control them in one way or another, may rein them in, plan them, etc., but it cannot totally "abolish" them until the objective process of production does that all by itself, until there exists a need to equalize this piece of work with that, and the value of this piece of work with that one.* Such a need will remain as long as differences in the kind of work persist, no matter what the character of ownership itself. For the need does not arise merely from the development of

---

*The term "abolish" is absurd in itself. No person has ever introduced goods, value, and the like, nor can anyone ever abolish them. They arose historically in the process of production, and it is only in that objective process that they will cease to exist. "Abolition" or "introduction" are words that only reveal how often people imagine that what they do is something happening independently of them. Nor is Stalin a "materialist." Nor, it scarcely need be said, has he "freed himself" of materialism.

ownership, which can and does change, but from a particular degree of development in the forces of production, which naturally have a fundamental impact on change in the nature of property itself but do not coincide with it. (The USSR served as an excellent example of this. There the forces of production were less well developed than in the United States and yet, even so, state ownership held sway, whereas in the United States it is private ownership that predominates.) Doing away with all exploitation, like eliminating state ownership, was linked closely with the character of ownership, with law, with the way in which surplus labor was divided. But it was not identical, nor could it ever be, with abolishing commodities and value as categories; it could never be the same as commodity turnover itself. With a change in the character of ownership, the categories of commodities, money, value, goods turnover, and the like really could lose their specific social form and content, be it capitalist, be it bureaucratic. But they could not fully cease to exist as long as there were differences in the division of labor.

In the same way, Stalin failed to understand the problem of differences fading away between urban and country settlements under communism. As he saw it, under socialism cities would suddenly come into being and there would be less differentiation: New cities would simply spread about in the countryside, engulfing the smaller settlements. However, vast cities are the result of concentrating production, concentrating economic functions in fewer and fewer hands (monopolies, monopolism in general). Hence their abrupt growth in the USSR. With the abolition of a concentration of management (abolition of state capitalism and bureaucracy), cities would lose all the conditions for rapid growth. And as for erasing the distinctions between the city and the small town, in every case elevating town to the level of city— living conditions, technology, and modern transportation will play a most important role, perhaps even more so than the abrupt expansion of existing cities and the appearance of new ones. Proceeding from the premises of state capitalism—that is, from the premises of ever greater concentration of management—Stalin again could not help but arrive at an anti-Marxist and antisocialist position when it came to abolishing the differences between city and town.

But for him this shallow, vulgar, confused assumption really was indispensable if he wanted to achieve something totally new. For Stalin was working to stretch the all-powerful bureaucracy's wings still farther: over agriculture, over industry itself. Here is a sample of his line of argument:

> However, the operation of the law of value is not limited to the sphere of commodity turnover. It also extends to production. True, the law of value does not have the significance of a regulator in our socialist production, but it still has an impact on production and must be taken account of when production is managed.
>
> Is this a good thing? It is not a bad thing. It is not bad because it teaches our production officials systematically to improve production methods, to minimize production costs, to carry out cost accounting and to make their enterprises show a profit. It is a good, practical school which accelerates the development of our economic cadres and their transformation into genuine leaders of socialist production at the present stage of development.
>
> The trouble is not so much that in our country the law of value influences production but that our economic and planning officials, with rare exceptions, have a poor understanding of the way it behaves; they neither study it nor know how to take account of it in their budgets. This in fact helps to explain the chaos that keeps getting the upper hand in our price policy. Here is one of numerous examples. Some time ago it was decided to adjust the relation of cotton and grain prices in the interest of cotton production. The prices of grain sold to cotton producers should be more accurately fixed, and the prices of cotton delivered to the state should be raised. So our economic officials and planners submitted a proposal which had the unintended effect of shocking members of the Central Committee. It was proposed to fix the price of a ton of grain at nearly the same level as that of a ton of cotton. At the same time the price of a ton of grain was made identical to that of a ton of baked bread. The authors of the proposal were unable to give any coherent reply to comments by members of the Central Committee to the effect that the price of a ton of baked bread ought to be higher than a ton of grain because of the additional expense of milling and baking. Or that cotton was generally much higher than grain, as witness the world prices of grain and cotton. Therefore the Central Committee was

obliged to take the matter into its own hands, lowering the prices of grain and raising those of cotton. What if the proposal of these comrades had attained legal force? We should have ruined cotton producers and ourselves been left without cotton.

This excerpt shows how well Stalin tutored the economic bureaucracy. He even waxed tenderly paternal toward them. But not toward the working class! Of them he desired—but again this did not pertain to the working class!—that they take account of the law of value. And all this precisely so that that bureaucracy might be in a position to wring sweat out of the proletariat. For if it were not really thus there would have been no reason to speak of it, seeing as how the action of that law was clear as crystal to the workers. They might not understand it as a complex theory but they did as daily practice, from the process of production itself whose results could be seen in the marketplace. And once again one saw with what issues "wise leadership" had to be concerned, issues that in truth would not have concerned it had it really a shred of socialist brains. The value of cotton, grain, and flour would have been seen in commerce itself. Prices would have been set with far more precision. They would be set more simply and, for society, more cheaply. There was no need of the wise men of this world here, only intelligent calculators, with or without Stalin.

But Stalin had no grasp of the essence of the categories of goods, value, and the like; and he constructed a theory around them exclusively for the sake of the bureaucracy's immediate practical, state capitalist needs (mainly for the sake of giving bureaucracy and state capitalism a stronger hand in the collective farms). And so he excluded these categories—whose validity he had to acknowledge in the realm of trade turnover between cities and towns—wherever society (i.e., the state) carried on goods turnover, especially when it came to weapons production. Their value for Stalin was only a formal calculation, but it was one that nonetheless even he had to carry out, though it supposedly was not subject to the economic category of value.

But only when he passed to the issue of safeguarding his "socialist" society from more significant and deeper disharmony between the forces of production and production relations did Stalin stand revealed not only as a theoretician of state capitalism but also as a subjective idealist of the most vulgar type:

Comrade Yaroshenko is mistaken when he asserts that under socialism there is no contradiction between the relations of production and the productive forces of society. Our present relations of production are of course going through a period when they fully conform to the growth of the forces of production and advance them with seven-league strides. But it would be wrong to rest easy at this and to imagine that there exists no opposition between our forces of production and production relations. Contradictions certainly do exist and will continue to exist, since the development of the relations of production lags and will continue to lag behind the development of the forces of production. Given a correct policy on the part of the directing bodies, these contradictions cannot grow into antagonism and matters cannot come down to a conflict between the forces of production and production relations in society. It would be a different matter if we were to begin conducting an erroneous policy, such as that recommended to us by Comrade Yaroshenko. In that case conflict would be inevitable and our production relations would be turned into a very serious brake on the further development of our productive forces.

Seen from socialism's point of view it was these very premises that best showed Stalin to be spinning in a circle. Generally, he no sooner touched on socialism than he became a prisoner of this charmed circle. It is a circle he broke out of, even attaining a certain boldness and clarity, only when he openly passed over to state-capitalist theory. And especially practice. Here Stalin was king. He was in his element. No more was there any twisting in circles, only a brave foot forward.

What did it look like, this "socialist" circle of his, subjective and idealistic? Who would guarantee society—socialist, indeed!—against potential mistakes by the leadership? Who would guarantee that they not lead to social conflicts between the forces of production and production relations? A "correct policy" by that same leadership! That was his only reply. But just how could society know, how was it supposed to know, if the policy was correct? It knew only by the fact that its leadership was leading them! Such was their vicious circle.

From the standpoint of socialism, however, matters stood quite differently, assuming that what was at issue was socialist social relations in this or that country. Above all, the economic laws of socialism had to have free rein. The social forces of production, together with their character, had to have free rein. All the shackles had to be shattered that hobbled those forces, that enchained them and prevented the free play of economic laws by uneconomic, administrative methods. This meant that the working class had to be given management rights over production and the right to decide on the division of surplus labor and surplus production, which only it made possible. For the working class alone provided natural, legitimate representation to the tools of production. By its labor it set these tools in motion. This meant that the role of the state had to be shifted to that of guarding socialist property and socialist relations. It meant that democracy for working people had to be introduced. In a word, it meant that state capitalist social relations had to be abolished. Let management then make its mistakes. Management need not be so infallible, management may even conduct an incorrect policy. Society, though, will not be led thereby into stagnation. To move forward and to give rise to gifted people in all areas, socialism and the socialist movement had to free itself of a system in which geniuses issue ukases, "geniuses" who become "geniuses" only by virtue of having a certain function. If the objective laws of socialism were free to act after socialist forces in the economy had prevailed over capitalism; if these laws were not hobbled by bureaucratic chains, meaning social relations contrary to them; if a socialist democracy were to come into being, develop, and grow strong—then the social process itself, society itself, would be capable of correcting potential errors and any erroneous policy by management; it could replace such a management, could cast up to the surface new, young forces ready for new relationships, new conditions. Therein consisted the problem. Only then did the problem become one of this or that management's competence or incompetence, ingenuity or mediocrity.

This time Stalin was not mounting an oblique attack only on certain of Engels's positions as "incomplete," "unsatisfactory," and the like, he was attacking Marx himself and, above all, *Das Kapital*. Here is the way he deigned to frame his thoughts about this fundamental work of political economy and socialism (again from the same source):

> Moreover, I think it necessary to discard certain other concepts taken from Marx's *Das Kapital*, where he analyzed capitalism,

concepts that were artificially applied to our socialist relations. I am thinking among other things of such concepts as "necessary labor" and "surplus labor," "necessary product" and "surplus product," "necessary time" and "surplus time." Marx analyzed capitalism in order to discover the source of working-class exploitation, which was surplus value, and to arm a working class bereft of the means of production with a spiritual weapon for the overthrow of capitalism. It is understandable that Marx was served by concepts (categories) that fully correspond to capitalist relations. But it is more than strange that today such concepts are still in use when the working class is not only not without power and the means of production but on the contrary holds power in its hands and is in possession of those means of production. Today under our system, talk of labor power as a commodity and of "hiring" a laborer, as if the working class which possesses the means of production hires itself out and sells its labor power to itself—these words sound quite absurd. It is just as strange to hear talk of "necessary" and "surplus" labor. As if under our conditions the labor contributed to society to extend production, to promote education and the public health, to organize defense, etc., is not just as necessary to a working class now in power as the labor expended to cover a worker's personal needs and those of his family.

I do not think it necessary to go into whether Marx's *Das Kapital* means only this and only what Stalin said it did. It was apparent that what was pinching His Majesty was that cursed surplus labor, surplus value, and surplus production. These could not be conveniently concealed as long as a class society existed, in spite of all the magicians, prophets, priests, gendarmes, professors, kings, prostitutes, bankers, and bureaucrats. But the trouble with this surplus labor and surplus production was the fact that society could not get along without it, regardless of the kind of society—slave, feudal, capitalist, or Communist—for without them extended reproduction could not be carried out nor, accordingly, survive and develop further.

Not a single bourgeois economist, not even the most vulgar and superficial, denies the existence of surplus labor and surplus product, for they exist and indeed have to exist independent of social relations. What they keep overlooking (to take the worst case) is how this surplus labor turns into surplus value and how the capitalist takes it over. In other words, they ignore the exploitation that arises from such appropriation. Stalin thought that the smartest thing to do was to declare that these concepts had been "artificially inserted into our socialist relations." That is, he felt the most useful thing to do (for people in the USSR) was simply to abolish the concepts. From the standpoint of science that was just as stupid as to maintain that people do not have to produce (in the USSR) to live. But let us set aside this and similar Stalinesque stupidities and his ignorance not only of Marxist but also of every other political economy (surplus labor was discovered long before Marx, and the discovery of surplus value is not just Marxist but also Ricardian). Actually we are dealing here with a highly reactionary attempt to paper over Soviet social realities by "abolishing" these objective categories, which exist in every society. By suppressing the evidence, Stalin could hide the way surplus labor and surplus product (not to speak of surplus value) were distributed and who got to distribute them. Here, stupidity and ignorance were only serving as the "effective" instrument of unclean intentions and an unclean conscience.*

The whole problem of both capitalism and socialism and democracy and indeed any system revolves—will revolve, all the way to communism—precisely around these diabolical, disobedient categories of surplus labor and surplus product. For the quality of a society and all its values depends in the end on who has the right to distribute them and how and with what aims. It is understandable why to Stalin it was "more than strange that such concepts are in use today," and that in Marx's *Das Kapital* he saw only an explanation for the cause of capitalist exploitation and not also a *critique of political economy*. Stalin overlooked, in other words, Marx's systematic explication of the fundamental laws of a new, anticapitalist socialist economy and of a new, socialist society.

On the question of what was happening to surplus labor in the USSR Stalin revealed something more than total ignorance of Marxist political economy plus equivocation (he cared no more about the subject than did the pope of Rome). He revealed himself to be

---

*And it is such a person and such people, with such a knowledge of economics and such social impulses, who administer the economic development of a great country! A country that by their reckoning (naturally) is destined to lead humanity to communism!

ultrareactionary when it came to socialism and a most consistent ideologue of state capitalism. He would abolish a thing that could not be abolished, a thing without which no society can survive, for the simple reason that he wanted to hide what was going on in the USSR, hide how surplus labor was being used and for what purpose, hide what kind of rights those who produced it had when it was a matter of distributing their surplus labor.

Concealing thus the essence of social relations based on the bureaucratic privilege to distribute surplus labor in the name of society, social relations that hold back the development of production forces, Stalin somehow had to explain why so many industries and sectors in his country were unprofitable and why this state of affairs was both necessary and even useful to the Soviet Union. He illustrated this with a new concept—"permanently higher profitability." Allegedly this was unknown to capitalism.* It aimed at disabling competition and anarchy in production (permanent profitability) and enabling the later development of productive forces in other sectors (higher profitability). However, Stalin was not successful in papering over the essential fact that in the USSR there existed a whole string of unprofitable sectors and industrial enterprises and that this situation had existed for a long time and that it showed no signs of coming to an end. So we can understand why workers in the USSR had low living standards—they had to carry out Stalin's Great Power economic plans (above all, the military-industrial complex and associated economic sectors). In classical capitalism such sectors and such industries would have ceased functioning at once; unemployment, crises, and so on would have ensued; and in a word not a trace of any "higher and permanent profitability" would have remained. But there would also not have been left to vegetate a rather large number of the backward at the expense of a rather smaller number of the developed.

We can understand that for political, first, and only then for economic reasons there can and even must be unprofitable enterprises in

---

*However, state capitalism in the West likewise knows such a "higher profitability" when it needs it to lay a foundation for future production in certain industries or economic sectors. This was not only historically true of war production but is true today as well. What else, for example, are U.S. agricultural price supports? Or, say, the measures taken by the British government in coal production after the war? Precisely this same "higher and permanent profitability" of Stalin's!

a country wanting to preserve its independence and secure the basic direction of its development. But this can only be a temporary or sporadic phenomenon if the whole system does not want to come to a dead impasse. In the USSR this was actually a permanent and in no way sporadic phenomenon for the national economy as a whole. So it became quite clear that the disappearance of unemployment and crises in the USSR was not the result of some advantage in the social system over capitalism but a consequence of low real wages. Unemployment and the absence of economic cycles were the direct result of impoverishing the whole working class. For the sake of "higher profitability"—in actual fact for the sake of higher Great Power interests and bureaucratic privilege—it was the working class that had to pay for planned unprofitability in individual enterprises and economic sectors.

Socialism itself, if it were not effecting more savings in human labor than capitalism by utilizing surplus labor to raise real wages and the cultural standards of the masses and to develop profitable production, would have no justification or advantage—not economic, not social—by comparison with capitalism. The social system in the USSR was surely losing every advantage in the face of contemporary capitalism, and this by the very fact that it was state capitalism and not socialism.

Just as he would like to avoid facing up to the way surplus labor and surplus product are distributed in the USSR by pronouncing them "artificially injected," Stalin fancied that contemporary capitalism would appear more black if he saddled it with "not . . . average profit, nor even super-profit . . . but maximum profit" as its "basic law" and "moving force." As science sees it, again, this was being just as asinine as when Stalin prattled about surplus labor and product. Obviously he knew neither what profit is nor how it is created, nor had he any idea of a rate of profit. He confused the wish with the reality: Individual capitalists wish to attain a maximum profit for themselves, but do they actually fulfill such wishes? If we assume that all capitalists have "done" all that must be done to maximize profit, the profit that is made can only be average, for all have made the same profit. But in reality this is not the way the market works, for some make a middling profit and survive on that, some make more of a profit, and some fall below the middle and are ruined.

"Some say," said Stalin, "that an average profit might be regarded as sufficient for capitalist development under today's conditions . . . but no . . . they must maximize profits." Stalin offered no explanation for this statement, this "discovery" of a basic law of today's capitalism. All he had to do was assert something and one was obligated to believe him on his word alone. Here too, however, ignorance went hand in hand with an unclean conscience. Inasmuch as his own system was no more fair and just for the primary producers than the harshest forms of contemporary capitalist exploitation, and inasmuch also as he had to strengthen his kingdom internally and expand it externally, painting it in rosy colors, it would be best to blacken the enemy as much as possible and to reveal "new," still blacker laws of contemporary capitalism. Here lay the root of that foolish babbling of Soviet propaganda about contemporary capitalism. They had no connection with reality. Or they had very little connection, and that very rarely. Propaganda neither weakened capitalism nor helped anyone to combat it. The only thing this babbling could do was to deceive the domestic masses as to the advantage of the Soviet system over the capitalist one. Capitalism all by itself, by its inner laws, is quite black enough for the proletariat, and any more blackening vis-à-vis the Marxist and Leninist system was counterproductive, sowing confusion in the ranks of the proletariat and muddling its tactics. But the brilliant heir of Marx, Engels, and Lenin thought that the devil was not black enough if he could be painted blacker still. This does not cause the devil to cease being a devil, of course. He does not become the devil of devils, either. But for the painter himself, matters stand differently. Is he by any chance painting his own features? "The monkey sees himself in the mirror."

Nor have the basic laws of today's capitalism changed: Hired labor has remained hired labor, profit remains just that, profit, and the average profit rate behaves as it always has behaved. But some things indeed have changed. The state, above all, has intruded, and no longer only as a monopoly power but also as an "independent"—state capitalist—factor. Colonies of the classic type have in the main vanished. National brands of capitalism have become more complicated.

But to expect Stalin and his theoreticians to explain these new phenomena and changes would have made no more sense than to try milking a billy goat into a sieve. They not only were incapable of explaining anything but also dared not do it, for to reveal the new phenomena in today's capitalism would only reveal that they themselves were state capitalists. And it would have shown their social system and social relations to be reactionary in today's world, especially by comparison to true socialism.

And since he didn't understand these questions and never would understand them or many others besides—or actually he understood them very well from his state capitalist point of view—Stalin failed to comprehend the changes in the postwar world, and especially in postwar capitalism. (To tell the truth, he did not exactly need such understanding, inasmuch as he was not fighting to extend socialism through the world and make it victorious but to expand his state capitalist empire and invigorate his bureaucracy.)

Stalin was partly right in noting that World War II led to the destruction of a single world market and its division into two world markets, a capitalist one and, in his words, a socialist one (the USSR plus the so-called people's democracies plus China). He saw this as the greatest and most progressive result of World War II.

However, it must be stressed that a world market finally took shape in the middle of the nineteenth century, at a particular stage in the development of the forces of production. Every Marxist, going back to Marx himself and forward past Lenin, regarded the creation of a world market and all that it brought about (strengthening each and every link among peoples, tearing down the barriers between nations, etc.) as a progressive fact of capitalism and a necessary condition for proletarian internationalism itself and the true convergence of peoples in socialism. Today the forces of production have reached a stage that necessarily demands the existence of a world market, and its every setback spells a setback for them as well. In fact this world market exists on a higher plane than its predecessor in the previous century. No longer is it possible for the forces of production to develop in isolation, within a single country, without damage to the development of production forces worldwide and to every nation's own domestic development. And since this process is under way while capitalism still reigns, under the hegemony of a high level of the forces of capitalist production in the United States, it cannot help but bring exploitation and oppression in its trail and in turn all sorts of trade quarantines, isolation, and self-defense among individual nations and national economies. The Soviet Union was only able to fend off that process, at the same time preserving its state-capitalist shell and bureaucratic rule, if it broke down the world market and also interfered with the associated—though socially contradictory—development of world production forces. Hence the "iron curtain," an ever greater isolation from the rest of the world, hegemony over Eastern European countries, and an aggressive foreign policy became social necessities for the USSR. Either Russia had to proceed along the path of socialist social relations and a socialist foreign policy, whereby capitalism would be compelled to lower an "iron curtain" (as it did during the Revolution), or Russia had to continue developing and consolidating itself as a product of bureaucracy and state capitalism. The social forces that could have turned this process in a democratic and socialist direction were too weak in the USSR.

This explains much else besides, as for example why the USSR was objectively the most reactionary great power. (For the Soviet Union was destroying the world market instead of stimulating it further—while preserving its independent socialist development, at a time when capitalism had already created such a market during its period of progressive development.) And why the East-West conflict (or in the last analysis the confrontation of the United States with the USSR) was not and could not be a confrontation of communism-socialism and capitalism but instead the confrontation of two supreme blocs, the one aiming to establish a world marketplace so it might thereby guarantee itself extra profits, the other aiming to destroy any such world market and to create its own market so it might preserve its state capitalist system on the basis of low real wages, the plundering of subjugated peoples, and unprofitable production.

But this also explains something else, something much more important. Stalin asserted that in fact contradictions among the capitalist countries were greater than between them and the USSR, but this was incorrect, based as it was on analogies from before World War II when there still existed a world marketplace. Again, this does not mean that contradictions among the capitalist countries cannot or will not grow. It does not mean that such contradictions will not lead to conflicts. But until a fairly well integrated world market becomes established, the East-West conflict will remain dominant, dragging various other countries into its maelstrom.

Proceeding from the premise that by the destruction of the global marketplace the possibility of finding a market for goods and capital had shrunk, Stalin regarded as out of date Lenin's thesis that contemporary (Western) capitalism "even apart from the rottenness of capitalism . . . on the whole is growing much faster than earlier." It may be true of a number of capitalist countries that they are slowing down, but only an analysis that is economic and solidly statistical can show that it is true for *capitalism as a whole*, that is, for capitalism independent of national borders. And, of course, there can be no doubt that such a capitalism is taking production further.

All these postulates about contemporary capitalism that more or less—though only in a formal sense—maintain Lenin's positions of a good seventy years ago, as if nothing in capitalism had changed, served as the basis for Stalin's foreign policy and his statement that the contradictions among the capitalist states, as a practical matter, were still greater than between the Western and Eastern blocs. This, of course, explains why the government of the USSR would not undertake the first hostility but waited in secret for a contradiction to develop in the capitalist camp. But Moscow's aggressive policy and the aggressive and reactionary character of the very social system of the USSR did not cease to exist as such. In fact, only the following possibility is explained: Moscow could rest satisfied temporarily with the conquests it made, for in view of its relatively low level of productive forces and in view of the internal obstacles to a further consolidation of state capitalism, the USSR was not capable of quickly digesting such a big mouthful. But that might have been only a "peace-loving" phase in its policy, always one and the same predatory policy, which flows from the inner nature of the system itself. Low real wages, unprofitability of production, and bound up with all this a system of repression and exploitation of the working masses in the USSR, together with an unbridled, elemental growth in the bureaucracy, with bureaucratic despotism and bureaucratic privileges—it all would have propelled the entire system into a blind alley if the USSR had not been able to plunder other peoples and to conduct an aggressive policy of conquest.*

And truly all that was taking place in the USSR, all this confusion of ideas and spiritual stagnation in all domains, the ever less disguised falsification of socialism and ever more unbridled and conceited strutting of revolutionary and socialist phrases—all this was no more than a symptom, a warning. Already there had begun a concealed, muffled, invisible crisis in the "Soviet" system that no measures could put off for

---

*In this connection it sounds like a cruel irony and mockery of repressed peoples to hear Stalin say that the USSR is giving "highly qualified" and cheap technical aid to China and the countries of Eastern Europe (aid that, according to him, not a single capitalist country is capable of rendering). Yet even if this were so it would not in the slightest degree change the fact that such "assistance" is really only a form—less pernicious, shall we assume, than the capitalist one—of domination and exploitation.

long. On the contrary, the course taken by the bureaucracy was becoming still more intensified, was growing broader and deeper. The "theoretical" work by Stalin under discussion affirmed all this more clearly than anything that had been published on this earth since the infamous 1948 resolution of the Cominform against socialist Yugoslavia.

In conclusion, I want to deal with the way this pinnacle of "theoretical," "socialist," and "Marxist" thought looked in the kingdom of gray mediocrity.

After all is said and done, it would appear that Stalin stood out as the brightest individual in that wondrous kingdom of mediocrity, of brains in uniform and of petty bureaucratic careers, careers just as creative in the arts and sciences as behind the office desk. True, this aging brain had had ever more openly to occupy its time with falsifying materialism and socialism. Intrusively, arrogantly, this brain insisted on the exclusive right to speak out in its master's name. All this was made plain in two articles, the one concerned with linguistics, the other addressing theoretical, economic problems. The theories then in fashion (in fashion, that is, up to the publication of Stalin's articles) in the USSR on these topics were so stupid, so unlearned, so shallow and childish that a question was almost forced upon us. Why had it come to such a pass that in this great country, this great Russia, which for a full century and a half before Stalin glittered with all kinds of talent—why, how, could such a steep decline take place in human and scientific thought that Stalin himself felt compelled to affirm from on high such acclaimed and eternal verities as for instance that "language is the instrument of human communication," or "production and productive forces do not and cannot exist without productive social relations"? And when one listened to and read these gobs of drivel, dreamed up by moldy clerks responsible for the development of art, science, and philosophy, one could not but acknowledge that the bureaucratic genius and leader, Stalin, quite justifiably attained that title and that role, for he was brighter than all of them. It is also correct to note that Stalin had to have been the first to choke off and cut down everyone with any talent or giving promise of future talent so that his own mediocre mind, knowledge, and talent might appear to be higher than the average clerical mediocrity.

Sanctimony and hypocrisy regarding issues of theory and learning, by virtue of being the expression of power over all domains of human activity, its vehicle in all things, were bound to have given rise to many wondrous forms of pharisaism in the immediate political and social practice of the bureaucracy. This really did become the "Stalinist style" in work and in manner.

It would be a mistake to treat Stalin from the standpoint of how and to what degree he departed from Marxism and socialism. First of all, it would be naive. In the last analysis it would play only into his own designs, which were not in the least theoretical. Stalin was once a Marxist, it is true, and a socialist. But he was these things in a primitive way, shallowly, vulgarly, often irresolutely, and quite often in the service of practical goals. As the USSR evolved from its socialist beginnings in revolutionary democracy to state capitalism and bureaucratism, Stalin himself, being at the head of that process, changed from a Marxist, a socialist, and a revolutionary (of that kind) into a theoretician and practitioner of state capitalism. He changed into the spiritual leader, the most immediate leader and teacher, of a privileged bureaucracy and a bureaucratic dictatorship. And as both a theoretician and a practitioner, Stalin was, of course, not without significance. Nor was he incompetent, on the contrary. It's only that those theories of Stalin's, those talents of his, caused more unhappiness and suffering to the working class and more defeat for socialism than all the bourgeois theories combined, from World War I to the present. But his theories were capable of causing such unhappy effects only because of being able to take cover behind the October Revolution. October was the first offspring of the proletariat, both international and Russian. They could take cover behind Lenin's councils (the soviets), which were a new form of revolutionary power and were democratic, inasmuch as they were supported by the workers and peasants. For all their harshness these soviets were nonetheless democratic. In a word, they took cover behind socialism.

Often, though, Stalin's manner of exposition was confusing. He generally proceeded from a handful of Marxist and socialist commonplaces, coming out foursquare in their favor in order to take cover behind them while eventually pushing through his own state capitalist and bureaucratic positions.* His procedure was not to be explained as

---

*Most often Stalin bandied the so-called eternal verities about as if they were "proofs." Thus: "Language is a means of communication among people"; "the law of value . . . just as did the production of goods . . . came into being before capitalism"; "working conditions for miners differ from working conditions in a mechanized footwear factory," etc. The Volga empties into the Caspian Sea!

that of a Marxist and a socialist who had to this or that degree diverged from Marxism and socialism, for he was neither the one nor the other. It could only be explained by his "revolutionary" origins and by the "revolutionary" origins of the social system itself whose incarnation Stalin was. It could only be explained by the demands of his reactionary foreign and domestic policies, policies that could appear in no other guise than a falsified revolutionary and socialist past, a false Marxism and a false socialism.

But even Soviet reality was not sitting still. In the 1950s it moved in the direction of more and more tension between the forces of production and production relations, tension between a state capitalist superstructure and the socialist base, tension between the bureaucracy and the primary producers. So Marx and socialism became more and more falsified in the USSR, with ever more shamelessness and deceit. "Old" positions were renounced ever more openly and loudly and new ones developed that were increasingly silly, shallow, and vulgar.

Theories that resemble Stalin's in substance and social practice down to the last detail were the same ones being professed today by the majority of Western theoreticians of state capitalism, and to a degree even by Hitler's supporters in his time. There was only the difference that those theoreticians did not present themselves as either Marxist or socialist, not having grown up on our soil.

The truth about the essence of social relations in the USSR and about the nature of its so-called socialism would inevitably force its way into the consciousness of the masses. The truth would penetrate with a strength equal to that with which it was once stamped out, whether by official Soviet propaganda or by bourgeois propaganda, stupid, conservative, and reactionary bourgeois propaganda against socialism and communism as such, propaganda that only made Stalin's dark task easier as he played with socialism for the sake of consolidating state capitalism within his country and imperialist conquests without.

The basic conclusions and moral lessons to be learned from the "socialist" text by Stalin might look something like this, contrary to his intent. Nor are these all the conclusions or lessons to be learned, nor are they even the fundamental ones, for as I said, those would require specialized and detailed analysis. Still, I shall put forward certain secondary facts as well, facts that are closely connected with Stalin's basic positions and with the essence of the USSR's social system.

After he had set out in this way the basic "Marxist" and "socialist" directives for his future textbook on political economy, Stalin underscored its international and domestic significance and defined the working conditions of those who would write it.

The need for such a textbook became just as essential for Russia's social system as, in its time, was the need to falsify the history of the Soviet Communist Party with the help of a history of that Party. Work was begun on this textbook even before the war, but it dragged on and was not regarded as urgent. A scientific work would not come of all this, nor indeed could it. But that it might be serviceable to official Moscow propaganda in papering over the essence of the USSR's social being as seen from the outside and from within—of that there could be no doubt.

Stalin saw very well the urgency of such a task from a propagandistic, ideological viewpoint and ordered that those working on the textbook be freed from every other task and given material security so they might offer such a volume to the Central Committee for approval in the course of the year.

Thus was scholarly work accomplished in this land of "the most advanced scholarship" and "the most advanced culture," this "land of socialism" and "the highest form of democracy"!*

---

*I replaced the formula "state capitalism" in the 1980s by "industrial feudalism," as closer to reality. Of course, all such formulas describing one or another system suffer from one-sidedness and generalization. But formulations of a social order, as so often elsewhere, are unavoidable when one tries to reduce a thing to its essence. The postulate of state capitalism corresponded to my understanding at the time, was formulated from a Marxist perspective, and depended somewhat both on the position of Yugoslavia and the state of affairs in its ruling Party. Vozlensky, author of the well-known book *Nomenklatura,* also worked out a postulate of industrial feudalism in conversation with me which closely resembled my own formula.

7

TO HAVE
A PERSONAL OPINION
IN
THE COMMUNIST PARTY
IS DANGEROUS

Stalin's death was greeted with relief and even rejoicing by the Yugoslav leadership, but there were distinctions among us, apparently minor, when it came to anticipating changes in the Soviet Union. Tito and Ranković, I recall, looked for more shifts in the power structure than Kardelj. I myself saw privilege and expansionism as so ingrained in the Soviet Party bureaucracy that the disappearance of even so dominant a figure as Stalin would have no essential impact.

No one in or out of the top leadership was aware how deep were the divergences triggered by the death of Stalin, nor their far-reaching nature. Once these differences emerged into the open, each person was already living through them in his own way and had his own attitude. I remember, soon after Stalin's death, how I gave a start when Kardelj, returning from the island of Brioni, said in answer to my inquiry after Tito and his work that he was engrossed in the effect of Stalin's death and expecting serious change. At this time Tito began to stress the need for dispensing with American aid as soon as possible. "Without an independent foreign policy there is no true independence," he would say. We all agreed on putting an end to the aid and thereby our dependence on the West. But the way he harped on it hinted at the coming reversal in domestic policy, when the process of democratization would be halted. It took effect especially on the intellectual front, where we had advanced the furthest. That was the sphere where incipient differences could first be detected. The more insistently Tito talked about the West's "negative influences" on culture and youth the more I, in my own mind, rejected the idea of dividing the fruits of the intellect and the spirit between "West" and "East," or even decadent and progressive. Differences also started to emerge in the way we viewed the League of Communists. Tito was now publicly concerned about the league, claiming that it was fading into ineffectiveness and that it was above all growing weaker ideologically, no longer monolithic. A number of us, including Kardelj, Bakarić, Vukmanović, and myself, believed that the league should exercise leadership ideologically but not tactically, that it should function through free discussion rather than by giving orders, imposing interdictions, and applying labels.

The critical juncture in putting the brakes on democratization, or in other words in returning to Leninist norms and a "dictatorship of the proletariat," came at the Second Plenum, held at the end of June 1953 at Tito's residence on Brioni.[1] That plenum's setting and its most important agenda item—the status of ideology in the Party—were strictly Tito's ideas.

I had the feeling at the time that both venue and agenda were directed against our "democratic currents" and, moreover, suspected Tito of taking "factionalist" measures with individual comrades. Too much, he kept saying, was being written and spoken against the bureaucracy and bureaucratism. The fact that guards officers were lounging about in every corner of the hotel where we were staying and even in Tito's villa itself where the plenum was being held caught my attention. There were no grounds for such security measures since the island was guarded by both the army and the navy. I do not know for certain how other people felt, but I believe I was not alone in having the painful sensation of having been enticed to a conference in a conspirator's lair.

Tito's behavior at the beginning of the session, while we were taking our seats, caught me unawares and embarrassed me. Motioning me to sit on his left, he said in a soft, significant tone of voice: "You have to speak too, so that they won't think we're not united." This was not just factionalist recruitment, to which I had never before submitted, but pressure to speak as Tito wished even though that might be contrary to my conviction. And I did speak, irresolutely, confusedly, reconciling my private views with those I thought to be—in fact, knew to be—Tito's.

But overnight I pulled myself together and came to my senses. My convictions hardened. On our way back from the plenum I suggested to Kardelj that we go trout-fishing in the Gacka River in the Lika region. It was a warm summer day and there came a moment as we were circling up the serpentine road above the town of Senj[2] when I told him I could not support the new "Brioni" line. Throwing a dejected glance at me, Kardelj said that I was overstating things, after which we lapsed into silence.

I had to rush back to Belgrade because the next day I was to greet the leader of the left wing of the British Labour Party, Aneurin Bevan,[3] and his wife, Jennie Lee. Between Bevan and me there was a certain affinity in our perception of the crisis into which Eastern communism and Western social democracy were plunging. We both believed there ought to be moral boundaries in politics, even though politics as such neither can nor need be moral. Such boundaries do not coincide with the striving for truth, the insistence on truth. But they are not totally distinct from it, either. To the end, Bevan and his wife stubbornly protested against my imprisonment and the pressures brought to bear on me, he turning for help to the Socialist International.

Jennie Lee came twice to Belgrade on my account, first when I was arrested in 1956 and again when I was originally released in 1961. The 1956 trip was without question a solace to Štefica and our small circle of sympathizers, but its impact on officials was probably limited to their meting out to me a "gentler" punishment. She and I continued corresponding infrequently but warmly for many years. When Štefica and I visited London in 1969, we were in effect guests of Jennie Lee's and under her constant care.

No sooner did I return to Belgrade after leaving the Bevans in Cetinje than I got down to work on our periodical *Nova Misao* (New Thought). In the Soviet Union change was in the wind, stirring our top leaders with hopes, no less for a change in the Soviet system than for a normalization of our relations. If it did not take the form of a radical shift, at least such a change might, like our own, open new horizons. I did not share that thinking, not believing that any radical transformation was in store there. With this thought in mind, and in the spirit and style of the times, I wrote an extensive and complicated article titled "The Beginning of the End and the End of the Beginning." It met with a mixed reaction in leading circles. Democrats waxed enthusiastic but bureaucrats were not so sure. They thought it might hinder normalizing our relations with Moscow. To some extent they were justified, but they entertained doubts chiefly because I criticized Yugoslav parallels with the Soviet order. One Soviet diplomat, visiting our Ministry of Foreign Affairs, remarked that such articles did not encourage normalization.

New elections were set for November 22, 1953, while at the same time a fresh and this time decisive crisis broke out over Trieste. Far from abating, the intellectual and ideological ferment associated with *Nova Misao*—at least as far as I was involved—was stimulated all the more by these events.

Tito gave such a fierce speech on October 10 in Leskovac[4] as to leave no doubt that if Italian troops did enter Zone A (Trieste itself) our forces would march in also. He spoke similarly the next day in Skoplje.[5] That same day *Borba* printed the first in a series of articles written by me that were to result in my being driven off the Central Committee in January and that were eventually, by degrees, to lead me into adopting a critical stance toward Marxism.

THE CLOSED CIRCLE OF THE PRIVILEGED[6]

No one, least of all this young woman, could have anticipated how cheerless life would suddenly become in that very milieu which as seen from the outside looked so clean and pure, so much more spiritual, even ethereal, than the life she came from. Such had been the grassroots perspective, one might say, the point of view of the masses as they looked upward from below. There, there surely could be none of this petty, crude malice and greed she was so accustomed to, plain for all to see and the natural outgrowth of poverty and backwardness. Her childhood and youth up to the moment she married had been expended in fighting it. At the moment she married, the bright summer days had seemed to sing. But to her now those same days took on an ugly, somber cast.

She was a singer in the opera, twenty-one years of age and beautiful. Without giving herself airs over her looks, even to herself, she was aware of them generally. But as for her body, slender and strong, she was quite aware of that and relished it in the way one enjoys something that does not actually belong to one. She had no strongly marked passions, no particular delights, but simply was pleased by everything. And she really was a stranger to sorrow, or at least the kind that seeps up from the depths and cannot be cured, the kind that comes from disappointment in life. Only music had irresistible charms for her. She gave herself to music more than with her mind alone, she surrendered to it with that extraordinary passion which can be seen in persons who are musically educated and possess an exceptional ear. It was a passion that insatiably burned in every fiber, fired her imagination, drew her into the music schools, and, in the end, brought her to the stage. Having come from a poor family with many children, she had preserved, even now after marriage, striking, almost glaring, habits of frugality. But she likewise kept her spiritual simplicity, directness, and modesty. Had her husband not reacted to everything in ways that were a little unexpected and hasty, especially when personal considerations were involved, she might have had no other troubles and cares than those which life, always offering us something new, brings to everyone, including the comfortable and carefree. In the presence of others her husband treated her like an inexperienced little girl, as in fact she was, despite having to live and work in the precincts of the theater (not so much for gainful employment as for the sake of singing and music). But when the two of them were alone together she liked the tutelage of this strong, virile man, and felt as though she had never left her own family nest. Poor it may have been, but the nest was warm. Or had she not merely exchanged it for a new nest? One that was perhaps more ungiving but was also more enduring and deeper?

So here was a typical young, beautiful woman such as grow up and are given in marriage by the thousands year after year all over this young and beautiful land. She resembled them all, resembled all humanity, in fact: She had her own individuality, her small cares, her big dreams. What might have been considered unusual for the world looking on was only that she was an opera singer and the wife of a high official at the same time. But she, in her enthusiasm and simplicity, did not feel this to be anything awful because, my God, don't we live in modern times in a socialist country?

She had known full well that many would envy her her good marriage: He was handsome, mature, virile, and strong, and above all he wore the legendary halo of a wartime commander. And this always titillates the vivid imaginations of women, putting them in mind of happiness lost. He, however, after spending his entire youth in battles and prisons and finally winning a peacetime life (deceptive though that might be), commenced to amuse himself on a rather large scale. He did so without regard for Party or other restrictions and heedless of any remorse that might ensue. This not so much because opportunity came easily as because that was how he wanted things to be. She was well aware of it all from the passing remarks he made, added to which he had the look of a scapegrace sometimes, which told her still more. Although she was imbued by inheritance with very strong, almost unbending, moral precepts, she was still a modern woman. A modern woman does not construct her life in advance, neither ethical code nor marriage, but instead fights for them, fights to make them come true. And so this particular modern woman calmly and good-naturedly accepted her husband's past, even adopting that relaxed, almost cheerful, attitude which people assume in the face of what once happened but cannot now be undone. For after all it is not so terrible if it only used to be so and will never happen again. She therefore expected other women to turn up, one way or another: the women with whom her husband had been intimate, but also the women who had not been lucky enough to share his bachelor adventures and yet could claim to know something about them. She anticipated their petty intrigues by way of the telephone, and looked for anonymous letters. Such intrigues might have been meaningful to a woman belonging to the old school. For her, though, as for practically all the new generation, intrigues were naive and without any impact.

She was also encouraged by the thought that all such annoyances would become utterly trivial once she set foot in that new, pure, spiritually refined milieu alongside her husband and surrounded by the wives of higher officials who, she thought, were for the most part simple, unpretentious people. Such petty, loose-tongued, malicious gossip would fade away in time, once the outside world could see for itself the inner solidity of their marriage.

As first the days and then the weeks passed by, all those petty, mean, deliberate provocations indeed did begin to subside—the telephone calls to her husband, the shocking details communicated to her in private, the anonymous letters. Nevertheless, even so, and contrary to all expectations, she was not accepted by her new milieu, still less taken to its bosom. What confronted her was a massive, icy, impenetrable wall that no one could have foreseen, least of all herself. As a young, postwar woman and Party member she shared the values and ideas of her generation and could have had no notion that such a wall existed. Besides, as a new wife prey to anxieties and perplexities over all the newness of married life, she was nevertheless immersed in the rosy glow of happiness, the fire of first love.

Whatever its inner relationships and outer forms, matrimony has always been one of the basic building blocks in the life of society. It is one of the hard-won legacies of human civilization, something that does not belong exclusively to this class or that but has accrued over a long time owing to the ceaseless process of civilizing human relations. The state of marriage has thus transformed itself into a set of conventions without which society would regress and turn savage. One of these is to help a young married couple, a broadly human value. The duty of friends is to support the new relationship and make it as natural and warm as it can be. Even among the most primitive people and cultures it has long been accepted that friends and acquaintances, family and even casual guests, far from disrupting a relationship, will do all within their power to see that it is as stable as possible. They will give feasts, confer gifts, devote their best attentions and good wishes to a bond that might otherwise be very hard to cement. For the newly married have different ideas and habits, come from different surroundings and the like, and cannot help but react differently to conditions so new to them. We are talking of unwritten codes but they incorporate a great many of society's aspirations, of which society is both conscious and unconscious as it makes its slow, tortuous way toward ever greater humanization. Deviations occur, but not by an entire society or class, only by a great many individuals and groups. Groups are impelled by class relations to be selfish and greedy and to hold fast to their social position no matter what others suffer. Over time, consideration and kindness have become one of the unspoken and intangible measures of a humane person and a humane society as a whole.

The young woman knew nothing of this, nor could she or anyone else have given expression to it, but deep in her heart she was aware of it, again like everybody else. For simply by living in human society is the quality of humanity absorbed.

Both as a woman and wife and as a human being she was therefore confused and crushed when this new, idealized milieu, or the greater and decisive part of it, went for her jugular at her very first step, greeting her and her marriage with the naked edge of hatred. The coterie of women displayed its hatred with a fierce insistence incomprehensible by any recognizable personal or known social standards. It could be comprehended only as a raw determination to hang on to social position. But this animal lust is actually more monstrous and ruthless than any fight between animals. Look what happened! The social positions of that clique were suddenly threatened by the appearance of the young wife, fatally menaced in some strange way. For she was one of those unknown, undeserving people who failed to serve in the war. She was incapable of becoming an ordinary member of some ordinary regional or student committee. But on top of that, she was an actress, and like all actresses, God only knows how, she'd "sneaked into" the Party. Today's Party has room for all kinds of people.

At this point a minor difference opened up between the husbands and their wives. The husbands were indifferent, or put on a show of indifference, to the appearance of this new member in their secluded, closed world. Once outside their glittering, pretentious offices these upstarts always followed the same routes. They all had their summer homes, they all belonged to the same clubs, they all had their town houses and their boxes at theaters and stadiums. Their wives, on the other hand, waxed indignant over this new marriage and would not be reconciled to it, greeting it with open hatred and contempt. It was they who proved to be the self-appointed watchdogs of morality. It was all their own, a moral system created to meet the needs of a coterie confined to specific functional levels, one that in practice was closed to all other ranks if these were noticeably lower.

True, for the most part they were model wives and mothers who would sermonize—in public—about equality and women's freedom. Some had in fact held offices in the women's movement, had even been high officials. And yet they had never remonstrated particularly with the husband for having married "someone who had nothing in common with us." (They had themselves in mind, women on a certain level with a certain job position.) Such blind prejudice was quick to detect incompatibility. He was almost twice her age, they would point out, and incomparably more experienced than she in every way. Besides, he was a veteran Communist. Even judging by the prevailing morality in that milieu, he ought to have been judged more severely. But . . . well . . . but she never had any connections "with us" at all. They meant, she never had any connections with communism. She never had any connections with people; with human society as a whole! In a word, a freeloader! Scum!

Any "blame" attached to the bridegroom was easily dismissed. The worst that happened was that he might be taken to task in passing because he was getting along in years and because he'd developed a taste—may the reader forgive me these and other such expressions!—for "chicken meat." Actually, it was she who was being blamed when you heard facetious phrases like "she hooked him by her bare leg," or "he couldn't stand up to that last enemy offensive," or "our comrade got a little battle-worn, it only took one lifted skirt. . . ."

That world and its lifestyle being what they were, there was a twisted kind of logic in the fact that it did not turn its knives against him. Many young women had ended the war as soldiers who were then bundled into offices, stuck onto committees, enlisted as private secretaries, and from such vantage points they would gaze with yearning at the famous, smart, good-looking war commander. Today they were wives with the past in mind and feeling a little regretful over the unhappy fate of their brave comrade-in-arms. He had finally got bogged down, they would say, let himself be caught or hooked, grabbed, even whistled for. But this was by the way. There was a better reason for their sympathy, closer to reality, and this was the stubborn fact that he was a man of their own blood. There couldn't be any doubt about that. And then, too, he had preserved his original job. He had the aptitude for it, the talent and the reliability, politically. That couldn't be denied either. He belonged to us by right, was no interloper among us, no Johnny-come-lately in our communism.

No one took a serious look at the young woman—who could do so, in that closed society?—no one asked who or what she was, where she came from, who her parents were, her brothers and sisters. All they needed to know was that she belonged to another world and had sneaked illegally, they would say, into ours. We were the ones who had gone to war, it was we who had gained political power and the freedom we now enjoyed. We're the ones who went to work after the war and achieved high office, it's we who drive around in autos or take parlor cars when we travel by train. We go to special stores for our food and clothing, spend the summers in secluded villas and summer homes. Isn't it obvious that we must be exceptionally meritorious? Here was a society that had convinced itself by degrees that this was all so natural and logical that only some manifest fool or else a confirmed enemy could fail to grasp it.

Under these conditions of a closed way of life and a closed psychology arose the ideas typical of such a world. Such ideas pretended to have universal validity. Only they were binding, only they were permanent.

And even if this could not really be true exactly, seeing as how the dialectic we were taught in the high Party schools and institutes knows no such thing as permanence, anyway they hold good for the Communist world, the socialist world, and even the human world.

This is why the wife of a high official can only be a woman of certain specific high Party qualifications and have a certain, specific Party past, a substantial one. No common woman could be his spouse, unless, of course, she's not his wedded wife.

And as for a dowry, we know that real property no longer exists, at least in the city, unless you count all those benefits that go with the job. So there can't be any dowry either. Beauty, spiritual distinction, physical attraction? Such things never have constituted a dowry in any society that maintained the custom. Beauty may have intensified and sweetened a dowry, if there was one to begin with, but it has always belonged in the realm of individual feelings, personal inclinations, compatibility. Beauty was never any social category. For today's good match and for the right official, the dowry can only be a job of similar status. Something a little lower on the scale, perhaps, seeing as it's only a wife we're talking about, but something on the same order as the fiancé's in terms of function and merit. Spiritual sympathies, bodily inclinations don't ever come into it, and they are certainly not part of the idea. As a rule love is calibrated and—enslaved.

Beauty our bride did have. And she had love. But she did not have this new kind of dowry that could cover everything with a coating of gold. She had nothing to offer the new regime.

She was an ordinary woman. Only an actress. That was the only unusual thing about her. And it was that which served as the basic motive for the covert hatred, scorn, and icy boycott she faced, all the more incomprehensible and spine-chilling because it was spontaneous and tacit.

The new partners were received with hostility by the very people who regarded themselves as the most qualified (indeed, the only qualified) persons to nourish and support the holiness of matrimony and who were regarded by others, moreover, as more or less well married. But in this case the general principle, marriage, was easily set aside and despised when it came into conflict with their own instinctive interests, now aroused. A sense of caste solidarity lurked unsleeping at the cornerstone of their interests. To dismiss sacred principles was as nothing when caste interest was threatened. Here we see the hypocrisy of that morality espoused by the majority of these respected wives.

They will maintain, and are even convinced of it, that they married for love. Maybe it really is true. Love does not exist in a vacuum apart from a social context, is not something only emotional. Love is the sentimental expression of an endless series of influences—ideas, habits, psychological and physical attraction—compressed into one experience. These women, though, denied it to anyone not close to or inside their circle. As for someone outside the circle, no one has the right to love anyone inside it. Call it whatever you like, but not love!

The individual's right to some sort of free life was thus lost to view and brought to ruin. The right to make mistakes, the right to commit sin, to explore one's personal destiny and that of man generally, to have failings—none of these could be accommodated by the arid, hidebound spirit of caste, which was all the more resistant and unyielding for having so recently come into being.

So it went in this circle, one of the higher ones. The spirit of rejection had arisen insensibly but logically from the need to create good working and living conditions for the leaders. As an attitude and a system, this spirit proliferated on all sides, up, down, and sideways, pigeonholing particular layers and associated layers and particular and kindred professions into such closed circles that they felt interconnected only by the common spirit of solidarity. It was a spirit whose shape was determined not so much by ideological and moral unity as by a common way of life and a coincidence of interests. It was a product of political power and the way power had been arrived at.

In the pigeonholes lower down on the scale all this was more open, more bestial, coarse, and savage. The wife of a district secretary turned overnight, you might say, into the first lady of the district, whatever her qualifications, intellectual and otherwise. She became most particular in her choice of friends. To join her exalted circle was real happiness.

Since political relationships within the circle could shift with the rise and fall of function, friendships between men and between women as well were made or unmade accordingly. In one respect, however, every circle remained closed and impenetrable: It would not allow an "unworthy" newcomer, or anyone not on approximately the same rung of the ladder of power, to participate in that circle's private, inner life, its real life.

An endless series of secret tragedies inevitably ensued. The young woman began to experience them at first hand from the start.

On the very day of her marriage she was standing with her husband and his best man, a spry little fellow, conceited and candid and also a young general, on the terrace in front of the entrance to the state box of a new, large soccer field. She knew nothing about this box and who possessed or didn't possess the right to sit in it, not even that they were going to go in, only that she had been invited to the game and had gone along with the group and so found herself with them now after the wedding luncheon. It was an early summer afternoon, warm but not muggy, a rare thing in this city, and the young woman was truly happy. She felt as if her body were somehow light and unnoticeable, though she was at the same time a little sad in the knowledge that she was parting from her girlhood. From the platform in front of the box the crowds seemed to flow slowly and unhurriedly into the new stadium, which from her vantage point looked like a giant stone beehive. Many times before in her life when she was experiencing something beautiful and fresh, especially when faced by a mass of moving but indifferent people, the young woman had had the thought that people were good even if they did inflict on each other their little outbreaks of egoism, ill will, and malice. This could happen sometimes out of pure boredom, she thought, but most often people were in the grip of difficulties from which they did not know how to extricate themselves.

Carried away by these thoughts and feelings, she was gazing vaguely down at the crowd and experiencing it as one vast, colorful, and kindly entity, when all at once she noticed a slender woman, still young, talking with her, the actress's, bridegroom at the entrance to the box two or three yards away. Even at first glance this person stood out by her unobtrusive elegance and cheerful manner. The bride felt a sudden rush of pleasure at the sight of her. They were not acquainted, but she recognized the woman from having seen her on the street and in a picture. She had heard only good things about the intelligence and simplicity of this woman, whom she knew to be the wife of a high economic official, determined and active and very popular with the people. She knew too about the student circles in which this wife had been living until recently. Just as the husband was known as a very human man, upright and modest and full of a deep, unaffected understanding for people's misfortunes, so his wife had the reputation of a cheerful, pleasant, sensible, and simple woman.

Our bride was not especially moved just then by a desire to meet this person, although she had a feeling that it would be nice to chat with her anyway and she might hear some bit of wisdom, now that she herself was entering upon a new life and open to fresh impressions. But as no one saw fit to introduce them, she did not venture to stare openly at the lady, and only when she overheard something rough in her own husband's tone of voice, something that seemed hard and sharp, did she turn to her bridegroom. He had narrowed his eyes, always a sign of suppressed anger gathering within. The woman, though, laughed ironically as she made some jesting remark, shooting an expressionless glance at the young actress the way we look at lifeless, broken, unwanted objects. The wife quickly went on into the lobby, following her husband.

Our bride had a sense that something had happened. Who was that woman? What meaning did she have for her new bridegroom?

It never occurred to her that it might be one of the ones who had phoned, as in fact the woman was not. What had taken place? was her only thought. She glanced inquiringly at her husband, expressing nothing more than a question. He only laughed uncertainly (but it seemed to her a grim and protective laugh) and then put his arm around her waist, pressing the tips of his fingers against her upper arm just beneath the armpit and drawing her over to him, lightly so that no one would notice but still strongly enough for her to feel the pressure clearly and understand the gesture. It was one of his gestures that now belonged to them together. She smiled too and laughed as though nothing out of the ordinary had happened, responding to his movement with one of her own, one just as unnoticeable. With a light, shadowy touch, not even that but the barest of motions, she pressed the back of her head and shoulders against his chest.

But *something* really had happened.

As she later found out, the woman and her husband had had the following conversation: *She:* Is that your beauty? *He:* It is. Do you like her? *She:* Well, it depends. Judging by her looks she's all right, but she doesn't seem to have smelled much powder. *He:* How could she, she wasn't even thirteen— *She:* I know, I know. But neither could you have had a hard time finding her. It was she that found you. Only I can't understand why you married her! With so many women around who are Party members, tried and true. . . . *He:* I married her out of love, because I liked her, and not . . . *She:* Sure, sure, love. Love burns like a wet blanket in the Sava River. Weren't you in too much of a hurry, running after youth and beauty? *He:* It's not some public meeting that gets married, it's a human being.

To the bride, entering with her husband's arm about her, it seemed that this had been but a momentary, chance encounter. Now she was threading her way between chairs and taking in new impressions. She forgot all about it.

No impression left by such an ambiguous, unpleasant meeting would have lived long beside the thrill of a crowded stadium, with its softened colors and spattering of applause on all sides, now here, now there, as the city's beloved team darted around the field. She could not avoid encountering the other women in that box, however, which chilled and dumbfounded her. As the players, waiting for the referee to come on the field, warmed up in front of the goals, her husband's friend, the best man, introduced her to some of the Party members, including the four women in the box. Here was the lady from the entrance. Now she aroused the bride's curiosity even more. The men politely shook hands, only to turn back at once to what was going on on the field, as if ignoring her. The women, however, shook hands limply and without a word, somehow distantly, turning their heads away from her with obvious intent. They did not even look at the game, in order to make their gesture quite clear. *She,* though, the one from the entrance, the one who looked the most refined and intelligent of the lot, *she* did not even take her hand but only vouchsafed a little bow. It was scarcely noticeable. She accompanied this small gesture with a reproachful jibe: "You're an actress? Yes, so they told me. Those others married to our generals never come here." She was indifferent. And cold.

What was that supposed to mean? the bride wondered all during halftime. Those pokerlike greetings? Those words?

It was as if a wall had suddenly gone up across the loge, erected by dozens of strong arms. A wall between the rest of them and her, even between her husband and her. Passionately, innocently following the game, he seemed to be just another soccer fan.

She herself saw nothing of the game. It was her own team playing, and like all the other young people in the stands (she had seen them growing up) she felt the impulse at times to yell with enthusiasm or whistle indignantly when the wrong call was made. But she couldn't. She couldn't move a muscle. She couldn't think. She was sitting in a box where people were wrapped up in affairs of state and concerned for their reputations. It would be strange and unexpected to yell or whistle, it was even unthinkable that anyone there might give way to such childish impulses. But she also was petrified by these introductions. It was as if she were embedded in ice, impenetrable, incomprehensible ice, frozen solid to undisclosed depths. Everything within her stayed exactly as it was—thoughts, desires, feelings. Everything was at a standstill, paralyzed. She felt the gaze of many eyes directed at her from the left, from the right, and from the rear, as though she were some strange phenomenon that had materialized all of a sudden in their midst from the hidden darkness. It was like something tangible, soft but unyielding, like ice-wrapped pressure. She made herself turn around once or twice as if to leave, only to find their gaze turned aside. The women would not be caught. She must have no suspicion that they might be curious; must not think that she, a young girl and a newcomer, might arouse any other feeling than that of a shocked amazement.

Later, she never could explain to herself how it happened that during the intermission she went up to that very woman whom she had met at the entrance. Was she perhaps totally confused and disconsolate? Had perhaps a latent sense of human dignity awakened in her, hitherto unknown but stubbornly alive? Perhaps she wanted to say something nice, something that would dissolve the barriers between her and that woman, who was to all appearances educated and discriminating. Self-improvement was the woman's hallmark (though actually she had managed to polish her own husband a little). Refinement had come by dint of unremitting labor and study. After raising herself out of a lower-middle-class Serbian milieu that was practically peasant, she had known the hardships of war, had worked tenaciously in the Party apparatus, and was now a woman of political savvy and decided cultivation. Our bride, though, did not know what to say when she approached. The woman listened in silence, looking her in the face while doggedly tapping her fingers on her purse. "I . . ." began our bride, wondering why she had started to stammer, "I have never been the sort of person you think actresses are. Maybe there are some like that. I—" Here the woman cut in. "I'm not saying you are. But your profession is the sort that . . . And yet why should I be explaining myself to you and making you feel uncomfortable? Still, one thing must be clear to you—and I say this with the best of intentions and for your own sake—you can never be the right company for our comrades, men or women." Thereupon the woman turned on her heel as if she were performing a pirouette and moved away. Our bride had no chance to reply and later regretted not at least having made the point that she wasn't begging for friendship. She collapsed and sat down, all alone.[7]

She wanted to leave. Her head echoed with noises, only not from the stands. These were internal and like tiny, rapid drumbeats. Feeling lost, she looked over at her husband and down onto the field. The men were all having a good time, and no one paid her any attention. At one point—when was that?—she heard one of the women remarking to the others as well as the woman from the entrance, in a tone meant to be overheard by the bride: "You really told her off, congratulations!" A quiet murmur of approval from the other women greeted her words.

But she could not run off. Where would she go? And how could she manage it? Could she really make a scandal for her husband right here in front of everybody? Today, on his wedding day, when he doesn't suspect a thing? The young woman wanted to scream, even tried to scream, tried to give way to tears, but she was too numb, weak, and bewildered even for that. She felt herself shrinking, growing cold as ice; felt her heart, contracted with the pain, giving frightened, faint beats.

Only when she was alone that evening with her husband did the bride give way to bitter, inconsolable tears.

That was their first, wholly free evening in her husband's apartment, their first night as a married couple, nor was this true in a purely formal sense for her, since it marked the beginning of another life in another person's house and in other surroundings. The young woman implored her husband not to abandon her, only to beg him in the next breath to go ahead and leave her and not to part company with his own people, his own Party comrades, just for her sake. In a sense that would mean making a break with his whole life up to that point. She swore to leave the stage the very next day, only to break out sobbing a moment later that she would have to do this, as she now said, but it was the only thing she never could do because her whole life, body and soul, was linked to music, to melody, to an inner need to sing that was beyond life itself. She tensely listened to the music in her mind's ear, to the arias that were ever more different and new. This sensation of music was so hopelessly full at this moment that she thought her body would be reverberating and ringing with undiscovered harmonies even after she was dead.

Thus it was that the first day of her wedding, her first great happiness, began to disintegrate and her expectations of harmony to come crumbled away to nothingness. Personal life collided with her new social relations; personal desires, hopes, and dreams were thwarted by artificial norms of behavior imposed from above; the tumultuous violence of her inner life came to be harnessed by received dogmas and rules. A boundless desert began to spread in her soul, her mind, her life, whose existence she had never before suspected. The specter of total ruin appeared.

But it was only the beginning of this star-crossed love match.

In that world, the meaning and worth of a person have come to be encompassed more and more by one's rank in the hierarchy, the role one plays, and above all by the real power one wields. This has been mainly an outgrowth of the Revolution and its immediate aftermath. So too have most of the wives gradually lost any pronounced personal traits, any personal worth of their own, a development that holds good both for the world outside and among themselves as well. The wives have assumed the value of their husbands, little by little making their husbands' habits and ideas their own. That is why the attitude of the woman our bride had first met at the entrance began to spread very quickly, not so much on her own intrinsic authority as on her husband's. This, despite a little fact that wouldn't go away: He himself was impartial, even well disposed, toward the new couple.

And this was a lady who could be numbered among the best of the lot, one of the more cultured, more humane and moral. Even so, she aided and abetted arrogance. Her exalted circle imagined itself to be sacred and behaved as if it were in very truth a hallowed place. This only encouraged illusions to luxuriate like weeds and the phantoms of past greatness to roister unchecked. It is an old truth that people are not what they imagine themselves to be but what conditions have made them. This truth stands, alas. People are conditioned by the relationships they defend and by which they live; by how they deal with reality.

The lady from the entrance had derived her own moral standards from tradition, religious and small-town morals, with an overlay of dogmatic and bureaucratic morality. After sizing up prevailing relationships and how they had gotten that way, she proceeded to truckle to them, in the process becoming their willing tool. But, and this was very rare, she did not lose anything of her manner, which was to all outward appearances civilized. She should have had qualms about her behavior. Her maintaining an outward appearance of civility should have led her to be more considerate, more indulgent, toward people who lack the natural advantage of a rung on the hierarchical ladder and have not entered higher society. Yes, people had once entertained second thoughts. That was when the spirit of democracy was on the upswing and we were engaged in a struggle against the Cominform and the spirit of bureaucracy. But when the tide was out and we were simply waiting for it to turn, all that acquired mentality awoke in a new form. This mentality was even more abstract and unreal, even more caustic on questions of ethics, morality, and ideology, in proportion as it saw all kinds of its privileges being undermined and to the extent living conditions slowly improved and notions about them changed.

The lady from the entrance took this in much more rapidly and intelligently than many another. She grasped the inevitability of change. But her code of morals, once revolutionary, which had first been inherited only to become dogmatic, grew less indulgent and thereby more monstrous. Her morality had its roots in her personality, in her girlhood. It had been no girlhood at all but a series of hard struggles and personal sacrifice. Then, too, she had gone to a lot of trouble to get her foot in the door to the higher circle, and after that to be accepted there. Once a personnel officer in the institution where her husband worked (at the time he was an old bachelor), then marrying him, she too had encountered cruel resistance and calumny from this preexisting social set. That, though, was now forgotten. A fighter, she had been in the war and had won a place for herself in the circle. Now this other woman was quite, quite different, an actress, a singer, "our little songstress," as she was scornfully dubbed.

Such was the logic of hierarchy: to get on top yourself and not let the "unworthy," the "immoral," get up there with you. It was the terrible logic of reality, hierarchy, and privilege, and it had turned these once heroic women and men into monsters.

Practically all of them, in fact, had been half peasant and semi-educated until yesterday. There were indeed some who, even in these conditions, had retained their modesty and had not essentially changed, especially if they had been formed politically and emotionally before the war. But there were few such people in any case, and they were looked upon as conservatives displaying false modesty. All at the same time but imperceptibly, the majority began to put on airs. Not only to the outside world but to each other as well. These amounted to a kind of studied, aristocratic style. It was calculated, stiff, and awkward, but plotted and gauged down to the last detail.

Many of them began to make all sorts of fine comparisons, each to each, searching for wartime or other services previously unknown or unimagined for some while, in the meantime belittling everyone else. Next they set themselves up as their husbands' equals; their own "rights" were the same as those of their husbands; each played the same role. Many would go beyond this. But what was ugliest of all and most laughable was that some began to vie for expensive, usually tasteless, furniture and works of art, displaying thereby not only a primitive greed and a fabricated, overblown sense of what was first-class but also the pretentious omniscience of the ignorant.

These latter types were quite different from the lady our bride had met at the soccer match. They were, though, in the majority and were still more coarse, more categorical, more uncouth.

Especially conspicuous for their rudeness were the women who in their own youth had lacked any of the virtues they now demanded of others, including our bride.

One said, borrowing a line from pulp fiction, that "I just smell the stinking odor of debauchery if I'm even in the same room with her." Another had been young during the period when S K O J [the Communist Youth Organization] deemed the first sign of women's emancipation to be liberation from "bourgeois" moral prejudices about virginity and fidelity to one man. These people were pleased to opine that "you don't know who our women comrades are anymore. You can't tell who's a whore and who's a Party member"! Another claimed that "her occupation is the same as being a prostitute." And that was the "statement" that became the most widespread. One evening, circumstances brought the young woman in company with her husband into the apartment of a certain friend of his. There, her hostess, seated in an armchair, reached behind her shoulders to extend a limp handshake, and that was all her welcome. Not a single word did she bestow on her guest. It was this woman who was known for having had no chastity to boast of before she got married. She was now engaged in putting forward her cultivated elegance and was learning the piano and English. But here in her own apartment she took the position that the young actress had done something she never had done, in effect throwing the accusation in her face. The husband abruptly rose and, taking his wife by the hand, went out without saying a word. It was a difficult evening.

So the wife, and her husband too, were everywhere met by an icy ostracism that she had done nothing to provoke. If she sat down in a restaurant banquette where some other woman was already seated, a third would soon turn up to summon number two off to the side. Everywhere it was the same.

It did not lie in the husband's power, or else he had no wish, to stand out from the crowd. Slowly there yawned a gulf between the two of them, and the husband, a self-possessed, tough, vigorous man, began to experience inner conflicts which were always rising to the surface and provoking questions like: "How is this possible? Where does it come from? Among people like *these?* Are these the new ethics? Is this communism? Is it socialism?"

Being a woman and fastidious, the young wife found every excuse to hang back whenever they had to go out somewhere so that he would not again stumble into a situation that isolated them and that would only lead to his flying into a rage. He gradually fell into the habit of going out by himself while she stayed home alone.

But as a human being, especially given her youth, her preferences, and her profession, the actress could not live in isolation and more and more found friendship in the world of the theater. Earlier, she had been as little inclined toward this world as she was irresistibly attracted by the stage itself, by rhythm and melody. As a young person and a Communist, while still a schoolgirl she had been carried away by thoughts of introducing to the world of the theater a new morality, a new zeal for work, new relationships. Now, under socialism, this became possible. No longer did one have to reach the stage by way of princely bedrooms or bankers' town houses. Her ideals were only further nourished by marriage to such a prominent and good man as her husband. But life proved to be different. The old stage world, eaten away by intrigues and corroded by careerism and belligerent self-assertion, had already been morally undercut by the German occupation and additionally was inured to the frivolous entertainments linked to such a mentality and way of life. Now that same world began aligning itself with the new political power. It was a fact of life that could not be avoided. "Show business is show business," they would say. True, some individuals and groups came into conflict with the new regime. On the whole, though, it would seem that some sort of accommodation was possible without necessitating any inner, structural change. To the young actress this fundamental immutability of things, of stage relations, now began to seem all the more credible because neither had that brave new world to which she had trustingly given her childlike commitment only to be dropped out of hand, entirely disengaged itself from the old one. So much was obvious.

Thus in every way, as a spouse and a person and an actress, she found herself transfixed between wish and possibility, ideal and reality, and goaded from all sides. Meanwhile the unplumbed depths of the old, Bohemian life of the artist drew her down by degrees. That was a life that at least promised to drown her tragic disappointments and unhappiness in easy joys, however temporary they might be.

Life, with the force of an avalanche, was driving her to fulfill the prophetic words of one of the women from that closed circle: "Sooner or later she'll take a tumble like the others. Such is her world." But the young actress kept struggling. For her own sake and that of her feelings, her love, she did not give in. Meanwhile, the women from the social circle would boast of being harbingers of the new, but the longer they ceased to be so the more their stupid, irrational behavior thrust the young actress deeper into a world and a way of life that she neither could nor wanted to leave but instead wanted to change.

Therein lay the hypocrisy, the inconsistency, of such a moral code: On the one hand the wives sat in judgment and ostensibly condemned her for being an actress, but on the other hand they kept propelling her in that very direction, even setting her up to become (by the usual norms) one of the lowest kind of actresses. . . . When one of these days it is verified that she, too, like so many others, "lowered herself," she really will merit scorn and ostracism. And we will never tire of repeating, just as they used to say in the days of proper middle-class wives, that the world of actors simply cannot give rise to a respectable woman. A woman formed down there amid "low life," we say, can never rise to the level of "one of ours."

In the course of that painful existence, hounded on all sides, torn by inner crises, the young actress made the acquaintance of other despised women, including some who were trampled and abandoned despite the fact of having been soldiers—and what soldiers they were!—in the war. Only then did the brutal social reality of an opposition that knew no bounds and stopped at nothing yawn before her eyes in all its depth and scope. Neither her profession nor even her potential immorality was the root cause of such resistance. No, those were all pretexts! She was unworthy of a social circle that had anointed itself in order to set itself apart and gain preeminence. Precisely here, the spuriousness of the cause, lay the hypocrisy of this morality.

No, to be "one of us" was not possible for her, she had no right to this status. That was the heart of it.

But to their way of thinking, "one of us" more and more stood for man in general, man as an ideal, one and only. It is an old truism that the further we diverge from objective reality, from social life and its problems, the more our own world appears to be the objective one and our interests, our ideas and morality, while actually becoming ever more abstract, take on an absolute value. They become society's only interests. They become the only authentic truths, the only authentic morality. It is as if the old, "eternal" truths long ago discovered by Aristotle had been forgotten. Those social circles and their "communism" had forgotten them too. Forgotten that no moral code or ethical system need be invented anew. These can be discerned well enough in reality and in the facts of life, can be formulated as they already exist, can then be fought for. And this too had been lost sight of, again an Aristotelian truth: One of the first duties of a politician is to study the human soul— its ethics.

Morality and ethics do not concern sexual norms alone, which cover only a tiny part of human relationships. People have lived together for a long time, and their relationships are constantly being "reformulated" in response to new social realities. To reduce morals and ethics purely to sexuality would be to ignore reality, the totality of social relations, the problem of social ethics. Sexual morals have always been understood in terms of open (and thereby more human) relationships; in terms of open personal and open social (i.e., matrimonial) relations between man and woman, and among people in general. Immorality is something exceptional, be it asocial or antisocial, and regardless of its social roots. It is a category apart.

There was a period when chastity was a necessary means for tempering and hardening our revolutionary ranks. Our cadres were conditioned to forget all personal interests for the sake of the common cause, to assimilate the personal to the general. Over time, however, this drive for sexual chastity underwent a change in the airless atmosphere created when circles both high and low on the social scale closed their doors and decay became rampant behind those doors with the rotting of bureaucratism. Chastity became transformed either into the crudest sexual perversions or, alternatively, into a brutal, malicious asceticism.

The social milieu under discussion, which was often much too moral in terms of quasi-religious dogma, had great difficulties in understanding these things. Some never did. Basically, theirs has been a morality of details. Concrete acts and specific conduct mattered. The fact that a kingdom of blindness reigned on all sides did not. Real ethics, social ethics, civilized human relationships, were a matter of indifference. What was important was this or that moral detail and the presumed immorality of a young actress. Disdain for a human being, the destruction of a person—all that was secondary. Dogmatism grew alongside bureaucratism, corroding all ethical values, including even the ascetic, dogmatic, "purist" values behind which these closed circles found shelter and which they took their oath upon. In the name of marital fidelity, marital happiness was ripped to shreds. In the name of love, hatred was fostered. In the name of human dignity, a living being was despised. In the name of a new social order, living people, living relationships, were treated like academic postulates—and violated.

All this appeared in telescoped form precisely in the case of the young actress.

We know that disasters never stop halfway, and so it was with her: Disaster had to be played out to the bitter end. But this meant as well exposing the real ugliness and inhumanity of that closed moral system. Their morality had arisen for the most part spontaneously and unplanned, taking its shape from a special way of life reinforced by bureaucratic practice. But it had also arisen in the name of humanity and the highest known moral law.

In the first month of her marriage the young actress became pregnant. Even that circle always rejoiced in motherhood and newborn babies, but only if they were their own. Many women belonging to it were the heads of various humanitarian, children's, maternity, and the like, institutes and organizations. It could not be said of them that they were inactive, still less that they were not conscientious and careful in their work. But when it came to the young actress . . . didn't she belong to a different world than they did? Weren't most of them saying that her profession ipso facto "predestined" her to prostitution? And practically everybody believed it too!

Like an electric shock, a bolt of summer lightning, the whisper ran the rounds of their circle: The actress is pregnant! In its wake came the remarks, peculiar and partisan: "Ah! the poor child! That's all she needed! So quickly!" It was not convenient to say openly that the child was not her husband's, for that would have been illogical and unnatural and besides would have damaged the reputation of someone who was, after all, a member of their set. Instead we heard: "Now it's all clear." She caught "our comrade" by playing on his "human weaknesses" (weaknesses never before recognized!); he "sired" this kid on her before they even got married and then he couldn't get out of it.

Intrigue and gossip have always been the stock-in-trade of all such closed circles, circles set apart, nor was this one exempt from the rule. And it was decaying from within. There were, it is true, the periodic reactions that took place when scandals accumulated to the point of disturbing established relationships and the general serenity, but these were short-lived because no intrinsic change occurred, or if it did, it came with glacial slowness. Intrigues spontaneously started up again, always based on some logical germ of fact that seemed true. Intrigues involving the circle's unanointed members were especially cutting and ruthless.

Could one of our people really fall in love with such a woman? Since the answer was no, it could only mean that he'd been trapped, and if you granted that he'd been trapped, then you had to allow for his being pinned down. The kid was planted on him deliberately, we might say, so that he'd be tied up forever. After that he had to get married, the poor man; he'd nowhere to go. What a stupid thing to do! Why didn't he drop her? Why let a baby lead him by the nose?

No one stopped to ask if this was factually so or not. For that world, it was logical. It was a world that had lost touch with logic along with reality.

So it came about that even motherhood was attacked. Besmirched. Profaned. Turned into a disgusting, willful, commercial transaction.

And though the young actress secretly rejoiced at seeing her slender shape grow more round by the day and rejoiced in realizing that her girlish, maternal instincts were stirring and growing into something tangible and enduring, at every step these new feelings of hers were met by jeers and hatred. Her profession, her origins, her inglorious past were incompatible, it seemed, with motherhood. Can "such a woman" really be a mother? It's only a question of fraud and deceit, isn't it?

How the story ended is not important here, nor what happened to its main participants. What our heroine had to pass through is unimportant too, at least in its concrete details, while she struggled to survive and put down roots in that boundless, heartless desert, at the same time fighting for the unwritten, imperishable rights of a mother.

One evening at the very beginning of the theatrical season, she was performing under the brilliant sheaves of the spotlights at a premiere.

Her role in the drama was secondary but still quite substantial. She was playing the part of the gay, mischievous chambermaid of a queen who knows of the queen's love and guesses her intentions. An old Renaissance motif carried over to a modern opera. Just when she was reaching the end of her cheerful, playful, popular aria she felt the spasmodic but quiet stretching of the child inside her womb. The auditorium was packed. In the mezzanine boxes she could make out the first-night audience in the half-darkness, among whom were the women from her circle, so many that the theater seemed filled with them alone. They hated her to death, they despised her to the point of trampling her underfoot, and yet they sat there in rapture over the destinies and the melodies of a Marguerite or a Butterfly. They applauded her arias too and, forgetting everything, they were enchanted by the surge of song rising from her young, uninhibited voice, they were delighted by this revelation in song of a rich inner life.

Meanwhile, the little being in her womb did in fact exist. And while she, self-forgetting, gave herself to the happy play of notes that poured out of her on every side, at the same time, just as if the sharp tip of a knife were working its way into her thoughts, she was thinking this: Right here on the stage I am myself taking part in the same tragic drama that we find invented for operas; I have to go on singing and smiling while pains and doubts are tearing at my heart. Everything suddenly began to seem unreal, as in a dream or a vision: her life, the auditorium, those women sitting out there, her songs—everything. No one else could see how her throat tightened and her breast heaved with every kick in her womb. It was like the old, now almost-forgotten pieces she had once acted in, where she trembled at the thought of bursting into tears when her songs, her gestures, and her feelings all had to express joy and happiness.

When the curtain fell at last, she stumbled to a sofa and buried her head in her arms, sobbing.

What for? How did it happen? Where to now?

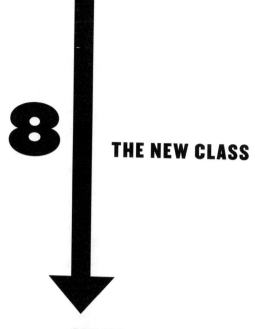

8

THE NEW CLASS

PRELUDE

Once I had set out along a new path entirely my own, my thinking lost its constraints and grew clearer and more steady. Clouds of disapproval were gathering all around, though on occasion I found enthusiastic support. I was torn between existing relationships that were real and well ordered and my own knowledge and inspiration. By the end of November, I suspected that it would all end in confrontation, but kept on hoping for some mutually acceptable solution. Even if forbidden the highest forum, I might still be allowed to advance my views, by agreement if necessary with the rest of the leadership.

These hopes reflected the intellectual atmosphere in which I moved and the democratic atmosphere prevailing in the Party itself, an atmosphere evident from the positive response to my articles. *Borba* was receiving more letters with each article, and the total approached thirty thousand.

It was clear to me from the start that my side was the weaker and that I would be pushed out. This was not, though, the reason for my failing to organize some faction or group. No, I wished to answer for my actions and ideas all alone. During that entire period of heretical intellectual and journalistic activity I did not attempt by a single word or act to win anyone over to my views. To the end, I stayed clean and loyal to the leadership of which I was a member. I regarded my articles as merely a seed, was in bondage to my ideas, and felt myself to be blameless, having taken no action contrary to the Party rules and my own conscience.

Within me, however, experiences accumulated of their own accord, verdicts were rendered. On the night of December 7–8 I suddenly awoke knowing that I had to part company with my comrades, and that in fact I had already done so. It was a piercing, irrevocable conviction.

Štefica and I had already begun to isolate ourselves so as not to draw suspicion to others. We proceeded to organize a life for ourselves—long walks, movies, reading.

Then, at the beginning of January 1954, a plenary meeting of the Central Committee (the Third Plenum) was called to take up "The Case of Comrade Djilas." This "Comrade Djilas," though, was not told a thing about it, neither then nor later. It was contrary to Party rules but completely in the spirit of the factionalism and behind-the-scenes mobilization practiced in Leninist parties against "deviationists" and "turncoats." Only through the newspapers several days afterward would I learn that such a plenum had been called.

I walked about without feeling my body; the city and its people seemed alien, dreamlike. To the extent that anyone addressed me at all, he looked unnatural and could not find the right words, as if he were communicating with someone who had come down from the scaffold or was about to be forced up it. Everyone in the house lost their appetite. My insomnia tightened its grip.

Štefica accompanied me whenever she had a chance. We would walk down paths trodden through the snow and along the uncleared sidewalks, numb with cold and apprehension. Anticipating hard times, we did not turn on the heat in our bedroom. Yet it was not from the cold but from a desire to be close that Štefica shared my bed. Whenever, anxious and sleepless, I turned over or asked some question, I was met by a wakeful, reassuring answer. A suicide pact crossed our minds. Štefica was readier for it than I. But we were beset by doubts. Did we have the right to die? Could we live like this? And how could we abandon Aleksa, our son of barely a year, to such a world?

We heard a rumor—was it planted or were we prompted by panic?—that the secret police, the UDBA, was now preparing lists of "Djilasites." The shadow of Goli Otok [Bare Island], the concentration camp for pro-Soviets, loomed also over us. And with it the awful fear, ever suspected, ever dismissed, that there existed a secret, inconceivable place of torment for separatists and turncoats. Across my mind flashed the thought that remaining a Communist led not just to defeat but to hopeless, boundless shame. Was it not precisely for this reason that Trotsky, Bukharin, and so many thousands of other luckless heretics had not simply lost their battles but been lost from living memory?

My whole past—my work in the Party, my long years of sacrifice and struggle for it—rose before me in all its unimagined, appalling truth. I thought I should write it down for some future, truth-loving generation. But the ideas I had been trying to formulate up till now seemed timid, only partly put into words, and even that with great care.

I walked to the plenum with Štefica by my side, arriving there feeling numb, bodiless. A heretic, beyond doubt. One who was to be burned at the stake by yesterday's closest comrades, fellow fighters in decisive, momentous battles.

Though I realized that the verdict had already been reached, I had no way of knowing the nature or severity of my punishment. It had been my secret hope that even while repudiating and dissociating itself from my opinions the Central Committee would not expel me from the Party, perhaps not even from its plenum. But all these democratic and comradely hopes were dashed once the contest was joined. Tito's speech was a piece of bitingly intolerant demagoguery. The reckoning it defined and articulated was not with an adversary who had simply gone astray or been disloyal, but with one who had betrayed principle itself.

The longer the plenum lasted, with its monotonous drumbeat of dogma, hatred, and resentment, the more conscious I became of its utter lack of open-minded, principled argument. It was a Stalinist show trial, pure and simple. Bloodless it may have been, but no less Stalinist in every other dimension—intellectual, moral, and political.

Surmise, though, demands its own confirmation. My suspicions had to be lived through. The experience was bound to be depressing and demoralizing. In my mental perceptions, also my style of life, I had struck out along my own path, yet I felt bound to my prosecutors and judges by some ancient, still unbroken, cord. Was this, perhaps, because of the suddenness with which I had been made a model victim of the Stalinism of yesterday's anti-Stalinist comrades-in-arms? In my rational and moral self I was now detached, sundered, but in my memory and sensibility I was a slave in shackles. In short, I was still a

Communist. Revolutionary ideals and comrades held me fast. At the plenum I would pay for this with a halfhearted show of remorse. It took the speeches of my comrades and the harassment that came later to provoke my decisive turnabout, one that would liberate me.

Sometime during the morning of the second day of the session I conceived the idea—or rather, a malicious way of punishing myself and the comrades who had till then been closest to me—of beating a retreat. Why not, since my ideas were unacceptable to the Party? I was still in thrall to the doctrine that ideas are without value if not corroborated in practice, and for me "practice" was still equated with what the Communist Party did.

Over lunch I told Štefica that I ought to yield a little so as not to break with the Party. The thought of Goli Otok oppressed me like a leaden weight. "That's where they'll send people who take my side," I thought, "and there are not a few such. Out there they'll break them and mistreat them worse than any Cominformist. There's no organization to take up the fight for 'my' ideas, to do battle on behalf of these spontaneous supporters. I dare not drag the innocent into suffering and misery. If I pull back, everyone will have a chance to take cover and collect themselves—then we'll see."

My wife was adamantly opposed to any self-criticism, but at the same time she was considerate and tender. "I don't think you should do this. It will be a mistake. But I won't keep after you. Do as you think best. I would tell them if I were you that I'm tired and would like some time to think it over and await developments."

At the conclusion of the plenum, I did offer repentance. But no one, least of all Tito and Ranković, believed in the sincerity of my self-criticism or in its finality. This was confirmed by the campaign begun against me in the Party—my "Bernsteinism" was being condemned in the most remote little villages!—and even more drastically by the attitude of the top Party and government leaders, which virtually the next day turned threatening and hostile.

At the plenum I had a hunch that my last rendering of dues to communism would cost me dearly. For years to come the realization of error and weakness would drive me to prove myself, to correct my views, to look deeper into myself and communism.

Štefica was waiting for me, as I knew she would be, on the path in "our" snow-covered garden. She was subdued but unwavering. Indoors,

I found my mother, concerned but steadfast as ever. "It would have been better not to come out with that last part, but now it doesn't matter. You know best."

No support was anywhere to be found; everything lay in ruins, nor had we any savings, any food supplies. We huddled in my mother's room, the only one we kept heated. I was now forty-three years old. The most important, perhaps most vital, part of my life had passed. Perhaps my whole life. Was another life possible? A new one? Hope and confidence broke through, and an old truism kept running through my head: Life can always be started over.

Barely three or four days had passed since the plenum when I was at my writing again. I was taking refuge in a new, more exalted reality, but more than that, was indulging a long and deeply felt desire to express my thoughts in my own way. Bruised and alone but unbroken and free, I continued to work out my ideas with even greater intensity and to set my thoughts down on paper with painstaking care.

We lived, Štefica and I, an ever more solitary existence. I with my speculations and conclusions, which at one and the same time intoxicated and alarmed me. Intoxicated by my "originality" and alarmed by my renunciation of Communist reality.

My wife found work at the beginning of March 1954. We were far from prosperous, though we would not go hungry. A couple of days later I tendered my resignation from the Party, and then Štefica—without any prompting from me—did so as well.

Even on the eve of the plenum, but especially after it, I was haunted by the idea of writing my memoirs, telling the story of the Communist movement from the inside, from personal recollection and experience. Side by side with the memoirs, I set to work on theoretical texts, too, including drafting and writing out portions of "Freedom and Ownership," from which, in the second half of 1956, *The New Class* would emerge.

It looked as though I would welcome in the year 1955 without major incident. But then, late in the fall, the Central Committee began to settle accounts with Dedijer. They had obviously been waiting for the matter of Djilas to blow over in the Western press and for the dust to settle on the Party's dogmatic, antidemocratic course.

Dedijer, however, rebelled. Refusing to respond to a Party committee, he took his case to foreign correspondents. The whole business flared up anew in the Western media. Although I was not involved at the beginning, I was quickly drawn into the affair, if only because foreign newsmen turned to me as well. To be honest, I was glad of the chance, not only from feelings of solidarity with him but, still more, so that I could finally and publicly draw a line between myself and the Party leadership, the regime.

More journalists visited me. I gave a statement to Jack Raymond of *The New York Times* in which I characterized the present system in Yugoslavia as totalitarian. That was the first time I mentioned that the way out of this impasse might be the creation of a second Party.

The regime being what it was, it could not remain indifferent to the statements being made by Dedijer and myself, for that would suggest indecision regarding these new, socialist oppositionists. Almost one full year after the judgment against me at the Central Committee plenum, criminal charges were lodged against the two of us for "hostile propaganda."

The trial lasted one day and was held behind closed doors. We were conditionally sentenced—Dedijer to six months and I to a year and a half.

Early in the summer of 1956 I had taken the manuscript of *Land Without Justice,* my childhood memories of Montenegro, to the Srpska Književna Zadruga [Serbian Literary Cooperative] for possible publication by that distinguished publishing house. But when I returned a couple of weeks later to inquire about my manuscript I was informed that it had been rejected—on the pretext that it was below standard.

The rejection of *Land Without Justice* had great, not to say paramount, significance for me. Here was bitter, painful confirmation that the state authorities, after casting me out politically and blackening my name, were determined to finish me off spiritually, as a writer, since I had not knuckled under and repented. I didn't know how to knuckle under and couldn't repent without destroying everything that constituted my individuality, my opinions, and my character.[1]

Only a few days after being turned down by the Srpska Književna Zadruga I set to work on *The New Class.* I had a manuscript to work from, titled "Freedom and Ownership," but it had not been thought through and lacked organization. Thunderstruck by the rejection, I was now bent on creating a work with broader and more devastating impact. The sum total of my experience, thought, and inspiration converged into clear, finished thematic units, or chapters. I used the existing material but refined it, deepened it, and welded it into a harmonious, cohesive whole. The book was rewritten from scratch, and in one go. *The New Class* was completed in three months, and written in the greatest secrecy: Štefica was already retyping the final pages in early November 1956, just before my arrest.

As soon as half of the book was ready, I gave it to the reporter Catherine Clark, asking her to look for a U.S. publisher. The other half Štefica passed to her in confidence a few days after my arrest.

I was arrested because of a statement to Agence France Presse opposed to Yugoslavia's abstention in the U.N. vote condemning Soviet intervention in Hungary, and also because of an article in *The New Leader* about the uprising.

From my account the reader might gather the impression that my ideas were formed simply, step by deliberate step, without any second thoughts. Not so. To be sure, I had no second thoughts when it came to ideas and personal knowledge. But how I struggled to acknowledge that I had no choice in publishing my views other than in the capitalist West! It needed no special brains to realize that I was opening myself to attacks from the Yugoslav leadership for having "betrayed socialism," for having sold out to "reactionary intelligence services" and who knows what other reactionary circles besides.

I was held for about four months prior to sentencing in a cell of the Central Jail—the very place I had planned in 1946. Sentencing was carried out in secret, so my voluminous notes and defense preparations came to nothing. During a recess, while I was whispering conspiratorially with Štefica and my lawyer, Veljko Kovačević, the question of *The New Class* arose. The two of them were in favor of printing it but left the decision to me. Jennie Lee had come to Belgrade in connection with my arrest and, when my wife told her about the book, had suggested that we abort its publication. But I emphatically said to Štefica and Kovačević that the decision was ours alone to make. "The book has to be published, no matter what. . . ." I was sentenced to three years in prison.

When the verdict was rendered—and I didn't have to wait long for it—I was taken to Sremska Mitrovica Prison. That was where I had served time before the war with some of the same comrades who were now sending me back to prison.

THE NEW CLASS

In the Soviet Union as in the other Communist countries, everything turned out differently than had been anticipated by such prominent men as Lenin and Stalin, or by Trotsky and Bukharin. These leaders had predicted that the machinery of state in the Soviet Union would swiftly weaken and that democracy would grow stronger. But the reverse happened. They also predicted a rapid rise in the standard of living. But again, it hardly changed at all, while in the subjugated countries of Eastern Europe it even fell. In every case, the standard of living failed to keep pace with industrialization. Instead, it was industrialization that moved ahead the faster. It was believed that the contradictions would gradually dissolve between city and country and between white-collar and blue-collar labor. On the contrary, they intensified. Other fields of activity had a similar story to tell, and the same can be said of developments foreseen for the rest of the world, the non-Communist world.

But the greatest illusion of all was that the Soviet Union would see a classless society come to pass as it industrialized and collectivized, that is to say, as capitalist property was destroyed. When in 1936 Stalin, on the occasion of promulgating a new Soviet constitution, announced that in the USSR the exploiting classes had disappeared, in reality what had then been achieved was not merely the destruction of capitalists as a class, as well as the other classes belonging to the old order. What had been achieved was the formation of a class quite new to history.

Understandably, this class, like all its predecessors, took its hegemony to mean that ultimate happiness and freedom had materialized. And that went for all peoples. The only difference, however, between this new class and its predecessors was that challengers were dealt with more harshly whenever they questioned its illusions or contested its supremacy. In this way it made certain that its supremacy would be more extensive than any other had been, historically. But also its class illusions and prejudices proved to be that much greater.

This new class, the bureaucracy, or more precisely the political bureaucracy, bore all the earmarks of earlier classes in the history of human society. But there was also something peculiar to it, something new, something that stamped all its endeavors, even though they resembled the endeavors of other classes.

Other classes in history, too, came to power mostly by revolutionary means, dissolving whatever political, social, and other relationships they happened across. But, practically without exception, all reached power after new economic forms already prevailed in the old society. With the new class in the Communist systems, the case was reversed: It did not come to power for the purpose of perfecting new economic relationships but to create still newer ones, and in so doing to establish its primacy.

In earlier eras, when some class or part of one, or some party, arrived in power, this was the final act of its formation and its awareness of selfhood. In the case of the USSR, the cart and the horse were reversed. There the new class was finally formed only after it itself had come to power. Similarly, it became aware of itself as an entity in advance of possessing real economic or physical power. The cart had to come before the horse because this class had not taken root in the life of the nation beforehand. It therefore embellished its own role while picturing the world in an idealized way. Its practical capabilities were not diminished thereby. On the contrary. For all its illusions, the class did represent the objective readiness to industrialize. Hence its practical bent. The ideal world promised by this new class stiffened faith in the ranks while sowing illusions in the masses, at the same time galvanizing and inspiring it to undertake gigantic, practical projects.

Because it had not been formed within society or the economy before coming to power, the new class could only have originated in a special kind of organization, one distinguished by discipline. This was the discipline of an identical and obligatory philosophy and ideology shared by its members. From the outset, the new class had to compensate for the weakness of its objective position in the economy and in the life of the nation by special, subjective characteristics, which were the unity of its self-awareness and an iron discipline.

The roots of the new class lay in a special type of Party—the Bolshevik Party. Lenin really was correct to consider his Party exceptional in the history of human society, even though he had no suspicion that it was the beginning of a new class.

To be more precise, the roots of this new class lay not in a Party of the Bolshevik type as a whole but in that stratum of professional revolutionaries which constituted its core before the Party as a whole came to power. It is no accident that after the 1905 Revolution had failed, Lenin asserted that professional revolutionaries alone—that is, people for whom revolutionary work was their sole occupation—could build a Party of this new, Bolshevik type. It is still less a coincidence that it was precisely Stalin, the future creator of the new class, who was the most developed type of such a professional revolutionary. Out of that very thin layer of revolutionaries there developed by degrees a completely new ruling class. These revolutionaries long constituted its core. Trotsky observed that the origins of Stalin's bureaucratism to come were to be found among the professional revolutionaries before the Revolution. What he did not grasp was that this was in fact the beginning of a new class of owners and exploiters.

No Party that was not materially interested in production, no Party that did not contain the new class and its property both as potential and as actuality, could ever wreak such havoc ideologically and morally as did the Communist Party. Still less could any Party lacking material incentives sustain itself in power for so long. After the first five-year plan, Stalin exclaimed: "If we had not created the apparatus, we would have failed!" He should have said, "created a new class." Then everything would have been clearer.[2]

This meant that the new Party and the new class were identical. The Party constituted its core and its foundation. In practice it was very hard, even impossible, to define the boundaries of the new class and determine just who were its adherents. The same was true, generally speaking, for other classes as well. We can approach the truth by stating that the new class included those with exceptional privileges and material advantages exclusively owing to their monopoly of management.

Society cannot do without management, however. Thus it happens that necessary functions may coexist with parasitical ones in the same individual. Not every Party member belonged to the class, any more than every craftsman or member of a municipal party is a bourgeois.

Broadly stated, one could say that in proportion to its strength and to the degree the new class gained a clear profile, to that same degree there took place a decline in the role of the Party itself. Within the Party and among its top leadership, as also within the political organs of government, was forged the kernel, the cornerstone, of the new class. The Party, which at one time took initiatives and was a living, compact organism, inevitably faded away, becoming a traditional perquisite of each individual member of the new class. Ever more irresistibly, the Party attracted into its ranks those spurred on by greed who wished only to insinuate themselves into this new class and climb its rungs, while pushing out those whose eyes were still fastened on ideals.

The Party spawned the class. But the class then grew on its own, using the Party as a basis. The class grew stronger, the Party declined—that was the unavoidable fate of every Communist Party in power.

It seems unusual for a political party to give rise to a new class. It is parties that are usually the product of classes and strata already tempered economically and spiritually. But if we understand Russia's actual relationships, if we understand that communism gained the victory in other countries through predominantly national forces, it will be clear that parties of precisely this type are the products of specific circumstances and that they are no accident. Although it is true that the roots of Bolshevism reach far back into Russian history, Bolshevism was also the product of the unsettled international relations entangling Russian national life at the end of the nineteenth and the beginning of the twentieth century. Russia could not survive any longer in the modern world as an absolute monarchy, and its capitalism was too weak and dependent upon the interests of outside powers to carry out an industrial revolution. That could only be done by a new class, operating, of course, on the basis of different property relationships.

Such a class did not yet exist.

History does not care who will carry out a certain process and is only concerned that it be carried out. So it was in Russia, as, too, in the other countries that saw Communist revolutions. The Revolution created the forces—the leaders, organizations, and ideas—that it needed. Objective conditions gave rise to a new class, thanks to the will, the political awareness, and the actions of those who manipulated these conditions.

The social origin of the new class was to be found in the proletariat. Just as the peasantry gave rise to the nobility and the bourgeoisie originated in the merchants, craftsmen, and peasants of the Middle Ages, so this new class comes predominantly from the proletariat. In keeping with national conditions, exceptions existed, but the backward proletariat of an undeveloped country furnished the raw material for this class.

That, however, was not the sole reason why the new class always championed the working class. Such a position was necessary for other reasons. On the one hand, being anticapitalist, the new class quite logically leaned on the working strata, while on the other it drew strength from the proletariat's struggles and antagonisms and from that proletariat's traditional aspiration of achieving a socialist and Communist society where brutal exploitation would not exist. Apart from such factors, it was vitally important for the new class to secure a normal flow of production, another reason for endeavoring to maintain its tie to the proletariat. But what was most important was that it could not carry out industrialization and consolidate power without the working class. And the workers likewise, for their part, saw salvation from poverty and despair, their own and the nation's, in the growth of industry. Over a long period of time the interests, ideas, and hopes of the new class coincided and united with those of a part of the working class and the poor peasantry. Mergers such as these were not unknown in the past between classes at opposite ends of the spectrum. Did not the bourgeoisie represent the peasantry in their struggle against the feudal lords?

The new class proceeded on the path to power only thanks to the efforts of the proletariat and the poor. These were the core groups on which the Party, or new class, had to lean and with which its interests most coincided until it finally established its power and authority. After that it took no interest in the proletariat or the poor except to the extent necessary to keep production flowing and to maintain in subjugation these most volatile and most rebellious social forces.

The monopoly imposed by the new class in the name of the workers over the whole of society was above all a monopoly over the working class itself. This was first of all intellectual and exercised upon the "vanguard" of the proletariat, followed by others. That was the biggest deception the class could carry out. But it also showed that the power and interest of the new class lay primarily in industry. Without industry it could neither stabilize its position nor establish its supremacy.

Former working-class sons were the steadiest members of the new class. It was always the fate of slaves to provide for their lords and masters their most farsighted and gifted representatives. Here too we saw a new class of exploiters, or, essentially, owners, growing directly out of the class that had been exploited.

The new class, having destroyed private property, could not reconstruct itself on the basis of some sort of new private property. Not only were private property relations inappropriate for achieving its primacy but also the economic transformation of the nation was conditional upon abolishing such relations. The new class drew its power, its privileges, ideology, and practices from a special kind of property, collective property. Collective property was property it administered and assigned "in the name of" the nation, "in the name of" society.

When Communist systems are being critically analyzed, it is usually assumed that their essential distinction lies in the fact that a bureaucracy, organized into a special stratum, rules over the people. That is so, generally. But a more detailed analysis will show that only a certain layer of bureaucrats, those who are not actually administrative officials, make up the core of the ruling bureaucracy, or, in my terminology, of the new class. This is in point of fact a Party, or political, bureaucracy. The rest of the employees are only an apparatus under their control, clumsy perhaps and slow to act, but something that has to exist in every society. Sociologists may be able to distinguish the one from the other, but in practice they are hardly to be told apart. This is true for two reasons: The Communist system is by nature bureaucratic, spreading its umbrella with ease over political and administrative bureaucracy alike, but also it consists of Communists who handle various functions that are necessarily administrative. Over and above these reasons the political bureaucrats cannot relish their privileges if they do not toss out crumbs to the other bureaucratic categories.

Now, it is important to note some essential differences between the political bureaucracy under discussion and the kind of bureaucracy that makes its appearance whenever a modern economy concentrates its forces, especially concentrations such as monopolies, companies, and state ownership that can be termed collective forms of property. It is an established fact that in capitalist monopolies the number of employees is growing by leaps and bounds. A similar phenomenon has been seen in nationalized industries in the West. Robert Dubin (in *Human Relations in Administration,* New York, 1951, pp. 165–66) points out how state officials or functionaries in the economy become transformed into a special stratum or layer:

> . . . Functionaries have the sense of a common destiny for all those who work together. They share the same interests, especially since there is relatively little competition insofar as promotion is in terms of seniority. In-group aggression is thus minimized and this arrangement is therefore conceived to be positively functional for the bureaucracy. However, the *esprit*

de corps and informal social organization which typically develop in such situations often lead the personnel to defend their entrenched interests rather than to assist their clientele and elected higher officials. . . .[3]

While Communist bureaucrats have much in common with such functionaries, especially as regards *esprit de corps,* the two are not identical. The difference is this: State and other bureaucrats in the non-Communist systems do form a special stratum but make no decisions regarding ownership as such. Communists, though, do just that. Exercising power over bureaucrats in a non-Communist state are political masters, usually elected, or else themselves proprietors. Communists have neither masters nor proprietors over them. The former are employees of a modern state, a modern, capitalist economy, whereas the latter are something new and different—a new class.

As with other proprietary classes, the proof that we are dealing here with a distinct class lies in its ownership and its unique relationship to other classes. Similarly, the fact of belonging to this class is demonstrated by the material and other advantages that ownership brings.

By "ownership" is understood what scholars have long accepted under Roman law: the use, enjoyment, and disposition of material goods *(usus, fructus, abusus).* The political bureaucracy under communism treats nationalized property in precisely this way. Membership in that bureaucracy—in the new ownership class—has to be seen in the light of the advantages brought by property, in this case nationalized, material wealth. To be a member of the new Party class (the political bureaucracy) is apparent by having a material income greater than that which society would otherwise have to pay for such a function. In other words, class membership brings one a privileged position in society, which in turn confers all sorts of advantages. In practice, property belonging to the new class comes in the form of an exclusive right, a monopoly exercised by the Party political bureaucracy over the distribution of the national income; the exclusive right to determine wages, direct economic development, and dispose of the national wealth. To the man on the street, however, the life of a Communist functionary simply seems richer, even somewhat idle.

More than any other form of ownership, Communist ownership has a tendency to reduce itself to one relationship in particular, the relationship between management, whose function is exercised by one narrow and exclusive stratum of society, and on the other hand producers without any rights: peasants, manual workers, and white-collar workers. However, this relationship is not entirely valid because the Communist bureaucracy enjoys also a monopoly over the ultimate disposition of material goods.

Hence any fundamental shift in the relationship between those who have a monopoly of management and those who work should inevitably be reflected in property relations. And vice versa: Weakening or abrogating outright the monopoly over the disposition of material goods would alter the aforesaid social relationship, consisting in the fact that some have the exclusive right to manage while others have the obligation to work.

Public and political relations, on the one hand, and property relations, on the other—the totalitarianism of political power and the monopoly of ownership—have been perfected and brought into accord under communism more fully than in any other system.

To deprive Communists of their ownership rights would mean to eliminate them as a class. To force them into allowing other social categories to participate in ownership, or rather to make decisions about it—as labor strikes and parliament forced capitalists into permitting workers to participate directly in property decisions—would mean depriving them of their monopoly over property, ideology, and political power. It would mean the beginning of democracy and freedom under communism. Essential change would therefore mean abolishing Communist monopoly, or in other words, doing away with totalitarianism. For the present, there is no sign of this.

Ownership, like class membership, comes about by administering—as we have said, it is a privilege of administration. This privilege extends over all forms of public life, from state governance and the administration of economic enterprises to that of sports and humanitarian organizations. Political and Party management ("general management," as this is called) constitutes the heart of the system, the nuts and bolts of administration as a whole. And it carries privileges with it. In his book *Stalin au pouvoir* (Paris, 1951, pp. 201 and 215) Uralov states that the average pay of a worker in the USSR in 1935 was 1,800 rubles per annum, while the pay and allowances of a regional committee secretary amounted to about 45,000 rubles per annum.[4] The numbers may have changed since, for both the worker and the Party functionary, but the proportions have stayed the same. Many other authors have arrived at similar conclusions. And that relationships really are such could not be hidden from visitors to the USSR or other Communist countries in recent years.

Other systems have their professional politicians too. One can think well or ill of persons of this sort, but they must exist. Society cannot live without a state. It cannot survive in a vacuum of political power. Nor can society get along without the people who fight for this power.

But between the professional politicians of other systems and those we are discussing there are basic differences. In the worst case, politicians in other systems do take advantage of power to secure privileges for themselves and those who think as they do, or to favor the economic interests of one or another social stratum. Under communism it is quite different. Here the government itself, political power itself, is identical with the "use, enjoyment, and disposition" of practically the entire national product. Whoever has seized power has also seized privilege and—indirectly—property. As a consequence, under communism, power or politics as a profession becomes every man's ideal. It may not be the ideal profession of literally all people, that being a practical impossibility, but it is such for those who cannot suppress the urge to live the parasitical life, those who hope to live at others' expense.

Hence if membership in the Communist Party before the Revolution meant sacrifice; if being a professional revolutionary was the greatest possible honor; later, when the Party consolidated itself in power, membership then meant belonging to a privileged class, and to have been a revolutionary by profession meant belonging to its nucleus of all-powerful exploiters and masters.

The Communist revolution and the Communist system cloaked their true nature for a long time. The appearance of a new class was camouflaged not only by socialist phraseology but also, more importantly, by new, collective forms of ownership. The new, collective, or "socialist" ownership was simply ownership by the political bureaucracy in disguise. In the beginning this was necessary so that industrialization could be carried through to completion. Property hid its class composition by pretending to be generally national.

The growth of modern communism and the emergence of a new class are reflected in the varied character and role of those who inspired them.

From Marx through Lenin to Stalin and Khrushchev and beyond, leaders have changed in their way of serving an idea. Marx too was exclusive by temperament, but it never so much as crossed his mind to prevent others from laying out their ideas. Lenin still tolerated freedom of discussion in his Party and did not consider that the Party forums, not to speak of the Party chief, ought to prescribe what was "ideologically correct" or "ideologically incorrect." Stalin eliminated any intraparty discussion and appropriated ideology as the exclusive right of the central forum—in other words, of his own self. To these phases correspond the names of their movements: Marx's International Workers' Union (the so-called First International) was not Marxist in ideology but a gathering of various groups that adopted only the resolutions on which its members more or less agreed. Lenin's Party was an avantgarde group combining an internal revolutionary morality with a monolithic ideological structure, based on which there was democracy of a kind. Under Stalin the Party became a mass of people who took no interest in ideology—inasmuch as they got their ideas from above—but who were wholehearted and unanimous in defense of a system that assured them unquestionable privileges. Marx never actually created a Party; Lenin destroyed all parties except his own, including the socialist one; while Stalin relegated even the Bolshevik Party to subordinate rank, transforming its core into the core of his new class and converting the Party itself into a social stratum that was privileged, impersonal, and colorless.

Marx made a system out of class roles and class warfare within society, without having discovered these things himself, seeing mankind predominantly in terms of class allegiances. Even here he was only restating Terence's Stoic maxim *Nihil humani a me alienum puto* [I consider nothing human to be alien to me]. Lenin viewed men more in terms of the ideas they share than the classes they belong to. Stalin saw men only as obedient subjects or outright enemies. Marx died a poor emigrant in London but was esteemed by the intelligent and valued in the movement. Lenin died the leader of one of the greatest revolutions, but he also died as a dictator about whom a cult had begun to form. Stalin had already metamorphosed himself into a divinity.

These personal transformations only reflect changes already carried out in actuality and, need it be said, in the "soul" of the movement.

The spiritual and physical initiator of the new class, though he had no idea this was taking place, was Lenin, with his creation of a Party along Bolshevik lines and his theories about its unique and leading role in building a new society. This, of course, was but one aspect of his many-sided and enormous work. But it is precisely what issued from his actions rather than his wishes and on account of which the new class regards Lenin as its spiritual father.

With his narrow shoulders, long arms and legs, and short, potbellied torso, Stalin may have been a little fellow, but he had the rather handsome head of a peasant, yellow eyes with a soft, dead glow and a laugh that delighted in appearing sarcastic and sly. His reflexes were quick, and he had a tendency toward coarse humor. He was not very well educated or particularly well-read and was a weak speaker, but he did possess a brilliant feel for organizing, was an implacable dogmatician and a great administrator, a Georgian who grasped better than anyone else where the new overlords of Great Russia were taking her. It was Stalin who created the new class, using the most barbaric methods and not even sparing the new class itself. Of course, it was this stratum that first made Stalin what he was and brought him up to the surface, only to submit thereafter to his ungovernable and brutal nature. He was its true leader as long as it was building itself up and gaining strength.

The new class was born in revolutionary struggle out of the Communist Party, but it created itself in the industrial revolution—without this revolution, without industry, its position would not have been secure nor its strength complete. The realization of an act that had national significance, the transformation of industry, was at one and the same time its victory as a class. Those are two different things, but they are simultaneous and linked by the decisive influence of circumstance.

While industrialization was in full swing, Stalin began to introduce major differences in wages, at the same time giving full scope to the appropriation of all kinds of privileges. He realized that industrialization would come to nothing if the new class were not given a material interest in it, if it did not really dip its hands into some property. And without that, without industrialization, the new class would have been hard put to hold its own. It would have lacked both the theoretical justification and the material resources for its existence.

The increase in Party membership, or more exactly the bureaucracy, was closely connected with all this. In 1927, on the eve of industrialization, the Soviet Communist Party had 887,233 members. In 1934, at the close of the first five-year plan, its membership had grown to 1,874,488. This was a new phenomenon obviously connected with industrialization: Prospects for the new class and privileges for its members were improving. What is more, class privileges had grown at a faster pace than industrialization itself. It is hard to cite any statistics on this point, but such a conclusion is self-evident even from a cursory inspection if one keeps in mind that living standards had not kept pace at all with industrial output. The new class had obviously seized the lion's share of the country's economic progress, which had cost the masses sacrifice and effort.

The appearance of a new class did not proceed smoothly, nor could it. It encountered bitter opposition from existing classes and parties as well as revolutionaries who could not reconcile reality with the ideals of their revolutionary struggle. In the USSR the resistance of revolutionaries was most visible in the discord between Trotsky and Stalin. This conflict, the conflict of the Party opposition with Stalin, was like that of the regime with the peasantry, and it sharpened, with good reason, as industrialization itself intensified, or in other words as the power and supremacy of the new class increased.

Trotsky, an excellent speaker, brilliant stylist, and sharp polemicist, a man of rich culture and resourceful intelligence, was lacking in only one quality: a sense of reality. He wanted to be a revolutionary at a time when life demanded the humdrum. He wanted to resurrect a revolutionary Party at a time when it had turned into something completely different—a new class indifferent to great ideals and interested chiefly in life's everyday satisfactions. He wanted action from the masses, who were by now tired of war, hunger, and death, at a time when the new class already firmly held the reins, had begun to taste the sweetness of privilege, and was pointing out to others the cozy corner of normal human life. Trotsky's fireworks lit up the distant heavens but were not capable of kindling fires in weary people. He was a sharp observer of the presence of new phenomena but failed to grasp their meaning. Besides, he never had been a Bolshevik. That was both a shortcoming and a virtue. His non-Bolshevik past made him feel chronically worthless. Attacking the Party bureaucracy in the name of revolution, he was, without being aware of it himself, attacking the cult of the Party and, in point of fact, the new class.

Stalin did not look far ahead, nor did he look behind. He had seated himself in the eye of a storm in the process of being born—a new class, a political bureaucracy, bureaucratism—and became its leader and organizer. He did not preach, he made decisions. He, too, it is true, promised a shining future but one that could seem to the bureaucracy all the more real because life was getting better every day and it was consolidating its position. Stalin spoke without fire and color, but the new class found this all the easier to understand, a language that for it was the language of reality. Trotsky wished to extend the revolution to Europe and promised it the world, something Stalin was not against. But such a risky enterprise did not obviate a concern on Stalin's part for Mother Russia. It did not dilute his concern for those who were to consolidate the new system. Nor did it hamper his strengthening of the might and fame of the Russian state. Trotsky was a man of revolution past. Stalin was a man of the present day, and so of the future too.

In Stalin's victory, Trotsky perceived the Thermidoric reaction against revolution—bureaucratic distortion in Soviet power, corruption of the revolutionary heritage. He was therefore overly affected by the amorality of Stalin's methods. Though we cannot deny Trotsky the merit of being the first who, however unconsciously, in trying to save contemporary communism, had begun to discover its inner essence, it must be said that he was not capable of penetrating communism to the core. Trotsky proceeded from the assumption that here was a momentary, bureaucratic phenomenon that was corrupting the Party and the Revolution, and he concluded that the way out lay in a change at the top, a "palace revolution." But when such an overturn actually did happen after Stalin's death, it was apparent that there had been no essential change. We could see that something deeper and more permanent was involved. Stalin's Thermidor[5] had meant the enthronement of a government more despotic than the previous one, but it had also meant the enthronement of a class. It represented the continuation of that other—violent—side of the Revolution, the one that inevitably gave birth to and sustained a new class.

Stalin could, with as much right as Trotsky if not more, invoke Lenin and the Revolution. He was their legitimate, though evil, progeny.

History knows no one like Lenin, who, with such versatility and perseverance, generated one of the greatest revolutions in history. Nor does it know anyone like Stalin, who took on the enormous, onerous task of empowering and consolidating the property of a new class, born of a great revolution in one of the largest countries in the world. After Lenin, all passion and thought, came the dull, gray little figure of Joseph Stalin, like a symbol of the difficult, ruthless, unscrupulous ascent of a new class to its final power.

After Stalin came what had to come if the new class was to grow in maturity: mediocrity. The so-called collective leadership and that "man of the people," Nikita Khrushchev, to all appearances kind-hearted and nonintellectual. The new class no longer needed revolutionaries or dogmaticians to the same degree. It was satisfied with simple personalities such as Khrushchev, Malenkov, Bulganin, and Shepilov, men whose every word projected the average man. This was a class weary of dogmatic purges and training sessions. It wanted to live in peace. It had to defend itself from its own leader once it felt strong enough to do so. For it changed while Stalin remained just what he had been when the class was truly new and weak, and cruel methods were necessary even against people from its own ranks who were wavering or who seemed capable of wavering. To come into being, the new class needed a person like Stalin, with his theories about the intensification of "class warfare" even after the "victory of socialism." But after Stalin, this was a bit too much. While not disowning anything it had brought into being under Stalin's leadership, the new class now disowned his reign in the earlier years, and only that. No, not even his reign, only his methods which had so traumatized this class or, in Khrushchev's words, "good Communists."

The revolutionary era of Lenin was succeeded by the era of Stalin with its consolidation of power and ownership, meaning industrialization, all with the object of letting the new class get on with its life, that so ardently desired life of tranquillity and small pleasures. Lenin's revolutionary communism was exchanged for Stalin's dogmatic communism, and this in turn was replaced by undogmatic communism, the so-called collective leadership—a group of oligarchs.

Here were three phases in the development of the new class in the USSR, under Russian communism. And in the development of every other communism, one way or another.

It was the fate of Yugoslav communism to unite these three phases in the single personality of Tito, combined with the national and the personal. Tito was a great revolutionary but lacking in original ideas. He attained personal power without Stalin's morbid distrustfulness or dogmatism. Like Khrushchev, Tito represented "the people"—that is, the middle Party strata. The road traveled by Yugoslav communism in carrying out a revolution was at first a carbon copy of Stalinism, then a renunciation of Stalinism while seeking its own path, and this road was reflected best in Tito. He was always consistent, more consistent than anybody else, in keeping the essence of communism and not rejecting any form that might be of use.

The three stages in the evolution of a new class—Lenin, Stalin, and "collective leadership"—were not completely divorced from one another, in either substance or ideas.

Lenin was a dogmatist, too, and Stalin was a revolutionary, just as the "collective leadership" resorted to both dogmatic and revolutionary methods if they had any use. What is more, the nondogmatism of the collective leadership referred only to it, to the top leaders of the new class. The people at large were obliged to be all the more stubbornly "reeducated" in the spirit of dogma, of Marxism-Leninism. By relaxing its dogmatic severity and exclusiveness, the new class, now economically strong, had prospects of acquiring even more elasticity and practicality.

The heroic epoch of communism had passed. The epoch of its great leaders had ended. The epoch of practical men had commenced. A new class had been created. It was at the height of its power and wealth, but it was without new ideas. It had nothing more to say to the world. The only thing remaining was to explain it.

When we consider today's communism we actually are considering a new class of owners and exploiters and not just a passing spasm of arbitrary, bureaucratic dictatorship. It would not be especially important to affirm this fact if certain anti-Stalinist Communists and some social democrats, including Trotsky, had not presented this ruling stratum as but a passing phenomenon. The new society, went their argument, had to learn to crawl before it could walk. Every embryonic, "ideal," classless society had to suffer in swaddling clothes under its own bureaucracy. Wasn't the bourgeoisie subjected to growing pains under the despotic reigns of a Cromwell or a Napoleon?

We indeed are talking about a new class, with the emphasis on "new." This was a deeper, more stable phenomenon than any "passing spasm." That it was a special—new—class with a special kind of property and special power does not mean, however, that it was not a class. On the contrary.

By any scientific definition of "class," even the Marxist one, according to which classes are ranked by their place in the production process, we can only conclude that a new class existed in the USSR and the other Communist countries. A class of owners and exploiters. This is not to say that this class was identical with other ruling classes throughout history, nor that it was eternal, only that we are not talking about the short-lived caprice of this or that bureaucratic magnate, who by some chance concurrence of circumstances has grabbed power during a revolution.

The special feature of this class was its collective ownership. Communist theoreticians stated, some even believed, that only under communism had this kind of ownership appeared.

In various forms, collective ownership existed in all previous social formations. All the ancient, Eastern despotisms were based on the predominance of state ("imperial") property.

In ancient Egypt, only after the fifteenth century B.C. did arable lands pass to private ownership, while before that time just the houses and farmsteads were individually owned. It was state land that was given over to tillage (exceptionally, it was made imperial property); it was state officials who administered it and collected taxes on it. Canals and plumbing installations, also the more important public works, were state-owned. State property was the dominant form of ownership until Egypt lost its independence in the first century B.C.

If this array of facts is disregarded, we cannot fully explain the deification of Egypt's pharaohs, that is to say, the emperors whose sort one encounters in all the ancient Eastern despotisms. Nor can one understand completely the undertaking of gigantic public works—construction of temples, imperial tombs and palaces, canals, roads, and fortifications.

Rome treated new conquests as state property and possessed slaves in considerable numbers. The medieval church had its own collective property.

Capitalism, by its very nature, was the enemy of collective property up to the appearance of joint-stock companies. And essentially, so it remained, even though it could not prevail over the new forms of collective ownership.

What Communists managed to dream up with regard to collective ownership was not collective ownership as such but its all-embracing nature. They made the property belonging to a new class more all-embracing than had been the case in the Egypt of the pharaohs.

And that is all.

Ownership by the new class, like its character, was not an instantaneous formation but took place over a long period of time and underwent constant change. At first the nation itself, or rather one part of it, for the sake of industrial transformation felt the need to surrender all economic powers into the hands of a political Party. The Party, in the form of the "vanguard of the proletariat" and "the most enlightened force of socialism," pressed for this centralization, which could be attained only by a change in ownership. The actual change was formally carried out by nationalizing, first the big enterprises, then the little ones. Elimination of private property was the prerequisite for both industrialization and the rise of a new class. However, without their special role as society's managers with the right to dispose of property, the Communists could not have converted themselves into a new class nor could this class have been formed and have taken root as something permanent. Little by little, material goods formally became national goods, and in very fact, through the right of *usus, fructus,* and *abusus* they became the property of a particular stratum within the Party and within the bureaucracy that collected around it.

The fact that this was a relatively slow process might help the illusion take root that under communism we are not talking about the property of a new class but about the property of society, of the nation as a whole.

Once the Party bureaucracy realized how important ownership was for its power and had taken a sweet bite of property, it could not help but continue extending its ownership over small producers. Further, because of its totalitarianism and monopolism having found itself in a state of hostility with every form of property that it did not administer and that it did not dispose of, the new class was quite consciously inclined to wipe out these forms of property, to take them over as its own.

Stalin, on the eve of collectivization, exclaimed that the question had arisen of "who will do what to whom,"[6] even though the Soviet government was not seriously threatened by any danger from a politically and economically disunited peasantry. But the new class felt insecure as long as there were any other owners of property besides itself. It dared not risk sabotage in the food supply or in agricultural raw materials. That was the immediate justification for its attack on the peasantry. But there was another reason, the class reason: The peasants could, in an unstable situation, have posed a threat to the new class. Through the collective farms and the machine-tractor stations the new class was obliged to subordinate the peasantry economically and administratively. That accounted for the elemental growth of the new class in the villages themselves, where the bureaucracy simply mushroomed.

Although seizing property from other classes, especially from the small owners, oftentimes led to a fall in production and to chaos in the economy, for the new class this was of small consequence. What was most important—as for every property owner throughout history—was to get its hands on private property and then to hang on to it. New property was worth acquiring even if the nation lost thereby. Collectivization of village property, which as we all know was economically unjustified, was inescapable if the new class was to be invested with power and ownership.

It cannot be said that per-hectare yields either increased or decreased in the USSR by comparison with Tsarist Russia; no reliable figures exist. Yields were low in any case. Yugoslav economists calculated—during the confrontation with the USSR, of course—that in fertile Ukraine, wheat yields amounted to only about one thousand kilograms per hectare. The number of cattle and livestock, according to various authorities (including Watson), in the course of collectivization fell by more than 50 percent, approximately, and even today has not climbed back to what it was in backward Tsarist Russia.

But even if these losses could be calculated, the losses in people, in the millions of peasants thrown into labor camps, are incalculable. Collectivization was a terrible, devastating war, a madman's insane undertaking, if one overlooks the fact that it profited the new class by assuring its supremacy.

By various methods—nationalization, compulsory collaboration, high taxes, market inequalities—private property, once destroyed, was transformed into "collective" property belonging to the new class, regardless of whether foreign labor was used or whether there were economic reasons for it.

The appearance of the new class, of ownership by it, was, of course, evident in a change in psychology and lifestyle, as also in the material situation of its adherents, depending on the position they occupied on the hierarchical ladder. Special quarters and closed rest and recreation areas were set up for the highest bureaucracy, the elite of the new class. The Party secretary and Secret Police chief in some places became not just the ultimate authority but also people who had the best housing, the best automobiles, the best everything. State budgets, "gifts," construction and reconstruction ostensibly to meet the needs of the state and its representatives—all became a permanent, inexhaustible boon for the political bureaucracy.

Only in cases where the new class was incapable of maintaining available property, or where such ownership came too dear and posed a political danger, were concessions made to other strata, were other forms of ownership devised. For example, it made sense to abandon collectivization in Yugoslavia because the peasants were resisting it and there was a steady fall in output, which presented a latent danger to the regime. But the new class never, anywhere, gave up its right to seize abandoned property in such cases, or in other words to finish the process of collectivizing.

The new class could not renounce this right without forgoing what it in fact possessed, a totalitarian monopoly.

No bureaucracy, however, could ever have been so tenacious in pursuing its purposes and aims. Only those engaged in opening a path toward new forms of ownership and new forms of production were capable of being so consistently stubborn.

Marx foresaw that the proletariat after its victory would be exposed to danger from the deposed classes and from its own bureaucracy. Whenever Communists, especially Yugoslav Communists, criticized Stalin's management and bureaucratic methods, they generally appealed to this idea of Marx's. However, what happened in communism had very little to do with Marx and certainly not with the position he took on this question. He was thinking of the danger lurking in any increase in a parasitic bureaucracy, which indeed did exist under communism, but Marx was scarcely thinking of modern Communist potentates, who disposed of material goods only on behalf of their narrow Communist caste and not at all in the interests of the bureaucracy as a whole. Here Marx was serving Communists only as a convenient excuse to criticize the extravagant tastes of individual layers of the new class or else to criticize slovenly administration.

It was not a question, therefore, only of bureaucratic self-will, perversions, and depravity—though the Communist regimes offered an abundance of these things, even more than other governments—but about the appropriation exclusively for Communists of the right to administer and distribute the national wealth. This was what really constituted the core of the new class of owners; it was this on which their totalitarianism was based.

Communism was not only a Party of a certain type or the bureaucratism that springs from a monopoly on property. Nor was it the state's excessive involvement in the economy. Communism consisted above all of a new class of owners and exploiters.

Not a single class has ever arisen of its own accord, even when its ascent is the result of an organized, conscious struggle. This holds good generally for the new Communist class, with the exception of some special features.

The new class, because it was quite weak economically and socially and of necessity began in a single Party, was compelled to establish the most rigorous organizational structure possible and to think through its public statements with extreme care. It was therefore more class-conscious and more highly organized than any class in recorded history.

This proposition is true if understood relative to the outside world, to other classes, parties, and social forces. Not one class in history was so cohesive and single-minded in defending itself or in making itself the complete master of what it held in common—collective and monopolistic property and totalitarian power.

However, this was a class greatly burdened with delusions and very little aware of itself as a class with new and special features. Every private capitalist or feudal lord was conscious of belonging to a separate and distinct social bracket, and as a general rule every one of them was convinced that his kind had been given the role of making the human race happy and that without such people chaos and universal ruin would ensue.

Likewise a Communist belonging to the new class believed that without his Party human society would regress and go down in ruin. Yet he was not at the same time aware of belonging to a new ownership class, did not feel himself to be an owner, regardless of whatever material privileges he enjoyed. The moment he parted company with this class, of course, his privileges vanished as if they had never been. What he thought he belonged to was a group with prescribed ideas and aims, with a prescribed mentality and role to play. And that was all there was to it. He could not see himself as belonging at the same time to a particular social category, a class of owners. Collective ownership, which acts to reduce and compress the class, at the same time acts to make it unaware of its class essence. Each member of the class taken individually was obsessed by the notion that he belonged uniquely to a movement devoted to doing away entirely with a class society.

A comparison of the remaining characteristics of the new class with those of other ownership classes reveals many similarities, together with some major differences.

The new class was insatiably greedy, just as the bourgeoisie was, but there was none of the bourgeois frugality and economy. The new class was as compact and exclusive as the aristocracy was, but there was none of the aristocracy's spiritual sophistication and proud chivalry.

But the new class did have advantages over other classes. Being more compact than any other class, it was more prepared for greater sacrifices and heroic achievements. The individual was subordinated to the whole down to the last atom in his being—at least such was the ideal, even though that individual was grabbing everything for himself and climbing higher by hook or by crook. There was plenty of arrogance to go around, but also plenty of devotion to the collective. Like no other class before it, the new class was capable of carrying out material and other ventures, and for this there existed material and other conditions. Possessing all the goods of the nation, it could measure up religiously to the goals it had set for itself and could direct all the forces of the people to their furtherance.

The new ownership did not coincide entirely with the government, but it was created and aided by that government. The use, enjoyment, and disposal of property was above all the province of the Party and the Party's top people.

Pushiness, duplicity, toadyism, and jealousy unavoidably grew with the feeling that power to dispose of the nation's wealth brought in its wake all the blessings of this world. Careerism and an ever-expanding bureaucracy were the incurable diseases of communism. Precisely because Communists turned themselves into owners and there was no other road to power and material blessings than "devotion" to the Party—to the class, to "socialism," and to "property"—unscrupulous pushiness had to become one of the fundamental pathways along which communism got ahead.

Careerism and aggressive pushiness in the non-Communist systems were signs that it paid more to be a bureaucrat, or signs that the owners themselves had become parasites and that property management was being left in the hands of employees. Under communism these same vices were a sign of the irresistible drive toward ownership itself and the privileges conferred by managing it, managing people.

Just as being a member of other ownership classes was not identical with possessing a particular property, so under communism was this even less the case, given that property was collective. To be an owner or joint owner under communism meant to have entered the ranks of the ruling political bureaucracy and nothing more than this.

Here as elsewhere, some individuals were always falling by the wayside while others went up the ladder. In private-ownership classes, one left one's property to descendants, but here no one inherited anything essential save the aspiration to climb another rung. The new class was in fact formed out of the lowest, broadest strata of the people and was constantly in motion. Although sociologists, as we said earlier, might be in a position to determine who exactly belonged to the new class, as a practical matter this was harder to do than with any other class because this one was always "melting away," spilling over into the population as a whole, into other, lower classes. There was constant turnover.

The road to the top was open to all, in theory, just as every one of Napoleon's soldiers carried a marshal's baton in his knapsack, although only a few succeeded in grasping that baton. The sole criterion here was a real, sincere, deep, many-sided loyalty to the Party, to the new class. But such loyalty was the very hardest thing to have. Open at the bottom, toward the top this class grew mercilessly narrow. Not only was the desire to climb necessary, one also had to have a talent for grasping doctrine and developing it, one had to be decisive when struggling with antagonists, one had to be exceptionally agile and resourceful when fighting intraparty battles. Skill and a gift for consolidating one's class were demanded. Many were called, few chosen. More open in some ways than earlier ownership classes, this new class was at the same time more closed than they. And since one of its most basic features was the monopoly of power, its exclusiveness was made stronger by bureaucratic, hierarchical prejudices.

Perhaps nowhere at any time had the gate been so wide open to the true believer as under communism. But similarly the ascent to the heights had never, anywhere, been more difficult or demanded so much self-denial and so many sacrifices. Communism was open and helpful to everyone. But when it was a matter of its own followers, on the other hand, communism was exclusive and intolerant.

To say that there was a new ownership class in the Communist countries may not explain everything, but this was the key to understanding the changes that periodically took place there, the USSR in particular.

It hardly need be said that any such change must be analyzed on its own if one wishes to know its probable scope and to understand what it meant in the specific circumstances. Before this can be done, however, the system has to be grasped fairly well as a whole.

In the 1950s the USSR was seeing some change. What exactly was happening on the *kolkhozes* (collective farms)? The original organization of these farms together with governmental policy toward them threw into greater relief than anything else the exploitative nature of the new class.

Stalin did not regard, nor did Khrushchev, the collective farms as a "consistently socialist" form of ownership. As a practical matter, this signified that the new class had not quite managed to prevail in the villages. Such was the case. It had used the *kolkhoz* to enserf the peasantry; through this vehicle it managed to grab a share—and the lion's share, at that—of the peasant's income by means of forced deliveries; but these did not make it sole lord and master on the land. Stalin was quite aware of this before his death. In *Economic Problems of Socialism in the USSR* he predicted that the collective farm would have to become state property, which is to say that the bureaucracy should become the owner-in-fact. Khrushchev, while blaming Stalin for his excesses in the purges, did not repudiate Stalin's views on collective farm ownership. About thirty thousand Party workers were dispatched to these farms under the new regime, the majority being sent to be *kolkhoz* chairmen. This was only one of the measures taken in line with Stalin's prognosis.

Just as once under Stalin, the new class under this regime, while putting into effect what was called "liberalization," was simultaneously seeking to extend its own, "socialist," ownership. Decentralization in the economy did not betoken a change in ownership but merely the extension of greater rights over the disposition of their property to the lower levels of this class. If the policies of liberalizing and decentralizing were to have carried any other meaning they would have shown up as a political right, if not of the people as a whole, then a part of the people; they would have had some influence on the disposition of material goods. People would at least have had the right to criticize the oligarchy's arbitrariness. In practical terms that would lead to the creation of a new political movement, if only a loyal opposition. Not a word was spoken about this. Nor even about Party democracy. Liberalization and decentralization held good only for Communists, first for the oligarchy, the leaders of the new class, and then for the lower echelons. Given changed conditions, there had to be a new way of further consolidating and strengthening the monopolistic ownership of the new class and its totalitarian supremacy.

The fact that in the Communist countries there was a new class of owners, monopolistic and totalitarian, meant that any changes occurring at the initiative of Communist leaders were dictated above all by the interests and motives of that class itself. Such changes should not be underestimated. But only after first perceiving their substance can we then determine their scope and meaning.

Like every social group the new class, too, lived and reacted, defended itself, and made advances, always with the aim of strengthening its power. This did not mean that change had no significance for the rest of the world or even for the new class itself. But no change was capable of sapping the essence of the Communist system, let alone altering it.

Like other regimes, this one, too, had to take into account mood shifts within the masses. Communists were unable to observe, however, the real state of affairs there because of the exclusive nature of the Communist Party and the absence of free public opinion in its ranks. Nevertheless, protest from the masses did penetrate up to the top ranks. Despite its totalitarian preeminence, the new class was not totally immune to opposition.

Once in power, Communists had no problem settling accounts with the urban middle class and the owners of large estates, whether because the historical development itself was hostile to these and their property, or because it was not hard to turn the masses against them. Taking away their property from these classes was quite easy. The difficulties arose when small properties were taken away. But, having acquired power in the course of earlier expropriations, Communists could do this as well. Who was who rapidly became quite clear; the old classes and old owners were no more; society was "classless" or on the road to becoming such; and people started to live in a new way.

Under such conditions, any demands to return to the old, prerevolutionary relationships seemed unrealistic if not ludicrous, because the material and social bases for those relationships no longer existed. Communists dealt with demands like these, in the end, as if they were a joke.

But some demands the new class seemed to treat more seriously, and these were demands for freedom. Not for freedom in general, only for political freedom. Not freedoms for those seeking a return to the earlier status quo but a return to freedom of opinion, freedom to criticize within the framework of relationships now prevailing, within the framework of "socialism." These the new class was highly sensitive to, a sensitivity originating in its special situation.

Instinctively, the new class felt that the national wealth was in fact its own property and that the very term "property" was an everyday legal function, whether called "socialist," "social," or "state" property. So it was constantly on the lookout for any possible breach in its totalitarian supremacy, as imperiling its property. Hence the new class resisted any kind of freedom, allegedly so as to preserve the sanctity of "socialist" ownership. And the other way around: Criticism of its management habits generated fear that it might lose power. To the degree that such criticism mounted, to the same degree the new class grew more sensitive. It did not like demands that would lead to its exposure as essentially a ruling class of propertyholders.

Here we see that the new class was entangled in a basic, even crucial, contradiction: In a legal sense, property was social, national, but in point of fact it was controlled by one group in its own interest. Not only did this discrepancy between the legal and the actual constantly make for a state of unclarity and abnormality, but it was always putting the top rulers in the position of seeing their words fail to correspond to their deeds. Any measure they might undertake, in the last analysis, only added to the strength of existing property and political relations.

This contradiction could not be resolved without jeopardizing the position of the new class.

Other ruling, property-owning classes could not solve the contradiction either, before being forcibly deprived of their monopoly of power and property. In other words, the more freedom there was anywhere, the more the ownership classes were forced into surrendering their monopoly over property, one way or another. And vice versa: Where such a monopoly was not possible, some degree of freedom was inevitable.

Under communism, political power and ownership were almost always in one and the same hands. But this fact was concealed under a legal guise. Under classical capitalism, in the eyes of the law the worker enjoyed legal rights equal to those of the capitalist, whereas in material terms the one was exploited and the other did the exploiting. Here, on the contrary, it was with regard to material goods that all were equal before the law, the formal owner being the nation. Whereas in reality, through its monopoly of administration, a single, thin layer of managers enjoyed ownership.

Every real demand for freedom under communism, the kind of insistence that strikes at the heart of this system, boiled down to a cry that the real material and property relationships be reconciled with those that met purely legal requirements.

It would not be enough to cry out for empty freedom. At the same time, those who did demand freedom had to insist that the capital goods produced by the nation be managed by the nation. That at least would be more efficient than management by some private monopoly or private owner. They had also to insist that this could only be carried out by society's freely elected representatives. Then the issue would squarely be joined and the new class driven either to make concessions to other "forces" or to take off the mask and reveal its true face, the face of owners and exploiters. Ownership and exploitation were made possible by political power, which brought with it the privilege of management, but such was their nature that they had to be repudiated in words. Did not the new class itself stress that it used its political power, its management functions, in the name of the nation as a whole with the aim of safeguarding national property?

Even apart from such considerations, the contradiction we have pointed to was the source of great internal difficulties for the new class, for it made its legal position problematic. The problem was that a disparity was constantly being brought into the open between word and deed. While promising to abolish social distinctions, the new class found itself always enlarging them, always appropriating the labor of others without justification, always empowering its own adherents. The new class was obliged to staunchly uphold a dogma according to which its historic role, its world mission, was to "finally" emancipate the human race from all calamities and misfortunes. But in practice it behaved completely the opposite.

This contradiction between legal position and actual ownership position potentially provided a good basis for criticism, one capable of inciting the population and capable at the same time of corroding the new class itself, inasmuch as one, thin layer of that class in fact enjoyed all its privileges. If the contradiction had grown and intensified there might have been prospects for a real change in communism, with or without the assent of its ruling class. Only because the contradiction was so obvious did the new class carry out any changes at all in the direction of so-called liberalization and decentralization.

Forced to retreat and make concessions to individual substrata, the new class aimed at papering over a difficult situation and fortifying its own position. With its property and power intact, any measure, however democratically motivated it might be, tended to strengthen the rule of the political bureaucracy. The system itself was such that it created real possibilities out of democratic measures but thereby deflected them into measures for consolidating the ruling class. Thus did slavery, so prevalent in the ancient Orient, replicate itself in every nook and cranny of those societies, including family life. In the same way, the authoritarian tendencies of the ruling class under communism thrust their way into every aspect of social life, even when this was far from the intention of the top leaders.

In Yugoslavia we invented what we called workers' management and self-management. At the time of our altercation with Soviet imperialism it was a far-reaching, democratic measure holding the potential of depriving the Party itself of its monopoly on management. Workers' self-management, however, was gradually reduced to but one of the many aspects of Party work, impotent even to give the existing system a mild shake, let alone change it. We cherished a notion that workers' self-management would give rise to a new democracy of some kind. No such dream could ever have come to pass, though, since freedom cannot be reduced to a bigger piece of bread. But workers' management did not even lead to any essential participation in the division of profits, be it on the national level or within individual enterprises. Such management was increasingly squeezed into safe limits. Through various taxes and other channels the regime siphoned off even the share of profit that the workers had earned in hopes that it would be given to them. Workers were left with crumbs. Crumbs and illusions. In the absence of general freedom not even workers' management could become free. We saw confirmation that in an unfree society no one can freely decide a thing. When freedom is bestowed, the bestowers get the greatest use out of it.

None of this means that the new class could not make concessions to the people, even though its eyes were focused on its own interests. Workers' management, decentralization—these things meant conceding to the masses. Circumstances could drive the new class, no matter how monopolistic and totalitarian it might be, to retreat before mass pressure. In the year 1948, even though Yugoslavia and the USSR had already had their face-off, our leaders felt compelled to carry out a string of reforms. But they stopped right there. They started reforming and even took a step backward as soon as they believed themselves to be in jeopardy. But then they stopped in their tracks. Something like this is happening today in Eastern Europe.

In defending its supremacy, the ruling class needed to switch into a reform mode whenever it became too obvious that it was treating the formal property of the nation as its own. Its motives, need we say, did not appear as such but were billed as "the further development of socialism" or the evolution of "socialist democracy." A basis for reforms was laid when the discrepancy discussed above broke into the open. Looked at historically, the new class was always being forced to consolidate itself in power and property while running away from the truth. It felt compelled to keep showing how successful it was in creating a society of equals under the law, happy people freed of every form of exploitation. But the new class could not keep itself from falling into profound, internal contradictions. Its historical origins rendered it incapable of legalizing its property. But at the same time neither could it relinquish its property, for to do so would be to undermine its legitimacy. It was forced to justify its ever more complete rule by invoking ever more abstract and unreal goals.

True, this was a class whose power over people was the most complete known to history. For that very reason it was a class of extremely limited views with false, shaky horizons. Ingrown, totally supreme, the new class had only unrealistic grounds on which to size up its own role and form an estimate of its surroundings.

Having carried out industrialization and so responsible for the national rebirth (that being unavoidable), the new class had nothing more in view but to go on strengthening itself through brute force and plundering the people. It ceased to create. Lying inevitably become its main weapon. It lived in a kingdom of darkness and ice.

It was a very great exploit to accomplish a revolution. The dominion of this new class, though, was one of the most shameful pages in human history. People will wonder at the grandiose projects it executed and will be ashamed of the means chosen to carry them out.

When the new class departs the historical scene, as depart it must, there will be less regret over its passing than for any class before it. Smothering everything but what touches its own self-interest, the new class has doomed itself to grief and a shameful death.

LEADERS

ON LEADERS GENERALLY

Communist leaders are no different from other leaders, essentially. All leaders are hungry for power, and they all get upset when they lose it. We are of course dealing here with real political leaders and not with unscrupulous bandits such as Bokassa or Idi Amin, men who have seized power by chance. True leaders, be they Communist or non-Communist, in their love of power share the motivation of doing something great for their people or for humanity. More exactly, while wanting to change the course of history, at the same time and no less ardently they desire to ensure themselves a special, lasting place in that history. Is this not one aspect of the general human thirst (nature has not endowed other beings with this capability) to prolong one's existence into eternity, or at least the "eternity" that is human and historical? It is a thirst worth enormous effort and boundless sacrifice. Such unsparing efforts, however, are hardly selective when it comes to the means of slaking that thirst. On the contrary, no moral consideration whatever raises a barrier to accomplishing "something great," in the sense of one's place in history; after all, one's rivals stop at nothing, either. A person becomes particular as to means and considers questions of morality only if social conscience and the organization of society force him into it—that is, if to transgress them were to disrupt and interfere with his ascent as a leader.

Non-Communist leaders—I have in mind leaders in democratic countries who are capable of reining themselves in when they find themselves in transports of power hunger—are realists and pragmatists more or less aware of the parameters of action.

It is quite implausible to assume that Churchill, for example, and De Gaulle were not autocratic, not to say dictatorial, in their intellectual and psychological makeup. Their nature, however, did not diminish their value, their greatness. On the contrary, without such traits of character they would not have been what they were—would not have altered the course of political history, would not have merited a place of their own in it. It was precisely because they were quite aware of the conditions in which they were operating that they were able to restrain themselves. Aware of their value and the role they had already played, they withdrew from the political/historical scene with dignity and without resentment.

While I was in power, and afterward even more (through television), I would notice how certain foreign statesmen, including those from democratic states who held political views contrary to Tito's, looked upon his omnipotence with stifled envy. This was still more striking when it came to the servile degradation and imperial luxury that always accompanied and surrounded him. Here, of course, I am not thinking of such men as Churchill and De Gaulle, statesmen conscious of the transience of fame during one's lifetime, aware that their work was going to endure, sensible of their own inner, real value. The envy to which I allude, particularly on the part of Westerners, was all too obvious during Tito's funeral in 1980. Tito, of course, had been a leader of many years' standing who positioned Yugoslavia between the two power blocs while fostering good relations with each, and this perhaps accounted for the unprecedented number and high esteem of those in attendance. The envy I could see, however, lay in their immoderate eulogies, eulogies that were contrary to Tito's ideas and that were moreover blind and deaf to the bad sides of his rule and his personality.

It never crossed a single Communist leader's mind—I am speaking of true leaders who broke through to the summit of power by their own intellect and energy—to step down from power, even though he had already played out his historical role to the end. True, no political or other circumstances compel such behavior. Once having reached power and having consolidated it, consolidated the political organization that has made power possible, such a leader slyly and systematically adjusts these factors to sustain him in such a way that *nothing* will undermine and *everything* will contribute to the ongoing consolidation and perpetuation of his place in history.

It is not easy to become a leader, just as it is not easy to become an artist or a scholar. If it were easy, there would be no leaders. Without leaders the world might sometimes be more happy, but it might also grind to a halt and turn gray. The world might also abandon itself to evil, demonic leaders. Without multiplying instances, there are two in the recent past who are quite infamous.

It is incomparably harder to become a leader under communism (or fascism, for that matter) than in a democracy. In a democracy one has to get elected through talent and skill and by plausible promises of change for the better, if not through victory in war. All that, more or less, is also necessary under communism. With the crucial difference that under communism one must be elected to leadership in the Party in the face of the guardians of ideological and statutory tradition and in the face of innovators. These latter are frequently more eloquent and better versed in adapting dogmas to their own visions. The Communist leader, to become such, must change relationships in a Party where ways of living and working are operating smoothly and set in stone. He must revise—most often convinced that he alone can faithfully defend and interpret them—the relevant propositions of an already adopted, hallowed dogma.

Such obstacles had to be overcome by every true Communist leader, of course in ways that varied by the conditions and the persons involved.

Marx never succeeded in becoming the absolute leader of his political movement (the so-called First International). His undefeated and unbeatable opponent was the popular, passionate Bakunin.[1] Nor did Marx overcome Blanquism[2] or Proudhonism.[3] During the first great, tragic appearance of a "dictatorship of the proletariat," at the time of the Paris Commune in 1871, Marx's followers played a secondary role.

But in socialist (Communist) teaching, Marx was without peer. He was the most convincingly learned. With time, after his death and within the socialist movements, Marx was understood to be the Messiah, the unquestioned prophet of an inevitable "happy new world." His doctrines reigned in the socialist and Communist movements of Europe, and after the October Revolution of 1917 they spread abruptly across the whole world.

Lenin, before ever coming to power (and afterward, in milder form) had to wage a stubborn struggle which was not particularly principled within his own Party against adversaries enjoying greater theoretical respect (Plekhanov,[4] Martov[5]). Often his opponents enjoyed more influence, too. Lenin's object was to single out within social democracy generally a Bolshevik faction of his own. This was to be a Party based on new principles, *a Party of a new type,* a Party that would serve as an instrument of totalitarian power and as a tool for transforming society into a "classless" one. The initial structure of that Party contains in embryonic form what was already present in the form of an idea: The "professional revolutionaries"—that is, the professional, leading apparatus—embodied the future new class.

And so if Marx, to develop his original teaching, had to revise Hegel[6]—"to stand him on his feet from having been on his head," in the process replacing utopian socialism with "scientific" socialism, Lenin then revised Marx in his turn by developing the revolutionary side of his teaching. That is where Lenin exhibited the highest degree of originality. Suppressing or slighting the humanistic side of Marx and thereby abandoning even the idea of democratic socialism and social democracy, Lenin expanded his own Party and his own ideology. A Communist International (Comintern) was set up, as opposed to a Socialist International. Herein lay Lenin's significance for history, for the world.

But it was really Stalin who took the trouble to seize absolute power. His opponents, to name only Trotsky and Bukharin, excelled Stalin in their role in the Revolution. They excelled him in general culture, in their eloquence, in their fruitful gift with the pen, and chiefly in their deep knowledge of Marx's and Lenin's teachings. Above all, these adversaries made use of the so-called Lenin Testament, wherein Lenin described Stalin as unfit for Party leadership because of his crudity.

In history a personality so cautious, so patient in making his way to the apogee of power is scarcely to be found, not to speak of possessing, from the very start, so infallible a feeling for the springs and levers of power. And Stalin was working within a faceless, young, ever-more-numerous Party apparatus greedy for privilege. If no one took note of the potential for absolute rule, no one had any suspicion either of the terrible future tyrant. At that time of bitter, factional struggles, in the middle of the 1920s, Stalin was criticized by his adversaries for being too soft and for defending the peasants. Those were the same peasants whom he would a few years later decimate with deportations, whose traditional economic structures he would destroy, whom he would collectivize by force.

One might have expected this incomparable, infallible realist, whose power was no longer in question and who reigned over a consolidated system, a ruler who had been victorious in the greatest and most horrible of wars—one might have expected some moderation in his terror, some imposition of reasonable limits on what had been excess. But it turned out otherwise: The terror spread and intensified. The pursuit of ideological goals had to continue, and for Stalin this was unthinkable without a comprehensive strengthening of the terror and in it of his bloody, brilliant role. In the final years of Stalin's rule we saw a feeble, lonely, suspicious old man, still insanely hanging on to his personal power and his artificial bureaucratic empire.

Nor did Mao climb to power without noise and turbulence, not to mention campaigning against a domestic enemy and various warlords in the course of twenty-two years. Mao enjoyed one advantage, which was China's separateness in communications and culture. At the decisive moment he got rid of (in fact, he arrested) the pro-Moscow Central Committee, thereby literally saving his Revolution and leading it to victory. Mao cared not a fig for the wise advice of Moscow and Stalin, and certainly did not take it.

Mao once remarked that the Chinese Party too had not been spared transformation into a privileged layer, into a *new class*. But instead of seeking a way out in total liberation of the economy and in the democratization of political institutions, he abused his authority by inflating the foolish, so-called Cultural Revolution into a popular frenzy with himself as its leader and by puffing up his "Little Red Book" into an irrational codification of dogma. (This was a kind of Chinese Communist prayer book composed of Mao's—for the most part banal and trite—dogmatic maxims.)

Tito underwent difficulty before becoming a Communist, perhaps great difficulty. He came from a large, poor family with many children and was expected to take up the locksmith's trade, but he hungered for and felt himself capable of a more sublime and exalted role. Making his way from workshop to workshop through German-speaking lands, he learned to speak German (as he would later learn to speak Russian while being held as a POW in Russia), neither correctly nor bookishly, but enviably, and enough for a self-taught man. He was attracted by

Social Democrats and trade unions, but not so much as to ignite his ambitions. The workers' bureaucracy held him firmly in its impenetrable layers and determined his functions. Tito intended, sometimes even began, to climb the military hierarchy but was wounded in World War I and captured on the Russian Front. There he became caught up in the Russian Revolution and communism. No higher education was required, and indeed he suited the Communists because he was from a lower class.

Upon his return from captivity to Yugoslavia, again Tito passed through the revolving door of workshops, but now it happened because he was thrown out for his activities as a Communist. At this point Tito stood out for his quick resourcefulness and energetic activity, but he was not known for any originality or innovativeness in the Party until factionalist struggles among prominent leaders threatened its existence as a united organization. By 1928, Tito had worked his way up to be head of the Zagreb organization, but was otherwise little known within the Party. He now came out with a demand for purging the Party of factions, for making it monolithic. This happened just when Stalin was forcing his own faction on the Party and identifying the Party with it.

The authorities quickly sent Tito off to five years at hard labor. In 1934 he found himself in Moscow. There the top leaders among the émigré Communists were plagued by factional bickering, very often unprincipled. Wisely, Tito stood to one side, obediently loyal to the Stalinized Comintern.

So when, in 1937–38, Moscow through arrests purged the Yugoslav and other émigré top leadership, and Tito himself was threatened, the Comintern put him at the head of the Party with the right of veto. This right of veto he skillfully and unwaveringly maintained to the end of his life, when both the Comintern and Stalin had long since ceased to exist.

A patriotic revolt against the forces of occupation in Yugoslavia was raised by the Communists led by Tito. To everyone's misfortune the revolt quickly became entangled in a civil war. This revolt did assist the Soviet peoples in their mortal struggle with the Nazi-Fascist attack, but it was not always and in every way to the liking of the Soviet government. Tito did not reject advice and criticism but nevertheless went his own way. How otherwise, when both his people and his Party, in still more difficult circumstances than the Soviets, were at war with a deadly enemy bent on extermination?

Such a war, and the victory that came with it, would later provide the moral and political point of departure from which Tito would muster up the courage to oppose Stalin in 1948, thereby initiating a crisis in world communism. That was a crisis in the ideology to which he had sacrificed his best years, and it continued to claim his allegiance. For Tito believed in communism, if not as a final truth, then as a means to power that could not be disregarded.

After Tito, as also after other Communist leaders, came political desolation, economic ruin, and infighting among the leaders of the national republics. It was a disastrous prelude to the national wars and today's "ethnic cleansing" in what was once Yugoslavia.

I have treated with special emphasis only those Communist leaders who revised and changed outmoded beliefs and relationships. But the movement otherwise had many talented and clever senior people.

The Bulgarian Georgi Dimitrov and the Italian Palmiro Togliatti can be numbered among those prewar leaders in at least one respect. Dimitrov may not have turned around Communist politics as it had been, but with his heroic and politically astute behavior at the Leipzig trial of 1933— a trial by which the Nazis intended to terrify the world with the Communist danger—he undoubtedly inspired and initiated an anti-Fascist partnership. That same Dimitrov, however, in the 1948 showdown turned out to be inconsistent and frightened. This was typical of Communists: brave and resourceful against an enemy, confused and faint-hearted within their own Party.

Togliatti, too, though endowed with a fine Latin intelligence, did not possess the intellectual and moral strength to set himself apart from Moscow and the Soviet model. Still, however dimly and supercautiously, he sensed the inevitability of separation from Stalinism. This would be worked out bravely and unambiguously by Berlinguer,[7] with his idea of EuroCommunism,[8] thereby rendering the largest Communist Party in the West independent and transforming it into a leftist social democracy.

Communist leaders are more absolute than the most absolute rulers of all time, but they leave no heirs. Not because they cannot find any, nor even because they cannot think of themselves as expendable, but because they simply do not want to be replaced. Megalomaniacs, they are convinced of their irreplaceability, convinced that they will endlessly endure in an endless, indestructible Party, convinced of their eternal presence in the life of the nation.

ON STALIN
STALIN'S PERSONALITY

I cannot recall any figure from history with as little in common between the public persona and the private one. No sooner did Stalin utter his first few words than all would vanish as if it had never been: that martial air, that grotesque good humor characteristic of his public photographs. ("Photographs" that were actually artistic portraits fashioned mainly from documentary films.) In place of the public figure fabricated by a propaganda office, there appeared before one a private, workaday Stalin. This Stalin was all nerves. He was intelligent and vain, but his lifestyle was modest. I was received by this man for the first time in the spring of 1944. By that point he had dressed himself up in the uniform of a marshal, never again to take it off, but that starched military dress would instantly turn into simple and everyday attire, inhabited by an unsoldierly, lively, unconventional person. Something of the sort also happened with the topics one would discuss with Stalin. The most complicated issues had a trick of metamorphosing into straightforward everyday ones.

When brought into immediate contact, one forgot all about Stalin's slyness and manipulativeness. This was so even though he made no special effort to hide such traits, regarding them as inseparable from any true politician. It even happened that he would give grotesque vent to his own sly calculations. Thus at the end of the war, after advising the Yugoslav Communists to come to terms with King Peter II, he added: "And then when you've gotten strong enough—stick a knife in his back." Leading Communists, even those from foreign parties, knew all about the man's character. At first it seemed admirable and a reason to chuckle. Afterward, though, it came to be held against him, being seen as a means of strengthening Moscow's position as the center of a world movement.

His calculation and slyness created an impression of Stalin as possessed of a cold, affectless personality. But he was in fact a man of powerful, at times easily aroused, emotions. Yet those feelings were, naturally, carefully tailored to the situation, the end he had in view. Stalin could get well wrought up if the occasion warranted, but if there was no good purpose to be served, he could not be aroused.

Stalin possessed an exceptional memory. Without fail he would recall the personalities of heroes from books or of characters from real life, even if he had forgotten their names. In a similar way he enjoyed total recall of situations in all their detail, or, say, the merits and weaknesses of states and statesmen. Often he made a fuss over seeming trifles that later usually turned out to be important. It was as though there were nothing, either in the objective world or in his own mind, that could not become important. To me, he had a better memory for bad things than for good ones. Perhaps Stalin suspected that the system he had built could not exist in any world other than a hostile one.

Essentially, he was self-taught. Not just in the sense that every gifted man is self-taught; I am talking of real, solid knowledge. Stalin moved about easily in the domain of history and in that of classical literature. He was, of course, highly conversant with current events. But one never noticed him concealing his ignorance. One never noticed him ashamed of ignorance. If it so happened that he was not abreast of something, he listened carefully while impatiently awaiting a change of topic.

A stiff, monotonous dogmatism seemed a constant feature of his public side. Ideology—Marxism as a closed, strictly prescribed system of thought—was to Stalin the spiritual basis of totalitarian power, the consecration of that power as a weapon in the hands of the classless society. He clung to Marxist doctrine, never deviating, never yielding. Stalin was no slave to Marxism: It only required that he serve the government and the Party bureaucracy, and not they him. Stalin never shrank from contradicting von Clausewitz[9] in public, even though the great German strategist was Lenin's military model. In the same way he did not hesitate to criticize the dependence of Marx and Engels[10] on German classical, idealistic philosophy. This he would do in his inner circle, and only after victory over Hitler's Germany. He certainly was aware of having blundered more than once, though he made no public mention of his failures. Thus one could hear from Stalin such expressions as "they made asses of us," referring to one or another "they." At the victory celebration he even mentioned wartime mistakes, and at the beginning of 1948 he said that the Chinese Communists, and not he, were in the right when it came to evaluating their capabilities.

One's initial impression of Stalin as a brave, clever man did not fade but rather deepened in the course of a conversation with him. This impression was strengthened by his incessant alertness. Stalin was a bundle of nerves sticking out in all directions. In his presence it was impossible to make even the most remote allusion, impossible to even change the expression of one's eyes, without his taking note.

These days serious, scholarly circles in the West see the traits of a madman in Stalin; even criminal traits are ascribed to him. I cannot subscribe to such views based on our meetings. I would only say that anyone who tears down in order to create anew, as he did a new empire, bears within a tendency toward transports of excess and devastating despair. Crazed anger and unbridled joy would come over Stalin at times. His joys could look like the fits of a buffoon. It truly would be abnormal to exterminate several generations of your comrades-in-arms and all their relations while at the same time remaining calm and confident and sure of yourself. It seems to me that any explanation of Stalin's "craziness" and "criminality" should be sought in the ideology and the order they created. The very idea of constructing any kind of society, especially one without conflicts, is at heart mythomaniacal and irrational, while an order founded on illegality is in itself criminal.

Stalin was exceedingly small. His extremities were too long by comparison with his short torso for him not to have suffered on this account. Only his head was good-looking, even handsome, with its lively expression of intelligence and common-man directness, its eyes with their yellowish cast and changing sparks. Millions he destroyed, millions died with his name on their lips, while all the time he accepted both the one and the other as a necessity. Nothing of all this could ever be noticed on his face, although it is true that he forced himself to hate the former deeply and to care fervently for the latter. The Party bureaucracy felt him to be its leader even as he hounded it and cut it to pieces. Not for one moment when I was with him did I have the impression that Stalin had ever known unalloyed joy or altruistic happiness. These were states of being that were simply outside his world. They had to be absent to allow him to identify with the idea and the movement.

I was convinced that my *Conversations with Stalin* had taken their last breath. But in this I was wrong, as in so much else besides. It was rather like my more recent hopes that after *The Unperfect Society* I would not have to bother myself anymore with "ideological questions."

Stalin, though, is a vampire still flying about the world. And he will long continue to do so. His legacy has been renounced by everyone, yet for all that, many draw strength from it. Multitudes of people take Stalin as a model, even unwittingly. Khrushchev denied him, but at the same time he worshipped him. Later Soviet leaders may not have worshipped Stalin but they warmed themselves nonetheless in his sun.

Fifteen years after breaking with Stalin, respect for his statesmanship came alive for Tito. And so I too have to ask myself whether all this pondering over Stalin is not a sign in itself that he continues to live on within me.

Who was Stalin? A great statesman? A demonic genius? A sacrifice to dogma? Or a maniac and criminal who grabbed power? Or again, what did Marxist ideology mean to him? And how did ideas serve him? What did he think of his own work? Of himself and his place in history?

These are just a few of the questions provoked by Stalin's personality. I bring them to the fore as much because they touch upon the fate of the contemporary world (especially the Communist world) as because of what I might call their broader, timeless significance.

STALIN, LENIN'S HEIR

From my meetings with Stalin, two attitudes of his keep recurring to me. The first, if I recall, was expressed in 1945; the second—of this I am sure—at the beginning of 1948.

The earlier position might be spelled out as premise and consequence: If our ideological assumptions are correct, then all the rest must follow of itself. The second point of view had to do with Marx and Engels. In conversation someone—I think it was I—underlined the living value of Marx's and Engels's worldview, to which Stalin observed, as one who had thought long on that subject and had arrived at a firm conclusion, perhaps even against his will: Yes, doubtless they were founding fathers. No doubt. But they had their shortcomings. We must not forget that Marx and Engels were too much under the powerful influence of German classical philosophy, especially Kant and Hegel. Lenin, however, was free of such influences.

At first glance, these positions do not seem especially original. Communists are well known for classifying all points of view and all behavior by how closely they coincide with sectarian belief and feasibility. They are either "correct" or "incorrect." Communists are likewise notorious extollers of Lenin as the sole defender and perpetuator of Marx's teaching. But these positions as taken by Stalin have certain features which make them not only special but also for our purposes extremely significant.

What does it mean to claim that ideology is the foundation and the condition of victory? More to the point, what did Stalin mean by it?

Didn't this contradict a basic doctrine of Marx, namely that "the economic structure of society" forms the basis of all ideas?* Does such a viewpoint not approximate, however unwittingly, philosophical idealism? Namely, that mind and ideas are primary and decisive? Stalin was clearly not taking aim at Marx's thought that "theory becomes a material force as soon as it embraces the masses" but rather at theories, or ideas, before ever they do "embrace the masses."† How is all this to be harmonized with what Bukharin, talking with Kamenev[11] in July 1928, said of Stalin: "At any given moment he will change his theories if only to get rid of somebody"?‡ And where, finally, did Stalin get his tardy, unpremeditated criticism of Marx and Engels?

Despite the flood of questions, in these assertions by Stalin there is no essential inconsistency. Further, I do not think that Bukharin's judgment about Stalin's lack of principle, even if one ignores that it was distorted in factional bickering, undermines Stalin's attribution of crucial importance to ideas.

If not the most essential, then one of the essential reasons why Stalin's adversaries in the Party—Trotsky, Bukharin, Zinoviev,[12] and others—lost the battle with him lies in the fact that he was a more original, more creative Marxist than any of them. His style had none of Trotsky's fireworks, naturally, nor in his analyses was there anything of Bukharin's thoroughgoing shrewdness. But for that very reason Stalin's statements are the rational aspect of social actuality, road signs and inspirations for the new, victorious forces. Ripped from the given reality, from the atmosphere that conditioned it, Stalin's thinking does indeed seem gray, monotonous, even feeble. But that is only the outside.

The essence of Marx's teachings is the indivisibility of theory and practice: "Philosophers have interpreted the world differently, the point is to change it."** Communism and Communists have been invincible whenever and as long as they could bring teaching into harmony with practice. But Stalin derived inconceivable force, force like that of a demon, by stubbornly and skillfully combining Marxist-Leninist teaching with power, with the strength of the state. For Stalin

---

*Karl Marx, "Preface" to "Contribution to a Criticism of Political Economy" in K. Marx and F. Engels, *Selected Works*, Vol. I (Belgrade: Kultura, 1949), p. 338.

†K. Marx and F. Engels, *Early Works* (Zagreb: Naprijed, 1967), p. 98.

‡Cited from Robert Conquest, *The Great Terror* (New York: Macmillan, 1968), p. 81.

**Marx and Engels, *Early Works*, p. 339.

was not a theoretician in the true sense of that word. He wrote and spoke only when compelled to do so by political struggle, be it within the Party or within society, or most often at the same time in both. That combination of reality and thought, that unimaginative, unreflecting pragmatism, accounts for the force and originality of Stalin's views. One might add that by overlooking or underrating this aspect of Stalin's views, by dealing formalistically with his texts, both dogmatists in the East and many conscientious students of Stalin in the West are hindered from penetrating into his personality and the conditions of his rise.

We must stress again that Stalin's views, Stalin's Marxism, never appeared apart from the needs of postrevolutionary Soviet society and the Soviet state. It was as if they didn't even exist. Such was the Marxism of a Party turning into political power out of a living need to do so; turning into a "leading," ruling power structure. Trotsky called Stalin "the most outstanding mediocrity in our Party,"* and Bukharin mocked him for being devoured by a vain hunger for renown as a theoretician.† Those are only opinions in the end, eloquent, factionalist— and unreal. Stalin's thinking was actually not theoretical in the usual sense of that word—that is, was neither studious nor analytic. But as a fusion of ideology and the needs of the Party, the Party bureaucracy as a new elite, his thinking was far more theoretical than that of any adversary. It is no accident that the Party bureaucracy lined up behind Stalin. Hitler's tirades, which today seem like the purest folly, sent millions of "sensible" Germans into ecstasy and caused them to commit themselves to lethal offensives. That, too, was no accident. Stalin did not win because he "distorted" Marxism but because he made it real. Trotsky was always showing off with his paradoxes and vain imagining of world revolution; Bukharin dug deeply into dogmatic minutiae and into turning the colonies into bourgeois models; Stalin, though, with his "as the following facts show us," identified the existence and the privileges of a transformed, newborn Party bureaucracy with industrialization and the empowering of Russia.

Like any other authentic politician and nimble administrator, Stalin borrowed other people's ideas and dressed them up to be truer to nature. His best-known initiative, "building socialism in one country"

---

*Cited in Conquest, *The Great Terror,* p. 71.
†Ibid.

(i.e., in the USSR), was a theory that originated with Bukharin and was developed by Bukharin, and in the struggle against Trotsky at that. Look at it as literary theft, look at it as unoriginality, but in politics this is the way to utilize what is possible.

No one, however, ever disputed when he was alive that Stalin was a Marxist, and a distinguished one. Nor does any sensible person deny this today. Differences continue to arise only in the weighing of his qualities as a theoretician and of his consistency as Lenin's heir.

I was just describing what seemed to me the most important of Stalin's qualities.

Taking the measure of heirs, however, is superficial and irrelevant, or so I think. Who is whose heir? And to what degree? True heirs are only those who are not endowed with visionary and creative powers. In politics, the general subject of this discussion, myths cannot be avoided, myths are everyday phenomena. But in the case at hand the issue is how to avoid treating Lenin's legacy too dogmatically and with a mouthful of quotations. Quotations can be used to prove that any one of Lenin's possible heirs was true to him; alternatively, that not a one was true to him. Only by comparing Lenin's intentions with those carried out by Stalin and with those that Stalin's adversaries proposed can we approach the truth.

Even so, we cannot avoid analyzing "Lenin's Testament," as it is called. That document played a great role in dogmatic discussion, especially discussion that was anti-Stalinist. And it continues to do so. What we call Lenin's Testament is simply a letter dictated by him after the stroke paralyzing his right arm and leg on the night of December 22, 1922. Lenin was thereafter restricted by his doctors to four minutes of dictation per day. The next day he began dictating this letter, continued it on December 25, and finished it the day after.

The December 23 portion, addressed to the Congress, proposed increasing the Central Committee by fifty to one hundred members and supported Trotsky on the question of the state plan. It was sent to Stalin, as general secretary of the Party, that very day. Judging by all the evidence, Stalin was on that account overwhelmed with suspicions that a rapprochement was taking place between Lenin and Trotsky. Over the telephone he showered Lenin's wife, Krupskaya, with oaths and threats, accusing her of jeopardizing the health of Comrade Lenin by involving him in political disputes, contrary to the advice of his physicians. It is not known whether she complained to Lenin, though this is quite plausible. The December 25 portion of his dictation stated that "Comrade Stalin, having become *gensek* [general secretary— M.D.], has gathered into his own hands unlimited power."* And ten days later, January 4, 1923, Lenin added the following note: "Stalin is too coarse and this shortcoming, tolerable enough in relations among us Communists, becomes intolerable in the position of *gensek*. I therefore propose to the comrades that they consider removing Stalin from this position and placing in it another man who in every other respect might differ from Comrade Stalin only in the one advantage [I believe this part of the sentence should read: who might in no way differ from Comrade Stalin except in one respect—M.D.], that he is more patient, more loyal, more courteous and considerate, less capricious, etc. That circumstance might appear to be an unimportant detail. But I think that from the standpoint of preventing a schism and taking into consideration what I stated above concerning the relationship between Stalin and Trotsky, this is no tiny detail. Or it is the sort of detail capable of taking on crucial significance."†

We are at once aware of the absence of Lenin's usual sharp, precise manner of expression. His Testament is everywhere equivocal and ambiguous, especially when it touches on issues of significance. Lenin obviously knows of the Stalin-Trotsky conflict; it in fact strikes him with foreboding. And yet in the first phase of his dictation, on December 23, he avoids speaking of this directly, instead proposing a palliative: He wants to raise the number of members of the Central Committee by between fifty and a hundred. (Up to then this body had consisted of twenty-seven members.) His reasons are "to increase the authority of the CC and to work seriously on Bolshevizing our apparatus and to prevent conflicts between minor segments of the CC from attaining too exaggerated an importance for all the fates of the Party. [Lenin ought to have written, probably, "for the very fate of the Party"—M.D.]"

To put it simply, it sounds naive and incomprehensible that so perspicacious a man—a man with so much political experience, a man accustomed to chipping away at the face of his Party until it looked like

---

*V. I. Lenin, *Works* (Moscow: Gosizdat, 1967), Vol. 36, p. 544.
†Ibid., pp. 545–46.

what he imagined it should look like, a man who now found himself at the head of the greatest of revolutions and the greatest of national states as well, one who had personally tasted the poisonous narcotic of "history" and power—that such a man should now see a virtual revelation and redemption "for all the fates of the Party" in an enlargement of the Central Committee. What on earth had happened to Lenin? Had his mind grown so weak that in place of principles and power, which had always been his essence, he now attributed importance to numbers? Was he really not mindful of the dialectic—the inevitability of contradiction in every phenomenon? Where was Lenin's ability to penetrate into the essence of the Stalin-Trotsky argument? It was as though he had taken fright for the first time at the sight of destruction looming over the Party he had molded and to which he had given purpose.

Nor is it clear why only in his next piece of dictation, on December 24, did Lenin mention Stalin and Trotsky and their potential disagreement. As though he had changed his mind overnight and gotten up the courage to be more candid. "Our Party," he dictated that day, "relies on two classes and on that account can become unstable. It will inevitably fall if those two classes cannot reach an agreement."* In very imprecise form, and forgetting his irreplaceable, hallowed "dictatorship of the proletariat," Lenin here grows fearful that the "union" of workers and peasants will dissolve; that's obvious. But it is just as obvious that this sentence has no good logical connection with the text that shortly follows: "I am thinking of stability as a guarantee against schism in the near future, and wish to set forth here some views of a strictly personal nature. I believe that such members of the CC as Stalin and Trotsky are very important when it comes to stability from that point of view. [What point of view?—M.D.] The relationship between them constitutes in my opinion more than half the danger of schism. This schism could be averted by, in my opinion and among other measures, raising the number of CC members by fifty to one hundred persons. [Lenin is still under the spell of yesterday's bewitchment with numbers!—M.D.] Comrade Stalin, having become *Gensek,* has gathered into his hands unlimited power and I am not convinced that he always knows how to use that power with enough care and consideration. On the other hand Comrade Trotsky, as has already been confirmed by his struggle against

---

*Lenin, *Works,* Vol. 36, p. 544.

the CC in connection with the NKPS question [Commissariat for Transport—M.D.], does not stand out just for his great abilities. Personally, he is probably the most gifted man on today's CC. But he is far too enraptured with himself, and far too preoccupied with the purely administrative side of his work.*

It did not so much as cross Lenin's mind, at least to his own self and in the hour of his dying, to explain how it could happen that under "Soviet power, a million times more democratic than the most democratic bourgeois republic,"† one man "has gathered into his own hands unlimited power." It would appear that he had taken fright not only for his Party but also for his own power, power far greater than anything his *gensek,* Stalin, then possessed. And so it is that with Lenin too we see emerging into view that well-known "human weakness" by which one identifies idea with power and power with one's own person. It is all the more apparent the more visible the "historical role" being played.

Speculation like this, though, pulls us too far away from the question as to which of his colleagues Lenin regarded as his heir. Neither Stalin nor Trotsky, that is obvious. The one was too coarse and vulgar, while the second was a conceited administrator. But Lenin found no other distinguished member of the Central Committee worthy of his legacy, either. "I do not wish further to characterize the personal traits of the remaining members of the CC," he goes on, "I merely make mention that the October episode of Zinoviev and Kamenev was, naturally, no accident [Lenin was thinking that these two had protested the uprising, i.e., the October Revolution—M.D.], but I cannot personally accuse them of this any more than I can Trotsky of not being a Bolshevik.‡ [Trotsky up to 1917 had belonged to the faction opposed to Lenin's Bolsheviks—M.D.]" Pay attention to logic, also to loyalty: Why does Lenin choose to talk about the "October episode of Zinoviev and Kamenev," stressing that this "was . . . no accident," if they cannot be accused of it? Why does he proclaim Trotsky's "non-Bolshevism"? In any case, when political power is at issue it may turn out to be of some use to bring up errors that have by now been forgiven.

Lenin does mention two young members of the CC, but like all the rest he praises them in one sentence only to find fault with them in the

---

*Ibid., p. 544.

†Lenin, *Selected Works,* Vol. II, Book 2 (Belgrade: Kultura, 1950), p. 38.

‡Ibid., p. 545.

next: "Bukharin is not only the most valuable and the most substantial theoretician belonging to the Party, he is also justifiably regarded as the favorite of the entire Party. But it is most doubtful that we can count his theoretical views as totally Marxist, for in Bukharin there is something scholastic (he has never made a study of these things and I think never completely understood the dialectic)." Next, Pyatakov:[13] "Here is a man who undoubtedly stands out for his strong will and distinguished abilities, but who is too carried away by administration and the administrative side of his work to be relied on when the issue is serious and political."*

To all this must be added that the following Party Congress, the Twelfth, held in April 1923, did increase the number of Central Committee members to forty, while the Thirteenth Congress, held in May 1924 (i.e., after Lenin's death), increased it to sixty-three. At the Thirteenth Congress, Lenin's Testament was read aloud, but it was unanimously decided not to publish it. Further, Trotsky denied the existence of the Testament†—of course, while he was still a Party member. And Stalin did not conceal what was written about him in the Testament‡—of course, while he was not in a position to subject even Lenin to censorship.

Lenin's Testament deserves analysis all by itself and from all points of view. From what has been said, it is already quite clear that he transferred power to no one. Clear too is the fact that in Stalin, Lenin found no political failings but only personal ones, and that this was true of no one else. This corresponds to the historical fact that Stalin alone had always been a Bolshevik and a follower of Lenin. Stalin had reason to boast at the Central Committee Plenum of October 23, 1927: "It is a matter of record that there is not a word, not even a whisper, in the Testament about mistakes on the part of Stalin. Stalin is simply vulgar and unpolished. Being unpolished, though, can never constitute a deficiency in political work or in the positions adopted by Stalin."**

So how do things now stand with regard to Lenin's legacy? Who really did continue his work?

In his study *A Life of Lenin,* Louis Fischer[14] concluded that the quarrel between Trotsky and Stalin would never have assumed such dark

---

*Ibid.

†Cited from J. V. Stalin, *On the Opposition* (Moscow: Gosizdat, 1928), p. 723.

‡Ibid.

**Ibid., p. 725.

hues, nor would the Soviet Union have sunk into total violence, had Lenin remained alive at least one more decade. His opinion can plausibly be defended; also, it has a wider, theoretical importance. But Lenin did not, after all, live on. And as for the question of who carried on Lenin's work we have to look at it through a number of prisms, all of them quite real: A Stalin-Trotsky conflict did take place, a Stalin-opposition conflict did take place, Stalinist terror did exist, and finally one has to take account of the actual Soviet political and social structure that took shape under Stalin.

It need hardly be said that differences in interpretation are unavoidable, if only because the Soviet Union's Stalinist past and the past history generally of Communist movements are, even today, in many ways a living reality generating a variety of ideas and opposing currents of opinion. Assuming we discard the deterministic view that so backward a Russia and so total an ideology could not have existed without the help of total administrative violence, it seems to me that Stalin is the most consistent, most natural, heir to Lenin. Such a conclusion need not run counter to the conjecture that Stalin may have encompassed Lenin's own death. For the very essence of Lenin's teachings ineluctably leads us in this direction: He espoused specific political power, total power, with the goal, and in the name, of building an ideal society. Here Lenin set himself off from all those who merely preached an ideal society, including Marx himself. Like Marx, Lenin too tagged that political power with the name of "dictatorship of the proletariat." But while Marx conceived of it as a controlling pressure exerted by the working masses, for Lenin such pressure was exerted only by a "vanguard of the proletariat"—in one word, the Party. To a hypothetical ideal society there stands opposed another ideal, one that is not at all hypothetical, and that is total power.

One could lay at Stalin's door every conceivable sin except that of betraying the structure of power Lenin had created. Such an accusation was beyond Khrushchev's comprehension, or at least his willingness to comprehend. He proclaimed Stalin's absolute authority "a sin" and a retreat from Lenin and Leninism. This was the reason he could never put down roots in the affections of either the educated classes or the people at large but instead kept undermining his position in the Party bureaucracy. For it, as for any community, its own history

is a constituent part of its existence. George F. Kennan once observed
that in postwar Germany the powers-that-be failed to repudiate the
crimes of the Nazis even though the measures being taken against
those same Nazis were inadequate. The continuity of power had been
broken in Germany after 1945. In the Soviet Union, by contrast, not a
single leader fails to prolong an analogous Party and to continue an
analogous history. Lenin's power, with certain alterations in the mechanism, was carried on by Stalin. And not only his power; but power,
political authority, was the essential thing. Power that, give or take a
few modifications, endures to the present day.

To one degree or another, Stalin's intraparty opponents lived,
moved, and had their being in an unreal world. Trotsky was obsessed
with revolution, and no more nor less than a worldwide one. Bukharin
was obsessed with the economy and naturally saw economics as the
foundation of anything and everything. They all grieved for the "comradeship" that had passed away while projecting an "ideal" future. As
for Stalin, who was concerned with attaching himself to Lenin as a
kind of extension of this founding father, he gradually came to realize
that the new system could not be maintained without changing the
position and role of the Party. Revolution represented a power-Party
fusion. But the greater of these was Party. Change consisted in the
greater of them becoming power, the power structure, the government.
That would have accorded precisely with Lenin's reduction of the state
to compulsion, to the organs of violence, meaning the Secret Police and
its troops. This realignment emerged gradually, of course, while the
Party ostensibly retained its "leading role." But such a leading role
amounted only to the formal preservation of ideological prejudices. If
at the same time one does not lose sight of the fact that power as such
brings privilege and "a place in history," it will be clear why from the
very first day of Party rule a ruling current materialized. It was not
Stalin who invented the totalitarian Party bureaucracy. Rather, it was
that very bureaucracy which found in Stalin its natural leader.

Precisely because he had this grasp of a potential reality in the
process of emerging, Stalin was able to bedazzle and outmaneuver his
adversaries. Their spiritual ties to a traditional, by now uncreative
Party became over time their weakness and his main tool. "Laying oneself bare before the Party" demanded its own corroboration: The most
heinous crimes—betrayals, acts of sabotage, murders—demanded to
be acknowledged. Today it is known that Soviet instructors in the

postwar trials of Slánský[15] in Czechoslovakia and Rajk in Hungary, and probably others, too, transmitted this "ideological" experience to their young Eastern European brethren. Naturally, none of it could have been undertaken without torture rooms and hangmen, just as with the medieval heretics and witches. The only novel aspects were motives and means.

Stalin did not destroy the Party, he transformed it, "cleansed it," and made it a mighty weapon. Like the Grand Inquisitor in Dostoyevsky's *The Brothers Karamazov,* Stalin too realized that God had to be slain ("God" in this case being Party comradeship and a society of equals), with the object of saving the institution (institution in this case being the Soviet system and Communist organizations). And he was obediently followed, not only by the political bureaucracy but also by most Communists the world over, Communists compelled by circumstances to tie their existence to the Soviet state and even identify their existence with that state. How could one explain otherwise the fact that refined minds like that of Togliatti or heroic personalities like that of Dimitrov failed to comprehend Stalin's clumsy lies and bent the knee before his monstrous terror?

In the process of winning his "victories," not only did Stalin's prestige rise but also he himself grew drunk on them: Political power and the idea of communism became identified with him and he himself with them. It was as if Hegel's Absolute Spirit, in its arrogant identification with the world, had finally found its own two aspects—the mystically materialist in Stalin, the intuitively mystic in Hitler.

Stalin was the first to set forth a complete theory of Leninism, something that happened three months after Lenin's death (in Stalin's lectures "On Questions of Leninism," April 1924). These lectures broadened dogma but also institutionalized it. Just so did Engels's "Anti-Dühring" systematize Marx into dogma and ideology. Stalin, of course, was not acting in haste and did not throw together his talks. He had already grasped the "essence of Leninism" and made it his own banner. His ideas and projects prevailed in the Soviet Union and all the Communist movements. Successes, victories—these are reality as politicians see reality, and they provided Stalin with an abundance of what he called proofs that confirmed the decisive importance of "our," meaning his own, ideological positions.

I believe that for these very same reasons Marx's teaching diminished in his eyes, even though Stalin did remain loyal to the essential
nature of Marxist doctrine: materialism as the cornerstone of a "scientific" view of the world, and the building of an ideal—Communist—
society. Although he was attacked by angry people precipitously and
cruelly, Stalin knew he could follow a certain issue or a possible adversary and probe them carefully and thoughtfully for months, even years.
That is how he behaved when it came to ideas. The shortcomings of
Marx and Engels he probably suspected even as he was formulating
"Leninism," very soon after the death of Lenin. Yet it would seem that
in this regard the war against Nazi Germany was crucial. Stalin must
have been shaken to the marrow by an invasion coming from the very
nation that had given birth to Marx and Engels—an invasion of the one
country in which their ideas had borne fruit.

Stalin had long since made the activities of world communism
dependent on the Soviet Party. War and the outcome of war appeared
to confirm that the power of Communists was being maintained only
within the Soviet sphere. Nor did he institutionalize a political bureaucracy or stoke the fires of Russian nationalism only because he could
build a nest for his personal power that way. He did these things
because they presented themselves to him as the only possible forms by
which the Russian Revolution and communism could be extended.
Soon after the war, Stalin was to brush aside Clausewitz, even though
Lenin himself had placed a high value on the famous military theorist.
Stalin did not do this, however, because of the discovery of some better
theoretician but simply because this German belonged to a nation
whose army the Soviet army had destroyed in what was perhaps the
most decisive war ever waged by the people of Russia.

It goes without saying that Stalin never publicly undertook a reeval-
uation of Marx and Engels. That would have threatened the faith of the
true believer, and hence his own political power and his work. He
knew that the crushing defeat of all his enemies had more than likely
come about because he had been the most consistent in developing
those forms that fuse dogma and action, consciousness and reality.

To Stalin, it was unimportant and secondary whether he had or had
not modified this or that principle of Marxism. Had not all great Marxists, and most assuredly Lenin, emphasized that Marxism was "management in action"? That it was not a collection of dogmas? That

practice was the one criterion of truth? The problem is, however, broader and more complex than this. Every system, especially one that is despotic, tends toward stability. Marx's teachings, dogmatic in any case, had to harden into dogma as soon as they became official, the moment they became state and social ideology. A nation and a ruling class, after all, would fall to pieces if they were to change their robes every day, not to speak of their ideals. They must live by adjusting to changing reality, foreign and domestic. Leaders are compelled to back away from their ideals, but they must retreat in such a way that the halo seen by their followers and by the people at large is kept up and if possible heightened. The finality of Marxism, or its claim to be a science; the hermeticism of Stalin's society; and the comprehensive nature of his power—all these drove him to exterminate anyone who committed a "mistake" ideologically and then to be unshakable in his decision. That meant that he employed the harshest measures. At the same time, life compelled Stalin to "betray" his "most holy" principles. And that meant that he changed his principles. Stalin watched over ideology with an eagle eye but only because of its value for power and because ideology was a way of nourishing what he called "Russia" and of confirming his own prestige.

It is therefore understandable that the Party bureaucracy, identifying itself with the people of Russia, with Russia herself and the Soviet Union, to this very day utters soft, approving murmurs and cooing sounds to the effect that Stalin, despite what they are pleased to call his errors, "did so much for Russia," "did so much for the Soviet people."

It is likewise understandable that under Stalin lies and violence had to be raised to the level of high principle. Who knows? Perhaps Stalin in his penetrating, ruthless mind thought that these things, lies and violence, were the dialectic negation by which Russia and the human race would at length attain to absolute truth and absolute happiness.

Stalin took the idea of communism to the extreme limits of dogma and living faith, at which point both the idea and the social structure it had created began to crumble. No sooner had he wiped out his domestic adversaries and proclaimed that a socialist society had been constructed in the Soviet Union, no sooner was the war over, than there began to appear new signs of change in Soviet society and in the Communist movements. In any case, when Stalin brought out the crucial importance of "ideological positions," he was simply articulating his own system in the language of his own reality, the language of his own ideology, and articulating the very same thing that other political leaders said in their own way: If by our ideology we have discovered the direction society moves in; if we are capable of inspiring people to move in the same direction to the point that they get well organized—then we are on the right path and are bound to win.

Stalin possessed an unusually watchful and tenacious mind. I remember how in his presence it was not possible to make the slightest move, to say anything however remotely, without his taking notice. In saying so, one may have in mind how much importance Stalin attached to ideas, for all that they served him only as a means. Still, one is forced to conclude that he was quite aware that the movement which had taken shape under his guidance failed to correspond to any ideal whatsoever. On this subject we have plenty of evidence at our disposal today, especially in the writings of his daughter Svetlana. Thus she quotes her father as crying out, upon discovering that a special school had been organized in Kuibyshev for the evacuated children of Moscow functionaries: "Ah! you . . . Ah! you accursed caste."*

The wiliest of his opponents, Leon Trotsky, affirmed the very same thing, that a caste of bureaucrats had come into being under Stalin. The monstrous purges, millions shot, millions annihilated, only deepened the sense of social injustice and strengthened the demand for still more violence, still more suffering. The demand that accounts be settled. In the course of his purges and generally harsh measures Stalin destroyed even his own family. Around this man there spread in the end only horror and desolation. Before he died he glued all over the walls of his room photographs cut out of periodicals, pictures of other people's children. At the same time, he declined to see his own grandchildren. It could serve as an important lesson, especially for dogmatic "one-dimensional" minds who run up the flag of "historical necessity" in the face of human life and human endeavor. For although Stalin belongs among the greatest conquerors known to history, he is in fact one of the most defeated of all human beings. He left behind not a single lasting,

---

*Svetlana Alliluyeva, *Twenty Letters to a Friend*, Russian edition (New York: Harper & Row, 1967), p. 157.

indisputable value. Victory turned to defeat, defeat in personal terms and the defeat of an idea.

In Stalin can be found the features of all earlier tyrants—from Nero and Caligula to Ivan the Terrible, Robespierre, and Hitler. And just as each of them was unique, Stalin too was a new and original phenomenon. He was the most complete and most successful tyrant. But although his tyranny was the most perfidious and most total of all, to regard him as simply a sadist or criminal seems to me both oversimplified and inaccurate.

In his biography of Stalin, Trotsky states that Stalin took pleasure in the slaughter of animals. Khrushchev once said that in his last years Stalin suffered from a persecution complex. I am not aware of any facts that might confirm or refute their observations. All things considered, Stalin did enjoy the execution of his enemies. Etched in my memory is the expression that broke out on his face one time when the Bulgarian and Yugoslav delegations were talking with him and his henchmen on February 10, 1948, in the Kremlin. What I saw was a cold, dark satisfaction over a victim whose fate had just then been sealed. I used to see such expressions on the faces of other politicians at moments when they "cracked the whip" over their so-to-speak "debauched" colleagues, colleagues who shared the same opinions. But none of this, however accurate it may be, is enough to explain the phenomenon that was Stalin. In particular, *Life* magazine ran an unfounded assertion that Stalin was a spy for the Tsarist secret police (the Okhrana). That does not help. Nor does it help when a certain American historian claims that Stalin got the Tsarist police, without their realizing what was going on, to arrest Mensheviks and other non-Bolshevik oppositionists. His claim is not all that implausible, but it does not help explain the Stalin phenomenon. The Stalin phenomenon is very complicated and does not involve merely the Communist movement or the domestic and foreign possibilities open to the Soviet Union at the time. The Stalin phenomenon encourages us to look into the relationship between man and idea, leader and movement; the role of force in society; and the role of myths in human activity. Stalin belongs to the past, but disputes about these issues and others like them have hardly begun.

When all is said and done, I should like to add that Stalin was a lively person, passionate, very abrupt, but also highly organized and self-controlled. So much I could see for myself. Could he otherwise have

governed such a huge, modern country? Made such terrible, complicated war?

So I think that such notions as criminality, derangement, and the like
are secondary and unreal when political personality is at issue. We
shall have to live with ambivalence. In reality there is no politics undefiled by the so-called low passions and impulses. By the very fact that
it represents the sum total of human endeavors, politics cannot be
purged of either criminal or insane elements. As a consequence, to discover some valid boundary between evil deeds and political violence
is difficult, even impossible. With the appearance of every new leader,
especially a tyrant, thinkers are forced to resort to explorations, new
analyses, and new generalizations.

What if we do grant that there exists a boundary between the rational and the emotional, between the necessary and the subjective? In
that case Stalin, though we have not found in him anything criminal or
insane, belongs among the most monstrous bullies history knows. For
even if we assume that collectivization, for example, was reasonable
and necessary under the given circumstances, obviously it did not need
to be imposed at the price of destroying millions of kulaks. To this very
day one can find people who object on dogmatic grounds to raising
such doubts. Stalin, they will say, was carried away by the building of
a socialist society; the criticism of Trotskyites for his alleged oppor-
tunism pressed him hard, they will say; his country was under the
threat of a German invasion that might find support in the class enemy,
they will say. But what can be said to excuse his concocting accusations
and conducting bloody purges of oppositionists within the Party?
These were people who posed no threat to the movement and its ideology and indeed revealed only impotence and confusion by their dogmatic bonds to it.

Stalin's terror was not confined to the purges alone, but they were its
most distinctive aspect. All the Party oppositionists were more or less
in agreement with the repressions carried out against the kulaks and
other class enemies. They all voluntarily placed their necks under the
yoke of ideology. They all shared goals and ideals identical with those
of Stalin. Criticizing him for not being engaged in any definite occupation, Bukharin only confirmed his own illusions about being engaged
in science, meaning economics and philosophy. Not one of them had
any essentially new vision, had any other ideal. And not one of them
failed to be astounded by the purges. By engaging in purges, Stalin

separated himself from all the rest, became what he was, and laid the foundations of his life's work.

Through those unbridled purges of the thirties, Stalin identified his own power with an idea, identified his own person with the nation. Could it have turned out otherwise? In a world of ultimate truths, a world with faith in a classless, perfect society? All by itself, the goal justified the means. Stalin's life's work lacked any moral foundation and thereby lacked anything vital that would endure. Here is the mystery of his personality. Here is the true measure of his life's work.

STALIN'S SHADOW OVER HIS HEIRS

Many, among them Trotsky of course, lay great emphasis on Stalin's criminal, bloodthirsty instincts. I am in no position to either deny or confirm it, not knowing the facts that well. Back in Khrushchev's time it was published in Moscow that it was probably Stalin who did away with Kirov, secretary of the Party's Leningrad branch, thereby creating an excuse to settle accounts with the opposition within the Party. Stalin's fingers were also very likely entangled in the death of the writer Maxim Gorky, for Gorky's demise was far too loudly trumpeted by Stalin's propaganda machine as an opposition initiative. Trotsky even suspected that he killed Lenin on the pretext of shortening his agonies. It is whispered that Stalin killed his wife, Alliluyeva, or at least drove her to suicide by his crudity. At any rate, the story spread by Stalin's agents (one that came to my own ears) to the effect that his wife poisoned herself inadvertently by acting as a food-taster in the presence of her fine, dashing husband really is only a naive and romantic legend.

Stalin was capable of any crime; and there was no crime he did not commit. By whatever measure that might be applied, he deserves—let us hope for all time—the glory of being the greatest criminal in history. For he combined the criminal senselessness of a Caligula with the refinement of a Borgia and the brutality of an Ivan the Terrible.

But over and above all that, my own concern has been, and still is, how so dark, deceitful, and cruel a person could govern one of the largest and most powerful nations on earth, and not for just a day or a year at that, but for thirty years. If this cannot be explained by today's critics of Stalin (I am thinking of his heirs), they would at least agree that in many ways they continued his work; that the same juices run in their own veins, the same ideas, patterns, and methods that drove him. Stalin, it is true, wanted to set in motion certain projects, and he found that an exhausted, desperate, postrevolutionary Russian society set the stage for him. But more than that, the kind of man he was—ruthless, decisive, practical in his very fanaticism—was just what was needed then by certain classes in that society, or more precisely, by the ruling political-Party bureaucracy. This Party really did follow his lead, persistently and obediently, and he led it from victory to victory, up to the point where, drunk with power, he began to commit sins against the Party itself. Later this Party found fault with Stalin only for doing that. As for all the rest—silence. Stalin sinned more copiously, and of course no less brutally, against the "class enemy" (the peasantry and the intelligentsia); likewise against the left and right currents within the Party and outside it. And as long as this Party in theory and in practice (especially in practice) does not put behind it for good and all what was the most original thing about Stalin and Stalinism, an undeviating, ideological unity—this will be an evil but sure sign that it has not emerged from under Stalin's shadow.

Hence I think that liquidating Molotov's so-called anti-Party group was superficial and premature, despite the odiousness of his personality and the rabid darkness of his views. The essence of the problem was not that one group was better than another but that they existed at all; the problem was whether monopoly as such had been abolished. For in the USSR, a single group enjoyed every kind of monopoly, not simply ideological and political. Stalin's shadow extended over all. As a person, Stalin may be cursed while living on in his society's social and spiritual foundations.

Returning to Lenin in words and solemn declarations cannot change fundamentals. It is one thing to disclose this or that crime of Stalin's, but quite another to hide the fact that this was the very man who "built socialism," who laid the foundations of Soviet society and the Soviet empire. For all its transformation technologically and perhaps precisely for that reason, Russia for decades lay under the spell of its framework of Stalinist dogma.

If we were to take the point of view of humanity and freedom, then history has never known so brutal and cynical a despot as Stalin. Relative to the people he led, he had more opportunity than Hitler and was more methodical. He was one of those rare and fearsome dogmatists capable of destroying nine-tenths of the human race so as to make the remaining one-tenth of it "happy."[16]

But on the other hand, if we look at what Stalin really signified in the history of communism, then next to Lenin he is a most grandiose figure indeed. Without essentially developing the ideas of communism, he defended them and fulfilled them by creating a Communist society and nation. An ideal society? No, that he did not create. It is not in the nature of human beings or human society. But he did turn backward Russia into an industrial power and also into an empire with stubborn, relentless pretensions to world domination.

Seen in terms of success and political resourcefulness, Stalin can hardly be surpassed by any statesman of our era.

I am, of course, far from looking upon success in the political struggle as the one and only value. It certainly has never crossed my mind to identify politics with amorality. I do not deny that politics, by the very fact that it involves a struggle for their very existence on the part of specific human communities, includes a certain neglect for moral norms. Great politics and great statesmen to me are those capable of combining ideals with reality and those capable of proceeding toward their goals without turning back while adhering to basic moral values.

Taken all in all, Stalin was a monster. While holding to abstract, absolute, and, at bottom, utopian ideas, in practice he only knew, only could know, success. Success defined as violence, as physical and spiritual extermination.

But let us not be unfair even to Stalin. What he wanted to carry out and what he did carry out could not have been accomplished in any other way, essentially. The forces that drove him and that he led, with their absolute ideals, their closed forms of property and power, could have had no other leader than him at that particular stage of Russian and world relations; they could not have been served by other methods. As the creator of a closed social system, Stalin was at the same time its tool. Under changed circumstances and too late he became its sacrifice. Unsurpassed in violence and crime, Stalin is not diminished by being the leader and organizer of a particular social system. Today he is of little worth because he stands out only for making "mistakes." By spotting and correcting Stalin's mistakes, the post-Stalin leaders of that same system hoped to redeem both the system and themselves.

And yet for all that, Khrushchev's dethronement of Stalin, resembling an operetta as it did, inconsistent as it was, told us that truth will out even long after the destruction of those who once fought for it. Conscience cannot be pacified. Conscience is indestructible.

Again, unhappily, after de-Stalinization as before, it might now be supposed that those who wish to live and survive in a world different from the one created by Stalin have had to fight for it. Force may be diminished, but it is still the law.

LENIN, HEIR TO THE CULT OF STALIN

The post-Stalin, Khrushchevian cult of Lenin was in reality a variant on and a continuation of the cult of Stalin.

Such a claim may seem whimsical, even malicious, and draws attention to itself all the more because to any ordinary person Lenin and Stalin are opposites in so many ways and their times are equally different. But any impartial, nonideological analysis leads only to just such a conclusion.

We remind the reader that the Lenin cult was resurrected under Khrushchev only after the revelation of Stalin's "errors" at the Twentieth Party Congress. Up to that time the cult of a living Stalin included a Lenin cult, as expressed by the formula "Lenin-Stalin." The Stalin cult further embraced both Marx and Engels: Marx-Engels-Lenin-Stalin.

Many will note that tying Stalin to Lenin and beyond Lenin to Marx and Engels was just another aspect of Stalin's falsifications and of that forced growth we call "the cult of personality." To say this is not inaccurate, touching as it does upon both Stalin's intent and his actual operations. But again, it leaves a question open: Why did Khrushchev resort to the cult of Lenin—a cult that Communists the world over have understood one way or another as that same Stalin cult now reapplied to their own times?

Khrushchev was impelled to do this for both ideological and practical reasons.

Every ideology is potentially totalitarian. No ideology can prevail save through total power over the spirit and over labor. To the degree, then, that it makes itself totalitarian, every ideology invents a leader and supports him. Though not all human relations are hierarchic, political power is indisputably just that, and only as such, as hierarchy, can it function. For that reason, totalitarianism, which is the most extreme form of dictatorship, cannot be what it is save under a leader. By the same token, a leader's elimination, as we have seen with the "cult of personality," or an oligarchy's advancement, as we see in the present "collective leadership," is a reliable sign that totalitarianism is declining.

Khrushchev himself came out of the Party apparatus, that of professional Party workers. The apparatus, where resided by definition all political, social, and economic power and which constituted the ruling class both in society and within the Party itself, could not find justification even to its own self without idealizing itself, or in a word, without ideology. The apparatus renounced Stalin's "errors" all the more readily because its stability was threatened by the terror. But that same apparatus could not abandon ideology, since ideology alone, though uncreative and self-deluded, was the *raison d'être* for its rule and its very existence. Furthermore, it could not do so without a "new," charismatic leader. This could only be Lenin, the "uncompromised" source of the apparatus and the man who put the finishing touches on its ideology. A living continuity, historical and spiritual, was thereby established for the Party bureaucracy. Mistakes may have been made by yesterday's leader, but no such "mistakes" could possibly alter the essence of the system, the "worthiness" of Leninism. A living Stalin was replaced by a dead Lenin, but the bond of uncritical worship, the cult of the leader—that remained. Oh! wondrous, "inconceivable" inversion, such as only life, which is to say politics, can bring about.

The state of affairs in the Communist Parties, Soviet and foreign, at once, even daily, forced Khrushchev to "renew" the cult of Lenin. Domestically, he was obliged to suppress decisively all those Stalinists who had grown accustomed to Stalin's lawlessness and purges. He hoped that by returning to Lenin he might resurrect the unity of world communism, now splintered and demoralized by those very same Leninist-Stalinist methods and ideas that had established such unity in their time. Whether Khrushchev succeeded in this and to what degree is up to historians. Here we must emphasize that he did not dream up that cult but took it over from the impoverished arsenal of a panic-stricken bureaucracy. So when he fell, the cult of Lenin grew even stronger, by the very fact that the new leadership, while more conservative, was more collective in nature than Khrushchev's own leadership.

But if the cult of Lenin was only a variation on the cult of Stalin, making it more authentic, is this so in historical and social actuality?

Are Lenin and Stalin two persons in one, belonging in essence to the very same system and very same ideas?

The cult of the leader had already begun during Lenin's lifetime: It was he who created a Party apparatus and was repaid by a cult of himself. Of course, the cult of Lenin did not attain such monstrous, idolatrous forms as did the cult of Stalin, but personal power over the Party, the state, and its ideology was all there in embryo. Having acquired unparalleled authority, Lenin—as opposed to his successors, who concealed the truth about themselves like the snake its legs[17]— Lenin could be open toward the new political power and his own role within it. Thus by taking over power he could reaffirm the dictatorship of the proletariat as the dictatorship of the Party: "The Party absorbs, so to speak, the cutting edge of the proletariat and, now a vanguard, carries out a dictatorship." Add to those words the following: ". . . Soviet socialist centralism is not in the least opposed to personal power and dictatorship . . . the will of a social class may from time to time create a dictator who can occasionally accomplish more by himself and frequently becomes more necessary."

In vain did later admirers of Lenin grasp at his tolerance for differences within the Party. Lenin did indeed tolerate differences before taking power, to the degree that they did not threaten his dogmatic and operational leadership. But no sooner did power become consolidated in the political apparatus, no sooner, that is, was a real—real, and not dogmatic—goal realized, than Lenin forbade ideological differences. Platform groups were forbidden at the Tenth Party Congress in 1921. "Purges," not yet bloody, began under Lenin. And concentration camps too. Not only for "class enemies" but also for allied socialist parties, for Social Democrats ("Mensheviks") and Social Revolutionaries ("SRs").

Hidden and indecipherable, Stalin ripened within Lenin, just as revolutionary violence begets totalitarian violence.

This is affirmed by all investigations—memoirs, historical studies, theoretical, belletristic—of both Soviet and foreign authors (Nadezhda Mandelshtam, A. Avtorkhanov, Solzhenitsyn, Robert Tucker, Louis Fischer, Robert Conquest, and others). It does not mean that Lenin could not have begotten other possibilities. Some were rendered impossible by Lenin himself (e.g., the "workers' opposition" of Shlyapnikov); others were disabled by Stalin (Trotsky, Bukharin). The Stalinist "possibility" carried the day, as the most Leninist current of all. And won by methods that would have horrified Lenin himself. Such is the natural course of revolution that has accepted violence as a means of realizing a utopian, classless society.

Taking refuge in Lenin may have mitigated Stalinist violence but did not change its course. Taking refuge in Lenin only prolonged the existence of a bureaucracy in violence and delusion. But neither that way out nor its remote inception in Marx, be it the "old" Marx or the "young" Marx, was able to conceal the noncreativity of violence. That noncreativity was so thoroughgoing that it has destroyed its own ideal.

POSTULATES ON STALIN

1. Stalin was a Marxist, a revolutionary Marxist. The cult of his personality, however, as well as his policy of terror, can in no way be considered an outgrowth of Marx and his doctrines.

2. Stalin was a student of Lenin's and his comrade-in-arms. He was also the most fully developed and consistent of Leninists. All that Stalin worked for and all he accomplished—from concentration camps and industrialization to the enslavement of the countries of Eastern Europe—Lenin began. Stalin did not destroy something that Lenin had established, aside from what were called the old cadres who stood in the way of his personal tyranny and hindered him from faithfully pursuing Lenin's work.

3. Stalinism exists only as total terror. Stalinism means Leninism in the sense that the system whose cornerstone Lenin laid is built to the end. Stalin consolidated, as a monopolistic class, the Party bureaucracy that had been founded by Lenin even before the Revolution. In doing so he codified Leninism, although not even Leninism exists save as a variant of revolutionary Marxism. Leninism, or Stalinism, could today be formulated as the Marxist doctrine concerning an ideological Party as the ruling class. Leninism-Stalinism was Soviet, or pro-Soviet, internationalism and until quite recently was an ideology of world expansionism on the part of the Soviet state.

4. The cult of Lenin in the Communist movements continues and replaces the compromised cult of Stalin. An ideological, totalitarian movement is not possible without a cult of personality.

5. Stalinism is the most total, most tyrannical of all systems, not only today but possibly in all of history. Hitler admired only Stalin. And even Hitler could only dream of such total power.

6. Stalin continued the despotism of the Tsars through a centralized, bureaucratic apparatus. But Tsarist Russia and Stalin's Russia were not the same: The first was agrarian and mainly oriented toward expansion in the direction of Asia, while the second was industrial (military-industrial) and oriented toward subjugating the capitalist, industrialized West. In this regard, after Stalin, there was change only in the sense that the Soviet Union was substantially stronger and in the sense that the country pursued its great-power goals by the mechanism of "fraternal assistance" rendered to the various revolutionary regimes and movements in a methodical, systematic way.

7. In the Soviet Union, no one after Khrushchev ever spoke of de-Stalinization. And even he thought that Stalin had "only" gone too far with his policy of terror. It was merely foreign Communists who prattled about de-Stalinization within the Soviet Union. They did this to legitimize kinship with their Soviet comrades. This is not to say that the Soviet Union remained exactly as it was under Stalin. The system was the very same, but it was not completely closed, and terror was mitigated. The Stalinist system had reached the point of self-destruction.

8. Stalin and Stalinism are still alive, here less, there more. Wherever we find the Party bureaucracy flourishing, there, too, we find ideas in the ascendancy about building—with the help of dictatorial power—a new, classless society.

9. Not one Communist Party has completely freed itself from Stalinism—that is to say, Leninism. This is because not one has ever freed itself from a penchant to monopolize power. Whether in spirit or habits of thought and action, not one Party has ever become pluralistic for good.

10. Stalin's shadow still spreads over the world. And it will keep spreading until the monopolistic forces of the Party are rendered harmless and wiped out.

STALIN'S COMMUNISM

There is one question left unresolved in the much too voluminous literature dealing with the Soviet movement and with Stalin. We do not find this question addressed by anyone who has approached the issue with circumspection and objectivity: Ulam, Tucker, Conquest, Fischer, Pipes, Voslensky, Kennan, Avtorkhanov, Geler, Nekrich, Brzezinski, and others. The question is whether Stalin believed in communism. Put another way, the question becomes: If Stalin did believe in communism, how did he picture it?

The writers mentioned above and many others as well have, it is true, posed this question, but mainly from the standpoint of history and sociopolitics. I, on the contrary, have long wanted to find an answer that proceeds from Communist ideology, from Stalin's place in that ideology and its "realization." Perhaps somewhere someone has come upon the answer from this perspective, but not I. Yet it appears to me that the answer is important if we wish to understand Communist ideology and as a consequence the appearance of Stalin himself and his role.

If Stalin was not a believer in communism there is no real proof of this. So conclusions must be drawn from his behavior and his views, and also from the way others thought of him.

From a Western, rationalist point of view this question is not essential: Westerners analyze the nature of power and the nature of the Communist movement just as they do Stalin's personality. Disillusioned Communists quite often imagine that for the sake of personal power Stalin, if he did not abandon Leninist ideology altogether, at least quit following it. Adherents of Stalin, Communist dogmatists (there still are such) see in him the greatest—after Lenin, naturally—theoretician and consistent perfecter of a socialist society. Religious thinkers see in him the embodiment of a demonic demiurge and a warning to men and nations from God when they get drunk with sin and fall into evil ways. Besides these there are many other views. They, however, can be accommodated as nuances in the above classification—schematically, obviously, for the sake of simplicity in exposition.

There were in Stalin two constant, unchanging features. One is that from youth on, after abandoning theology, he belonged to the Leninist, or Bolshevik, current in Russia's socialist movement. The other was a perverse obstinacy whose outward face was coarseness. Stalin's obstinacy pulled back only in the presence of Lenin, but not because he was fainthearted or feared for his position but because he genuinely admired and believed in the ideal embodied in Lenin's mind and will. As for his adherence to Bolshevism and not some other current, even as a young man Stalin had written of the Party's need for ideological unity. This necessity was implicit in a Leninist Party and in Leninism as a political doctrine. Only under Stalin, however, would it come to be understood as holy dogma that was interpreted and developed by the leader himself. And this was a leader who annihilated any who, in their naïveté and ignorance, might be attracted to "hostile teachings," as confirmed after the fact.

Stalin, therefore, was from the beginning the truest of true believers. But he was his own man too, possessing a tough streak of stubbornness—six times he escaped from prison and exile. He was deterred by nothing when it came to putting into effect the Party's (Lenin's) plans and decisions.

In connection with the Lenin-Stalin relationship we cannot avoid the so-called Lenin Testament,[18] set forth in his letter to the Congress of 1922 and his 1923 addendum to that same letter. Lenin dictated these texts to his secretaries after he had been stricken by sclerotic paralysis. We cannot avoid the Testament, if only because Stalin's Party opponents made their own use of it as proof of Lenin's vision and Stalin's non-Leninism. In these texts, which in their incoherence were unlike Lenin, the author furnished thumbnail sketches of his closest colleagues as potential future leaders. In each colleague by turn he found ideological and political shortcomings. But not in Stalin. Stalin was only coarse and vulgar, a man who had grabbed too much power and whose replacement as general secretary needed to be considered. Lenin saw no heir for himself: If only Stalin were not too crude, it would seem that politically the most appropriate man for the job would be he.

And that was no accident. Unlike the majority of leaders, Stalin did not puff himself up as a theoretician and speaker but was valued more as a "practical man." Precisely for this reason, Lenin raised him to the rank of general secretary. Communism had no existence apart from practice, practice before all things, practice above all. Communism meant organization and political power.

And yet that undervalued "practical man" proved to be the most realistic, most practical theoretician, or ideologist of the new, dynamic, and unruly class that was the Party bureaucracy. This class had been brought into being by Lenin, it gave birth in its turn to the Revolution, and it was the only group capable of exploring the true possibilities of that Revolution with powers it truly disposed of.

Lenin hardly lay cold in his grave, so to speak, when Stalin gave a series of lectures, *On the Foundations of Leninism,* which set forth the essence of Leninism simply and compactly. This unappreciated but priceless little work exercised enormous influence on the Communist movement. If it could not be compared with the Communist Manifesto of Marx and Engels, there is no doubt that to compare it with Lenin's *The State and Revolution* is valid. Not one of Stalin's adversaries, neither Trotsky nor Bukharin, for all their luxuriant style and great knowledge, offered anything that might be compared with these meager postulates, similar to mathematical formulas in language and style and in their decisive, categorical nature. Communist parties the world over as well as the newborn Party bureaucracy in the "first land of socialism" had acquired a guide, a "Communist catechism," distilled from Lenin's enormous work, which was scattered and (taking into account its offshoots) contradictory. The greater part of Stalin's later writings as well, those that were germane, would be gathered together as *Questions of Leninism,* but would have nothing like the importance of this brochure.

Stalin was not significant and original, even as a Marxist. His originality lay rather in what he chose to draw from other people's ideas. (Tito did the same, by the way.) But *On the Foundations of Leninism* is original insofar as he explained Leninism more compactly and clearly than others. Stalin thereby tied his thinking and his activity—his destiny—to Lenin, that is, to the social class and the state that had arisen from the revolutionary transformation. His theories, however, exacerbated class warfare in the very building of socialism. His notion that the state would wither away by being strengthened distorted not just Marxism but also theoretical thinking as such. In reality, his ideas sustained the senselessness of the Communist movement by serving the Party bureaucracy's total rule and Stalin's personal tyranny.

In the internecine warfare that ensued between Trotsky and Stalin, which had already been foreseen by Lenin in his addendum of January 1923, Stalin formed all kinds of alliances at the top, continually strengthening his position and the role of the Party bureaucracy—the nomenklatura, the Partocracy, the new class on which he relied and whose representative he was. Stalin without doubt was unsurpassable as an intriguer. But it was not a question only of a struggle for power; there were essential issues at stake here involving the further course of the Revolution and the role of power. Trotsky looked on Soviet Russia and Soviet power as the germ of a world revolutionary process (the "permanent revolution"), inasmuch as socialism could not possibly be built in one country, meaning in backward Russia. Stalin and his allies held the view that priority must be given to consolidating the Soviet state and that building socialism in one country was indeed possible, and precisely in Russia. Everyone, of course, appealed to Lenin. Theoretically Lenin, too, understood Soviet Russia to be the beginning of a world revolutionary process, but in practice he gave first priority to strengthening the power of the Soviet Russian system.

The theory that building socialism in one country was possible, and in Soviet Russia at that, came originally from Bukharin, but it was Stalin who mainly saw to its fulfillment, and even the theory itself is most often ascribed to him.

Up to the end of the twenties, Stalin was rightly looked on as a moderate, especially by Trotskyites; he was seen as a centrist within the Party. It was thanks to the Party opposition that he had to prove that it was indeed possible to build socialism in one country, even in backward Russia. And at the same time, he had to remain true to the ideal of world communism, though naturally under the leadership of the Soviet state as "the main force."

"Building socialism" roughly coincides with definitive rule by the Party bureaucracy and the enthronement of Stalin, the enshrining of his cult. True, Stalin himself fortified his cult with all the stubborn arrogance characteristic of him. But even the cult of Stalin would have lacked any potency if it had not been created in the first place by social reality, by the restructuring of society in an ever more totalitarian way.

The international situation pointed ahead to fascism and war; the prevailing ideology was "scientific," which meant that it was totalitarian; and the Party, with its built-in tendency to be monopolistic, had to "build socialism" as a matter of survival. Under those circumstances, neither industrialization nor collectivization could have been carried out other than by "revolutionary," terroristic methods. Terror struck fear into the builder and added to his enthusiasm. The builder became carried away by building.

And once it had been "successfully" carried out, or so goes the supposition (this time one that was original to Stalin), once a socialist society had been built—then the road was open to a Communist society. According to both Marx and Lenin, by that point the state would have withered away. So Stalin was now obliged to explain this, too, in theoretical terms: The state would wither away in proportion as it got stronger. So went the claim. On the surface this looked like mere dialectics. But in reality it meant abandoning all distinctions. It meant naked power. Stalin probably supposed that it meant a final break away from the salons of class societies in the direction of a perfect society. He probably envisioned motion away from "the Empire of necessity to the Empire of freedom." Stalin was aware of the weaknesses and shortcomings of his system, thinking of them as relics of the past that survived mainly in people's thoughts. But his efforts did succeed for reasons that could readily be seen. No longer were there any class enemies, even in the countryside, who could stop the victorious march toward a perfect Communist society.

And in truth—this may well seem absurd—Stalin did come very close to realizing a classless society. As a sharp-witted and talented realist, he realized that he had to lean on a ruling class already in existence, namely on the Party bureaucracy, consolidating and reinforcing its privileges. But he could not afford to let them become a class of private owners, certainly not large magnates who could possibly threaten his personal power as the vehicle—nay, the incarnation—of an ideological and social transformation beyond anybody's wildest dreams. Stalin's cult was the cult of an inaccessible divinity, as distinct from Tito's cult, which was predominantly folkloric. And society? Society as a thing fairly independent and spontaneous in its development— such a society was suppressed and destroyed. And with it the human being as a unit within society; for all intents and purposes, Aristotle's "social animal" was abandoned. Hence aside from professional differences, there are no classes. The Party bureaucracy may be defined as a class by its power and privileges but not by property. As for what kind of a society we saw before us, classless as it now was, its outlines were clear enough: The further it had "advanced," the more self-destructive it was becoming, the more insufferable, the more senseless. And the less productive.

The human race, however—man—is not perfect. And especially not perfect in the way Stalin conceived of the perfect "new man." Even though a socialist society had now been built, all kinds of opponents and malcontents began to appear. Very frequently as individuals and small groups. But very numerous. There were all those onetime Party leaders, embittered at having been deprived of political power and at having such an un-Leninist socialism forced down their throats. But look at these concentration camps (they had existed all this time)! Why not enlarge them, spread them around, make good use of them for the building of socialism? All the more because the work performed by so-called free workers did not differ essentially from the work done in the camps? And those former leaders, that eternal, grumbling throng of intriguers who sow confusion and delusions in the Party—those people really needed to be excluded from the heart and mind of the system once and for all. Of course, they had to be accused of betrayal and sabotage. The fear of God had to be instilled into this Old Guard. Any sparks of memory for those times of Revolution had to be stamped out. Camps and purges, lies and slander, thus became both social and political necessities for the tyrant's new society.

Along with this there came, naturally, one more original, Stalinist theory: Class warfare intensifies with the building of socialism. Senseless, futile—true—but not for such a system and its leader and builder. The thought must have occurred to Stalin: Have not all great religions and all new societies gained victory in such a way?

There are serious analysts who maintain that Stalin was paranoid. At one time I could not have been among their number, though I have been in the process of changing my mind. If it really were true, however, then we had a paranoiac who persevered in carrying out his plans with self-confidence and a zest for organization. Stalin did scorn people who were necessarily burdened by earlier class evils and sins. He was carried away. He behaved more and more like some pagan priest who would stop at nothing and who could not be satiated by any human sacrifice in consummating his "most sublime idea." Tyranny feeds on successes and sacrifices.

So, yes! Stalin did believe in communism. Communism consummated by exterminating unbelievers and fence-sitters, communism fulfilled by uprooting—precisely that word was adopted in Stalinist propaganda after the war—uprooting from the conscious awareness of people all "remnants" of earlier social formations. And was any other method possible on the path toward such a future society? Had the "mistakes" not been present in the idea itself, in the ideology, rather than in Stalin?

Stalin's communism—and really every other kind, too—was a community of "perfected" people. A community of robots or insects. A community without personality. A community without real, possible, error-prone people. Stalin knew that he was a tyrant, but his considered opinion was that only through tyranny could one arrive at communism. In that future state, once one got there, his tyranny would be justified and exalted by the fulfillment of a social order formerly only the subject of dreams. Its possibility had first to be proven "scientifically" and, yes, "practically."

Stalin combined the crazed believer with the realistic tyrant. Utopia as practice, as political power in the service of building a new society, creating a new man.

MAO: GENIUS OF GUERRILLA REVOLUTION

Mao Zedong brought China and the world no new doctrine, no enrichment of Marxism. But he was without doubt responsible for fusing Marxist doctrines with Chinese reality. From that synthesis, from form that was new, living, and adequate, there arose action. This was revolution in the most populous nation on earth.

When we assess Mao's work, we cannot go far wrong by taking the "Little Red Book" of his quotations as a guide. Wherever he elaborated on Marxist dogmas—and the "Little Red Book" is a collection of abstract fragments—his thought was dry, oversimplified, and even scholastic. It is quite clear that Mao had no very thorough knowledge of Marx, and took his Marxism mainly from popular sources. If we can say that Mao's Marxism existed at all, if indeed anyone's Marxism exists outside of the practice of it, it never went beyond the level of student circles and Party schools.

But in his Marxism, such as it was, there did exist two features characteristic of Mao, and they were a self-confidence similar to that of Lenin and a capacity to adapt on the order of Stalin's own adaptability. As a formulation of Lenin's basic principles Mao's Marxism might have come down to organizing cells and distributing illegal leaflets, but for the fact that he instilled a belief in comprehending and changing the conditions of China, and to a degree also a method for doing so. To the extent that that faith was confirmed—and without doubt it has been, as revolution—and to the extent that that method brought about new patterns—and without doubt it did, in the form of guerrilla war as the path to power, Mao was not only an important Marxist but also one of those giants who fashion their own fate and thereby the fate of the world with their own hands.

Mao Zedong did not find the path to his life's work swift and easy. All his prior experience and all his schooling, including his schooling in Marxism, pointed to the crucial role of cities in a revolution. In 1926 (in his *Analysis of Class in Chinese Society*) he had already taken note of the significance of the peasantry. But only the urban defeats suffered by the revolution in the course of the year 1927 would give Mao inspiration and teach him that the villages of China offered an inexhaustible source and an indestructible base for revolution. In the autumn of that year, 1927, he directed a peasant rebellion in his home province of Hunan, and at the beginning of 1928, together with Zhu De,[19] he gathered the remnants of his troops and led them into the mountains, there creating a "revolutionary base" (a free territory). That same year he published his essay "Why Soviet Power Can Survive in China."

The text just mentioned envisions a program of future struggles and achievements. China's weaknesses—her provincial fragmentation, her semicolonial nature, her uneven development, her half century of latent, agrarian revolution—were considered by Mao as evidence of revolutionary potential, and he sought for ways by which a revolution could be set in motion and sustained. In the forlorn provinces, especially along the borders, revolutionary bases could be established and military units organized. In Mao's vision, revolution was not a single event nor even a string of connected ones but a long-lasting struggle on the part of scattered detachments united only by ideology and an ideological Party.

Mao may have thought this, but he could fulfill it only through error, suffering, and revolutionary blood. His guerrilla units and "revolutionary bases" had to overcome Jiang Gaishek's (Chiang Kai-shek's) attacks as well as infighting within his own ranks.[20] Inspired by Mao's precise analyses, guerrilla forces outmaneuvered four "sieges meant to destroy." One of these campaigns brought about the lifting of Changsha's blockade. In breaking that siege, Mao disobeyed the orders of the leaders of his Central Committee, who were schooled and approved in Moscow, but he saved his troops and his Party from collapse.

At that time, 1931, Japan began its invasion of China by attacking Manchuria. Two months later, Mao held a congress of soviets (councils) at which he would be elected president of the Soviet Republic of China. For him, Japanese aggression presented a new revolutionary possibility, but for Jiang that same aggression discouraged what might have been a wise decision to call off the civil war in the face of general danger. Jiang methodically and obstinately continued his operations against the Communists.

In the final offensive, the fifth, which lasted almost the whole of 1934, Jiang succeeded in "cleansing" Communist territory. His success owed much to the refusal of those Moscow fledglings sent out by the Party leadership to adopt Mao's strategy of maneuver. To escape annihilation, Communist units began—at the initiative of Mao and his followers—the so-called Long March from southeastern to northwestern China. In the course of a year Mao's soldiers traversed about eight thousand kilometers, encompassing twelve provinces. They forced their way across twenty-four large rivers and eighteen mountain chains, among them five covered with perpetual snow. And as they marched, they battled the troops of ten provincial warlords.

The Long March was an incomparable military and human exploit. Losses were frightful. But Mao's views of war and his leadership became engraved in our consciousness as symbol and action. Until then he had been only fifth or sixth in the leadership. Moscow's protégés regarded him as an opportunist and inveterate peasant who couldn't be gotten rid of because of his popularity among the troops. In the course of the Long March, with all the fatal bloodshed that entailed, the revolution found its prototype and its leader. On January 6, 1935, in Tsunyi, the Maoist current within the Party replaced the Muscovite intruders and elected Mao Zedong president of the Party. Moscow no longer found it possible to replace the leadership. Mao would go to Moscow, but only at the end of 1949, and as victor in the revolution and leader of the world's most populous nation.

The Long March and Mao's assumption of leadership were tragic for China and constituted a sacred obligation. Only then did he set down in concrete, even stunning, detail his way of making war and the form that revolution would now take in China. This was done in writings such as the following: "Questions of Revolutionary War Strategy in China," "Questions of Partisan War Strategy Against the Japanese Conquerors," and "On Prolonged War." It is noteworthy that neither Mao's views nor war as it was waged under his leadership underwent any essential change when the Japanese invaded or when an armistice occurred with Jiang Gaishek and the two sides began to coordinate. War with Japan only enriched Mao's guerrilla strategy and broadened the social base he had inherited from the civil war within his country.

The two-decades-long guerrilla campaigning in China did not contribute anything essentially new in the purely military aspect. Such questions never entered Mao's mind. Mao was no field commander, never even donned a military uniform. It was war itself that was new, or Mao's idea of it. For such a war, regular troops do not play a decisive role. Decision is up to the masses in action, the people as a whole plus mobile units. Such a war cannot be planned or conducted by generals, no matter how gifted, only by those gifted political leaders who possess insight into their times and conditions and identify themselves with an ideal and with their fellow soldiers. Mao grasped the long-lasting character of the Chinese revolution, and he understood Japan's impotence when it came to occupying the whole of China. Consequently, what was fundamental for him was preserving his army and broadening guerrilla warfare, not defending territory or winning great, bloody battles.

Mao did not idealize guerrilla warfare, did not conceive of it in absolute terms. For him, it was a way of bringing on revolution and building a regular army. Generally speaking, it was only his final victories over Jiang Gaishek in 1948 and 1949 that introduced face-to-face warfare carried out by regular armies.

But that does not mean that his views had no influence on methods of warfare and how to build an army. Having discovered the form of warfare by which it was possible to hold out and to win, Mao gave his soldiers both self-confidence and a strategy.

In the Communist movement, Mao Zedong is the most important theorist of war. In the history of wars and revolutions he will occupy one of the most significant places, both as leader and as thinker.

Mao's teachings cannot be dissociated from circumstances, from the space and time in which they arose. He never in any way ceased to be Chinese. His appeal to Sun-tzu, China's greatest strategist (fifth century B.C.), was no accident. For that reason Mao's teachings are not applicable in other locales and other epochs. This does not diminish his greatness, nor the consequences of the Chinese revolution. New ideals and future struggles will extinguish all ideological estrangements and spates of madness. What remains are only admiration, lessons in sacrifice and creativity, and ever-expanding opportunities for men and nations. The guerrilla revolution in China together with its leader so abound in these traits that they keep growing into something universal and timeless.

TITO: THE STATE AS PERSONAL POWER

I have never known anybody with such an immediate, ferocious sense of danger. This, as I see it, was basic to Tito's personality. It would be fair neither to him nor to his historical role if this trait were not placed upon record in all its complexity. For a sense of danger to his own person was very often intertwined, even identified, with careful attention to principle and to his work.

In trying to understand this feeling in Tito, the fact that he identified political realities with his own private self, I am not saying that this represents some single, universal key to his personality and attainments. But without it, getting to the heart of either is not possible. In Tito, the sense of danger was overwhelming and amounted to a living instinct, a way of reacting.

Now, even if a sense of danger is characteristic of life and if politics represents the concentrated life of a nation and its social groups, in Tito's case this trait of character bulked large, surfaced in unexpected places, and never slept. Since it was elementary, instinctual, and very strong, it was a feeling that sometimes betrayed him, however, leading him astray. His instinct was reliable, almost infallible, when it came to assessing objective risks, but it could happen that he either belittled the perils threatening his own person or overreacted to them. During the war he invariably sniffed out danger and weighed it, but finding an exit was impeded by personal fears. At the very beginning of Germany's Operation Schwarz (in our historiography, the Fifth Offensive), he exclaimed to his closest associates that "never before have we been in such danger!" And in truth we did quickly establish that we were surrounded by all kinds of firepower in a deadly encirclement. We found an exit, and it was spotted with unerring accuracy. We could, however, have gotten out with more composure. Again, when he first stood up to Stalin, Tito went to the heart of the matter—that this was basically a frontal encounter between two nations. Risk to his country and to the course of revolution evidently combined and coincided with apprehension over his personal power and personal fate. Tito was tough, unyielding, and brave as he managed that conflict. However, he never finally or decisively set himself apart from the Soviet Leninist ideology, for that might have jeopardized his prestige in the Communist movement and lessened his role within his country.

Just when tensions were on the point of snapping between us and the Soviets, he and I had a talk, and I remarked that as a Communist I would have preferred prerevolutionary Yugoslavia to domination by Moscow. At this, Tito stared uncomprehendingly at me. It was not my preference as such that he could not absorb but the logic of putting homeland ahead of the Communist movement, ahead of his work, in which only Communists and he, Tito, had any role to play. A role that could not be questioned.

Tito could be thrown off and undone by his sense of danger only in a situation that arose suddenly, one that was filled with tension. Such a situation, though, he would quickly figure out and turn into reason for action. In doing so he would forget about suffering any errors and delusions, or else would explain them away capriciously.

Tito was first of all a man of practice and organization, not one to entertain second thoughts, especially if they were novel or original. What is more, his sense of danger made him distrustful of people who philosophized. Theory, meaning Marxism-Leninism, was for him a given that had been formulated once and for all. The slightest quiver of restless questioning in that domain he felt as a mortal danger for his work and his own person. Not only because he himself was no theoretician but also because all new theories herald the dissolution of fixed values. This Tito knew by both experience and instinct.

Danger and action both demand swift, penetrating thought. Tito possessed this ability. In public debate his thoughts could even be too swift, with confusion the result. His tongue being slow to catch up to his thoughts, it could happen that he combined two ideas into one, the outcome being disharmony and disarray.

His diverse political experience taught Tito to rein himself in and act with forethought. He might be confused or spurred into taking some hasty action only by sudden danger or novel circumstances. His penetration and ability to analyze grew out of these character traits. And above all, his courage in making decisions. The storms Yugoslavia passed through were, of course, not his fault alone. But they were his in the sense that he functioned on the ship of state as both the wind and the helmsman.

No one is born a Communist. But now and again there is born a rebel who then becomes whatever may be offered by the ideals and conditions of his time. So it was with Tito. In any system he would have performed some notable role. Only under communism, however, could he have become the leader of a revolution and absolute ruler of a country.

For this he possessed one other, special quality: He identified his political movement, both Party and the power it brought, with his own self. To each he transferred his personal apprehensions and problems. The particular fears and fortunes of each were experienced by him as if they were his own.

Tito was one of those who are born rebels. He learned during his second stay in the USSR (1934–36) that institutions like a Party and political power are more important than ideals. But he also learned that institutions inescapably erode if they do not maintain their ideals—ideals as an intellectual guidebook and as a code, a catechism. For in politics, all may be means to an end, and Tito, too, made ideals the means to an end, but an end that was not interchangeable with power and Party. He would never turn his back on ideals for power's sake. But his allegiance to the pure ideal was no end in itself. It arose because he realized that political power such as he had was only possible when it was informed by ideals, also such as he had. This is why he proved to be irresistible to the average Communist, who was more oriented to power than to any ideal. Communists were right in seeing in Tito their own, true representative. He was their leader, even their lord. He also was, though, the agent of their will, the architect of their aspirations.

By identifying himself with a movement and with the power of the state, and by taking on the major role in his nation's drama, a role associated with industrialism and an undogmatic approach to life, Tito always felt prompted to pay heed to his place in history. Being both concerned for this larger end and a sensible person as well, he held his impulsive temperament in check and refrained from rash actions. Of all the revolutionaries and Communists who have held power and who have traveled a similar road, Tito was one of the most rational and most moderate. As his personal power persisted and even increased, there is no question that he increasingly lost confidence in the Marxist theory about the state's withering away; there would be no quick realization of that idea. His uncertainty on this score only heightened Tito's concern for his own sustained endurance. Learning a lesson from the fate suffered by his earlier model, Stalin, he remarked to colleagues seven or eight months after Stalin's death: "It is hard to believe how quickly such a man gets forgotten." The odium and damnation heaped upon Stalin that flooded the world, especially after he died, prompted Tito to look for a balance between personal power and impersonal, legal, ways of governance. Yugoslavia did shift her position; the prevailing atmosphere did undergo a sea change. But none of that would have happened, particularly after the Soviet-Yugoslav confrontation, had Tito not realized how slippery any place in history could be if it were cemented in the blood of his fellow citizens and comrades-in-arms. In such a case, neither his personal adversaries nor Communist heretics would have had much prospect of surviving.

While not itself generating any fresh ideas, his mind did have the capacity to penetrate the minds of others with ease, to digest their ideas, and then to apply them. This, too, was part of Tito's practical gift as an executive. He thought in terms of practice; unrealizable ideas, ideas that could not be molded into organized form, were ideas without much significance for him. Something else again were ideas that had already acquired the nimbus of a cultural legacy. These he, as a statesman, had an obligation at least not to disavow.

Tito treated art in a similar way. Art that brought immediate benefit—that is to say, socialist trash—he clasped to his bosom. He once pointed out to me a certain woman author, quite untalented, sentimental, but to him a good writer, doubtless because she glorified him and his struggle. But he found modern sculptors and architects acceptable—once they became famous. Any established value, as long as it was innocuous, enjoyed Tito's easy approval; he had no ideological prejudices in these cases.

A Croat by nationality, Tito was oriented to a federation of South Slavs already in his youth. During the war his Yugoslav feelings were passionate and firm. Later on as well, he remained steady in his convictions, especially since the political power of his Party originated in the Yugoslav idea, as did his vision of a powerful Balkan and Central European state. Tito was conscious of being Croatian but not emotionally tied to his origins. One got the impression that he felt more sentimental attachment toward the Slovenes (Tito's mother was a Slovene) than toward Croatianism and the Croats. Serbs he respected, especially their spirit of pugnacity when it came to country-formation. He had the mind-set of a man from the Zagorje region, just to the north of Zagreb; it was a fervent, unquenchable love of home. Tito never managed to shake off the dialectal forms and expressions of his Zagorje,[21] even though he learned foreign languages with relative ease, such as German and Russian, and later, when he was already middle-aged, English.

In a conversation we had in 1953, when Yugoslavia's survival as an independent nation was no longer in question, Tito expressed an opinion I did not share, that at some point in the future the Yugoslav communities would fuse into one nation. For him a single state was the essential point, not ethnic kinship.

Tito attributed exceptional importance to the state and its power, which were creative and vital. He had taken an unconcealed liking to the Austro-Hungarian monarchy: order, laws, autonomy, together with a powerful, political center. No uniform, no medal or service stripe, was prescribed without his careful measurement. To the future state Tito did not bequeath only its foundations but also its external appearance. Once anything is established, he would say, change comes hard.

A man like this could never be caught off guard, naturally, when his prestige was in question. Even in wartime, with its mortal agonies or ecstasies of triumph, Tito kept his closest associates at a distance: Comrades may be comrades, but it should always be clear just who is who. He jested easily and had a sense of humor. One might play a joke on this man, but beware of injuring his sense of prestige. He was capable of splitting hairs in the pursuit of prestige, capable of being childishly petty. Whatever belonged to Tito had to be the most beautiful, the most costly, the most luxurious. Even the wild animals he shot had to be big game. This quality was the earliest cause for outrage among Party intellectuals and idealists, who immediately after the war still thronged his entourage. But Tito would not be budged.

Luxury was the hallmark of his palaces, his vehicles, his hunting grounds and yachts. More than merely an attachment to luxury, these manifested power. To Tito, flamboyance was inseparable from political leadership, from state administration. One was reminded of the crowned monarchs of old, some of them Austro-Hungarian, some Yugoslav. He took great pains to collect and appropriate all that had belonged to the former court. But he expanded also, built anew. He was surely aware that in all this ostentation there was much that did not conform to the professed modesty and simplicity of a Communist. Communist morality was simply a code of ethics that he never espoused. He never forbade anyone to live as he did, as long as they lived more modestly and more simply. Such an epicurean return to life helped the Party, and thus society as a whole, dissociate itself from class and dogma.

In this style of living Tito saw nothing at cross purposes with the man on the street. On the contrary: Humanity loves exceptional personalities, with all their glitter. Nor can it be denied that Tito tried his best for the people at large, that he sympathized with the poor in their daily lives, and that this lively interest did not arise from politics alone but because he remembered his own past privations. Tito viewed himself as just as much a popular ruler as a Party leader, and there can be no doubt that the former seemed more important and more lasting to him than the latter.

Skill at governing is quickly learned, assuming the gift for it. Luxury and leisure are learned still faster, especially with the assistance of "experts" who skim off a little luxury and leisure themselves. But Tito was a quick study in general. Once I had occasion to forewarn him over the pronunciation of a certain Latin phrase, and he never again mispronounced it. Something of the same sort used to happen before the war with regard to his spelling.

For all his love of hunting and entertainment, Tito was not a lazy man. And he never had second thoughts, or more precisely, he was so alert and aware that nothing important—important for politics, power, or personal prestige—ever got by him. He was preoccupied by what might be called pure politics. Wholly absorbed in it. Until things began moving along in their intended course, a course matching his intentions, Tito would watch unobtrusively. He never bothered officials with frequent calls. In my work, months could go by without his interfering. So it was with the others. His management was flexible and intelligent, though he could be anxiously persistent over details if these seemed important to him.

In no way an intriguer, Tito was loyal and attentive to colleagues—until, of course, there began to arise differences and "deviations." Once these made their appearance he became suspicious and sly, quick to denigrate, and uncompromising when it came to crushing resistance.

Tito privately never agreed with Marx's idea that it was the masses who had played the dominant role in history. Once, when we were both escorting the body of Boris Kidrič, our economics minister who died in 1953, by train to Ljubljana, I was expatiating on that theory, and his response was almost cutting. "How absurd!" he shot back. "Often the whole course of history has depended on one person." Obviously he had himself in mind, was thinking of the role he himself was playing in history.

I think a feeling for religion had not entirely died out in Tito. On that same occasion when we were sitting by Kidrič's corpse in the railroad carriage, I started talking about how nothing but chemical elements remain of a human being upon death. At this Tito broke in with an ambiguous little smile. "No more along that line now! Who knows?" And he insisted, with ill-concealed discomfort, that signing death warrants was in the hands of other organs of the government and not up to him as chief of state. Without a doubt this, too, reflected a concern for his "place in history." But also a repressed sense of sin.

He knew how to keep a confidence and avoid revenge. But when conflict did break out, vengefulness came alive in him and he would pass into a rage of accusation. Both forgiveness and reprisal were subordinated to political ends, despite any momentary flashes of anger.

Tito's bravery also fit the end in view. He was careful to avoid risks. And yet there is no question that he was ready to die for the sake of his work and his political power. And political death he viewed as the most terrible kind of death, the most final. After the conflict with the USSR in 1948, in a state of angry suspense while we were walking through the park on Brdo that had once belonged to Prince Paul, he exclaimed in a rush of furious conviction: "To die for one's own country! At least a memory remains."

Nor was the confrontation with me and the settling of accounts that ensued prompted by personal motives. What is more, I believe that the friction between us came hard to him, at first. I am not bringing this out just because death blunts all sharp edges and mitigates bitterness. I always thought this. When we last met, in company with Kardelj and Ranković, when our own confrontation was already public knowledge, Tito said to me: "You're a different case, and things will go differently with you." I think he meant by this: "You, when you get a bee in your bonnet, nothing can remove it."

Tito saw easily into people's motives. However, being more inclined to belief than disbelief in people, he found himself often led astray. Many were able to hoodwink Tito, but battles are not wars, and in the end he won his wars. Even when he believed most strongly in someone or something, in his mind there remained enough sovereign caution to hold him to that deadly, stormy path along which he had been traveling from his youth.

10 POWER AND DISSIDENTS

CAUSES OF DISSENT IN THE COUNTRIES OF EASTERN EUROPE

Dissent in the countries of Eastern Europe had a great many causes.

To penetrate to the heart of this topic sanely and sensibly, let us first agree that the root causes of any kind of dissent cannot be measured, and spring from the unrevealed depths of human nature. To this, Communist dissent was no exception. The term "human nature" has been employed from time immemorial. Our era, acquainted as it is with the psyche, has delved more deeply into this nature than ever before. Even so, human nature remains mysterious and endless. That such is the case is a good thing, for if human nature were ever to be explained to the end, then mankind would have no reason to seek outside itself. Man would become the last word. His creative restlessness would flicker out. Afterward, man himself would flicker out. For human nature harbors an ancient, congenital unwillingness to come to terms with reality, with the humdrum affairs of every day, with official values. This restlessness creates or destroys, according to the person involved. Very often within the same person, the same spirit, we find both creation and destruction. And what these forces may produce is unforeseeable and inconceivable.

Human nature, no matter how capable of patience and submission, in the last analysis rebels against any "final" values, any "perfect," closed society. The Eastern European and other such socialist systems were no doubt "true" societies, the "best" possible. But even if the ideals of total equality and total freedom were susceptible of achievement, let alone achieved, human nature someday would rise up in revolt against such a state of affairs, as if chafing at constriction and too much quiet. Generally speaking, human nature reveals its worst side first and foremost in leaders: There we see the insistence on power, there we see leadership cults of all kinds whether of petty leaders or major ones, there we see privilege available on the basis of hierarchy and ideology, the suppression of new ideas, new ways.

But if human nature as a reason for dissent in the lands of socialism could not be plumbed, other reasons could indeed be identified, and for the most part were indeed uncovered.

Doctrines dealing with building a perfect, classless society—whether based on justice and mercy or on science and rational methodology—have proven in historical practice to be only utopian. Such doctrines do not stop there. They also legitimize supreme command over all society by the very force administering the construction. This force is new, it is violent, it is exploitative, and it is the Party bureaucracy together with its satellite groups. Building society is in itself a foolish idea, inasmuch as we are not talking about the Great Pyramid of Cheops or the White Russian Canal but about the life of peoples and nations. So far as I know my Marx, such ideas are not to be found in him. Marx spoke of a transitional stage when the proletariat would have to watch out for the restoration of bourgeois dictatorship. Only then would they have to be on guard, he thought. But there is method in this madness, for the historical role of an avantgarde and its very real privileges find their motivation in the fabrication of such a transition, a transition that then has to be overseen and administered, until finally the building of this perfect society is completed.

Revolutionary societies had already begun to be stratified in the course of their revolutions: There were the leaders and the led, the self-aware forces and the unaware masses. But it took us a long time to realize this, and at the beginning we were conscious mainly of its moral and illusionistic aspects, as, for example, the revolt of the sailors on Kronstadt in 1921.[1]

Time, though, took its course. The ruts of stratification deepened; compulsion became grandfathered in by the doctrine that brute force would be necessary until the state should wither away; and there grew an awareness of the parasitic nature of bureaucracy, of its unproductive inequality and its illegitimate, irrational use of force.

Concrete events—the subjection of Eastern Europe to Soviet power and the revelation of Stalin's terror in all its frenzy—enabled critical spirits to see the system as a whole. Official ideology was growing sclerotic—hard and inflexible—and thereby tilling the soil for new ideas. Mental activity is likewise a condition for the individual and the community, and it becomes crucial when society stagnates and withdraws into a cocoon.

International conditions as well favored the growth and broadening of dissidence. Seen from afar, the Cold War facilitated a falling out among nations: First Yugoslavia broke off, next Albania and China fell out with the USSR, then this was followed by revolt in Hungary and restlessness in Poland, while at the same time détente permitted criticism of basic principles and promoted the inception of antidogmatic, democratic processes and various opposition movements (the Czechoslovak Spring of 1968, Croatian nationalism and Serbian liberalism in Yugoslavia at the end of the sixties, economic unrest in Poland).

In Eastern Europe, dissent took different forms from country to country, in both ideas and in intensity. But all were united by desiring respect for human rights. That also is the way in which individuals and movements attain a certain legality. The struggle for human rights ties together various miscellaneous currents of thought and clears the path for publicity, whatever kind of publicity that might be, and mostly in the Western press. For human rights are values that no one can deny openly, especially in the countries in question. After all, human rights are built into their legislation and are even recognized in their official ideology. And the systems of Eastern Europe, for all that they were closed by nature, could no longer isolate themselves from the West either spiritually or economically without provoking internal shock and protest.

In the 1960s it might have seemed that conditions did not exist for a dissident movement in the Soviet Union, if only because it was a stronghold of bureaucratic reaction and diehard ideologues. The dissident movement was extremely diverse and did things without warning. The authorities dispersed the dissidents, only to be faced with rancor more abundant and more unruly. Campaigns of slander provoked interest, and yet such campaigns could not be dispensed with when the "reactionary" and "imperialist" West set all bells ringing for even the least little dissidence, and these bells were so strong and modern that agitprop and the intelligence services were incapable of laying traps for them.

Dissident currents in the Soviet Union affirmed themselves through strong personalities: Sakharov[2] and Amalrik[3] representing rationalism and democracy, Solzhenitsyn[4] standing for Orthodoxy and conservatism, Roy Medvedev[5] for a reformed Leninism. The Soviet order had fallen into such an impasse that dissent there was inevitable, a force of nature.

There could be no question, however—judging by *Charter 77*[6]—that the dissident movement in Czechoslovakia attained the highest form of self-awareness and realism. The reasons for this were more than obvious. The people of Czechoslovakia—indeed, all of Europe—had endured Soviet intervention and control and a domestic administration consisting chiefly of lackeys and agents.

Charter 77 in reality was really not so much dissent as simply a gathering of the most intelligent and courageous sons of the Czech and Slovak peoples, who were emancipated by the 1968 tragedy both from any illusions about "the brotherly Soviet Union" and from the ideology of a "perfect" society. The conclusions and goals of *Charter 77* were applicable to every Eastern European country. It was no accident that the charter was not published in any of these countries save Yugoslavia, and in a quasi-pornographic periodical at that!

The attentive reader was amazed by the style of *Charter 77* even more than by its contents: calm harmony, dignified self-confidence. This was the most mature, most complete program to come out of the East after the war. No wonder: *Charter 77* was a continuation of the Czech Spring of 1968. It arose from life, from social and national reality, not from dogma. Through *Charter 77* the tolerant and indestructible spirit of democracy characteristic of the Czech and Slovak peoples began to speak out.

In *Charter 77* human rights were given full, vital substance. For that reason *Charter 77* pointed the way for dissidents and inspired them—persons deprived of rights, persons enslaved, the depersonalized peoples of Eastern Europe.

CREATIVITY IN DOGMA*

To emphasize the concise beauty of style or the refined penetration of thought in Leszek Kolakowski would today be no more than to repeat yesterday's acknowledgments of what in this

---

*On the books by Leszek Kolakowski, *Marxism and Beyond* (London: Pall Mall Press, 1969) and *Filkozofski eseji* (Belgrade: Nolit, 1964).

writer is most conspicuous and least debatable. Something similar could be said of his role in liberating contemporary Polish society from the myths and dogmas of Leninism-Stalinism; or could be said of the steadiness with which he carried this out, not only at the time of the Polish October but, what is most significant and bravest of all, after that Polish October failed to live up to expectations and was reduced to stabilizing the "legal," autonomous rights of the Party bureaucracy within the framework of the Polish state.

But even if these values in Kolakowski had already been appraised and even were I a literary critic, or a philosopher, or a historian, even then I would not linger over them or expand on them. For it seems to me that Kolakowski's attributes, however unarguable and important, are not those that make him in the highest degree special and set him apart from other writers and thinkers who also from within communism criticize Communist dogmatics and the noncorrespondence of Communist ideals with the privileges and lack of scruples of the Party bureaucracy. Defining these particularities is important and needful today both for a fuller evaluation of Kolakowski and because it is precisely they that make him a living presence in today's intellectual currents, especially those within communism.

Kolakowski passed through all the phases typical of a heretic of communism: ecstasy over Stalinism, moral revolt against the untruths and monstrosities of that same Stalinism, and a return to the sources of Marxism, including the young Marx, whom Kolakowski was among the first to discover. Even though this sequence looks typical at first glance, it is just there that we must seek first for the quality that makes him stand out as a personality and a thinker within communism, and for that matter within all other structures.

First of all, though, we must clarify the real meaning of the terms "Stalinist" and "Stalinism." These are words that are pinned to every former Communist regardless of whether anyone for any reason was an adherent of Stalin's and a champion of his writings. I find it indisputable that terms like these, originating at a time of the cruelties and oversimplifications of the Cold War, turned into stereotyped formulas. Later, such formulas tended to stifle the democratic ferment taking place within communism. They impeded the process of coming to one's senses within it. In short, they helped the Party aristocrats counter every real criticism and essential change through either de-Stalinization or re-Stalinization.

Stalinism was a crazed, fictional formula eagerly employed by yesterday's Communists (and not only by them) in an endeavor to rejuvenate and reform communism by denouncing Stalinism. Stalinism was not actually a "mistake" but the logical outcome of Marxism. Because Marxism, or communism, believes in its own hardheaded scientism, it is not possible to effect any sort of change in it, to create any sort of communism without this being Stalinism to one degree or another. And vice versa: The fall of Stalinism meant the disintegration of Marxism as an ideology and of Communist socialism as a social system. Now, to clarify that this person was an adherent of Stalin for certain reasons and that person for another set of reasons meant, of course, that we were determining someone's moral characteristics. But—and this is what is most essential—it meant that we were investigating everyone's aspirations and possibilities. For there were two quite different things involved in the distinction. Was the one person a Stalinist because he believed that Stalin fulfilled and perpetuated Marx? Was the other a Stalinist because he had bonded to Stalin's power and methods? In the first case it was a question of revolutionaries and idealists, in the second of bureaucrats and political careerists who were employing the dissolution of Stalinist forms to impose their own monopolies. I do not say by this that any person, simply by virtue of being a revolutionary, is spared from having shortcomings. Nor do I think that political idealism must always be a fateful attitude, disastrous for individuals and whole peoples, more disastrous, in fact, than the most egoistic and shortsighted realism. Nevertheless, we should not lose sight of the fact that Stalinist idealists and revolutionaries have it in them to criticize from a position within Stalinism, that is, within Marxism and the Communist systems. In fact, such people have long since begun to criticize, while the reformist and liberal bureaucracy of Party members maintains its own critical stance by further monopolizing power. Such a situation is not new to history, but it is new to communism, where heretics inspire change, even when they are not the beneficiaries of it.

Neo-Stalinist and anti-Stalinist bureaucrats doubtless enjoy an advantage in the politics of "real" rule. But the future does not belong to them. In the best scenario they can only prepare for change and then try to shepherd it along by making what they like to call "adjustments." Criticism from within actually removes a certain mythical, idealized luster from their own reality, eating away at its foundations, blazing new trails. For this is not criticism of an external, alien world but of the one which has evolved out of the evils and delusions of communism itself. Bureaucrats may repress such criticism but they cannot uproot it, for it emanates from the very roots of communism: Wherever Communism exists, corrosive criticism exists. Soviet bureaucrats were able to dismiss the prerevolutionary philosopher Berdyaev,[7] but could not dismiss the writer Solzhenitsyn, even though the latter lacks Berdyaev's depth and truth. Berdyaev was opposed to the Communists from the very moment they were enthroned. Solzhenitsyn, by contrast, is the creation of their own system.

It need hardly be said that Kolakowski belongs among the idealistic sort of former Stalinists. This camp includes the most important of today's theoreticians of Marxism: George Lukacs,[8] Herbert Marcuse,[9] Roger Garaudy,[10] and others. All these thinkers, like Kolakowski, were looked upon by the Kremlin censors of Marxism as revisionists and freaks. But the Kremlin bureaucrats were what they were because they had no feeling for nuances. Whatever was not part and parcel of their own grayness was for them the same color. The Marxist theoreticians mentioned above and others like them differed among themselves, threw their weight around, possessed their own values within the framework of Marxist literature and Communist movements.

But between them and Leszek Kolakowski there existed a difference that is essential and very significant. All of them reduced Stalinism to a distortion of the "good" Lenin and the "modest" Marx. Not one learned to ponder in freedom, not one began to reflect without first taking thought for his inherited Marxist foundations or considering the given conditions. I certainly do not find fault with these theoreticians for failing to see through those archaic and utopian Marxist formulas. Nor has it crossed my mind to fault them for failing to renounce Marxism. Especially not that. It is a question of something else. Those Marxists, unlike Kolakowski, who (so far as I am aware) remained within the framework of Marxism until he was forced out of Poland in 1968, were not behaving as investigators of the truth but as true believers in an inherited and irrefutable dogma. Hence not one of them was capable of noticing, to say nothing of foreseeing, the Marxist and particularly the Leninist roots of Stalinism, roots that made Stalinism what it was and accounted for what it could do. They could not understand the Communist movements of the sixties and seventies. Therefore even their criticism of Stalin's distortions of Marx and Lenin—distortions that undoubtedly existed—remained sterile. In place of analysis they all nourished hope; in place of awareness they were by and large embittered. Their truths remained half truths. They analyzed and took note, but none of them got up the courage to destroy their own comfortable, inherited world. So none of them was a true creator. Generally speaking, not one of them had the slightest desire to do anything but go on developing the original dogma.

Not a single hallowed truth stopped Kolakowski, however. In all things he was a free thinker and thereby a creative one. For this reason he had no need to renounce Marxism or to see through its unrealities. He kept looking into his own understanding and his own life experience, which I do not think was all that rich. Instead of reworking and redeeming his inherited doctrines, he investigated them. The dogma in terms of which he thought and lived, as it disintegrated within his consciousness, could only stimulate him inexorably and creatively. As dogma hardened and narrowed for him, it forced him to make new mental efforts, new moral exertions. Kolakowski was passionate, but no hater. His texts were shadowed with resigned irony but never with bitterness. His criticism, no matter how inspired by actual processes—by "mistakes," "distortions," "betrayals"—always encompassed a certain essence, which was that dogmatism and force, interlinked, constitute a human phenomenon. Then there were the civilizations of Europe, fatal for modern man and modern technology. Kolakowski was no revisionist, actually, and about him as a reformist we can speak only in connection with his political and social activity. He was simply a thinker who did not throw overboard his own dogma but outgrew it with his creativity.

Kolakowski's particularity lay in his not criticizing Marxism but on the contrary, and more often than not in parallel with it or even in terms of Marxism, developing new ideas and understandings. He discovered a thematic and motivational continuity between the scholastic teachings of the Middle Ages and modern dogmas, and he showed this with such clarity that no one could doubt that it was all about Marxism in the first place. Many writers before Kolakowski had noticed the scholastic side of Marxism, and especially of Leninism and Stalinism. But only he showed that in reality we were talking here about something more stubborn and longer-lasting—about one of the enduring features of European social and philosophical thought.

So he did not stop when faced with any hallowed, "unalterable" truth of Marxism. The destructive quality of his logic and resourcefulness seemed to have no limits. Kolakowski, therefore, all the time remaining within the fold of Marxism and developing many of his theses straight out of it, demolished its foundations: the primacy of matter* and the doctrine that history follows predictable laws.† Out of Marxist dogmatics and socialist reality in Poland and Eastern Europe, new truths spoke through him. Thereby he affirmed himself and—in a new way—the old, time-honored human knowledge that any dogma is impotent and ineffectual when faced with a free, creative spirit. And by situating modern dogmas within the framework of European history and human conditions, by demonstrating their inner poverty, and by proving their inappropriateness for modern human existence, Kolakowski confirmed that he was a thinker who did not belong just to a Polish, Eastern European, and Marxist "heresy" but to modern thought as a whole.

True, Kolakowski often discoursed about practical exits from the blind alleys and impasses of the Party bureaucracy's so-called omniscience and omnipotence, and this could have led people of the New Left to rely on him too. His rationales were sometimes implausible. But what was most essential in his thinking—that spiritual and personal freedoms are certain—has never had and never can have any place in the world of those "new" makers of human happiness who resort to the old, tried and true, methods of brute force. For courageous, critical endurance, which was the fundamental, inner motive in Kolakowski's work, is an aspect of freedom. None of today's "academic" or "auditorium" revolutionaries has anything essential to offer the world that has not already been tried by any number of countries and found to be a bloody and devil-ridden utopia, impossible of fulfilment, one which its own proponents would be glad to give up if only they had enough common sense and honor.

It has been observed that Kolakowski was not a modern philosopher in the narrow sense of that word. But no one can argue that he was not new and original within the limits and conditions in which he operated. In that sense, moreover, he was perhaps the most original philosophical phenomenon of socialist Eastern Europe.

---

*"For even our thoughts about reality are likewise a part of reality, no less important than other parts" (*Marxism and Beyond*, p. 56).

†See "Responsibility and History" in *Marxism and Beyond*, and "Cogito, Historical Materialism, and an Expressive Interpretation of Personality" in *Filozofski eseji*.

My own critical thinking developed in parallel to that of Kolakowski, but it was predominantly a product of political experience and literary forms. Marxist philosophy, however, has not yet passed through the fire of creative criticism; that is to say, criticisms have arisen out of its reality and its structure. Not yet has there appeared in Eastern Europe, nor even in all of communism, a person capable of taking up this task, if not Kolakowski. He it was who evoked my amazed excitement in prison, when first I came to know his work. Even without that, however, I was prepared to render homage to his gifts, his integrity. For Leszek Kolakowski has discovered and bestowed on the world new understandings and new decencies. I am confident that he will be regarded as one of those who engender future attainments and future truths about man—out of the dark gloom of force and frozen dogma.

ON THE "NEW LEFT"

1

It should come as no surprise that the rebellions of young people which flared up especially in 1968 throughout the universities of Europe and America elicited anxiety and resistance among the guardians of order and the theoreticians of social reform.

It is not puzzling that the majority of official Communist parties came into conflict with these rebellions: Insofar as the young rebels were Marxist, their Marxism repudiated the "distortions" emanating from Moscow, including bureaucratic Stalinism, and even Leninist oversimplifications.

But that is just one reason, and a secondary one to boot, for the resistance of Communist Parties to the views and methods of dissatisfied youth. The parties in Eastern Europe had become entrenched vehicles for their bureaucratic and hegemonistic systems, while those in the West—particularly the Italian and the French, which were the only ones to have any significant influence in their countries—could no longer avoid being turned into sectarian splinter groups save at the cost of fusing, however indirectly, with the technological or consumer societies in those countries.

These revolts by the youth delighted the Trotskyites, Maoists, Castroites, anarcho-Communists, anarchists, disillusioned Stalinists, and intellectuals generally of all kinds, university-department and drawing-room revolutionaries. All too eagerly they rushed to warm themselves at the revolutionary flames, although they neither had set them ablaze nor had enough breath to stoke them. They were deceived by an ossified, dogmatic faith that capitalism had got itself pregnant with revolution all by itself, that the purges, acts of violence, and privileges associated with socialism had not quite finished off their revolution. And while the politicians and thinkers of the movement sank ever deeper into the misfortunes brought upon them by the disorders in the universities and on the streets, true believers and the shipwrecked victims of long-ago revolutions were eager only to flatter and to give orders to the rebellious youth. It could not be otherwise: Like the call of the horn summoning us to the spoils and delights of the hunt, so the very thought of revolution makes the former revolutionary tingle with delight. But it also awakens fear of being late for the revolutionary train, a train ready to carry him to power and human beings to the kingdom of peace and equality.

I flatter myself at not being overcome by such weaknesses, although as a onetime revolutionary myself I ran the risk of being declared a traitor and deserter to the side of capitalism, imperialism, and counterrevolution. I never rose to the defense of the system, although I could be criticized for not having settled scores to the bitter end with my own past. Somebody might wish to explain my behavior by the fact that I had nothing to lose and that I had been broken of the habit of admiring anything. Well, I should reply that I was drawn into such a position by the knowledge that not one system is so righteous and open as to merit unconditional defense against attacks by young rebels. I should add that these young rebels were not exactly so idealistic and wise that they could get away without being criticized and having to cool down.

2

Protests by the young in the sixties were, taken as a whole, the first world movement that had not begun in someone's brilliant head or in some leading center but instead in reaction to bureaucratic arbitrariness and crass consumerism, in opposition to an atomic cataclysm, and in resistance to inhumane classifications, whether ideological, nationalistic, racial, or moral. The roots of this movement were not to be found mainly in politics but in nonconformism in clothing, morals, and behavior (existentialist beatniks, hippies, and others).

Maoist and Castroite currents were either sporadic or, more often, expressions of pride and protest against official, entrenched opinion.

Nonconformity and universal decency are what unite young, dissatisfied people both East and West. These are what have been and what will remain—though in the form of tradition—the most inspirational and most creative characteristics in the spontaneous protests of contemporary youth.

But these also are precisely what slackens and turns pale as soon as spontaneous movements turn into ideological and political ones. Institutionalization means taking things into consideration, manipulating; it leads to dogmatic exclusiveness and factional bickering. That is just what befell the youth movement the moment ideology—that is, an idealized goal and manipulation by leaders—started to become implanted in it.

Above all, the young Western rebels became stuck with the tag "New Left," like an evil omen. Although this tag implied that the old left had fallen, it failed to proclaim any new, more realizable, ideals. The New Left merely promised to be more true to an ideal than the old left had been. The ideal itself—a perfect society (Communist, anarchist)—remained unchanged. And owing to its being too weak to cut the umbilical cord binding it to the myths of revolutionary tradition, the New Left was unable to shed the sins of the old—too old—left. More on account of these dogmatic legacies than because of its breakup into currents and lines of descent, the New Left was not capable of creating any real, all-embracing program. Though no one can deny that its activities awakened many a sleeping conscience and opened up many an essential question in old issues (the war in Vietnam, race relations, emotional problems, reorganization of universities), nonetheless the New Left remained old in spirit.

For all these reasons the New Left movements were short-term ones, brave and effective in the concrete, moral dilemmas of life among young intellectuals but confused and powerless whenever it was a question of society as a whole and of our planet's common troubles and needs.

From country to country and in each country taken on its own, the New Left movements became ever more heterogeneous, fragmented into various factions and organizations. But from the beginning there was a noticeable and growing difference between the attitudes of dissatisfied youth in the West and in the East. In the so-called consumer societies of the West, solely because the broadest layers no longer felt the pinch of hunger and unemployment, nor were they oppressed by one Party's monopoly of power, young rebels were blinded by ideal dogmas and utopias. In Yugoslavia, too, together with tendencies toward more efficient production and political freedoms, there appeared, also predominantly at the universities, dogmatic groups of "humanist" Marxists and egalitarians. But in Eastern Europe as a whole, youth protests, to the degree that they managed to find expression at all (e.g., in Czechoslovakia, Poland, Yugoslavia, and among the Russian intelligentsia), had a predominantly democratic character oriented toward emancipation. It was no accident, therefore, that Rudi Dutschke,[11] the astute rehabilitator of "unspoiled" Marxism in West Berlin, was met by indignation among the students of Prague; or that the very clever Daniel Cohn-Bendit[12] in his little book *Obsolete Communism: The Left Wing Alternative* (London: André Deutsch, 1968), did not even mention the events in Czechoslovakia. The leader of the Czech students, Jan Kavan, put it this way: "For us, the classic civil liberties assume the utmost importance. In socialist society freedom of speech, freedom of the press, freedom of assembly, and freedom to organize are essential if the people are to have any kind of control. . . . I have often said to my friends in Western Europe that we are fighting only for bourgeois-democratic freedoms. But somehow I cannot seem to distinguish between capitalist freedoms and socialist freedoms. What I recognize are basic human freedoms."*

Clearly these distinctions emerged from different political arrangements and from the different tasks standing before the developed countries, and as a separate matter before the educated, both West and East (with the exception of backward China, where social and other differentiations are blinkered and blinded by transports of dogma, anathemas, and prohibitions). The inexhaustible and unceasing protests of young intellectuals were products of the new and heightened role of knowledge, and so of the educated, in a modern economy open to contemporary technology. Although there is no prospect that life's everyday toil (labor) will disappear, it is obvious that physical, industrial

---

*Cited from Stephen Spender, *The Year of the Young Rebels* (New York: Random House, 1969), p. 65.

labor (work) is on the wane.*[13] The working class to a considerable degree has merged with the middle class and been incorporated into the consumer society. Hopes that the young rebels had entertained of a union of workers and students had to come to nothing. Even in France, whose students in July 1968 served to detonate a general strike, the workers did not follow these dogmatic wise men and young idealists but simply went after higher wages. Private property is no longer the only form of property, even in the West, not to speak of its being an unconditional form. Moreover, it is obvious that the form property takes, though this can be a source of inequality that is unjust (i.e., unfreedom), by itself is not the controlling condition of a better or a worse society. A modern economy obviously functions effectively when managed by technocrats. For this there are more convincing and illustrative proofs in the West (Volkswagen, Renault, INA, atomic energy in the United States, etc.) than in the East, where the economy, merely by virtue of being nationalized, has been clogged by the Party bureaucracy and other bureaucrats. Educated people will soon become the most numerous, and judging by all the signs, the most significant social class. They have proliferated suddenly, thanks to the technological revolution, and neither they nor society as a whole have adjusted to these changes or been capable of understanding each other.

Put in the simplest terms, the structure of society and of politics is essentially the same as before today's technological revolution. And so are the ideals of the young rebels, by and large, dating from the times of Marx, Bakunin, Lenin, and W. D. Haywood.[14] Society's problems, however, are more rooted, while the aspirations of the educated are more far-reaching and their role more inevitable.

3

"The present generation of young people in our universities is the best-informed, the most intelligent, and the most idealistic this country has ever known."† This was my impression, too, of young, educated Americans during my stay in the United States in the fall of 1968. The same cannot be said of the young intellectuals of Europe, be they in the capitalist or in the socialist states. Other, even

---

*This distinction between "labor" *(trud)* and "work" *(rab)* is taken from Hannah Arendt, *The Human Condition* (Garden City, NY: Anchor Books, 1959).

†*Crisis at Columbia* (New York: Random House, 1968), p. 4.

better words could be found to apply to the new generations. But here we are speaking of the new generations as a whole. And when the subject is the young rebels, only the most fanatical reactionaries and the most bigoted dogmatists would benefit if their sterile dogmas were ignored and suppressed.

If the failures of the old left did not cease with the dissolution of its ideology, the failures of the New Left began just at this point. Hence those people are not correct—for example, Sidney Lens*—who maintain that the weaknesses of the New Left flow from their not having a simple, "constructed" ideology. No one has ever succeeded in constructing an ideology. Ideology is the sort of thing that grows out of innumerable conditions and finally synthesizes in someone's brilliant mind. In every way the unruly world daily stands revealed as diverse and indefinable. It lacks causality in the structure of nature, none of its human societies is ideal, the human psyche is quite indefinite, it is impossible to take the measure of the human mind. In such a world, constructing an ideology is especially impracticable. Modern society— like matter and man—cannot be explained through the prism of the eighteenth and nineteenth centuries, still less by an oversimplified adaptation of it. In the same way, neither can the protests of youth, who are products of both the atomic era and today's troubles, be fit back into the grooves of a nineteenth-century ideology by the most skillful manipulation. If it were possible for Marx and Bakunin to be reborn today it is quite certain that they would be neither Marxists nor anarchists. Change in society is a creative, not an imitative, act.

Social and political patterns are outmoded in many respects, in good part because in their appearance an enormous role has been played by dogmas dedicated to revolutions and privileges. On that account many forms of contemporary societies are hermetic and immobile. Social, racial, and other minorities often lack the wherewithal to publicize their troubles legally, still less to resolve them within periods that are for them vital and important. The opponents of unnecessary, unjustified wars, of poverty and slums; underappreciated, intellectual masses; unemployed workers; spirits terrorized by dogmatic dictators; citizens deprived of rights; and subjugated peoples—these cannot just sit and wait to win power in parliaments, wait to be granted consideration by despots, wait for totalitarian parties to resign voluntarily from power

---

Liberation (New York, November 1968), pp. 3–4.

and dogma or conquerors to abdicate empire. Illegal, violent methods are inescapable and justified whenever some group or community is forced to deny its own life, its own visions. And by the very fact that there are no perfect societies, groups and communities such as these— yes, even violence itself—must exist.

But this hardly justifies movements in which brute force and the violent destruction of society are a basic component of their goals and their tactics. We can speak about currents in the American New Left for whom the war in Vietnam, the stodginess of the universities, and the neglect of the blacks were the only good reasons for tearing down the old and building the ideal future society; these are the only true reasons a society ever will have for destroying a given social order. For the New Leftists, or at least their most ideological exponents, were already at war with society as a whole and already had worked out their own methods and final goals, had taken on their true appearance. That is why we must speak of them now as they really were and not as of some protest against particular evils and inequitable relationships.

These movements, fully formed as they are, have contributed very few new ideas despite their leaders' resourcefulness and devotion. For it was quite beside the point that the "undistorted" and "unrevised" Marxism of Rudi Dutschke was pure and ideal. The point is whether societies are ready to yield to the revolutionary changes he offered them. It is beside the point that revolutions become corrupted and devour their children. The remedy to this is certainly not Cohn-Bendit's "uncontrollable spontaneity,"* or in different words "the perpetual change called the Revolution,"† for anything of that sort is no kind of society at all, nor could any revolutionaries endure it.

Developed countries, East and West, are unready for revolutions of the classic type, not only on account of the terrible force that governments have at their disposal but also because human life within these countries has merged with modern technology, and modern technology is so complex and precise that any lasting disturbance can have consequences like an atomic cataclysm. Over and above that, production in these countries has either solved or is on the way to solving the basic material issues of the vast majority of people. Besides, the burden of

---

*From a conversation between Cohn-Bendit and Jean-Paul Sartre cited in Spender, *The Year of the Young Rebels,* p. 107.
†Ibid.

social conflicts moves in the direction of income redistribution, of managing both the state and the economy, even of managing moral dilemmas. Sensitive to disruptions, modern systems respond with relative ease to the limited pressures and reforms of their individual components and activities. Universities began to reorganize, Lyndon Johnson declared he would not run again for president, and yet even so, the student-worker revolutions were not carried out nor was capitalist society torn down.

To be a revolutionary can be wildly ecstatic and romantic, especially where one does not pay for it with one's head or with prison terms. But revolution is a serious enterprise, responsible in the extreme, and justified only where the nation extends its sway. Revolutionary violence, like every other kind of violence, turns into madness and tyranny as soon as it becomes the instrument of new, achievable changes and patterns. Up to now revolutions have changed the form of power and property, but not one of them has altered the nature of people or the character of a nation. Property relations in the developed countries are less important than ever before. That could not be said for political power itself. Its role, especially in coordinating an economy, has become greater and more significant.

If anyone were to ask me in what consists the essence of today's revolutionary mind-set and what ought to be the task of today's revolutionaries, I would reply that it is to seek out the possibilities of human material and spiritual freedom and to insist on these publicly, honorably, and unwaveringly while staying clear of dogmas and absolute truths. After so many failed hopes and tragic temptations in both counterrevolutionary and revolutionary despotisms and when mankind is about to be plucked from the bonds of Earth to unite with space, the human being also is discovering values that cannot be compensated by or crushed by any kind of ideology or any ultimate form of political power and property.

LITERATURE AS NEVER-ENDING PUNISHMENT

The writer actually is seeking himself by expressing the world he senses and knows. And the more fully and profoundly he has affirmed his world, the more authentically he has found himself.

Not by chance does Solzhenitsyn's *The Oak and the Calf* bring this generalization forcibly to mind (and as a generalization it is not all that original).[15] It is here that this writer discloses his personality most fully. This is because it is here that he has revealed most consistently and plastically the reality he has experienced and learned, or better, suffered. And that reality, which constitutes the theme of *The Oak and the Calf,* is the Soviet Union, Soviet society under Khrushchev and his heirs. More narrowly, more precisely: These are Solzhenitsyn's memoirs on writing in secret, on concealing, black-marketing, and smuggling his works abroad—from the publication of *One Day in the Life of Ivan Denisovich* in 1962 to achieving the Nobel Prize for literature in 1974 away from his homeland.

Solzhenitsyn's significance and power lie in his original witness, artistic and replete with facts. Writers had testified on the Soviet camps before him. But Solzhenitsyn is a writer-witness, one who brings to life an unfamiliar, uncomprehended labor camp reality. About these Soviet camps more or less everything was known even before him. But only with the advent of this writer, especially his *Gulag Archipelago,* did it become known what life was actually like there, the life (if such it can be called) of human beings, how conditions in the camps and the social order founded on them were lived through and experienced by both the tormented and the tormentors, the violators and the oppressed. Out of millions of those who were murdered, those who simply died and those who were deformed, there arose a writer-witness, a truth-teller, merciless because he was a gifted writer who also was a writer of conscience.

The Oak and the Calf concerns itself very little with ideas and ideologies, criticism and history of the Communist order. For that reason it is Solzhenitsyn's most compact and, literarily, most masterful work. This is a document about people and human interactions, about the closed Soviet system, and about a wonderful, cunning, heroic effort to drill a hole in the solid, fortress wall of police and ideology and through it to squeeze the creations of the spirit into the outside world, into life. The work is written as if in one breath. And we read it never ceasing to tremble in fear even while knowing that the spirit of Solzhenitsyn had already breached the system with the publication of *Ivan Denisovich,* the moment he had begun to re-create artistically the labor camp essence of the Soviet system and the undoubted but unimagined suffering of millions of innocent people in those camps.

For this memoir, or document, is basically a novel about the conspiratorial life of the artist, about the secret strategy of writing belles-lettres, about setting down in print whatever might disagree with the censor and all that refuses to knuckle under to "The Most Advanced Doctrine." Quite a few facts were known to me, including many incidents from *The Oak and the Calf.* Its basic theme, too. Yes, the theme most of all! For I, too, have been and still am driven into silence about my literary motifs and have been forced to conceal my manuscripts, typed in secret in a number of copies, in various places. I have even had to bury them in the ground. Secret Police agents brazenly issued orders directly in front of me and my wife to a blushing post office girl, telling her without so much as a by-your-leave that my letters should be set aside in a special little compartment. I would choose this post office and change another post office and in short would contrive to find all sorts of ways to get my manuscripts off to publishers. I was obliged, writing in prison, to change the roles of my heroes so that this or that one not be seen as a caricature of a Communist. I had to camp out on people's doorsteps on behalf of my manuscripts, slave to momentary caprice and the incessant endeavor to kill me in spirit. Where and what my homeland is, that I know, but in reality I, too, am hounded out of my own country by the taboo on being what I am, the ban on that by which I live. And yet despite knowing it all so well in advance and despite my own Solzhenitsyn-like struggle for spiritual, literary, existence, I read *Calf* without pause and with a wide-awake mind. For the magic of artistic work lies in the fact that what is known is made unknown, what is familiar is made strange and takes on a life of its own.

The Oak and the Calf in many ways represents a continuation of the *Gulag.* Nor could it be otherwise: This man carries within himself for good and all the camp sufferings, the Russia of the camps. But the link between the two books is more literal, more thematic. Finding a way for animal survival within the camp, contriving to find a way of which only the human spirit is capable, is a stratagem that becomes continued "in freedom." There, too, one contrives to find a way to preserve and disseminate the truth about the camps and the camp system, and it is a way of which only those are capable whose creativity is stronger than themselves, whose creativity is conscience, and whose conscience—creativity. The fusion of literary gift and the morally scrupulous took place in Solzhenitsyn.

Solzhenitsyn often refers to the role of "miracle," as he calls it, and the "finger of God" in his destiny. To me, what is miraculous is his intelligence and his loyalty to himself and the Russian nation. In him we see the "finger" of Russia and the people of Russia pointing at the wellsprings of the nation, pointing to the dignity of personality. Rational, critical Western thought is hard to comprehend. Solzhenitsyn's prerevolutionary Orthodoxy in particular cannot be understood as an ideology, even though he offers it as a replacement for the monopolistic Marxism of the Party bureaucracy. But this incomprehension does not diminish the role of Solzhenitsyn and his work as a whole, his witness-bearing and his convictions, which at times attain high, even the highest, reaches of Russian literature. These attainments have independent, permanent value, sometimes in the face of his social and ideological views. Who is this writer whose social views and religion are within the reach of all? Are the ideas of Tolstoy and Dostoyevsky really any more comprehensible today in the West—and not only in the West but in intellectual, rationalistic circles in the East as well? And yet their works are fundamental to both "Western" and "Eastern" literatures.

With Solzhenitsyn there began a literature about human life and the destiny of men and nations subjected to violence, ideological violence, political violence—total violence. This new, horrible, merciless epic is only starting to unroll, but it has already brought forth a number of gifted and uncompromised writers (V. Maksimov,[16] Andrei Sinyavsky,[17] Vladimir Voinovich[18]), and after them will come the thinkers and critics. However, no matter what one thinks about its achievements up to the present, this body of literature already stands as a verdict upon the system from which it has emerged, stands as a curse upon it. Camp literature damns that system not so much by telling the truths of history and filling them with facts—though the literature of the camps has already yielded significant results in this regard—as by the sincerity of its depiction of a monstrous life. It was a life couched in lies, a life led in the name of utopian dogma, a life conducted in accordance with the prescriptions of pragmatic, unbelieving Party bureaucrats. Tsarist Russia had been stigmatized and condemned by the writings of Gogol, Tolstoy, Nekrasov,[19] Gorky, and Bunin.[20] Most essentially, I might say, this was carried out by Dostoyevsky with his inimitable depiction of captive beings (in their Russian variant). The Tsarist order, of course, did not come unglued from the impact of their writings. But their writings disarmed that established order and made it seem senseless. Not without reason did Lenin lay claim to Tolstoy as the "mirror of the Russian Revolution." Soviet literature was harried and persecuted, for it was the legitimate heir of classical Russian literature. The direction of this literature and what it achieved spelled condemnation of a system impotent to tear itself away from its labor-camp, ideological foundations. These were not emigrants from Tsarist and bourgeois Russia, nor were they emigrants from the Russian intelligentsia. These were our own offspring, the negation of the prevailing state of affairs. Their testimony was saturated with life—and life is the one final truth, out of reach and unutterable.

Art and especially literature is the evil spirit of all unfreedoms; it is sublimated life, life spiritualized. So it must be. Conflicts with unfreedom by the negating of unfreedom, plus certain other features, turn into art. Art cannot lie, for in the presence of lies there can be no art, and no truth can be propagated.

The verdicts of art are eternal, as eternal as mankind itself. Those of Solzhenitsyn will endure beyond the system from which they arose. For functionaries and hangmen will vanish from the face of the earth, as will ideology and the power it has served, the political power by which it has been inspired. Concentration camps, however, and that human suffering which can be grasped in its infinite depth only through the achievements of writers and other artists—these will last forever by the very fact that art is forever. Because art is the memory of mankind. Memory is not the only authentic value, but it is imperishable because it is the most authentic value.

The Oak and the Calf bears witness to the birth of that kind of art and its penetration into the world, and it is a very powerful, exceptionally artistic, work.

PRISONS AND THE SEA

Old and gouty, I came down to the sea to put myself under the spell of the Boka Kotorska, down where the mountains join the sea and the human urge to create joins the elements in an encounter ever the same yet ever different.[21]

The first breath of that blue freshness invigorated me, the first splashes of the sunny waves. But however earnestly I plunged into the bliss of oblivion, memories would arise irresistibly, like life itself, insistent as the pangs of conscience.

It was the summer of 1933. It was a long time ago. I was imprisoned on the island of Ada Tsiganlija in the Sava River. My window opened onto the gray-hued, lazy Sava, ever the same. From dawn to dusk the river sparkled and splashed with the happy play of swimmers, re-

sounded to the tooting of little boats. Left behind were all the promises and pleasures of a life I called my own. All those empty, un-
slaked yearnings of mine were dismissed in the self-assured hope that
prisons could never extinguish human desire and ideals. Surely not
in my country, once fascism and capitalism were vanquished.

That was long ago. Now I am brokenhearted and inconsolable over
that onetime endurance, bathed in faith. Leaders and the banners they
struggled under have all changed, fighters and the ideas they used to
fight for. And yet nothing has changed, after all. For in my very own
country, generations after the victory over fascism and capitalism,
young and old are still being persecuted, former revolutionaries are
locked up with artists just coming into flower, all for the crime of having thought differently, all because they tried to express their ideas and
carry them out.

None of these people in Yugoslavia today who are condemned to be
thrown into prison—and they perhaps number in the hundreds—have
ideas like the ones I had. So why then does their fate unsettle me? Here,
with the sea noisily beating on the sand? Here, where swimmers come
from every corner of the globe? Is that conscience in rebellion against
life? Or is it life itself, life that becomes bare existence, inhuman and
vegetablelike, when thought is suppressed and conscience stilled?

Almost without exception, the persecuted were nationalists of various stripes. Yet not one of them favored brute force and a return to
prerevolutionary relationships, certainly not publicly and unconditionally. In Zagreb they included the student leaders gathered around
Budiša and Čiček, in Belgrade there was the lawyer Subotić, the eighty-
two-year-old historian Zubović, three students who called themselves
"Trotskyites," and the philosopher Djurić, while outside the major
cities . . . No, I did not know exactly the number of "the guilty," but
there were more than enough to send shivers up the spine and to
excuse lawlessness, especially in Croatia, plenty from all classes and all
walks of life.

From the very beginning I was against taking these people into cus-
tody and subjecting them to trial. In this, I was prompted by knowledge
and experience. Whether under capitalism or under socialism I had
learned that all political trials, excepting, of course, trials of terrorists
and spies, were judicial farces and stagings for propaganda's sake. But
at the same time knowledge and experience dictated a convenient and
practical course: not to expose myself to risk for the sake of people to

whom I felt obligated merely because they had kept silent or made little of things. For it seemed more intelligent and more useful to stand aside from disasters not your own. In that way you win favor from both prosecutors and victims. As for the sea, it offered cheerful peace and calm. These thousands of sunburned, relaxed bodies on the beaches and under the pine trees knew nothing of prisons and cared not a whit about the righteous resentments and understandable despair of martyrs to ideas and ideals.

I thought otherwise then, inside the prison on the island in the Sava River. Do knowledge and experience over time really destroy all ideals and all consistency of behavior? Did I really feel entirely satisfied with myself, my renown, and the comforts brought me by rebelling against dogmatic privilege based on violence? And what is freedom? The patient endurance of that time, and later in prisons? Or this bliss by the sea under the sun? This cultivated chitchat without strings attached?

There is no reply if we find none within ourselves. In vain do we justify ourselves, twist and turn. Today's arrests and trials in Yugoslavia resolve nothing. But they do affect everything and everyone. Persecutions are justified today, too, in the name of revolution and socialism, although the one bequeathed only political power and the other had already attained all it was ever capable of attaining. Only Marx is lacking, to reveal onetime tragedy as today's farce.

Revolution (every revolution, not just the Communist one) has discovered that revolutionary failures, the failures of revolutionary ideals, begin with depriving one's antagonists of their rights. Freedom is freedom only to the degree that it is freedom for others. And just as the traitor first betrays himself, so the oppressor first deprives himself of freedom. Oppression and lawlessness initially take merciless aim at those in whose name oppression and lawlessness are being carried out, and then finally at those who carry them out. One way or another, the persecuted will survive. But those who persecute will dig their own graves and bring themselves to ruin.

To insist on the revolutionary myths is too late, to take shelter behind them futile. Only the objective truth and life itself, unobtrusive and unrestrained, live on. Truth and life are the sole revolutionaries. But it is a waste of time to appeal for reason and democracy in those who are in love with power and are the slaves of dogma. Silence, though, is complicity and suicide.

Thus I took pity on myself by the seashore for not having interceded on behalf of those who suffered when I ought to have done so, or to the degree that I should have done. And regretted not having written down these words before sinking into the fragrant, blue waters of the Boka Kotorska.

And may my words, belated though they are, be a solace to me and comfort those in prison—even though they infuriate the jailers.

BUREAUCRATIC NATIONALISM

Bureaucratic nationalism (allowing for its different national variants) is an essential feature of any Communist Party, including those not in power. However, this has not been given sufficient analysis. Even the term itself, "bureaucratic nationalism," is not yet current. Understandably enough, for only when it has become a patterned response, even a way of life, can bureaucratic nationalism finally take shape and settle down on the tongue.

Bureaucratic nationalism is inherent in communism and enjoys a certain hidden evolution, one that continues to be concealed. Its preliminary stage was "national communism," a term that came into use in the course of the Yugoslav-Soviet confrontation of 1948. At the time, this term conveyed the contradictions and absurdities of present-day communism: A movement for which internationalism served as inspiration and intentional regulation was dissolving into its national components, and these components were starting to manage their own affairs in accordance with their own interests and potentials.

But even then the term "national communism," as usually happens with any political language, reflected reality in a simplified, one-sided way; reality was a living thing, and complex. And what was worse, a term like that lost sight of the fact that communism upon coming to power becomes embodied in a new class. This class maintains its hegemony only by becoming identified with "sacred national egoism." (The usual reservations must be applied, that the Party does this only to a certain degree and in a particular period.) Communism means first and foremost political power, after all, and this power can neither come into being nor survive save under concrete (i.e., national) conditions. Communists, at least ideologically, subscribe to internationalism as long as they are fighting for power, and once they get hold of it they turn into "national Communists" if they want to keep on holding it. And hanging on to power for Communists is always the most important thing.

At the time when "national communism" came into currency as a term, there may have been awareness of such a concept, but it was not supported. Classless societies had been transformed into class structures, shattering illusions; furthermore, Communist states were at daggers drawn. Hence the term "the nationalism of the Party bureaucracy," or more succinctly "bureaucratic nationalism," better expresses modern Communist movements and the relations between them.

Until the 1990s Eastern Europe was ruled by bureaucratic nationalisms, varying from country to country and not uniformly dependent on the Soviet center. So far as China and North Korea, Albania, Cuba, and Vietnam were concerned, that blanket statement was hardly appropriate. These countries in the 1970s were still in the phase of revolutionary, or bureaucratic, totalitarianism, preliminary to bureaucratic nationalism.

Among all its other firsts, the Soviet Party can also claim to be the first to have been transformed into a monopolistic and nationalistic bureaucracy. It was a complex and bloody process that finally was consummated under Stalin. But while the social privilege of the Party bureaucracy in the USSR was clear at a glance, its nationalistic character was veiled and differed from that of the other countries of Eastern Europe. Stalin favored the Russian bureaucracy's nationalism. Under Khrushchev there was more "equilibrium" in that the non-Russian bureaucratic structures grew stronger within the topmost Party organs. (First and foremost, this meant Ukrainian bureaucrats.) Nor did their role diminish under Brezhnev. But to conclude that any one national bureaucracy in the USSR played a dominant role was unwarranted. If Stalin's Great Russianism exploited the darkest impulses of the Russian nation for the sake of the new class as a whole and its imperial expansion, in the same way (at least on paper), subdivisions and conflicts within the Soviet bureaucracy became possible on the basis of nationalism.

The Yugoslav Party initiated an epochal disintegration of world communism into national parts. But communism is an ideology, a complete, closed doctrine: Take one prop away and all the other props pitch and sway—indeed, the whole edifice totters. By setting in train internationalism, incarnated as this was in the hegemony of Moscow, Yugoslavia grew stronger, but at the same time undermined the ideology.

There ensued two more great crises within the Yugoslav Party: a bureaucratic reaction after Stalin's death and at the time of "fraternal friendship" with Khrushchev; and finally, after the fall of Khrushchev and the failure of an economy permeated by bureaucracy, one that was a slave to ideology, the Secret Police disintegrated as the keeper of ideology and guardian of the Party bureaucracy's undeviating uniformity. An end was put to any new democratic visions, but at the cost of spiritual chaos and disintegration into national bureaucracies. True, national bureaucracies were scarcely Marxist except in name. But not one was democratic, or rather, each was less democratic than the next. None was sufficiently strong with respect to any other or within its own nation, and they not only conducted behind-the-scenes alliances with each other but also opened the gates to anti-Communist, undemocratic nationalisms. What it came to was a fusion of bureaucratic nationalism and chauvinism. In process of being born was a pluralism of a special kind: the pluralism of intolerant, undemocratic nationalisms. The Party bureaucracy did not evolve but fell apart, mostly turning into new, authoritative structures. Democratic currents appeared, too, of course. It all made for a chaotic, freer atmosphere, but one without democratic institutions. Yugoslavia became freer but also less stable. The unforgotten frenzies and heartaches of the Nazi invasion and the civil war threatened us.

But change in Yugoslavia did not have to unfold in the same way in the other countries of Eastern Europe, especially not in the USSR. In Czechoslovakia a democratic transformation was in prospect in 1968, in Romania not, despite the latter's relative independence. The Soviet bureaucracy was more stable thanks to its revolutionary traditions and the possibility of maintaining a closed system, plus its imperial interests. This despite the fact that its ideology had come to nothing and cracks were appearing in its monolithic facade.

When Party monopoly disintegrates, peoples and nations are freed from the monotony and horror of ideological and political totalitarianism. But this disintegration does not automatically deliver the freedoms for which these peoples and nations thirst. To escape into chauvinism and a nationalistic ideology, it is sufficient to rely on the irrational impulses and legacy of myth, while the way out of bureaucratic nationalism demands an effort all the greater and more conscious. The world is faced by a phenomenon offering new possibilities but also risks.

GORBACHEV'S LENINIST ILLUSIONS

There could be no doubt that Stalinism had reached its demise with Mikhail Gorbachev. But to return to Leninism, insisting that if Leninism was not being renewed, at least it was being preserved—all this led up a blind alley straight to stagnation. What is more, we saw here a Party bureaucracy insisting on keeping total power. And precisely the kind of power, the kind of monopoly over it, that had first been instituted by Lenin, with the finishing touches laid on by Stalin.

For Stalinism was but the main current of Lenin and Leninism, the one that emerged victorious. Without a grasp of this truth, bitter and fearsome especially for the Soviet leaders, there were no hopes that the system might turn itself into a real state and an efficient market and monetary economy. Not without quite serious upheavals. Poland and Hungary carried out the first, fundamental changes precisely because they had earlier gotten rid of Leninist ideology. That is the precondition of all change.

For it is not enough to expose the sterility of ideology. The parasitic quality of one-Party, autocratic political power should also be shown up for what it is, and for good measure the nonproductive, "socialist" properties piggybacked onto that power. This is what made our Yugoslav leaders agonize, even though they had long since shuffled off ideology as well as ideals. Because political power was not at issue, it was Leninism, meaning Stalinism as an ideology, that first died off in Western Europe.

It would not be good manners nor would it be very intelligent to find fault with Gorbachev for believing in a "good Lenin" and for believing (if only lukewarmly) in ideology. But hushing up the weakness and danger that lurked in this faith of Gorbachev's could only damage him and bring harm to the democratic process of reform in the Soviet Union.

Gorbachev was doubtless a resourceful, gifted politician. But he was not without flaws which proved fatal for both him and the cause of reform. That is to say, judging by his public statements, his theoretical horizon was narrow and out of date. Probably here was the major reason, though perhaps not the only one, for his excessive reliance on personal power rather than institutions. He arrived at the "legitimizing" of personal power by making concessions to a Party bureaucracy that were too great. A policy that is not pragmatic cannot be a success. But pragmatism in a policy has no chance of survival if it is not grounded in fundamental, theoretical knowledge. Western pragmatism is successful, more successful than Communist pragmatism, because it is based on a nonideological, rationalist philosophy.

Domestic events took Gorbachev by surprise because he believed that ideology is scientific and trusted to personal power. This at a time when personal power was compromised and ineffectual. The breakup of the system came to light first and most painfully through the breakup and disavowal of ideology. Gorbachev reacted with composure to daily events without foreseeing the volcanic eruptions to come.

And eruptions were unavoidable, both national and social. The social ones were more profound and decisive, while the national ones were more flammable and frenzied. Both system and empire faced an incurable crisis.

All Communist countries were entering a dramatic period, whether reformist (the Soviet Union, Poland, Hungary, Yugoslavia) or opposed to reform (Romania, China, and others). But the Soviet case was a special one, unique. The system was authentic, original, arising out of revolution and in essence remaining unchanged from 1917 to its demise. A multinational empire was politically more centralized than under the Tsars.

Ways and means differ. The pace may be faster or slower. Because the Russian nation failed to get its house in order deliberately and speedily via a free, pluralistic, political route; because conditions—even-handed conditions, real conditions—were not created for all forms of property; because the right to be informed was not made fair and impartial for all democratic currents, Gorbachev was overtaken by cataclysmic events. Confirmed authoritarians, social demagogues, nationalists, and religious extremists tried to coopt the "spirit of rescue."

The Soviet Union took a significant, irrevocable step in the direction of change. We recognized the first stirrings of parliamentarianism and of an organized opposition in a reorganized, supreme legislative organ, the Congress of People's Deputies. But along the way serious, unexpected vicissitudes lay in wait for society and the state, all the more serious and unexpected to the degree that advocates of democratic reform, both those in power and those in the opposition, failed to have any insight into the crisis of the political-social order, failed to see that the centralism of empire was at a critical point.

Communist states have long differed among themselves, and the process of bringing uniformity to them has only led to rebellion and intervention. With reform they will become—already are becoming—ever more differentiated, and intervention ever less probable. But Leninism as an inspiration, the order inspired by Leninism—this has come to an end. What is happening will clearly be a period neither easy nor short. Just as every country's domestic and foreign policy is individual and different, so changes will occur in various patterns and at different rates. To the degree that changes within the Soviet Union come first (of course, in democratic form), the process for the rest will be eased. Change will seem an uncopied pattern. Change will be helpful, an unprescribed form of aid, for these others.

THE KREMLIN'S PALACE-PARTY PUTSCH

The 1991 putsch in the Kremlin well illustrated Soviet political and social conditions. The organizers themselves of the putsch, the way they created it, revealed that decay had thoroughly set in. Once, political power was totalitarian. Now it was authoritarian. Either way, power had rotted away and could no longer spawn any fresh idea or hatch out any striking personality. The mutineers were known to come from the circle of Gorbachev's closest collaborators, as, for example, Yazov, minister of the armed forces; Kryuchkov, head of the Secret Police; and Vice President Yanayev. These men Gorbachev himself had selected and promoted over the grumbling of the military command and parliament.

It was a typical palace revolution, except that it was not one aimed squarely at the monarch. The rebels even sought from Gorbachev that he approve of being besieged! It was not his overthrow they announced but his replacement due to illness. And what a terrible, "incapacitating" illness it was: sciatica and high blood pressure. So this was a state of siege owing to illness in the chief of state. Were it not so fateful it would have been really funny.

Such a palace composition of the conspirators and rebels gave rise to suspicion among some that Gorbachev tacitly stood behind the whole conspiracy. The more the mutineers appeared on television, the more they kept leaving the impression of being men who were confused and frightened. There was none of that force or decisiveness characteristic of people bent on destroying a nation's leaders, people with pretensions to complete power. And the fact that they were not even aware of the mood of the broad masses was nothing to be surprised at: These were bureaucrats detached from social movements, immersed in sycophancy, overflowing with privileges. Nor did they know the mood of the Red Army or that of the security forces. They knew nothing, understood nothing. They were not even Stalinists. They were what they were: bureaucrats who had a feeling—or rather, the "hidden" top Party leaders did their feeling for them—that the political and imperial system had been dangerously compromised.

There was no doubt, however, that the putschists represented an outdated Party-bureaucratic system that had survived in the top ranks of power. And there was certainly a political backdrop of conservatives formed by the top ranks of the Party. These people had long resisted reforms and agitated for a renewal of their monopoly over society and the state, over the economy, and over the media.

When the putschists proclaimed that they had taken over power, in the outside world all sorts of Sovietologists began to speak out about the "mistakes" of Gorbachev. Taking as their point of departure the still-living bureaucratic structure of the Communist Party and the machinery of security (the KGB), they were even predicting that the new power would be in place for some time.

To fulfill his grandiose undertaking, his noble plan, which was to turn the Soviet Union from a sort of Eastern despotism into a democratic state and a modern society, Gorbachev would have had to possess divine powers to avoid making mistakes. However, in politics such powers really do not exist. Gorbachev was a gifted and very astute politician who hardly ever committed errors, save for failing to recognize till too late the essence of the Soviet order. That was without question a capital error, although it is easily explained: Gorbachev grew up in the Party apparatus and was imbued with Leninist doctrines that he idealistically took to be scientific. However, a powerful sense of reality and a clever comprehension of the totality of problems facing him saved Gorbachev from being too doctrinaire and going too far, saved him from acting in haste and making a slip, saved him from experimentation.

But the Leninist burden and legacy entangled his mind and held him back. Even while it cost him great pains, he was still slow to free himself from his lifelong ideal of reforming the Soviet system and elevating his homeland into the circle of modern, developed, democratic states.

His vision of Soviet socialism as democratic, in itself a contradiction in terms, was creative up to a point, but for Gorbachev it also was fateful, for to alter the Soviet system was not possible. A totalitarian system, especially one embedded in an empire and shot through with imperial aspirations, was not susceptible to reform by the very fact of being totalitarian. Such a system is enclosed within itself and, by virtue of its structure, complacent and self-satisfied. It changes through internal decomposition until there comes a point when strength is found to finally alter and eliminate it. Judging by all the signs, Gorbachev came to agree with this out of necessity. Experience led him to it, not conscious or conscientious thought. This happened only as he came to appreciate a market economy and free property.

Gorbachev was slow to understand this unalterable feature of the system. It was his one great error, a mistake only excused and explained by his evident good intentions, or by the fact that he was surely tolerant toward new political and social phenomena and the fact that his foreign policy was successful. His achievements in this domain were not in dispute. The Cold War was, essentially, shortened. Relations among the Great Powers did turn in the direction of peaceful coexistence. He may not have been the slave of his own system in foreign affairs, but he did have to take into account other, more stable systems, superior systems. His successes here owed much to his steady and intelligent minister of foreign affairs, Eduard Shevardnadze.

Gorbachev was authoritarian by nature; this was his style; at the same time, beyond his own circle, beyond his assumptions and his political milieu, he was tolerant, a sort of Soviet De Gaulle. It could not have been otherwise within the closed, intolerant, and suspicious Party-bureaucratic milieu. A milieu like that could never have fostered a more intelligent, more tolerant, and broader personality. On that account he chose (with the exception of Shevardnadze) obedient, colorless collaborators, though ones who were capable of carrying out his orders. Those collaborators would go along with their leader's plans as long as the plans stayed within the parameters of system reform. As soon as the system reached the point of self-destruction and was giving way to new democratic and national patterns that were antisystem and anti-imperialist, then his collaborators turned into opponents. Their chief had hesitations and second thoughts, which they noticed, and this made it all the easier to oppose him. The ferment of conspiracy swelled in the dough of a Party bureaucracy lacking in common sense and politically leaderless.

The putsch could not have turned out differently than it did. For that reason it was not only the mutineers who were defeated (or better "diminished," for they had not fought any battle) but also Gorbachev himself, to the degree that he was in thrall to his socialist, reformist prejudices while maintaining through it all a position of legality and legitimacy. This was his position at the moment of decision. Of course, it meant holding on to power and not only the hope of continuing his work.

Onto the stage there came—to the surprise of the putschists and even Gorbachev himself, to some extent—the people and the people's army. And a new leader, Gorbachev's old foe Boris Yeltsin. As a man opposed to Gorbachev and the product of an educated, reformist part of the apparatus, Yeltsin had distanced himself from that apparatus and, while not breaking off with reformist currents in the Party, was now becoming a product of the masses. And these were the Russian masses, a fact that has special meaning and weight, given that they were the biggest national group, historically dominant. Dynamic, free of ideological dogmas and his Party legacy, a man of radical, reformist views, Yeltsin, in resisting the putsch, played not only the decisive role but also a role that belongs among the classic examples of resourcefulness and courage at critical, historic turning points.

The Gorbachev era came to an end with the putsch and with the victory of the people, the people's army with Yeltsin at their head. That period had in reality closed at an earlier moment, when governance had suffered a rearrangement and imperial, political centralism began to unravel.

Folded into these events or a little preceding them there came the rise of Party pluralism and an orientation toward a market economy. The hopeless, failed putsch only added an operetta ending to the Gorbachev period. Neither Gorbachev nor his period really had deserved this, but the stormy course of history does not consider merits or past achievements.

What was this "Gorbachev period"? What did he deserve?

Gorbachev dismantled Stalinism; he put an end to terror of every kind. He had no intention of undermining Leninism. But insofar as Stalinism has no independent existence as a special, original ideology and was only a phase in the development of Leninism—Leninism driven to its uttermost limits—Gorbachev willy-nilly undermined Leninism itself. And this, in the final analysis, had its consequences. The two earlier leaders did not have the same personality, any more than their works were the same, but no longer was there a good Lenin or a bad Stalin. Lenin had been the dictator of a revolutionary Party, Stalin the tyrant of a bureaucratized revolutionary Party.

With the end of Gorbachev there began a new era for all the peoples of the Soviet Union, soon to collapse, but in particular for a Russian people deprived of individuality. This is a revolution set in motion by Gorbachev's reforms. A revolution that began there but will not stop with the destruction of the Communist Party's monopolistic power. This stupid, extemporized putsch has given it good reason not to stop. New problems, including new confrontations, only lie in wait. Perhaps, too, there will be challenges more turbulent and better prepared than a putsch by Kremlin palace bureaucrats. This revolution will continue to unfold until it has undermined and overthrown all formal structures, all remnants of Communist totalitarianism and governmental power, economic or imperial. For Russians are a long-suffering people and hard to get moving, but when they do move it is as if the immense land of Russia herself were moving along with them, crushing everything in its path before finally settling down.

As for us, knowing these events, we will adapt to the realities and will fulfill and enrich ourselves with new works of creation, tragically fruitful, conceived amid the ruins of a utopia brought about by force.[22]

11

THE END

IN

GRIEF AND SHAME

THE FATE OF MARXISM

Gandhi once said that one single man, inspired by a righteous idea, could bring down an empire. Marx believed he had revealed a doctrine that would transform the world. Few would deny that Gandhi confirmed his famous utterance on the strength of his own example. But also, no disinterested onlooker could argue that Marx was wrong either, even though his doctrine was not fulfilled in the manner foreseen by him, not even in the social systems, the developed nations, that he originally had in mind.

Marx's doctrine was not the first worldwide teaching, for many religious and social doctrines have aspired to be just that. But the various religions as well as the pre-Marxist social doctrines, however universal they were in their intentions, were neither victorious nor calculated to break out of the framework of particular civilizations. Marx's teachings were actually the first that—over the course of time and with varied intensity, naturally—spread throughout all nations and civilizations and touched all humanity to the core.

Marxist ideas could spread in this way because they espoused an essentially religious faith connecting human brotherhood and freedom for the human being with the technical and scientific progress that was irresistibly gaining ascendancy all over the world. Hence these teachings took on the aspect of systematic thinking and ascertainable fact that we call science. There were other reasons, of course. Social conditions, historical circumstances, philosophical and other legacies also had a significant share in the Marxist formulation of new doctrine. But his teachings could never have acquired such dimensions nor played the role they did had they not at the same time paid heed to science and technology, whose potential was endless. It was because science and technology could not be stopped that the world would surely come together and the human condition would surely change.

In Europe in particular, social movements inspired by Marx spread. The victory of Marxists in the October Revolution, specifically, could only contribute to the persuasiveness of Marxism as a "science."

Nations feel the need to transform themselves. Human beings need an ideal. Conditions differ. All these facilitated the spread of Marx's teachings throughout the world, frequently in very different guises. It was Marxist doctrine that transformed the systems of two great powers, Russia and China. Ten or so small and middling nations changed as well. The broad sweep and impact of his ideas generated a backlash that was perhaps no less powerful, as it provoked and compelled opposing systems to adapt and change.

This does not mean that humanity is now or will be Marxist. On the contrary. Circumstances have essentially changed: The industrialization of the world is no longer a tendency, nor are societies inspired by Marxism a remote dream. Both are living realities. And it is those realities that are what make Marxism old-fashioned. The world Marx envisioned, one that has already been achieved over a considerable portion of the globe, reveals first that his doctrine no longer can be an inspiring science—basically it never was!—and second that it is fast becoming the biggest obstacle to a world unity based on common production and a different, undogmatic, existential vision of man. If the world still is imbued with the spirit of Marxism, this spirit no longer behaves exclusively as a revolutionary force but as a predominantly governmental and conservative one.

However, let us put to one side the dispute about the degree to which Marxist doctrine is scientific and a science and the degree to which it is religious and a faith. Not that we think this is unimportant, it is even essential to an examination of Marx's doctrine as such. In any case, the fact cannot be disputed that in the past hundred years not one thinker nor any social teaching can be compared with Marx and Marxism in their effect on the human race.

For my goal is not to measure Marx's significance, still less to weigh the value of his teaching as doctrine. With Marx and his teaching there happened what happened with other great thinkers and reformers before him: Merely by being enacted, his teaching lost its creativeness and turned into stagnant dogma, while he himself ascended ever higher in history.

The most important causes, the greatest swings of the pendulum, and most striking forms of that transformation of Marxism did not act in isolation and can only be grasped as they interact together.

In historic perspective the first victory of Marxism (the October Revolution) also marked the start of its decline. Communism thereafter did indeed spread, but not exclusively thanks to its own visions or to the activity of the national Communist movements. It was the Soviet state that caused communism to spread, now less energetically, now more. And the ideal dried up in proportion as the reality legitimized by it grew stronger.

When the political focus of the Soviet leaders shifted to reinforcing their own nation and to stiffening the movement within it (a move that began under Lenin but was completed under Stalin), doctrine itself had to suffer. It was a process of strengthening the Party bureaucracy domestically and, externally within the Communist International, of subordinating to Soviet leaders the viewpoints, tactics, and even the staffs of the leading administrative organs of other Communist Parties.

The visible expressions of that process were the purges. Purges had begun already under Lenin, when he suppressed the "workers' opposition" and put down the rebellion of the sailors on Kronstadt, just outside Petrograd. Under Stalin, these purges rivaled forced collectivization in their staggering and irrational scope. Purges also were carried out in the Communist Parties abroad, especially those in Europe. At the same time, Soviet foreign policy grew ever more insensitive to anything but the interests and position of the Soviet Union. It perhaps is debatable whether Stalin had to choose precisely such a path and such methods, but it is impossible to deny, even without Khrushchev's revelations, that he did so choose.

National and state elements dominated the policies of the top Soviet ranks, and since a world Great Power was at issue, their coloration was perforce that of a Great Power. They assumed a worldly pretentiousness that was expressed in the doctrine of the Soviet Union's "leading

role" and the "leading role" of the Soviet Party. Their insistence on
Leninism as the highest stage of Marxism could be read as "Leninism
is a universally accepted socialist doctrine," and the only one deserving
of consideration. National communism actually first came into being
in the Soviet Union. Today we designate by these words the various
national forms of "socialist" construction and the various forms taken
by resentment of Soviet hegemony. But since this was a power laying
claim to world domination, the most natural thing for it to do was to
hide behind "internationalism" and "Marxism-Leninism."

Such relations were able to endure until other revolutions gained the
victory—the Yugoslav, the Albanian, and the Chinese, and through
such revolutions independent Communist states came into being. No
Communist Party, however international its inspiration, can help but
justify its political power by claiming a leading role in national politics,
even if the Soviet Union had never displayed pretensions toward hegemony, for an independent state and a special nationalism would and
could not ever have been independent and special had it not yearned
for its own confirmation and never ceased to ask for it.

The Soviet Union's becoming a kind of Eastern European empire
could only have led to confrontation with Yugoslavia as an independent, albeit Communist, nation. Additionally, pressure on Yugoslavia
was the condition of Moscow's hegemony in Eastern Europe and the
way in which that was to be embodied; it was the way the countries of
Eastern Europe and Communist Parties the world over would be brought
to heel. There were, of course, other factors, including the entry of the
United States onto the world stage, the atomic bomb, the Cold War,
modern technology, the breakup of colonies, the consolidation of Western societies, and the like. But Soviet hegemony would have appeared
even without these factors, eliciting national resentments within the
world of communism. The Soviet Union suppressed those resentments
but was unable to eliminate the aspirations of Communist countries
for their own affirmative forms. It was even forced to adapt to those
aspirations.

Finally, between the two Communist superpowers a bitter struggle
began for influence within the Communist movement. The results
were, roughly speaking, that the USSR won a dominant influence in
the Parties of the developed countries and China in the Parties of the
undeveloped ones; but the results were also that a number of Parties
gained independence, including those of Italy and Sweden.

Khrushchev, beginning a reform of Stalinist structures in the Soviet Union, also began to include agreement instead of command in his relationships with other Communist Parties. We now know that he was not able to be consistently radical, domestically, in this endeavor and so could not change the essence of relationships with other Communist countries and Communist Parties. Khrushchev's pressure on Albania reminded us of Stalin's anathematizing of Yugoslavia in 1948. And the rift with China in 1963 revealed how irreconcilable he could be with regard to Moscow's "leading role" within communism. His successors called a halt even to the unfinished reforms he had begun. Insisting on the unalterability and holiness of what they called Leninism, they stopped spiritual movement dead in its tracks, reinforced management by the Party bureaucracy, and hardened an imperialistic foreign policy.

Thus it happened in the postwar era that out of that single, simple doctrine and out of a unified Communist movement there grew different movements, nationalist ones, with different practices and different emphases on this or that aspect of Marxist doctrine. There appeared different theories about contemporary capitalism, about the role of the state, about religion, even about the possibility of building a Communist society and whether the Hegelian-Marxist dialectic has any value.

Not one ideal, let alone some dogmatic teaching, could avoid being altered in the course of its adaptation. Movements calling themselves socialist fell under the shadow of doubt as inadequate reflections of Marx's intentions, even those of Lenin. Their disputes, however ingenious, were only the reverse side of the manipulations engaged in by the Party bureaucrats. They, too, had authentic teachings ready at hand to justify their privileged position and their own vision of society. For it was not essential whether "socialist reality" more or less corresponded to Marxist teaching. What was essential was the sort of reality that, after all was said and done, emerged on the basis of those features deemed applicable—that is, what sort of reality we now had.

Now, it cannot be denied that (a) Marxist revolutions generally happened in countries that otherwise could not have carried out an industrial revolution (e.g., Russia, Yugoslavia, and China); and that (b) the societies that have emerged from Communist revolutions undergo differentiation from within, or—to use the Marxist term—become class societies; and that class differentiation does not diminish as these societies mature, but deepens. There will, of course, be found idealistic revolutionaries and people dissatisfied with an "electronic paradise" who (thinking of China, Cuba, and Albania) will deny any value to the above conclusion. Very often such people are not well informed about the real relationships and the real state of affairs in those countries. And in any case they lose sight of a reality that is now part of the past and has been historically verified, to wit: that more or less all the so-called socialist countries who have today "revised" Marxism—that is, those where societies are now undifferentiated—have passed through a similar stage of egalitarianism. China, Cuba, and Albania found themselves, generally speaking, at a lower stage of the kind of society that was characteristic of the countries of Eastern Europe. The difference between the two was that societies in the first group were still totalitarian—inspired and controlled by one single power, the Party—while those in the second group have now begun to cease being totalitarian. Class differentiation still existed even in these countries. Surely political power is all by itself a privilege! Even when it does not confer "a place in history" and material benefits! Only those in a transport of delusion could believe that Liu Shao-chi, for many years Mao Zedong's fellow fighter but later his Party adversary, turned overnight into an ideologue of capitalism and a servant of foreign imperialism.

Romantic revolutionaries and Marxist dogmaticians might gather from this that, yes, perhaps in other countries a revolution was made with the help of other social forces—for example, the working class instead of the peasantry and the radical intelligentsia—and that consequently a classless, or undifferentiated, society could be achieved. In our day such a hypothesis actually furnished the foundation for the doctrines of self-styled Marxist humanists and the main portion of the so-called New Left. In short, in place of Marxism and the despotism of the Party bureaucracy in those countries where revolution gained the victory and what is called socialism was established, this point of view offered revolution in the developed countries and a society of "free," meaning perfected, people.

Without going into a more detailed critique of such viewpoints, let us recall that Marx was thinking of societies not too far away from the age of steam (and in part the electric age of industrialization), and that it was known at the time that such views were utopian. And, what is no less important, the views spoken of above openly negate, if not ignore, revolutions already carried out in the name of Marxism and the social relationships that had developed out of them. There is not nor can there be a pure, undefiled Marxism, just as no other set of doctrines in this living, human, impure reality of ours can exist pure and unde-filed. Pure Marxism would constitute a denial of its own nature, would be a Marxism that had no stake in its own fulfillment, that did not insist on changing the world. In short, and without the least irony, such points of view offer a paradise in the name of visions that have already failed whenever they were actually applied.

The divisions and conflicts among Communist parties and the social differentiation within the so-called socialist countries were not the result of Marxism misapplied, nor did they happen because some peo-ple were dedicated to a "cult of personality." In reality, we are faced with the issue of what is real and possible in the world of Marxism and among the societies it spawned.

We already live in a world that is neither capitalist nor socialist. It is a world in which there hardly exists a national group that would not like to be a legitimate nation unto itself. But it is also a world where the United States, Russia, and the People's Republic of China still play their decisive roles as world powers, each in its own way, and will go on doing so for a long time to come. The ideological battle that contin-ues to agitate the mind and soul of contemporary man is in fact illusory. That struggle is today only a flimsy screen masking various national aspirations, including first of all those of the three great powers. Hap-pily, for the time being they cannot go to war against each other, and one hopes this will remain so. Not one is capable of mastering a rival by the use of classical weapons of destruction, let alone both rivals at the same time. The atomic weapon has turned this option into an absurdity; war is more than simply madness, it is madness that has to be organized and possess its own rationality and so cannot be embarked upon when the prospect of self-destruction is real.

In the world, of course, the major roles are played by the highly devel-oped, or capitalist powers and those middling or socialist powers which are on the way to being highly developed. The world is therefore divided into various systems, each of them making any changes first in accordance with its domestic concerns. It is as if there were something correct in Hegel's concept of the unity of opposites as a way of existing and thinking. This enlarges the possibilities for the small and medium-sized (though undeveloped) countries.

But this is not a complete picture of the world. Humanity is forced to unite by technological developments that cannot be slowed down or halted, and by an ever more accessible and growing body of knowledge about the generality of human beings. In such a world the thought is bound to arise that no system can exist with a claim to absolute superiority and as a consequence that neither a perfect society nor an independent, absolutely free, human being is possible.

The reason that not merely Marxist ideology but also no other ideology (ideology being defined as a closed, all-explaining system) has ever been put into effect nor ever can be, is not because people have no liking for ideologies—religions as well as philosophical systems are ideologies, too—but because of the great differences between today's social systems, forced to unite just as they are. It is good that this is so: The world always was varied, and uniformity would only mean stagnation and collapse.

In such a world Marxism cannot help becoming old-fashioned, cannot help but give way to new and more realistic human visions. In such a world the Communist revolutions, too, become anachronisms, before even considering the inevitable interference in them by the Great Powers. National groups already know what such revolutions are capable of giving and clearly see that they are unsuited for today's flights of technology and knowledge of society and mankind.

This, of course, does not mean that there will be no more revolutions or that Marx and Marxism were not among the heroic inspirations of human history, playing perhaps the widest prewar role in our history. Everything in its own time, as the wise maxim has it. Old-fashioned though it is.

It is as though the life of nations and social groups mocked those who inspire that life and shape it. Marxism is the ideology that first spread the world over, the first ideology that gave the world a significant push to unite. Perhaps this is precisely why Marxism is condemned to vanish and to deny its own mission.

COMMUNISM AND THE WORKING CLASS

Communist ideas did not originate in the working class but were fathered on it by dogmatists and political movements. Marx and Lenin were aware of the gulf between Communist theory and the working-class movement. Their advantage over other Communist theoreticians and leaders lay in the fact that revolution and a new socialist society represented for them a merger of what they termed their scientific views and the working class, or movement. No movement, no class activity not inspired by or led by their "science" was regarded by Marx, Lenin, and Communists generally as revolutionary and socialist, or even as faithful to the labor movement. This broadened the base for revolution and—what is much more significant—strengthened the convictions of revolutionaries.

Communists therefore, even against their better judgment, cannot regard the working class, its interests, and its situation as other than a function of revolution, or in other words—after victory—as a function of political power. Communist influence on the working class at various times might wax or wane as conditions fluctuated, but nowhere did matters go beyond influence to a total identification of Communist ideology with the working class. Furthermore, as time went on and Communists remained in power (read: industrialized), the gulf between ideology and class grew wider until in the end it was seen by all to be unbridgeable.

Ideology itself instigated that division. Just as Hegel's absolute spirit was predestined to subordinate the world, so the laws of history command the Marxist proletariat to pull down capitalism and build a "perfect"—classless—society. Life, though, commanded otherwise. The working class, like every other social class, entertained different hopes, ones that even stood opposed to the historic mission appointed to it by dogmatists and revolutionaries.

Marx's article of faith, however, that the working class would dig the grave of class society and erect a classless one to take its place was not superficial. It was not mere fantasy.

In Marx's time social classes, especially in Britain, the country to which he had paid the most careful attention, were clearly set apart and opposed to one another. That was an era that belonged to scientific technology and the bourgeoisie, but it was also one of cruel class struggles. All across Europe, now here, now there, erupted rebellions of the disenfranchised and enslaved proletarian masses. It was also an era when various philanthropic and reformist doctrines appeared, wishing to build equality and absolute freedom. Marx, though, grasped the fact that an industrial transformation of humanity was inevitable. His doing so meant that the working class, as the most significant human factor in such a transformation, took on a crucial social meaning. Workers needed neither pity nor understanding: Their very role in production made them strong and organized to appropriate their rights.

In this respect, earlier events indicated that Marx was right and affirmed him to be the most profound and many-sided prophet of modern times. European developments very closely tracked his analyses and specific forecasts. For that reason, Europe at the close of the nineteenth and beginning of the twentieth centuries would witness an equation of Communist ideology with the workers' movements such as had never been seen before nor would be seen again.

Marx, however, was not right when he predicted that the working class in the industrialized countries would become more and more impoverished and when on these grounds he concluded that a proletarian revolution was inevitable. Revolutions have indeed taken place, but in countries that could not rapidly industrialize without the old order being destroyed before it could ever happen, and destroyed violently. Also, the working class in those countries was very weak. Revolution there was mainly a matter for professional revolutionaries and for the impoverished and nationally endangered peasantry (who constituted the common soldiers). These were proletarian, ideological revolutions, not social ones.

Lenin's strength lay in the fact that he offset class weakness and lack of class consciousness by a Party vanguard, one pervaded by ideology. This was how the means was discovered whereby a revolution could be launched and new political power gained—a means that Marx had set in motion but that he could not elaborate in liberal, industrial Europe.

The working class seized its new, revolutionary power and fastened on the new property relationships, inasmuch as they regulated work relations and guaranteed workers their basic needs. But that did not eliminate the difference between this class and a Party pervaded by ideology—and it was the Party that wielded the power. Lenin would insist on the initiatives taken by the soviets (councils), just as he insisted on strengthening the workers' element in them. But he was never in bondage to the illusion that political power could be wielded directly, either by a class or by the masses. For his "leading role" in power and society he had ready at hand the Party that had carried out the Revolution, and that was what for the most part he would lean on.

The fact that the Communists and the working class did not identify with each other was a matter for open proclamation, both during the Revolution and in victory. The Communists would harass socialist and other labor activities as something "alien," thereby setting themselves off from class as such and placing themselves above it as representatives and interpreters of its mission. But that was still the idealistic, heroic period of communism. Communists conquered or died believing that they were the only genuine representatives of a class and its historic mission. If they did die, they died for their faith, and victory would be theirs alone.

Communists could hold out hopes that when they came to power the distinctions between them and the working class would disappear. According to Communist doctrine, political power need be nothing more than an instrument of the working class aimed at betrayal and intervention. That instrument should at once start to wither away and, in the end, could be expected to die off completely with the building of a classless (socialist) society.

But communism took a vow, so to speak, that all its prophecies, all its ideals, would turn into their diametric opposites just when Communists thought these prophecies and ideals might actually come true.

So it was that with the coming of Communists to power the working class and communism drew apart from one another, became alien. It did not happen uniformly, and it took various forms. By and large, this coincided with the metamorphosis of the Party bureaucracy into a privileged, monopolistic stratum of society. A special elite—the new class—justified its activity as the continuation of the revolution, and its raison d'être was absolute power as the way to industrialize. The revolutionary organs, or media, where the voice of the worker could be heard were preserved formally, but they were elected and acted under the immediate control of the Party apparatus. The working class selflessly took up the cause of industrialization and spared neither sweat nor blood against the Fascist conqueror. In that regard the interests of the Party bureaucracy and the worker were one.

For this reason the purges would affect the working class less than the other social strata (peasants, intelligentsia, urban dwellers). The bureaucracy squeezed the working class out of politics and turned it into a faceless labor force without which there could be neither industrialization nor industry. Workers were the one class that was not "alien" and socially guilty. It was as though the bureaucracy would have no reason to exist at all had it not organized labor. The bureaucracy could not have survived without appropriating someone else's labor as "our own."

The result of conditions like these was to turn the working class into a mass and to disrupt the bond between the individual and his social milieu. Here the worker was just that: a worker. He was not a member of a class, if by class we understand the expression of group aspirations and interests and not merely (as they write in the Communist textbooks) a special position in the production process. The interests and aspirations of the class were exhausted in Party resolutions. And how could it be otherwise? Class consciousness long since became identified with ideology, and the autonomy of a class became the same as activity at Party forums.

How to justify this? That's what the word "comrade" meant (they would say), at least as far as Eastern Europe went. So it came down to us from the days of Stalin's ideological darkness. But there was no way to justify why not a single country in Eastern Europe managed to understand or even was aware of the unique interests of the working class, let alone the autonomy of workers' organizations.

The syndicates had and still do have the least enviable role in this depersonalization and subordination of the workers. People outside of communism have scarcely any understanding of the reason for their existence. In Lenin's time, within the Soviet Party there were sharp polemics about the need for syndicates. What turned the scales was his view of them as a school of communism. If it was a school, though, it was one that remained embryonic, for society did not evolve toward communism but toward the hegemony of the new class. Stalin turned the syndicates, as he did other non-Party organizations, into transmission belts, so that the decisions of the Party center might be better understood. The actual work of the syndicates amounted to increasing production and raising productivity. This made some sort of sense during reconstruction and then during industrialization.[1] But today, after those countries have carried out an industrial transformation, the parasitic, syndicalist bureaucracy has fallen into oblivion and makes no sense, least of all in Yugoslavia. And not because syndicates here have been more subordinate to the Party and state apparatus than in the other Communist countries. On the contrary, Yugoslav syndicates have taken greater initiative and have been more resourceful. The crisis and sterility of Yugoslav syndicates have been more visible because Yugoslavia has gone the farthest in removing ideology from public debate and in creating a market economy without at the same time completing a transformation of the political system. Thus in

Yugoslavia the syndicate "still does more to explain government politics than it casts light on workers' wishes, while management, without consultations, wants to raise the labor base." ("Politika," Belgrade, February 24, 1972.)

The nature and methods of Communist power provoke the deepest doubt in communism as a workers' movement. But here too, one should be careful about categorical conclusions ripped from time and circumstance. There is no doubt that the ideas and practices of communism are far from those of the working class. But under certain conditions communism can be associated with the most militant part of that class (for example, in Italy and France) and can even carry out particular goals of the class as a whole (in restoration and industrialization). Communism, however, is no workers' movement: As in all things besides, to Communists the laboring class and its struggles and desires are but means to "higher" ends.

Enthralled by ideology and power, Communists have never, anywhere, completely understood the working class. This is a class that by its nature and its role is creative and nonexclusive. Marx could conceive of a world without an individual bourgeois; we can conceive of a world without a Party bureaucracy pervaded by ideology; but neither the past nor the present world is conceivable without a working class.

Communism in crisis helped change the situation and function of the working class. This was more surely indicated by the nature of its crisis than by the explosion of workers' discontent (as in Hungary in 1956 or Poland in 1970). True, the crisis of communism and discontent among the workers are connected. Moreover, worker discontents brought that crisis into the open and deepened it most drastically. Nevertheless, these expressions of unhappiness were more a reaction to shameful abuses and intolerable conditions than to the social position of the working class, which was monopolized by a dogmatic Party bureaucracy. The bureaucracy's crisis, however, was never-ending. It constantly rose to the surface. This resonated all through society and took its toll on social development.

It was most obvious that we were dealing with an ideological crisis. The motto of a utopian Communist society—"consumption in accordance with need"—was fulfilled and overfulfilled in terms of ideological "goods." This veritable flood of ideology was the most convincing proof of its sterility, its reduction to routine, its impoverishment.

The crisis in ideology I believe goes back to Lenin's banning of different currents within the Party and to his special rewards for political work. But only with Stalin's standardization of ideology and his organization of the Party bureaucracy into a privileged, monopolistic stratum (the new class) would the transition from creativity to ideological stagnation be complete. Under Stalin, communism grew ever stronger as it was spread in the whirlwind of war and chaotic disintegration by an ever-stronger Soviet state. Spatially, physically, communism enjoyed a sweeping scope but morally and intellectually—internally—communism was in decline. Ideology defeats and consumes itself even as it is in the process of being fulfilled; ideology exterminates its true believers.

The crisis of ideology today becomes most visible and sharp-edged when one sees how the world Communist movement has split into national Parties and observes the transformation of communism into bureaucratic nationalist movements. As this happened the USSR and China as superpowers took on special meaning, played special roles. The USSR might have been characterized as tending toward bureaucratic imperialism, while in China's case we are still dealing with revolutionary bureaucratism.

The crisis in ideology was at the same time a crisis of the "ideologized economy," where property division was treated dogmatically and bureaucratically.

And finally, it was a crisis of competition with the "capitalist" world.

The crisis of ideology turned into the structural crisis of communism. Communism itself contained all that was weakened and broken, all that was hopeless about this movement.

But society and the state are rather strengthened than weakened by this crisis. The crisis, paradoxically, emancipated both society and state from perspectives and models handed down from the Revolution which, over time, had grown dogmatized and bureaucratized. Societies under communism were quite similar to the postrevolutionary societies of earlier epochs and they will emerge from this movement, sooner or later, more free and more dynamic. The same can be said for the governments of "Communist" countries.

Within such societies there arose considerable differentiation. Most conspicuous in this differentiation was the rise of a special sort of middle class. Its roots lay in all the social groups, even in the Party bureaucracy. To it gravitated the upper strata of all these groups. The same was true for the working class as well. To be a worker is no choice of one's own; it is one's lot in life—good or bad, more often bad than good. Although the working class under socialism was closer to Marx's pauperized and disenfranchised proletarians than under capitalism, the transformation of today's socialist societies into consumer ones offers workers greater advantages and more security than would the tearing down of the existing economic structure. The working class is not content, nor can it ever be content, with the perverse, arbitrary division of the national product carried out by the bureaucracy. But workers need not destroy society itself, or destroy the way production is carried out, to enjoy a better division. They only claim the right to take action on their own behalf. They want abolition of bureaucratic monopoly over society, starting with the monopoly exercised over themselves.

That is part of a wider process, one which in the capitalist countries is farther along the road. The technological revolution, in which the developed nations are far advanced, makes it possible for the working class to change its living conditions together with its social position. Only in the dogmas of ideologues and the wishful thinking of revolutionaries was the working class absolutely revolutionary. Was it always, everywhere, and in all things revolutionary? Workers are stubborn, disciplined, and self-sacrificing fighters, but only when it is a question of their own interests, or when general human values are at stake, or when it is a matter of their country's equal rights.

All this means that neither socialism nor capitalism is pregnant with a "proletarian" revolution. Only in the minds of revolutionary fanatics, however, is the workers' function or importance thereby diminished.

The crisis in socialism is mainly a crisis in the politics of the superstructure. That being so, socialist societies, even if they have not already had enough of violence, are unsuited to revolutionary programs and civil wars. What they are suited to is reforms, strikes, and demonstrations.

Within socialism the driving social power of the working class will inevitably grow with the deepening crisis of the new class. Contemporary knowledge and contemporary production are intolerant of management that is ideological and bureaucratic. Marx's proletarian is unqualified, or is a badly paid foreign worker. The modern worker approaches the level of the professional in his knowledge, and because of his standards is growing into the middle class. Science and new production methods mean for the working class, as for professional people and scientists, not merely survival but also a greater potential freedom. The society Marx had in mind was, of course, different. But is not his vision being fulfilled after all? For Marx dreamed of eradicating the difference between mental and physical labor, dreamed that people who were slaves to their work would be transformed into integrated, free persons.

THE END IN GRIEF AND SHAME

Foreign powers led by NATO[2] bulked large in communism's fall. But it was not they, basically, who overthrew communism; communism overthrew itself. Communism collapsed in the most beggarly, shameful, and irrevocable way. The peoples living under this system only came to realize that they were living in filthy mud and dying in their chains after communism did, finally, fall apart. Never could they be pushed back into that condition of loathsome shame, not even if by some unlucky stroke the fag ends of communism were to grab power again. Nothing that rots away from within can ever be made whole.

When we speak of "communism," we think first of all of Soviet communism. It was Soviet ideological and military, imperial, power that kept the movement going. It is often said, and quite clear, that communism in this sense fell apart owing to an economic and political organization that could not keep up with today's changes, whether external or internal. It could not adapt, either by hook or by crook. So much is clear.

True enough. But the idea itself contained the seeds of its own inglorious, future collapse. They lay in wait within the very idea of communism.

I have long spoken out on the subject of communism. My writings have expressed all that I have come to understand about it over many years of often painful, equivocal meditation. Now that I have reached the end I feel an urge to round out what I have learned. An absence of certainty is inherent in any attempt to prophesy, but even so I am prompted to entertain prospects for the various post-Communist movements. It goes without saying that such predictions apply above all to my own world, the world of a people whose unkind fate was determined by the utopian dictatorship of Communists.

Precisely because of having first set down in compressed form all that I experienced and came to understand, the most important thing to do now is to subject the very idea of communism to criticism. For as I said above, it was here that the seeds of communism's own demise germinated and sprouted unseen.

That the Communist idea in its Marxist variant was basically a vision of a perfect society without classes, a vision that was scientific and at the same time mystical and utopian—truly the most utopian of all possible visions—was an idea familiar not only to political thinkers but to any tolerant, liberal politician as well. Many a religious community, many a sect with its sterile, aborted experiments, pointed in this direction. Such undertakings appeared at the beginning of Christianity, were characteristic of the whole Middle Ages, and materialized once again as the industrial transformation began. Those experiments come in the guise of holistic teachings concerned with social transformation, as, for example, the so-called utopian socialists: Owen,[3] Saint-Simon,[4] Fourier,[5] and others. Utopias aspire to eliminate injustice and violence from human communities, to root out evil from the human race. Utopias are the human spirit plus all noble acts. They defy the fact that all that is human is "unperfect." Perhaps that is just the reason for their existence.

What was not noticed, or not adequately observed, by critics who were contemporaries of Marx and by his later critics as well was that Marx's Communist idea was a utopia of a special kind. It was entirely explained by systematic proofs grounded in the supreme achievements of Western philosophy and economics; and it was oriented to industry. The possibilities of modern industry were as vast as they were certain. In other words, as distinct from earlier utopias moved by religious and humanitarian impulses, Marx's utopia was impelled by the inevitability of scientific and industrial progress and so was based on the "inevitable" possibilities of building a "perfect society." (Marx puts us in mind of Hegel's Absolute Idea: Both were pitiless.) That fusion of utopia with scientific methodology, of an absolute ideal with "objectively conditioned" and ruthless realism, furnished the basis and inspiration for revolutionary movements. It was the source of their victories in more than one country that was industrially backward.

A utopia like this, which was Marxist and idealistic and, under Lenin and Lenin's Party as an instrument of totalitarian power dedicated to total transformation, was at the same time a utopia that was realistic—such a utopia might come to be realized, given the prevailing circumstances, international and national. The building of a socialist society was not possible without total dominion over the basic existential factors of society and without the transformation, under Stalin, of a totalitarian Party into a privileged stratum. But once that had happened, this powerful, unconquerable, revolutionary ecstasy guttered out and retreated before the unbridled, rough, violence-prone realism of the Party and state oligarchies. Utopia never did come to be realized, nor could it be. Of the original ideal there remained only its element of methodical, "scientific," total violence. For utopia is not in itself evil— on the contrary, it is inspirational. What is evil is utopia as potential power containing the reality of Marxist doctrine. In Russia, Marx's utopia finally stood revealed in its concealed, essential aspect: Instead of force as the "midwife of a new society"—to use Engels's term—we had the abolition of society itself by force.

From a metaphysical point of view, communism is the idea of struggle, the inexorable and ruthless struggle of extremes, an absolute law of existence for this world. But taken out among human beings and their society, which is all that Communists really care about, that idea could only mean the unwavering struggle of Communists against everything and everyone—right down to the final transformation of human beings themselves. The evil in them is wiped out, opposed interests and contradictions in the human community are eliminated. In the last analysis, for social reality this means infinite tyranny, tyranny idealized, tyranny as a kind of Platonic "idea" of evil in the name of compassion. It is an idea that often goes about in disguise. But under certain historical circumstances such an idea need not go about always and everywhere in disguise. The idealism of Communists and Communist currents that *keep the faith* has the ability over time, in the struggle against an evil reality (e.g., fascism and other sorts of tyrannies), to bring to life that other aspect of the idea, its sacrificial and humanistic side.

The essence of force and utopianism, and above all, of this idea's tyrannical nature, lies in the fact that Communists work with living people and *use* these living people to build a "new" and abstract human being and to construct a "new" and chimerical society patterned after their own ideas. It is a social vision almost Manichean. A Kingdom of Heaven on Earth is indeed envisioned, but it is a vision that divides not only the earth but primarily people and their communities into darkness and light, into absolute evil and absolute good. *We,* of course, represent the good; *they,* the evil.

Even as such, the idea of communism bore death within itself. In the Communist world, the powers-that-be plus existing political circumstances together saw to it that no one killed communism off. The idea was left to rot away by itself. To all appearances it stood revealed as the purest banality, as a gross oversimplification and an extremely violent treatment of human beings and societies. The transformation of most Communists, even of once outstanding revolutionaries, into inveterate totalitarians and nationalists shows how far fighters for such an idea might go. Their consciences were capable of the most monstrous transformations—and those ideological combatants were not exactly overburdened with conscience to begin with! But on the other hand, to the credit of some, there was a handful of Communist idealists, mostly from the older generations, who found a way to be consistently democratic and by that token "utopian." It was their consolation. Future freedom can sprout from such seeds. Tolerance and civility germinate here.

It cannot be denied, though, whether we are talking of ideas, of political movements, or of leaders, that in the end all things return to their essential nature. It does not matter how well they may have been concealed or falsified. Or how thoroughly believed in.

Idealism works wonders and is a mighty force, but it behooves us to be cautious when faced with absolute, idealized visions. Such visions may encourage us to sacrifice and goad us into noble acts, but they are also opiate to the soul and can unseat the mind. Shun these visions, need we add. Do not jostle at the trough, do not give way to violence, do not exploit others. In the idea of communism there was something of the grand vision, but there was always a sufficient supply of the rest. The one being crushed by force, everything devolved upon the other.

The Communist ideal in its Marxist-Leninist aspect will never be restored. As an ideal it remains memorable for its sacrifices and battles, and for having shaken the whole world in revolution. But, alas, this ideal will be remembered also for the cheap and tawdry sufferings it brought, the humiliations it imposed. It will be remembered for its extermination of the innocent on ideological and pragmatic grounds. It will be remembered for its dark destruction of the human spirit. It will be remembered for robbing the living person of individuality.

Communism is an all-inclusive, holistic doctrine. It is more than simply a philosophic understanding of the world and history, more than a teaching about society. Communism gives guidance to artists of all kinds down to the most paltry level, telling writers in particular how they should write if they want to be first-rate, to be socialist. In its total integration communism brims over with humanistic injunctions (as we said earlier) touching on brotherhood, solidarity, equality, and so on. But for the essence of the idea and its practice, meaning totalitarian power for the purpose of building a utopian, classless society, these humanistic elements as a rule have no significance beyond legitimizing stern methods. They may be needful, but they are provisional. Communism's humanistic elements nourish the illusion that they themselves will become a reality once the final goal, as they call it, is reached.

But for events taking place within communism, those elements possess enormous significance.

However homogeneous and totalitarian, Communism is prey to incurable inner crises. These crises keep provoking discord between theory and practice, between the ideal and the real, between total power by the leadership and resistance to totality and uniformity. These crises could be labeled crises of conscience. (Naturally, we are talking about what might be called Communist conscience. People like this deny human conscience and in its place impose ideological consistency on themselves, or what they call *Party conscience.*)

The disharmony between an ideal and the actual practice of rulers usually manifests itself politically. Totalitarian power claims to interpret and carry out an idea, while on the other hand any such interpretation, any such path toward the ideal, is challenged. Both the powers that be and the challengers to it are total; each is consistent in the way it represents and interprets the idea. The difference is only that rulers regard power itself as the reality of an idea. Its incarnation is the only possible reality. While their adversaries look upon such a viewpoint and such behavior as retreat from that idea and as merely the means to power.

Humanism in communism, loyalty to an idea, consistency in fulfilling it—these are the curses of Communist rulers. Never have they managed to rid themselves of such values. Nor, for that matter, does the Communist idea allow itself to be gotten rid of. This contradiction between political power and the ideal, if it does not break out as an interpretation of some kind, smolders in the ashes until it is fanned into flames by the spontaneous reactions of "ideologically unbaked" Communists or by the fact that non-Communists quietly stick to indestructible values. Spontaneity, which is what ordinary real life is all about, has never submitted to dogma. No one has ever been able to alter it or to stamp it out.

The history of communism is the history of factional struggles. This has been so from the time of Marx. Through fierce factional struggles Lenin built a Party of a new type, one that served as the model and creator of a new society. And though when he took power Lenin condemned factional currents as "a luxury we cannot afford," illness kept him from outlawing them altogether. Still, it is more than likely that he would have done so if possible. Stalin, having consolidated his personal power, solved the issue of unavoidable factions (like other things that seemed unavoidable) in the simplest manner possible: He destroyed them physically from the moment he suspected their existence or even suspected people of thinking differently. He killed off the majority of his own Central Committee so as to finally "establish order," in his words. Thus he, Stalin, the greatest Communist—for so everyone thought him save the dogmatic purists and naive "quintessentialists"—the incarnation of the real essence, the real possibilities, of the ideal—this greatest of all Communists, killed off more Communists than did all the opponents of communism taken together, worldwide. He managed to impose his peremptory will on practically the whole of world communism. His will was a purified, exemplary model of communism. But not even Stalin in his own Party managed to keep doubts from germinating; he never succeeding in eradicating resentment of his "infallible" interpretation, of his "consistent" realization of dogma. It now is known that within the narrow circle of Stalin's cronies, a circle of men tested at every stage of the struggle, a circle that could be relied on for any criminal endeavor—within this circle there had formed a still smaller nucleus of the dissatisfied. This nucleus amounted to a palace conspiracy and included Khrushchev and Malenkov.

Factions and factional fights, the very appearance of differences, bestow on any political organization its dynamics, its mobility, and its willingness to be critical of itself. Intraparty struggles are the most reliable, most tested way of establishing the vitality of a party. In communism, too, this is so. And yet factionalism has a double meaning, a double dimension. Factions there, too, bestow dynamism and generate change. But at the same time the inner, essential nature of the idea is to be intolerant of factions and intolerant even of divergences in points of view, not to speak of methods.

Trends in the Party were suppressed; its top ranks thought as with one mind. This did indeed represent the victory of totalitarian, authoritarian tendencies. But it also was the harbinger of an inner decay within communism. Stalin, who consummated the idea the most consistently, dug its grave at the same time.

Whatever occurs within communism nearly always signifies a power struggle. So it is with factions. Even in the case of events liberally inspired, or relatively so compared to totalitarian approaches, or by comparison with the leader. Consistently liberal factions within communism cannot even exist when it comes to program, let alone practice. Not a single faction ever made its way farther than an attempt to "perfect" the system so it might last longer. Khrushchev dethroned Stalin wanting to imbue the system with more dynamism by revealing the inefficiency of tyranny. The result was that faith in the ideology tottered. Wasn't the system already perfect as it was? Similarly, Gorbachev too wished to breathe life into the system by democratic reforms. He wanted to facilitate peaceful world competition by this means. But his *glasnost*—more freedom of expression—only undermined the foundations of both system and empire. And being more candid was all the more effective because *perestroika,* or reconstruction of the economy, had led to its collapse and dissolution.

Solzhenitsyn displays no regrets when factions are wiped out and Communists liquidated; for thereby has been achieved what they have done to others. They have gotten what they deserved, have been done unto as they did unto others. This writer's deep compassion is engaged by the sufferings of millions of innocent peasants and non-Communists. And rightly so, from the standpoint of both human and divine justice.

But factions, factionalists, and deviationists of all kinds are very important politically when it comes to the breakup of communism. They chew away at ideology and the system from within. And this perhaps is of even greater weight than the millions of innocents who have suffered and died, for factions reveal that there is a worm in the apple.

To annihilate them brusquely and brazenly reveals that communism and Communists have no regard even for their own comrades and yesterday's leaders.

Factions, particularly after the seizure of power, are the first agents of crisis in a Party and in communism. They are the first harbingers of cracks and fissures within the monolith of power and ideology.

The transformation of the Party apparatus into a privileged monopoly (new class, *nomenklatura*) existed in embryonic form in Lenin's prerevolutionary book *Professional Revolutionaries,* and in his time was already well under way. It is just this which has been the major reason for the decay of communism. Not only was such a class, such a monopoly, an eyesore because it was so bold and open a violation of an ideal, so blatant a disregard of promises that had been made, but even apart from this, the new class was inherently incapable of building a social order that stood any chance of permanence. It could not consolidate into a durable force for leadership within society and the nation.

It is true that where a social revolution had been carried out (Russia, Yugoslavia, China) and where other classes had been either destroyed or expropriated, and where an industrial revolution was both myth and national necessity, the Party bureaucracy did have a rational reason to exist and to consolidate itself. Stalin was under no compulsion to exterminate his rivals and to uproot and destroy millions of peasants. However, without enthroning a privileged class through industrial transformation he could not set in motion an active majority nor keep his revolutionary power intact. No matter how futile, heartless, and mindless, Stalinist savagery did contain some elements of rational, historical justification up to the end of World War II. On the other hand, in the larger historical perspective, by undertaking this transformation the Party bureaucracy itself became transformed, turning into a parasitic layer of society that sabotaged its own work while squandering the ideology that legitimized it.

No society lets itself get built, just like that. A society builds itself— spontaneously, as it were—and over long periods of time. It does not get put together in private studies or open assemblies. This was surely the case with slave societies, and with feudal ones, and with capitalist ones too—with all such social orders. Communism and Communists simply took it into their heads, more boldly and thoroughly than anyone else ever had before, that they could construct a paradise by following their "scientific" blueprints and by applying brute force, legitimized by the state, to body and spirit.

Instead, they destroyed society as a living, active organism. They depersonalized the personality, robbing it of its individuality by tearing it away from its social milieu. And yet the shattered parts of the social organism lived on. Society continued to change in unpredictable ways that no force could control, let alone bridle.

However, this monopolistic Party bureaucracy, this new class, did not come into being as a social class in the usual meaning of the word, but was simply installed on a throne by an oligarchy led by a tyrant who then turned around and tyrannized the oligarchy itself. Those were times of political improvisation formed under particular historical circumstances. The new class disposed of material assets as if it were their owner, advancing their interests according to its own interests and sharing the wealth hierarchically. Those who belonged to it (meaning those in the top ranks) lived more spaciously and luxuriously than American multimillionaires. But they were not able to become owners of the means of production, for that clashed with the essence of their ideology and with the nature of their power. And it was all too easy to lose every privilege they had (often life itself) the moment they tried to back off even slightly from the established ideology and norms of their class. The path from glory and dominion to grief and shame was extremely short.

A class of owners that disposes of material goods at its own discretion, a class without productive or commercial assets of its own, is an absurdity. It means complete self-enclosure. It means a tortured, unscrupulous scrambling for power within a hierarchy that is the sole source of well-being, power, and prestige. It means blind subordination to the leadership, isolation from one's people and the world. A social stratum like this by its very nature was doomed to destruction the moment it had reached the point of being unable to resolve not just basic national problems by force but even to keep the peace within its own ranks.

Without the so-called cult of personality the Party bureaucracy could not have imposed its will nor kept itself in power, but this same personality cult also meant it could not last.

The expression "cult of personality" in Communist-Marxist literature was first used by Marx when he criticized the practice of glorifying leaders in the revolutionary movement. Immoderate, uncritical glorification of Marx himself existed even while he was yet alive. Only later, with the strengthening of socialist parties (the Second International) in Europe, did Marx's works come to be idolized for revealing history's laws scientifically and for predicting, again scientifically, that a classless society was inevitable in the future. And along with this he, too, came to be venerated as a person.

It was Lenin who took hold of Marx's doctrines with the greatest consistency, and also in the least critical way: They were the definitive revelation, as he saw it, of definitive truths. Before taking power, Lenin was known and valued as a leader in his own small faction, but his reputation in the Party taken as a whole was not without reservation. Once he did take power, the relationship suddenly underwent a change, with the result that when Lenin died he turned into a saint and his every word became a hallowed truth not subject to argument. Lenin was now "a Marx from the era of imperialism and proletarian revolutions."

Only with Stalin, though, did the cult of personality become a ritual obligation for everyone. Thanks to his own intimidating encouragement, of course, it was Stalin one appealed to, Stalin one deified. Proposers of toasts at private parties outdoors had to glorify him. Children still in nursery school had to venerate him aloud. Stalin's name was obligatory at every public announcement. Philosophers and artists as well were required to be obliged to Stalin.

The cult of personality belongs to the very pith and marrow of communism, is part of its nature. An infallible and universally valid doctrine, valid everywhere and at all times, particularly when it merges with totalitarian, hierarchical, political power cannot make do without some "infallible" interpreter and omnipotent leader. Khrushchev, who began the undermining of Stalin's tyranny, modestly nourished a cult of his own. This then was fed by all kinds of scribblers and flatterers, as is always appropriate and tolerable. Brezhnev's cult took on a grotesque shape for two reasons: He himself was intrinsically insignificant, and he degraded the Communist system morally and ideologically. Personality cults were fostered in all Communist countries and parties. They were persistently pampered with an intolerance and pretension to totality that depended on how deeply rooted and strong communism was under the concrete circumstances. Tito forced on the country his own cult, in a Yugoslav way, folkloristic and "liberal." Generally speaking, the cult spluttered out with Gorbachev, when both system and ideology fell apart.

At all times and places, however, the cult throttled every creative initiative in the Party, and through it, in society. It was the essential element of moral and intellectual degradation, both of the ideal and of its proponents.

In the spiritual sense, the Communist bureaucracy did not create a thing, literally not a thing. Culture generally it crippled, or choked off altogether. With its invented and false "ethic," this bureaucracy stamped out or caricatured the ethics of religions and philosophies. Whatever was created in the field of culture under communism arose from those of its true believers who had talent, or else was owing to the Aesopian language of the clever.

I have always believed, as I still do, that critics of communism who do not come out of the movement attach too great an importance to the economy in communism's demise. Such critics, chiefly from the West, live in a world where the economy's influence on politics is enormous, often decisive. In communism it is otherwise, even the reverse: Everything, including the economy, is subordinate to ideological power. One could even argue that if ideology had not collapsed, Communists might have succeeded in deceiving the people longer yet, all the while holding them down to a bare, vegetable existence. Only force was requisite, that and the manipulation of an economy over which they exercised total dominion.

Not that economics has been unimportant. On the contrary, we are only talking of the precedence of ideology over the economy, the subordination of the economy to the political authorities, to straightforward ideological aims. Communists, conscious that economic failure can deprive ideology of its value and undermine their own power, have always bestowed special attention on the economy. Sometimes they even go too far. Whenever such danger threatened, as, for example, at the time of Soviet collectivization of the villages, repression and propaganda would be intensified to the point of becoming an orgy of fury impacting whole social strata, touching the lives of millions. And yet Communists, rational and methodical in both idea and practice, knew that force had—had to have—its limits, even when it was out of control. And so, at the very moment when the individual peasant was being annihilated, the village paupers were being offered prospects for rapid industrialization. Agriculture may have been set back, the best peasant households may have been torn up by the roots, but an industry was, after all, created, and an empire, its political power reinforced, was made ready for defense and further conquest.

When it comes to appraising ideology, the two men who were best known and (in the post-Stalin period) most significant for abjuring the Soviet system and communism were Alexander Solzhenitsyn and Andrei Sakharov, and they differed in fundamental ways. True, it is on the broader plane that they differed. The one represented the traditional "pan-Slavist" current, the other the modern, or what might be called Western, current within Russian intellectual and political opinion. What their differences and even opposition may have meant stemmed largely from their different views on the role of ideology. These differences were all the more important because they heralded today's deep political and spiritual ferment within Russia, ferment that in my judgment is fateful both for that country and for the world at large. The ferment is absurd and astonishing only on its face: a coupling of former Communists and nationalists that seems to have inherited the mantle of "pan-Slavism," while the liberal-democratic contingent looks as if it were the heir of the "Westernizers."[6]

Solzhenitsyn, if he does not actually reduce all evils to ideology, thinks that all evils originate there. This position is not generally inaccurate. It simply does not bring out sufficiently the fact that as totalitarianism consolidated and strengthened, it turned ideology into its tool, a tool that may have been obligatory but had become ever more secondary. This was a gradual, long-lasting, and sporadic process, linked with the political purges of the so-called deviationists and revisionists. Ideology thereby petrified. Or better, the ruling class set it in concrete with the aid of the Party schools as they branched out and to the degree that well-paid "theorists" and popularizers multiplied.

When Solzhenitsyn declared ideology to be unalloyed evil and expressed the absurd desire to the Soviet leaders that they renounce it, ideology was already a rotting carcass and actually served only as a ritual expression of loyalty. Solzhenitsyn, though, was proceeding from an integrated religious understanding no less than from tragic knowledge of the destructiveness of ideology for all of life in Russia and for the life of the spirit in particular. Even if ideology had long been in-capable of being a living, potent, and demonic force, to Solzhenitsyn it seemed so. This writer's direct effect in bringing to life religious nationalism is indisputable.

Sakharov's approach to ideology was rational and pragmatic. Having taken note that ideology had grown desiccated and had shriveled to nothing, he considered that the focus of change lay in reforming the economy and broadening freedom, first and foremost in the media. Sakharov exerted a clear, though indirect, influence on Gorbachev.

The views of these two men on the importance of ideology represent extremes: Ideology may be the wellspring of evil, but on the other hand, it is not the greatest evil of all time. Be that as it may, granting that ide-ology has indeed withered away and turned into a mere instrument, still, a system cannot but stay on its feet even in the absence of such a "spiritual" crutch. A system breaks down completely only when it rec-ognizes that ideology no longer plays any role, including the function of ritual observance over a system that has turned into a mummy.

The significance of the economy in the fall of communism both in the Soviet Union and in the subjugated countries of Eastern Europe grew in proportion as all these countries turned inevitably to the world as a whole, including, above all, the West. Even so, they represented competition of a kind on the troubled, fragmented, but inescapable world market. Communist production lagged behind, not only by com-parison to the West but also by comparison to earlier periods in its own development. Communist countries, with their inert bureaucracies drenched in predatory extortion and their archaic concepts of eco-nomic life and its independence from ideologies, were completely unable to participate in what is known as the postindustrial transfor-mation. This, despite their resources and cadres: The Soviet Union, for example, had approximately twice the number of engineers the United States had, but the value of production there was no more than 50 per-cent that of American production.

Relations grew strained as if by a law that might be called Marxist. The Communist method of production, feudal-industrial, came into conflict with production forces, where people are the most important factor. Production methods had to be altered, either by revolution or evolution. Under communism, change began (or better, started to begin) only with the decay of the Communist ideology of political power, and only when the ruling class disintegrated in futile attempts to find itself a way out of its impasse by reforming the economic and governmental system.

A very great role, at times even decisive, was played by the sharp and unbridgeable face-off that took place over the long period of the Cold War. That the Soviet Union was losing this war could have been detected twenty years before the fall, as soon as it was forced to assume a defensive stance ideologically, or more exactly when it passed over to a defensive rivalry that was first military and then ideological instead of being both ideological and military, as before. Just when this happened is hard to pinpoint, for it continued over many incidents and many acts of defiance. It seems that the Cuban Missile Crisis, the orientation of Kennedy and Khrushchev toward ending the Cold War, and the policy of De Gaulle that tended in the same direction, were all very important in this matter, if not crucial.

The final turning point, in my judgment, happened when President Reagan undertook the decisive policy of rearmament in response to the Soviet challenge. The Communist empire collapsed; in the end, it had suffered a military defeat without war. The subjugated peoples of Eastern Europe, already in a state of readiness, were simply awaiting the moment. More abruptly than forecasters had foreseen (among them this writer), the empire imploded. Communism threw in the towel the moment its expansion was finally brought to a halt.

The term "national communism" has long been digested by the Western press and widely used; I do not know who first uttered it apropos of the Yugoslav-Soviet break in 1948. For the world, the year 1948 came as a sudden, surprising turn of events whose significance went unnoticed at first. There were few if any outside Yugoslavia who thought the Yugoslav Communists up to resisting, if only because we were regarded, and rightly so, as the most hard-line and most revolutionary of all Communists. But after the Cold War flared up and a year had passed, the chancelleries of the West, headed by the United States and Britain, started taking a lively interest.

As global relationships go, Yugoslavia's confrontation with Moscow may have been something new, but it had no crucial significance: a small, backward country could only be important strategically if by parting company with Moscow it crippled access to the Mediterranean by the Soviet bloc.

However, for the further course of communism as a world movement this event had epochal significance: All today are unanimous in holding that the inner disintegration of communism began right there and then.

Moscow's accusations were read in the light of clichés from the time when Stalin settled accounts with deviationists in the Soviet Party. They therefore seemed to be unlikely fabrications. But they were also understood to express imperialist subordination of the new Communist states. This was all the more clear because, though they might be reproached with many a sin, the Yugoslav Communists could not be criticized for lack of consistency. Indeed, it was they who in the war displayed incomparable self-sacrifice and unreserved solidarity with the Soviet Union. Moscow enjoyed the diligent support of all Communist parties. Some were less vigorous (the Italian, the Polish, the Chinese), some more (French, American), but doubts were implanted. Was Stalin really infallible? Was Moscow engaged in relationships that were only comradely and not oriented toward hegemony and imperialism? Such questions began to eat away at the smooth and unbroken surface of ideology and politics. Communism was not so monolithic as it appeared to be. Yugoslavia, while remaining Communist but with substantial material and political support from the West, resisted boycotts and armed threats. Soon after Stalin's death, Moscow was forced to admit to "error," and a delegation headed by Khrushchev set out for its Belgrade Canossa.[7]

The Yugoslav example was followed by those of other countries that had undergone revolution: China, Albania. The subjugated nations of Eastern Europe registered their own brands of protest: Hungary and Poland witnessed revolts, various forms of uncontrollable national resistance occurred elsewhere, and most Communist parties across the world started to see attrition in their ranks, for they could no longer blindly follow the Soviet Party without losing influence and prestige among their own peoples.

The Yugoslavs, with patriotic and moral courage, may have been the first to resist Soviet bullying, but they were not the first to invent national communism, nor the first to adopt it.

Pride of place in this case as well goes to the Bolsheviks. National communism was already present in Lenin's Russia quite concretely and unambiguously at the moment when Soviet power was in its birth pangs and the Brest-Litovsk peace treaty with Kaiser Wilhelm's Germany was signed in 1918. Lenin thereby saved his own national power as a vital goal now achieved, while maintaining his credibility as an internationalist, for he was expecting revolution to break out in Europe, starting with Germany. It was he in fact who prescribed the conditions for acceptance of the various parties in the Communist International, which came into being, essentially, by accepting the Soviet form of political power: dictatorship of the proletariat under Party leadership. Currents of opinion that were socialist and Communist and particularly social-democratic, but that did not accept this core belief, were simply excluded. And the leadership of the Russian Party and Lenin was taken for granted, since it was only they who had power and financial resources. But within the Comintern, discussions were tolerated. There was no noticeable cult of personality. And Communist parties had some sort of autonomy in national politics.

Soviet-Russian national communism consolidated itself through factional struggle under Stalin, within the Soviet Party and in the Comintern. By orienting himself to national communism, Stalin stoked the fires of Russian nationalism. Russians themselves had no need for it, but Stalin's own power certainly stood to gain and so did the new class.

Like the subjugation of the Soviet Party and state to Stalin's personal power and cult, subordination to his leadership and to the Soviet secret services as well was undoubtedly also put in place within the Comintern. The one Party that was not brought to heel thanks to its geography and specific political circumstances was that of the Chinese, headed by Mao Zedong. All Communist parties were in point of fact obligated to keep uppermost in mind the interests of what was called the first land of socialism.

Soviet national communism was incessantly dressed up in internationalist phraseology, whereas in reality it was an ideological cover for Soviet imperialism, and the international Communist movement was a political weapon of the Kremlin.

More than a few Communists noticed this in the curved mirror of their own indoctrinated state. It was viewed as inconsistency by Stalin in the application of an idea. Many of these people were killed; many were proclaimed traitors and agents of some enemy of the Soviet Union (actual enemies, "imperialists," or Fascists); some even found out the truth. (Few grasped it, and no one stood up for it.) Tito and Mao Zedong parted company. Tito, while staying in the Soviet Union during the purge that was taking place in even the Yugoslav Party, came to realize that ideology above all else has to serve institutions, serve the Party, serve political power. By not suffering any change within its ideology, political power attained stability and uniformity, became monolithic. Tito reasoned thus: Through the Comintern, Stalin and the powers that be have to be obeyed as a real force. But in secret one should not tamper with the workings and interests of one's own Party and one's own political position. Or, as Tito would say, of one's people and one's country. And Mao? In the vast reaches of China far from Moscow and in a revolution raging under his direct leadership, Mao cared very little or not at all about the positions and wishes of Moscow.

National communism never turned into a different system. It viewed democracy, with reason, as its most dangerous opponent. But national communism did have a fundamental impact on the breakdown of communism as a single world movement, and thereby on the collapse of the Soviet empire and the defeat of Soviet imperialism.

The political future, being a living reality (often all too alive), cannot be predicted. True, inspired individuals see how events are tending, as much by sixth sense as by conscious thought. There can be no doubt that Churchill felt defeat to be inevitable for the Nazi and Fascist forces, or he would not have let himself be drawn into the lonely adventure of resistance. After all is said and done, and whatever form political relationships may take, one can only hypothesize about these things. Hypotheses may have the look of logic but are essentially not to be relied on. In politics everything looks logical and reasonable. In fact, though, this is merely the rationalized outcome of irrational, unpredictable forces. For we think in terms of *this* world, *these* realities, while foreseeing some *future* world and *future* reality, even under the best of circumstances, as through a glass darkly. When we think in terms of post-communism, the same holds true.

It does seem safe to say this: Since the Communist governments had gone their separate ways even before the general collapse, therefore post-Communist development in each country would have its own special features. And though they are all different and each a case unto itself, for this or that country one can at least hypothetically make out the common features that will influence its future development.

Nationalism is the overriding fact of life in all the former Communist countries of Eastern Europe. Upon reflection I believe that this kind of nationalism has more force and potency than what we see in Western Europe and the United States, which is a different style altogether. The style of no ideology at all. Nationalism will be seen in the weakening role of the United Nations and the weakening of *human rights,* as also in a leaning toward policies pursued by each government in isolation.

This discussion, though, is about tendencies within the post-Communist states, and neither my knowledge nor my experience are great enough, nor do they give me the right, to draw any conclusions about phenomena in the countries of the West.

In all the post-Communist states, nationalism is in the ascendancy, and each brand of nationalism is different from the next. For the Czech Republic, what is in store is likely to be peaceful, democratic development and inclusion into Europe. Nationalist tendencies are strong in Poland and Hungary, but in neither country do there exist really potent claims to revise boundaries, meaning calls for the "autonomy" of compatriots in neighboring countries. What we have in Poland is anti-Semitism, even though there are no Jews there to speak of. In Romania there is less reaching out toward Europe and European models. But Romania has claims on Moldova, or more exactly on the special status of its national minority there. Official Bulgaria has opened itself up to Europe. But neither does Bulgaria renounce the "Bulgarian nationality" of Macedonians. Militant nationalism toward her neighbors is ready to flare up in Bulgaria if this country sees a convenient opportunity. Albania has only just begun to rally, save in the matter of its pretensions toward conationals in neighboring countries, mainly Yugoslavia and Macedonia. These claims are more intense than at the time of the Enver Hoxha tyranny, and they are being supported by outside powers, above all the United States—although for the time being, a peaceful resolution is sought.

But in not a single one of these countries, despite their inner social and ideological tensions, do we see any signs of civil war. I have never thought that the consequence of the fall of communism would be civil war. Nor did civil war account for communism's fall. The wars that have flared up in the former Yugoslavia and the former Soviet Union do not constitute civil wars but only a settling of scores between the various nationalisms within their respective territories and between different cultural and religious groups. The reason is simple: With the fall of Yugoslavia and of the Soviet Union, national communities, or rather nationalisms, have found themselves to be without boundaries.

And aspirations for wider horizons have only grown in strength with the creation of national states.[8]

Today's military actions in the former Yugoslavia and the former Soviet Union clamor to be dealt with separately, though briefly.

Communism did not succeed in altering cultural and religious communities, let alone in abolishing them. Like individual human beings, these national communities, if they can change at all, change only from within and after a lengthy evolution. When revolutions occur, cultural and religious identities do get hammered down, only to bounce back with elemental force unless precisely defined relationships have developed in a society: democratic institutions, a free economy, a middle class. In this regard communism left behind it a desert. Now that desert has erupted with ideologies and movements inflamed by the raw material of hatred and bitterness, by deep-rooted and bad memories, and above all by the ideologized belief that the blame for all failures, national and otherwise, is borne by other people and that these "other people" can be removed from the scene by creating "pure" national states.

The belligerent nationalist movements now waging war—as, for example, in Bosnia (and, I believe, the former Soviet Union in no wise differs from this case)—are all completely intolerant. They all breed a "biological hatred" toward members of other groups. They all seek ways and means of annihilating each other. And they are all characterized by undemocratic internal relations. In these respects they do not differ essentially from Nazism and Fascism. But they are not Fascist movements: They have no homogeneous ideology or social program, nor do they possess a disciplined, militarily organized party. They represent, again as in Bosnia, temporary improvisation combined with short-term aims. They represent the traditional, time-honored way of fighting a war in those parts of the world, following no rules. They are motivated by a mythic and uncritical grasp of their own history. These movements are half modern in their military and political, chauvinist organization, and half hereditary in their Balkan, political style of life, like the traditional *hajduks* (highway murderers) made to order for mayhem and robbery.

Political power, be it Serbian or Croatian, is not identical with these movements, at least not for the time being. But such centers of power prop them up, and they are willing (more or less) to be thus supported. Belgrade and Zagreb are motivated by impulses and interests that are both local, religious and ethnic, and nationalist. Serbia and Croatia are led by authoritarian, nationalistic regimes, Serbia's being the transformed heir to communism while Croatia's regime represents a conservative, state nationalism.

In Russia, the situation is different. There we see a conflict between modern, predominantly democratic currents under an authoritarian leader, Yeltsin, on the one hand, and conservative couplings of former Communists and nationalists aiming to restore the empire and its function, on the other. In Russia, any trend in the direction of a modern, democratic society is of exceptional importance because of that nation's sheer size and spiritual might. Also, such trends toward democratization politically and economically are incomparably more persistent and dynamic than in most of the other formerly Communist countries, not to mention Serbia and Croatia.

Before bringing the present text to a close, I should like to venture a shaky prediction as to the direction being taken by economic and social developments in the post-Communist states. As I have pointed out earlier, every government, every nation, will go its own way and adopt its own forms, even though the general direction might be similar in all cases. The countries belonging to the European Community, too, despite their economic unity and political coordination, are maintaining their own specificities and even developing them further.

That general direction is already pronounced. Change may proceed faster in some places, slower in others, but it amounts to denationalizing socialist, or rather the Party-bureaucratic, forms of property. The trend is toward a differentiated, class society. A restoration of sorts, but one that is more like a conscious effort to turn the clock back to pre-Communist relations than can ever really take place economically or socially. Feudal structures have no prospects of reinstatement, whereas capitalist ones, which are the most plausible, will be interwoven with spreading social legislation. This lack of correspondence between mind and reality will delay any normal, dynamic development, and in fact is already doing so. In all the formerly Communist countries, what used to be called socialist property is seeing the penetration of capitalist arrangements and ways of doing business. And the process is in a fever of excitement in most cases. These are the same structures and relationships of early, primitive capitalism that Marx brilliantly described in his book *Das Kapital* as primitive accumulation: speculation, extortion, heedless exploitation, all of which often take advantage of a corrupt government apparatus. But the process ought not to last long, considering that all these countries have by now embarked on an industrial revolution and are starting from a relatively advanced base. So when consolidation does take place, an efficient, incorrupt government apparatus plus an authoritative, democratic parliament will have an important role to play.

I have not touched on the problem of China and Asian communism, being insufficiently acquainted with any of these countries. In Asia other arrangements may well be possible: Already we can see the development of a market economy within the framework of the Communist political system, while at the same time the desire for political freedom is being suppressed. Does not all this signify some different and original path of development?

The West was caught off guard by the abrupt fall of communism. Accustomed to confronting communism, and wrapped comfortably in its own superiority, the West behaved with self-confidence and unconcern, as if this were a question of different planets. Now it can be seen that these planets were but the extreme ends of one and the same indivisible world.

The West's indifference is especially evident in the lukewarm and mainly declarative support being given to the new Russia, even though world trends, perhaps the destiny of mankind, depend greatly on how conflict develops and turns out in Russia. Once again, this can force Russia into a separate development, this illusion that she can no longer be a great world power. She has the strength, the will, and the means to become so. Even lacking these, she already is a great world power, and without Russia, weakened as she is, it will not be possible to solve a single significant issue. If today Russia is incapable of making her true weight felt, tomorrow she will make up for this as a country transformed, with rejuvenated strength.

As for the war in Bosnia, with its conquests and alterations of boundaries and territories, its senseless destruction of cities and places of worship, the rapes, the arbitrary exterminations, and above all the "ethnic cleansing" and forced displacement of hundreds of thousands—for the West it is as if all this were taking place in some faraway world not inhabited by human beings at all. The West is inefficient, confused, disunified. Its behavior is not motivated by any national interest. Above all, the West has turned away from the ideas and values by which it stood up to Communist tyranny and Soviet imperialism.

For these reasons the West lacks the vision or the will to play a decisive role in unifying or modernizing humanity in freedom.

The formerly Communist countries, including also Communist China, the countries of Communist Asia, and those of the Third World, must before all else find strength in themselves, as does every creative endeavor, as does human existence itself. And find it they will even though by singling out their own path they, and others too, may be led astray into monstrous political arrangements and dangerous, unfathomable relationships.

A BIOGRAPHICAL NOTE ON THE AUTHOR

BY ALEKSA DJILAS

Milovan Djilas was born on June 12, 1911, in the village of Podbišće near Mojkovac in the district of Kolašin, Montenegro. His father's name was Nikola, his mother's Vasilija, née Radenović. The Djilases traced their origins to the ancient clan of Vojnović from the region of Nikšić. Nikola Djilas was an officer in the imperial army and had been decorated with the Obilić Medal, the highest Montenegrin decoration. As commander of one of the Montenegrin companies that had guarded the retreat of the Serbian Army in the withdrawal across Albania in 1915, he was awarded the Albanian Certificate of Service.

Milovan Djilas attended the gymnasium in Kolašin and in Berani. He enrolled in the University of Belgrade (Philosophical Faculty, program in Yugoslav literature) in 1929. Upon arriving in Belgrade he began intensive literary work and published poems and stories in various reviews. At the same time he was politically active, being especially opposed to the dictatorship imposed by King Alexander in 1929. In the fall of 1931 he was one of the organizers of the student demonstrations against the single-candidate elections that had been prepared by the president of the government, General Petar Živković. He helped put together other demonstrations as well. In the united student movement he represented the Communist trend, although there was no official Party organization at that time at the university, nor in Belgrade itself.

In February 1932 he was arrested by the police but in the absence of evidence was released after ten days. In that same year he became a member of the Communist Party and secretary of the Party organization at the University of Belgrade. He initiated a policy of collaboration between the student organization and the worker-Communist group. When the latter's cover was blown, subsequent arrests swept him up as well. He was tortured by the police to disclose the student organization, but these efforts were without result. Djilas was sentenced to three years at hard labor, years mainly served in Sremska Mitrovica Prison.

After finishing his term in 1936 he and (shortly thereafter) Aleksandar-Leka Ranković were given leading roles in the renewed and broadened Party organization in Serbia, and in 1937 Djilas became a member of the Serbian Provincial Committee.

In 1937, when Josip Broz Tito arrived as head of the Communist Party of Yugoslavia, Djilas became a member of the innermost circles of the Yugoslav Party, the Politburo and the Central Committee. At the illegal Fifth World Conference, held in Zagreb in 1940, he was formally confirmed as a Politburo member.

On July 4, 1941, the Central Committee of the Communist Party of Yugoslavia decided to foment rebellion. Djilas was sent to Montenegro to organize this rebellion and set it in motion. There he remained till autumn, when he proceeded to the liberation of the city of Užica. In the course of the war he was a member of the Partisan General Staff. At the beginning of 1944 he attained the rank of lieutenant general, and in 1949, colonel general.

In 1942 Djilas also edited the newspaper *Borba* on the liberated territory.

In 1943 he took part in preparing the decisions that were then adopted by the anti-Fascist council, decisions that laid the formal foundations for today's Yugoslavia.

In April 1944 he went to Moscow as head of the Yugoslav military mission, and in 1945 again traveled to the Soviet Union as a member of the delegation led by Tito.

The entire Djilas family took part in the war. His father, Nikola, was killed, as were his sister Dobrana and his brothers Aleksa and Milivoje.

Djilas entered the first postwar Yugoslav government in 1945, first as minister for Montenegro and then as minister without portfolio. At the beginning of 1953 he was made vice president of the government, and at the end of that year president of the Federal People's Parliament.

In 1946 he participated in the preliminary peace conference in Paris. In that same year he traveled to Warsaw and Prague in a delegation headed by Tito.

In 1947 he took part, along with Edvard Kardelj, in founding the Cominform.

In 1948 Djilas headed a delegation to Moscow aiming at coordinating the policies of Yugoslavia and the Soviet Union and resolving equipment issues for the Yugoslav Army.

At the Fifth Congress of the Yugoslav Communist Party, held in 1948, Djilas was elected one of the Party secretaries. (Tito was elected general secretary, while Edvard Kardelj and Aleksandar-Leka Ranković were chosen as the other two secretaries.)

In 1949, at a U.N. conference in New York, Djilas delivered a speech in opposition to Soviet pressure on Yugoslavia.

In 1951, on a visit to Great Britain, he conducted conversations with Winston Churchill and Clement Attlee.

That year also, at a U.N. session in Paris, he defended Yugoslavia's position vis-à-vis the USSR.

At the beginning of 1953 Djilas led the Yugoslav delegation to the Asian Socialist Conference in Rangoon, also visiting India.

Milovan Djilas was one of the ideologists and theoreticians of the Yugoslav Party. During the confrontation between the Soviet Union and Yugoslavia that broke out into the open in 1948, he developed the concept of Yugoslavia's independence and worked out ideas with a bearing on democratization within the Yugoslav Party and Yugoslav society as a whole. The Sixth Party Congress, held in 1952 in Zagreb, adopted the majority of his ideas, and they entered the Party platform. At his suggestion, the Communist Party of Yugoslavia changed its name to the Yugoslav League of Communists.

Failure to put into effect the decisions of the Sixth Party Congress and resistance to democratic reforms intensified after the Plenum of the Central Committee on Brioni in July 1953, gradually leading to an ideological parting of the ways between Djilas and the Party leadership. In a series of articles published in *Borba* at the end of 1953, Djilas further developed his ideas concerning the democratization of Yugoslav society and began to criticize the Party bureaucracy.

At the Third Plenum of the Central Committee of the Yugoslav League of Communists, held in January 1954 in Belgrade, Djilas was accused of revisionism and expelled from the Central Committee.

Two months later he himself submitted his resignation of Party membership.

In January 1955 Djilas was sentenced conditionally to three years' imprisonment because of his interview in the *New York Times* in which he criticized the political state of affairs in Yugoslavia and expressed the need for an opposition party as a factor in democratization.

In November 1956 he was arrested and sentenced to three years' imprisonment for his criticism of Yugoslavia's position on the Hungarian uprising and Soviet intervention there.

In October 1957, while in prison in Sremska Mitrovica, Djilas was sentenced to seven years' imprisonment for his book *The New Class,* which had been published in the United States. By sentence of the court, all wartime and postwar decorations were taken from him, including the Order of People's Hero.

In January 1961 Djilas was provisionally released from prison.

In April 1962 he was again arrested, for his book *Conversations with Stalin,* and sentenced to five years' imprisonment. This term was combined with his previous terms so that the total length of time to which Djilas was sentenced amounted to thirteen years.

On 31 December 1966 he was freed unconditionally. In postwar Yugoslavia Djilas served altogether nine years in prison, of which two and one half years were in solitary confinement.[1]

Djilas was unable to publish in Yugoslavia a single political or literary text. The majority of his works were published abroad in various of the world's languages. He published more than one hundred articles and essays in Western European and American papers and journals, and gave numerous interviews to Western media.

He was prevented from traveling abroad from 1970 to 1986, because his request for a passport was always denied.

In 1989 Djilas was given permission to publish his works and speeches in the Yugoslav media.

Milovan Djilas lived in Belgrade at 8 Palmotić Street. He died in Belgrade on April 20, 1995.

IN LIEU OF AN
EPILOGUE

A CONVERSATION BETWEEN THE
AUTHOR AND VASILIJE KALEZIĆ
OCTOBER 1993

KALEZIĆ: So far as I am aware, you did not welcome the idea of working on this new book. If so, you surely had important reasons. For you, I know, like to work and are an enterprising kind of man, a writer disposed to work when you are inspired and have in mind a well-defined intention or goal. I would like you to say something about the actual reasons for possibly not working on this book and then how, overcoming all obstacles, you emerged victorious in the end.

DJILAS: Yes, in the beginning I didn't warm up to this book. The publisher's concept was not clear and it was presented to me abruptly, before I had thought through and come up with my own concept. Finding myself face to face with the problem, I did begin to think it through and would wake up at night, as I always have when confronted with a new task. But once the idea and the form of the book had taken shape in my head, a problem cropped up, seemingly hard to overcome. I had to define the basic themes, had to compose supplementary, related texts, had to cull out some superfluous material. As an expert and one very knowledgeable about my writings, you helped. All this was going on at a time when my wife Štefanija—Štefica—was seriously ill, with a condition that proved fatal. This kept breaking in on my time. However that may be, it should be noted first of all that her presence inspired me, ill as she was, painful as it was. So while I was meditating and working on the book I felt continually that I was fusing with my wife, that our work together over the decades was ongoing. She, after all, had been a constant participant in my writing, and not just techni-cally but also with suggestions of her own. Some of my best-known political works (*The New Class, Conversations with Stalin*) could never have appeared in print without her brave and steadfast participation: police control, after all, was total and totally ruthless. So, as I came to grasp and give coherent shape to the book's material, I warmed up more and more. I came to realize that the book was bound to embody in compact form my thoughts and my life; that it would represent the essence of all my experience as a critic of communism; and that this meant criticism of an idea and its origins to which I had devoted my life and about which I could feel assured of saying something authentic.

KALEZIĆ: In the course of your work on this book, you really did become much preoccupied with the pursuit of very complicated rela-tionships and goals. Describe, if you can, what concepts you were thinking through, how you struggled pro and con, what you finally settled on.

DJILAS: The work as I have composed it is itself an answer to this ques-tion. The hardest and most painful thing was to figure out the basic approach; even so, there ensued much wearisome labor. I pondered such questions as: Should the book be a selection of political texts with an admixture of literary and autobiographical elements? Or only a selection of political themes, and those the most basic? I decided to lay out my most fundamental ideas about communism while tracing at the same time the evolution of my political views. A critical stance toward communism developed gradually with me, *The New Class* being a watershed in the process, though not the last word. This was the reason—or, I should say, to enable the reader to understand that my ideas evolved in tandem with both my political biography and my personal biography—this was my reason, I say, for writing "The De-velopment of My Political Thinking" as an introduction to the work as a whole.

KALEZIĆ: All right. Even so, "The Development of My Political Think-ing" represents a particular approach to a particular theme and a par-ticular way of communicating your thought, chiefly journalistic. Have you now passed through some kind of catharsis? Have you given any thought to your legacy, to what is called a "last will and testament"? Or did all this emerge naturally, normally, in a commonplace way?

DJILAS: "The Development of My Political Thinking" is not new thinking, except insofar as I set it down for the first time. But as I passed under review all my criticism of communism I could not help but get excited. Still, in doing so, not for a moment did any kind of "last will and testament" come to mind. There was not the shadow of a thought about it. Testaments make sense only in real estate.

KALEZIĆ: For quite a while—after more than thirty-five years—you have been able to publish your own works in Yugoslavia, and there was a period when some of your previous books were actually printed. (They came as a kind of surprise, something of a curiosity, something of value. There were stories, a novel, even the proscribed books like *The New Class, Conversations with Stalin,* etc.). There was also a book *about* you. It would be interesting to hear yourself on the subject: How did you take the news after living this long? And what do you think generally about the reviews of your work?

DJILAS: Well, publication in itself of my books in Yugoslavia did not excite me much. It came as no surprise because it happened gradually: First I gave interviews in Ljubljana and Zagreb, then I was received by the Union of Writers, and then your own books about me opened the window still wider. Given this atmosphere of liberalization, the authorities in Belgrade as a consequence were no longer able to hold out. Some of my books—two books of memoirs and the two novels— could not be printed anyway. Publishing activity came to a standstill, and two of my publishers went bankrupt before paying me my fee. Exactly the same thing happened under capitalism: One publisher got away with not paying me a very considerable sum, while another even used up my savings, which I had deposited with him. As for reviews, criticism of my books in Yugoslavia has hardly existed. Criticism here is undeveloped, and I lose no sleep over it.

KALEZIĆ: As the author of a book about you, and more generally as editor of several of your books, I have always stood up for you as a writer, as an author and man of letters. You would seem to be regarded as far more interesting and more important for your political, ideological, and journalistic work than for what you have done as a writer of fiction—as an artist. My opinion has always been that this is unjust. You will live longer, and your memory will endure among the people and in history, because of your artistic work. Please tell us your thinking on this matter.

DJILAS: Not to be modest, I too regard my work in fiction as more important. But my political destiny was such that work like this attracted less attention. I comfort myself with the thought that if something is of any value, especially in art, sooner or later time will give it its due, its rightful place.

KALEZIĆ: Good, now let us cast our net a little more broadly and consider whether and in what sense you can be described as a writer *engagé*. As I see it, in various aspects of your work you do bear a certain resemblance to Miroslav Krleža and Jean-Paul Sartre. Dramatic works excluded, there are genres in common and sheer volume. (You have written a great deal.) Krleža and Sartre are writers who are highly thought of precisely owing to their being *engagés*. Do I deceive myself, and if so how, in asking you about this? I do not go into the value or lack thereof of any particular political or social involvement, but only into how a person views writing as an act, and an act without which the existence of certain people would be unthinkable.

DJILAS: I am no advocate of mixing politics and belles-lettres in one and the same work, and in my own writings have tried to practice what I preach. True, this is hard to achieve for a politically involved writer. And it can even happen that better results come from mixing the two. I think this was true in my memoir *Wartime* [in Serbian, *Revolucionarni rat*—"War of Revolution"]. But there is no need to blend—it is not right to blend—political involvement with politics as such, thematically, in literature. War, politics, social struggle—yes, those are perhaps the most frequent themes of all, and in the greatest works: *The Iliad, The Aeneid,* Shakespeare, *War and Peace,* Njegoš's *Mountain Wreath,* Hemingway's *For Whom the Bell Tolls.* As a political writer I was too *engagé,* thanks to political circumstances in an illegal Party, and above all thanks to war and revolution. It is true that had there not been such exceptional circumstances I would still have been *engagé,* only perhaps not to such an extreme extent. But on our Balkan soil there has never been any writer of significance who was not involved in this way. On soil where people's very existence is under constant threat it is simply impossible to take form as a creator of works of the spirit without being in some way politically *engagé.*

KALEZIĆ: Taking this occasion, I would like to explore possible literary friendships of yours: Whom do you see, under what circumstances, how often, and what are your thoughts about it? I do know that Dobrica Ćosić[1] appreciated your statement about his being replaced or (as they say) toppled from his position as chief of state, for I read it aloud to him over the telephone. It was in my possession, and was also given to the reporter for *Pobjeda,* Nikola Ivanović. Your statement is not very well known (indeed, hardly known at all, I think). Perhaps you might repeat it and explain better what you mean by "unification," from both the political and the literary standpoint?[2]

DJILAS: Matija Bećković[3] and I see each other on a regular basis every Saturday, so we are dubbed the "Saturday-ers." He and I have been on very good terms for a quarter century by now. I look upon him as a unique, extraordinary individual and one of the greatest poets of the Serbs, a people whose highest and best realm is the realm of poetry. The unusual aspect of our relationship, its broader, symbolic significance, if you like, is the fact that we are politically on opposite sides of the fence. Time, it is true, has dulled the sharpness of our differences, differences that continue to grow less and less significant. Bećković and I are like the leaders of two tribes who have shed each other's blood and are not yet reconciled. The tribes will disappear before that ever happens, in fact. But those leaders had the sense to rise above the bloodshed of their fellow tribesmen and now are inseparable friends, close in spirit, close in their moral essentials. You will agree: It is a rare phenomenon, quite exceptional on this ideologically poisoned soil, especially with well-known, *engagé* people. Evil times and an intolerant milieu have only strengthened the friendship between Bećković and myself. From time to time I receive visits from the writer and theater director Živojin Pavlović,[4] an independent and upright person with whom I am on good terms intellectually. I have long been friendly also with the author Borislav Mihailović-Mihiz,[5] a man of high morality and extraordinary intelligence. You mentioned Ćosić: We are good friends, although we are rarely in contact—since he became president he only calls on the telephone. Politically we differ, and my statement concerning him I gave only at the instance of the main editor, Mr. Ivanović, of *Pobjeda*. I have no other friends except those who belong to the liberal "renegade" group: Latinka Perović, Mirko Tepavac, General S. Daljvić, and a few others. By nature I am not very communicative, and since I have long lived in forced isolation I have grown used to living apart and in solitude.

KALEZIĆ: I ask you, as a writer of fiction, when were you first struck by the fateful urge to write? How did it happen and what did you hope for? From our previous conversations about literature, I know something of what you think of Dostoyevsky, Tolstoy, Chekhov, Maupassant, Jovan Skerlić,[6] Ivo Andrić,[7] Miroslav Krleža, and a few other contemporary authors. Perhaps it would not be inappropriate to once again say a few words about certain writers, especially those whom you perhaps have regarded as your models, whom you perhaps wanted more to read than to study and argue with.

DJILAS: To my way of thinking, no one has exerted any decisive influence over me; I have had no model. But that said, I do not mean to imply that I have not learned many a thing from many a writer, spontaneously, involuntarily. These have been chiefly the Russians and the French, and, after my fall from power, the Americans too.

KALEZIĆ: Now, along these same lines, here are also some questions from the domain of politics and ideology. This year there have been several anniversaries related to Marx (175 years since his birth, 110 years since his death). Even in our country these anniversaries have been marked, though the celebrations were niggardly and superficial. Professor Dr. Mihailo Marković wrote negatively under the title "The Importance of Marx Today." It is also known in Yugoslavia that Professor Nathan Rosenberg from the United States wrote an article entitled "Marx Was Not Entirely Mistaken." Your present book contains more than one piece where Marx and Marxism are brought up. Even so, it would seem important, today especially, that as a onetime ideologist as well as Marxist you take a look at Marx's role in the development of humanity. What part did he play in building communism and then in its fall? What did he mean for the relationship of utopia to reality?

DJILAS: Notwithstanding his ideology and its consequences, Marx undoubtedly belongs among the greatest social and moral thinkers of the nineteenth century. It goes without saying that he was right in many things: Industrialization *was* inevitable, technological advance could *not* be stopped, mankind *was* to achieve unification little by little, and the differences between city and country, town and village, would also gradually be erased. As for his criticism of early capitalism, Marx may have been unforgivably mistaken in his judgments as to how long capitalism would endure and how long the position of the working class would stay the same with respect to the progress of capitalist production. But his critique was never superseded, in either its literary skill and suppleness or the force of its moral revulsion. A similar capitalism is rising now on the ruins of communism, but no new Marx is in sight. There can be no disputing the fact that Marx was the founder of the world idea of socialism, an idea that the Communists fulfilled politically and organizationally. His influence was enormous, if only because he was attacked as few, or anyone at all, before him had ever been attacked, not to mention that he was the wellspring of all the major socialist movements that were based on his ideas. Marx was a utopian. His ideal of a perfect, classless society turned out in practice to be quite tragic for all those peoples who were made its guinea pigs. But there can be no argument that this ideal exerted a basic influence on capitalism itself, notably European capitalism, in resolving social issues and in bettering the position of the lower classes. Since the fall of communism, Marx and Marxism have faded into history and become the domain of departments teaching the evolution of political doctrines.

KALEZIĆ: And finally, one last question on this occasion. We began with a discussion about a "new world order," about a single, overwhelming force that presides over the world and that will introduce universal harmony. But along with this there is talk about Planet Earth—our planet—as consisting of worlds split, divided, and deranged, worlds for which there is no salvation. Typical of these evaluations and prophecies are the books by Francis Fukuyama, *The End of History,* and Paul Kennedy, *Getting Ready for the Twenty-first Century.* Before I ask my question, I would like to remind you of other judgments by people of your generation, Americans (one even mentions our Bosnia today), who write that "all Americans who served in the Pacific were racists" (William Styron), that now "chaos from the American Empire" has come into being, that "Somalia and Bosnia are the latest of our exploits," and that "we," meaning America, we as "Lord of the world," we are "above the law, which is nothing unusual for empires; more's the pity, we are above common sense." In consideration of these remarks, I would like to ask how you view the future in the light of the present, and what hope humanity might draw from politics and art.

DJILAS: "New world order"! Nothing of the sort exists. But since the idea has been uttered (first of all, to my knowledge, in the United States, on the lips of President Bush), it is hardly more attractive, let alone more realizable, than the old schism between East and West, which was a world order consisting of communism and democracy. It is no accident that the United States was the first to spawn this idea of a "new world order"; and even there, it has not struck very deep roots. With the disintegration of communism, and so of the Soviet Union, the United States has in fact become the one and only superpower. Ideology today, as a worldwide movement, means achieving human rights through the United Nations. And since there the United States plays the dominant role, the realization of any "new world order" would chiefly be under the leadership of Americans. It would be hard to find fault with the idea of human rights: This is the most exalted and universal idea of our time. But ideas in political practice can change their meaning and their attractiveness. The idea of human rights is at one and the same time the spiritual forerunner of American technology and of American finance; it undergirds the broadening of American influence in the world. Capital, though, cannot be expected to be in harmony with the spirit of human rights. And as a rule it is not, unless it obeys some hidden lever of political control. But these are all theoretical combinations and recombinations. The reality is that no "new world order" can ever be carried out, for the simple reason that most of the world could never bend its neck to American domination, no matter how hard U.S. capital tried to adhere to human rights. This would be so even if the world wished to adapt to American potential and American trends. The structures involved are too diverse. And it is even more important to make the following point: The idea of a world order does not fit either the American free market economy or American democracy. If some political group in the United States were to succeed in inflicting itself on American society and then were to try to impose its own world order by force, such a group would first have to impose a military-police-state order in the United States itself. Nothing like that even crosses the mind of anyone in the United States today. And as to the sort of resistance such a policy would provoke in the world, let us cite Robespierre's maxim, "No one loves armed missionaries." Fukuyama's *The End of History*? History will end only when the human race ends. Something of the sort was dreamed up by the Communists, and we have seen what it cost and how it all ended. Fukuyama's theory is violently rebutted right here, with the war that is going on between Serbs and Croats, and between both and the Bosnian Muslims. I do not think Fukuyama himself still holds to this theory. And as far as the future is concerned, relations between countries move in the opposite direction to any principle that is single-minded and oversimplified. The collapse of communism shook both the West and Western unity to their very foundations. Countries follow their own national interests. They form into groups independently, and may even oppose the tenets and edicts of the United Nations. Is that good? I grew up in the era of opposition to fascism, in the era of support for a United Nations where the idea of human rights was paramount. And I would like to avoid answering your question. To old men only the old ways are good—the patterns of life, the shapes of creation—even when there was more bad than good in them.

REMARKS
BY THE EDITOR

Milovan Djilas wrote several chapters especially for this book. They include the introductory and final discussions, plus the initial explanations for individual sections. In addition, the book as a whole contains for the first time the chronological and thematic basis of all his writings, in accordance with the title and subtitle. These writings have to do with the rise and fall of the new class, with criticism of communism and Bolshevism's self-destruction, with charismatic leaders, with dissidents and their significance in today's world, with communism and dogma, bureaucratic nationalism, and democracy. The collapse we see today is central to the book, and an assessment of that collapse. What can be expected in the future is also part of the book.

For the sake of thematic continuity and chronological consistency the author and his editor have expressly singled out essays published in the newspaper *Borba* and the journal *New Thought* in 1953 and 1954. These were exceptionally significant at the time they were published, and in the life of the author they were a watershed. Subsequently he was punished in various ways: by being stripped of his Party and state functions, by undergoing trial, and by being sentenced to imprisonment lasting some ten years.[1]

The editor has respected the ideas and intentions of the author, though he is not completely correct in asserting that in his book there is no place for several fragments drawn from other published works, which are of unusual value in the domains of fiction, memoirs, and journalism. Collaboration between author and editor was almost an everyday affair and was conducted through convivial and amicable discussions. When disagreements arose, compromise usually would prevail, solutions being mutually sought and found.

The interview at the end, which takes the form of a conversation between author and editor regarding the book, was intended as a unique kind of epilogue in which the author personally and critically looked back on certain events in his own life, and pondered the intellectual and moral stirrings of our time.

Data about the author were collected and put in order by Aleksa Djilas, publicist and writer, sociologist, and son of Milovan Djilas.

The intermediary in touch with publisher, author, and editor was the journalist and writer Miloje Popović, whom the author and editor during the whole of the work on the book considered to be their representative and agent.

> VASILIJE KALEZIĆ
> BELGRADE
> 13 OCTOBER 1993

TRANSLATOR'S
NOTES

1

1. Socialist realism was a theory of composition, conformity to which was incumbent on all Soviet writers, as well as other artists, from 1932 on. Their obligation was to promote socialist progress by creating positive protagonists and writing in terms easy to understand. Their heroes and heroines as a result usually turned out to be made of cardboard, and the final outcome to be slick propaganda.
2. Josip Broz Tito (1892–1980), wartime and postwar leader of Yugoslavia. Born in Croatia, he trained as a locksmith and metalworker. Arrested for antiwar propaganda during World War I, he was sent to the front with the Austrian army, was wounded and captured by the Russians, and subsequently fought with the Red Army during the civil war. Back in Yugoslavia, he became a member of the Communist Party in 1920 and rose in its ranks. In 1937 Tito became secretary-general of the Party in Yugoslavia and reorganized it. From 1941 he led the Partisan movement and in 1943 was made a marshal, a year when he also gained the Allied recognition previously accorded the Chetniks. In 1945 he became premier of a coalition government, then head of the People's Republic of Yugoslavia, and remained chief of state and head of the Party until his death. For many years following the 1948 break with Stalin, Tito was identified with the foreign policy of nonalignment.
3. Miroslav Krleža (1893–1982), Croatian dramatist, poet, novelist, and story writer, widely known for his progressive views. He edited a series of literary and political journals between the two world wars.
4. The first of four such "markers" in this chapter indicating stages in the author's political thinking. Each consists of a single sentence without full stops until the end, and the first three of these signposts begin with a lowercase letter. In translation, they have been indented to draw attention to their radical difference in

style from the surrounding text. Here, the original also underlines the first three words: *no greater misery.*

5. Comparison of the same passages in the installment of Djilas's memoirs translated as *Wartime,* pp. 284–85, is instructive. There the author included a certain amount of manifest content for what purported to be a waking dream; the experience was embedded in detail surrounding the Partisans' harrowing escape from the Sutjeska River gorge in Bosnia. Here, by contrast, both vision and thoughts are disembodied, as it were, and presented as a stage in the development of Djilas's "political thinking." I have left standing the italicized phrases, which were typed and underlined in the original. A similar hallucinatory moment would occur later to Djilas in April 1953, upon hearing of the death of his friend Boris Kidrič, back in Belgrade. Sitting at a table in Titograd, Montenegro, it appears to Djilas that his fingers have momentarily become detached from his folded hands. (*Rise and Fall,* p. 308).

6. The addition of some such phrase as "my dream up to that point . . ." would eliminate the apparent contradiction with the statement on page 7 that Stalin's authority "was not that of the incarnation of an idea and a movement."

7. The author underlined "first visit," "second visit," and "third visit," not in type but by hand when he proofed this passage. I have removed these, thinking the emphasis insufficiently motivated. But I have let stand the originally underlined (now italicized) *they* and also the capitalized "He." Djilas perhaps had Christian commentary on Jesus in mind here.

8. For Serbo-Croatian words, I use Croatian diacritics throughout this translation, including notes. Words in other Slavic languages are usually given their standard English spellings, without diacritics. Cf. Zhdanov, Zhukov, below. In *Rise and Fall,* Djilas's second wife is consistently called Štefica, the affectionate form of Štefaniya.

9. This fourth and last *profession de foi,* like the others, consists of one extended sentence (in the original language), with very little punctuation other than commas. There is not, of course, any paragraph break. The passage does begin with an uppercase "If." The original has a breathless, stream-of-consciousness quality that sharply sets it off from the paragraphs preceding and following.

10. Edvard Kardelj (1910–1979), a leading Slovenian Communist who received his prewar training in Moscow and was an organizer of the Partisan uprising in Slovenia in 1941. Kardelj later became a member of the Party's Central Committee and, in 1945, vice premier of the new Yugoslav government. For many years he was Tito's second-in-command and the paramount Party ideologist.

11. Eduard Bernstein (1850–1932). German Social Democrat and political theorist who was one of the first socialists (1891) to attempt a revision of Marx's tenets. He proposed a type of social democracy that combined private initiative with social reform.

12. Petrović Njegoš, Prince Peter II (1813–1851). Ruler of Montenegro and a major poet who composed two extensive, greatly renowned (among Serbs), and much-quoted literary epics, *Ray of the Microcosm* (1845) and *Mountain Wreath* (1847).

13. Djilas's autobiographical memoir of his childhood, *Crna Gora—Besudna zemlya,* would literally be translated *Montenegro, Land Without Law, Lawless Land,* or

the like, for *sud* means not "justice" but "court of law" and connotes codified law, the writ, the word. Justice they had in their rough-and-ready, Hatfields-and-McCoys way—justice, that is, in the sense of retribution, not of equality under the law. Justice in the latter sense the inhabitants of that mountain country had no use for or understanding of.

14. The author here crossed out his original word "literal" and wrote in "spiritual" above the line.

15. A five-word phrase in the original, *Udar nadje iskru u kamenu* (Blow finds spark in stone), quoted from Njegoš's *Mountain Wreath*. Another rendering one may run across is "Blows coax the spark from the stone, else it would have languished there."

16. *Tamnica je kuća neobična.*

17. I have chosen *un-* instead of *im*perfect to translate *nesavršen* because of its resonance with the author's earlier book, *The Unperfect Society* (New York: Harcourt, Brace & World, 1969), which was considered a sequel to *The New Class*. The title, involving a play on prefixes not available in Serbian, was intended to undercut the traditional Marxist assumption that a society can even attain perfection in the first place.

2

1. Jajce is a town in eastern Bosnia notable as a tourist attraction for its picturesque setting and as the site where the leaders of the Partisan movement met in 1943 to plan for the postwar period.

2. Peter II Karadjordjević (1923–1971) was king of Yugoslavia after his father, King Alexander, was assassinated in 1934. His cousin Prince Paul ruled as regent until March 27, 1941, when the regency was overthrown by an officers' coup opposed to collaboration with the Axis powers. When the latter invaded Yugoslavia, King Peter fled and established a government-in-exile in London. As the Partisans grew stronger he was forced to accept a coalition government, was forbidden to return to Yugoslavia, and in 1945 was deposed when Yugoslavia was declared a republic. King Peter spent the rest of his life in exile and died in the United States.

3. Sreten Žujović (1899–1976) was a longtime Communist who was a member of the Central Committee and the Politburo before World War II. He helped organize the Partisan uprising in Serbia in 1941 and became a member of the Supreme Staff. Finance minister in the postwar government, Žujović lost his Party membership and high office when he sided with Stalin against Tito in 1948.

4. Moša Pijade (1890–1957) was a prominent Yugoslav Communist of Serbian Jewish origin. With Djilas, he led the Partisan uprising in Montenegro in 1941. Pijade held high political posts during and after the war and was a member of the Central Committee and the Politburo.

5. Aleksandar-Leka Ranković (1909–1982) was a leading Yugoslav Communist of Serbian origin who was a member of the Politburo from 1940. Captured and tortured by the Gestapo in 1941, he was rescued in a daring Communist raid.

Ranković served on the Supreme Staff throughout the war. After it, he was minister of the interior and head of the military and secret police. He fell from power in 1964, ostensibly for abusing his authority, and was expelled from the Party two years later, in 1966.

6. Georgi Dimitrov (1882–1949) was a prominent Bulgarian Communist and a high-ranking official of the Comintern who lived in Moscow for many years. He returned to Bulgaria at the end of World War II to lead the Party there, becoming premier in 1946. Dimitrov died in Moscow, possibly at Stalin's instigation.

7. Ustashi (English plural, in Serbo-Croatian Ustaše) was the name given to members of a tiny, radical-right Croatian party that was brought over from exile in Fascist Italy and installed in 1941 as the government of the nominally independent state of Croatia, after the Axis powers dismembered prewar Yugoslavia. The Ustashi, under the command of Ante Pavelić, became a byword for the viciousness and brutality of their regime. They were responsible for the murder of several hundred thousand Serbs, Jews, and Gypsies during the war. (The exact numbers are disputed.)

8. Chetniks (Serbo-Croatian plural, Četnici) were members of the major Yugoslav resistance movement in World War II. They were organized originally by Draža Mihailović in 1941 to oppose the German invaders, but throughout the war fought chiefly against Tito's Partisans. In 1944 Britain formally transferred support from the Chetniks to the Partisans. After the war the Chetniks were proscribed for many decades. Recently the name has been revived for the Serbian (and Bosnian Serb) followers of Milošević.

9. The second session of AVNOJ and all that led up to it are covered in detail by Djilas in his book of memoirs, *Wartime,* pp. 353–63. The material in this present account is based consecutively (paragraph by paragraph) on the earlier one.

10. Antun Avgustinčić (b. 1899), representational sculptor whose best-known works were of kings and dictators he did not approve of or personally like. Sympathetic to the Communists before the war, but active only in intellectual discussions. Avgustinčić sculpted at one point a bust of the Croat puppet leader Ante Pavelić, and later busts of Tito and Politburo members. Because of his lack of Party involvement and his reputation as an artist, he was chosen to be vice president of AVNOJ on November 29, 1943.

11. Vladimir Dedijer (1914–1990) was a Serbian journalist and scholar, and author of more than a dozen books dealing with Yugoslavia and its history. He had come to know Tito in 1939, when the Party was illegal, and had concealed Tito several times in his Belgrade home. He joined Tito's staff in 1941 and later became a member of the Party's Central Committee. Dedijer wrote two important accounts of Partisan history, the first titled *Diary* and the second *Tito Speaks* (1953), both of which have been published in English. (His biography of Tito became standard and was translated into thirty-six languages.) Other than Djilas's former wife, Mitra Mitrović, Dedijer was the only Party member to take the side of Djilas in 1954. He broke with the Party that same year, thereafter devoting himself to writing history and teaching.

12. Vyacheslav Mikhailovich Molotov (1890–1987) was a Bolshevik from 1906 and a specialist in Party organization. Molotov ascended the ladder, largely as Stalin's lieutenant, until he was second in power only to Stalin himself. From 1926 he was

a member of the Politburo and of the Presidium of the Executive Committee of the Comintern. He was chairman of the Council of People's Commissars—that is, prime minister—throughout the thirties, and deputy chairman until 1957. Molotov was best known to the world as Soviet commissar (after 1946, minister) for foreign affairs. In 1957 he was stripped of power as a member of the "anti-Party group" in association with Malenkov, Kaganovich, and others, and thereafter held relatively minor posts.

13. Klement Gottwald (1896–1953) was the Communist Party leader in Czechoslovakia during the 1940s: Gottwald replaced Beneš as president of his country in June 1948. Earlier, he had been prime minister (from July 1946).

14. Dmitri Zakharovich Manuilsky (1883–1959) was a Soviet Communist Party official and diplomat of Ukrainian origin. He was active in the pre-Revolutionary underground in 1903 and as an underground activist experienced arrest and exile.

15. Pan-Slavism is a chapter from Russian intellectual history, a popular movement from the 1850s through the 1870s that espoused the cause of Russia's Orthodox coreligionists in the Balkans, especially Bulgaria. Pan-Slavism was never adopted as a policy by the Tsarist government, but it was accountable in part for the Russo-Turkish War of 1877–1878. The movement itself is dated, but the attitude that underlies it—sympathy for Orthodox Slavs—is very much alive today in Russia.

16. See above on p. 7, where the author specifically disavows such an "incarnation," only to corroborate it later (p. 15). Even apart from what Djilas reports to his editor later in "In Lieu of an Epilogue," much or all of his first chapter must have been written after the later ones. (These had, in any case, been previously published in either the original or translation.)

17. This particular Zhukov was a young man from the NKVD characterized in *Conversations with Stalin* as "a slender and pale blond" (p. 41). Not to be confused with the famous marshal (1894–1974) who during World War II conducted the defense of Moscow against the Germans, and broke the siege of both Leningrad (October 1942) and Stalingrad (January 1943).

18. Konstantin Mikhaylovich Simonov (1915–1979) was a Soviet lyric poet and novelist of the 1940s, known particularly for his sentimental, popular war poems such as *Wait for Me* and his war novel, *Days and Nights* (1944).

19. Wladyslaw Sikorski (1881–1943) was a Polish general and statesman who was prime minister (1922–1923) and then minister of military affairs (1924–1925). After Poland's collapse in 1939 Sikorsky became prime minister of the Polish government-in-exile in London.

20. Edvard Beneš (1884–1948) was a Czechoslovak statesman and follower of Masaryk, with whom he worked in the nationalist movement. Beneš was first elected president in 1935 but went into exile in 1938 upon Nazi occupation of the Sudetenland. He returned to his country at the conclusion of the war and was reelected to the presidency in 1946. Beneš again resigned the presidency in 1948, when Czechoslovakia became a Communist state.

21. Ivan Šubašić (1892–1955) was a Croatian politician who governed Croatia from August 1939 but who went into exile during the war. On June 1, 1944, he was appointed premier of the Yugoslav royal government-in-exile at the

insistence of the Allies. Šubašić merged his cabinet with Tito's after the Tito-Šubašić Agreement, concluded on the island of Vis. In this coalition provisional government he served for a time as foreign minister.

22. Leon Trotsky (1879–1940) was the Russian Communist leader and opponent of Stalin who had negotiated Russia's withdrawal from World War I at Brest-Litovsk and who later organized the armies that repelled attacks by the Whites and their allies on four fronts (1918–1921). After 1924 and Lenin's death, Trotsky was defeated by Stalin over control of the Party, was expelled from the Party (1927), banished from Russia altogether (1929), and finally found haven in Mexico (1937), where he was murdered in August 1940, at Stalin's instigation.

23. Nikolai Ivanovich Bukharin (1888–1938) was a Russian Communist leader and editor. With Lenin he published *Pravda* in Austria, and in New York, he edited *Novyj mir.* Returning to Russia after the Revolution, Bukharin became the leader of the left-wing Bolsheviks. Expelled from the Party in 1929, he was readmitted five years later, in 1934, only to be expelled again, in 1937, because of suspected support for Trotsky. The following year Bukharin was arrested, tried, and executed.

24. Lavrenty Pavlovich Beria (1899–1953), Georgian Communist who made a career in the Soviet Secret Police, starting with the CHEKA, followed by the GPU, the NKVD, and finally the MGB. Beria brought the Great Purge to a close by purging his predecessor, N. I. Yezhov, and many other officials. He also directed the reign of terror, not only in the Soviet Union but in the satellite states as well, that marked Stalin's last years. Beria himself, however, was shot in the power struggle that followed Stalin's death.

25. Up to this point Djilas generally follows the account of his first visits to Stalin published earlier in *Conversations with Stalin.* (See especially pp. 56ff. in the section "Raptures.") Very few passages in the original, however, seem to be quoted verbatim.

3

1. Valjevo is a small industrial town about fifty miles south-southwest of Belgrade, more than halfway to Srebrnica in Bosnia (as the crow flies), and a third of the way to Sarajevo.

2. Arandjelovac is a very small town almost directly east of Valjevo, in the center of the Šumadija region south of the capital, again about fifty miles from Belgrade.

3. Peko Dapčević (b. 1913) was a Yugoslav general who joined the Party in 1933 when a student at the University of Belgrade. With the invasion of Yugoslavia in 1941, Dapčević led the Partisan uprising in his native Montenegro and thereafter rose rapidly to the Supreme Headquarters of the Army of People's Liberation. From 1953 he served as chief of the Yugoslav General Staff, but was demoted as a result of being indirectly implicated in the Djilas affair. Though close to the author, Dapčević did not support him publicly in the January (1954) plenum of the Central Committee that in effect expelled Djilas. It was Dapčević's young actress wife, Milena Vrajak, whom Djilas defended against the "New Class" in his essay "Anatomy of a Moral," published in *Nova Misao* in the first weeks of 1954.

4. Vladislav Ribnikar (1900–1955) was the prewar editor of the Belgrade newspaper *Politika*. Ribnikar joined the Partisans in 1941 and became a director of their news agency, TANJUG. In the postwar government he was minister of education.

5. Andrei Aleksandrovich Zhdanov (1896–1948) was secretary of the Soviet Communist Party Central Committee from 1935, and became a full member of the Politburo in 1939. In charge of ideological affairs, Zhdanov made socialist realism obligatory in the arts and directed the postwar campaign against Western cultural influences. Earlier, he had been prominent in the founding of the Comintern.

6. Koča Popović (1908–1992) was the scion of a prominent Belgrade family who joined the Yugoslav Communist Party in 1933 and fought in the Spanish Civil War. Upon his return he was arrested but continued his underground activities after being released. He joined the Partisans in 1941, commanded various units, and rose to the highest military and government echelons. He was chief of the General Staff from 1945 to 1953, also becoming foreign minister of Yugoslavia in 1946.

7. Andrija Hebrang (1899–1948) was a prominent Croatian Communist and leader of the Partisan movement in Croatia during the war. He was a leader of the National Liberation Movement from the start, in 1941, and after the war was minister of industry, member of the Presidium of both the Yugoslav and Croatian Constituent Assemblies, and chairman of the Federal Planning Commission. In 1946 the Party's Central Committee investigated Hebrang's past and found him guilty of wartime cowardice and collaboration with the Ustashi. After being arrested while allegedly fleeing to Romania in 1948, he committed suicide while awaiting trial. Some sources, however, claim he was murdered in jail.

8. Arso Jovanović (1905?–1948), officer from Montenegro in the prewar Royal Army who joined the Partisans in 1941 and helped organize their army, serving as chief of the General Staff to 1946. When Tito broke with Moscow in 1948, Jovanović sided openly with the Soviet Union. He was shot by border guards while trying to escape to Romania.

9. Mitra Mitrović Djilas (b. 1912) was the Serbian-born first wife of Milovan Djilas. She joined the Partisans in 1941 and did Party organization work, after the war holding important education posts in Serbia.

10. The Timofeyev incident was earlier recounted in *Rise and Fall*, pp. 85–86.

11. Milan Grol (1876–1952) was primarily a dramatist, a professor, and an editor on the staff of various interwar publications. He was also, however, the prewar leader of the Serbian Democratic Party and briefly a member of the postwar coalition government.

12. Mikhail Ivanovich Kalinin (1875–1946) joined the Social Democratic Party in 1896 and took a prominent part in the Revolution. He was formally president of the USSR from 1923 till his death.

13. Georgi Maximilianovich Malenkov (1902–1988) was a Soviet Communist Party leader who became a member of the Central Committee by 1939, when he was placed in charge of the administration of cadres. In 1941 he was a candidate member of the Politburo and served on the State Defense Committee throughout World War II. After the war he served as secretary of the Central Committee and deputy prime minister. Malenkov succeeded Stalin after the latter's

death as prime minister in the era of "collective leadership" but was forced to step down after a public admission of failure in 1955.

14. Nikolai Alexandrovich Bulganin (1895–1975) was a Soviet politician who joined the Communist Party in 1917 and was a member of the Supreme Soviet from 1937 to 1958. He was chairman of the Council of Ministers (1955–1958), member of the Politburo (1948–1952), member of the Presidium (1952–1958), and prime minister (1955–1958).

15. This entire dinner conversation, or monologue, was told in greater detail in *Conversations with Stalin,* pp. 107–15, and again more briefly in *Rise and Fall,* pp. 155ff. Djilas often recycled his previously written work.

4

1. Maurice Thorez (1900–1964), was president of the French Communist Party at the time of his death and its secretary-general since 1930. At the height of its power just after World War II, Thorez led a Party of about 1 million; by 1964, however, its membership had fallen to about 240,000. It was in 1946 that Thorez nearly became premier of France, failing by only 29 votes out of more than 500 cast in the French Assembly. The French Communist Party was the most orthodox and unswerving in Western Europe in its allegiance to Moscow, and Thorez was considered the mainspring and symbol of that orthodoxy. Still, he overcame an early resentment of Khrushchev's 1956 denunciation of Stalin to become as devoted a follower of the later Soviet premier as he had once been of Stalin.

2. La Pasionaria, *nom de guerre* of Dolores Ibarruri (1895–1989), was the foremost Spanish Communist of the 1930s, whose oratory earned her this nickname. She went into exile in 1939 and lived in the USSR until the Communist Party was legalized in her native Spain (1977), when she returned home. La Pasionaria subsequently became a member of the national parliament, the Cortés.

3. Palmiro Togliatti (1893–1964), from 1943 leader of the Italian Communist Party, which at the time of his death in the Crimea numbered some 1.6 million and was the strongest Communist Party in the West. He was said to have been a close personal friend of Stalin's. In 1956, however, having been present at the Twentieth Party Congress in Moscow where Khrushchev denounced Stalin, and following a visit to Tito in Yugoslavia, Togliatti emerged as spokesman for what he called a new, "polycentric" communism, meaning that communism should no longer draw its inspiration exclusively from Moscow. He later supported Khrushchev in the ideological controversy with China and also in his policy of de-Stalinization.

4. Wilhelm Pieck (1876–1960) served three terms as president of East Germany. Pieck escaped Germany twice for exile in the Soviet Union, once after Germany's defeat in World War I and the second time after Hitler became chancellor in 1933. In Moscow he headed the Communist propaganda machine set up to communize Germany's war prisoners in Russia during World War II. Back in Berlin after 1945 and during his terms as president (from 1949), Pieck became a sort of Communist elder statesman, with actual control of public affairs being wielded by Walter Ulbricht.

5. This particular dacha dinner of Stalin's in May 1946, which focused on his opinions about Albania, was earlier related on pp. 104 and 105 in *Rise and Fall*. The paragraph on Stalin's opinions about other Communist leaders is quoted verbatim from p. 105. Djilas did not participate in this delegation.

6. Vassil Kolarov (1877–1950) was a Bulgarian Communist who succeeded Dimitrov as premier in 1949.

7. Traicho Kostov (1897–1949) was a Bulgarian Communist leader who was a member of the Politburo and deputy prime minister. Though an anti-Titoist, Kostov was associated with a "Bulgaria first" outlook. Stripped of power in March 1949 and indicted in December of that year, he created a sensation by repudiating his confession at his trial. Kostov was condemned and executed.

8. The foregoing paragraphs are largely taken from *Rise and Fall*, pp. 105–106.

9. Cf. *Rise and Fall*, p. 108.

10. Mijalko Todorović (1913–1989?) was a Yugoslav Communist leader who fought in the Partisan ranks during World War II. After the liberation, he served in the Ministry of Defense (as director of the Extraordinary Administration of Supply), as minister of agriculture, and as chief of the Council for Agriculture and Forestry.

11. Svetozar Vukmanović-Tempo (1912–1958) was a Montenegrin who became a Party member in 1935. During World War II he served in the Partisans' Supreme Headquarters and was Tito's personal representative in Macedonia. Vukmanović-Tempo was one of Tito's closest collaborators. It was his young wife, Milica S., whom the public identified as "the wife of a high official" at the stadium entrance in Djilas's essay (or story *à clef*) *Anatomy of a Moral*, which was published in *Nova Misao* early in 1954, just prior to the Third Plenum of the Central Committee. (See below in Chapter Seven, "The Closed Circle of the Privileged," and note 6.)

12. Andrei Aleksandrovich Zhdanov: see note 5, Chapter Three.

13. Both this Kremlin meeting and the dinner that followed are covered extensively in *Conversations with Stalin*, pp. 143–61.

14. Nako Spiru was an Albanian Communist leader at the head of the state planning commission in the 1940s "who was in direct contact with the Yugoslav officials and had to deal with their demands. He became convinced that the Yugoslav government wished to keep the country backward and to control it closely. Unable to change Albanian policy, he committed suicide in 1947." (Barbara Jelavich, *History of the Balkans,* Vol. II [New York: Cambridge University Press, 1983], p. 332.)

15. Enver Hoxha (1908–1985) was a founder of the Albanian Communist Party in 1941 and of the Albanian National Liberation Movement in 1942. In 1943 he became secretary-general of the Party, and by 1946 he was premier, foreign minister, defense minister, and commander in chief of Albania's armed forces. After the fall of Kochi Xoxe, Hoxha became the country's undisputed leader. He kept it internationally isolated, breaking ties with the USSR in 1961 and with China in 1976. He repressed religion and minorities, but was credited with the elimination of illiteracy.

16. Kochi Xoxe (d. 1948), Albanian Communist leader who, thanks to Yugoslav backing, became the most powerful man in the Albanian Communist Party just

after World War II, when he was minister of the interior and head of the secret police. At the time of the Tito-Cominform break, Xoxe was executed on charges of Trotskyite and Titoist activities.

17. Nikolai Alekseyevich Voznesensky (1903–1950) was a leading Soviet economist. During the Great Purge he was rapidly elevated to the post of chairman of the State Planning Commission (Gosplan), which coordinated the whole Soviet economy. He was also deputy prime minister in 1939 and, during the war, a member of the State Defense Committee. Voznesensky was stripped of all his posts in 1949 at the time of Malenkov's campaign against the followers of Zhdanov, and was arrested and shot on Stalin's orders.

18. Maxim Gorky (1868–1936) was Russia's most conspicuous revolutionary novelist. His works—notably *Mother, The Artamonov Business,* and *The Life of Klim Samgin*—embody a condemnation of capitalist society. Though he gave considerable financial support to the Bolsheviks, Gorky opposed their seizure of power and lived in exile from 1921 to 1928. Upon his return, he headed the Writers' Union and was declared the founder of the doctrine of socialist realism. A close friend of Stalin's, Gorky became a leading apologist for the Soviet regime. He died in mysterious circumstances.

19. Mikhail Mikhailovich Zoshchenko (1895–1958) was a Soviet author best known for his satirical works in the 1920s and his treatment of the "bewildered little man" in Soviet society. In 1946 Zhdanov made him a prime target of the campaign to impose Party control over cultural life. He was expelled from the Writers' Union and lived in obscurity until his death.

20. Aleksandr Mikhailovich Vasilevsky (1895–1978) was a prominent Soviet general and chief of the Soviet General Staff at the time of the Battle of Stalingrad. He was made a marshal in 1943 and in 1945 was commander of the Byelorussian front, later serving as minister of war.

21. Cf. *Conversations with Stalin,* pp. 162ff., in the section titled "Disappointments."

22. Vladimir Bakarić (1912–1983) was a Croatian who in 1941 joined the Partisans. After the war he became premier of Croatia. In 1946 he was a member of the Yugoslav delegation to the Peace Conference in Paris. He was for years the ranking Communist leader in Croatia.

23. Mikhail Andreyevich Suslov (1902–1982) was a Communist Party leader in the USSR. He entered the Central Committee in 1941, and was a high-ranking political officer during the war. From 1949 to 1950 he served as editor in chief of *Pravda.* Suslov's main posts thereafter were chairman of the Foreign Affairs Committee of the Soviet Union (1954) and member of the Central Committee's Presidium (1955). Generally regarded as doctrinaire in his views he nevertheless supported Khrushchev in defeating the "anti-Party group."

24. Valerian Alexandrovich Zorin (1902–1986) was a Soviet diplomat. Among the posts he held were assistant general secretary of the National Commissariat of Foreign Affairs (1941), ambassador to Czechoslovakia (1945–1948), deputy minister of foreign affairs (1948), and ambassador to the German Federal Republic (1956–1958). After 1960, Zorin was permanent Soviet representative to the United Nations.

25. Covered in the section of *Conversations with Stalin* called "Disappointments," pp. 173–84, and again the same material in *Rise and Fall,* pp. 163–70.

5

1. Anastas Ivanovich Mikoyan (1895–1979) was an Armenian Communist who was especially prominent as director of Soviet foreign trade (1938–1949) and the food industry (1934–1938). A candidate member of the Politburo as early as 1926, he had become a full member by 1934. He was also deputy prime minister (from 1937). After Stalin's death Mikoyan consistently supported Khrushchev and became one of the most influential leaders of the Soviet Communist Party. In 1964–65 he served as president of the USSR.

2. Bogdan Crnobrnya (1916–1981?) had been a teacher in prewar Yugoslavia who later joined the Partisans. In the years following the war he served as deputy minister of foreign trade and of foreign affairs and after 1955 as Yugoslav ambassador to India.

3. Kliment Yefremovich Voroshilov (1881–1969) was a Soviet soldier and politician. He supported Lenin in 1914 and was associated with Budenny in the First Cavalry Division of Civil War fame. He is credited with reorganizing the Russian general staff, mechanizing the army, and developing an air force while commissar for defense (1925–1940). At the outbreak of World War II he commanded the Leningrad front but lost his command of the northwestern armies that same year (1941) for failing to raise the German siege. (Together with Marshal Zhukov, Voroshilov did finally break the siege, in 1943.) Promoted to the rank of marshal, and as one of Stalin's closest friends and cronies, Voroshilov was made president of the Soviet Union in 1953 (to 1960).

4. In 1848 both the Croats and the Serbs of the Voyvodina area north of Belgrade were driven to ally themselves with the Habsburg monarchy against the Hungarian demand for a more fully representative government. A central moment in that year of revolt came when Baron Joseph Jelačić, who had been appointed *ban* (governor) of Croatia by the emperor in Vienna, invaded Hungary at the head of Croatian forces to suppress the Hungarian uprising (September 1848). Another fatal moment for the Hungarians occurred the following June, when a Russian army dispatched by Tsar Nicholas I invaded from the north.

5. Mátyás Rákosi (1893–1971) was a longtime leader of the Hungarian Communist Party. He held power from 1944 until mid-1956 and went back into exile in the Soviet Union after the Hungarian uprising that fall. He was a Soviet citizen, married to a Russian, and held the rank of brigadier general in the Soviet army at the time he returned to his own country to assume leadership of the Party there.

6. Boris Kidrič (1912–1953) was a leading Slovenian Communist who joined the Party in 1928 and lived the dangerous life of an underground activist. With Kardelj, Kidrič organized the Partisan uprising in Slovenia in 1941. In 1945 he was made premier of Slovenia and continued a harsh program of establishing Communist hegemony there. In 1946 Kidrič was sent to Moscow to study the Soviet economy. From his return in the fall of that year to his death, Kidrič was virtual director of the entire Yugoslav economy. His administration is associated with the ruthless collectivization of agriculture (abandoned after his death) and highly demanding production drives in industry.

7. Dedinje is a hilly district in the southern outskirts of Belgrade, a little to the east of the wooded park of Topčider. It is where the most elegant residences in the city were once located, including Tito's *Beli dvor* (White Palace).

8. Vlko Chervenkov (1900–1980) was one of the Eastern European Communist leaders who spent the 1930s in Moscow. He returned to his country, Bulgaria, only with the victorious Red Army (1944), taking over the secretariat of the Party. Married to Dimitrov's sister, Chervenkov was the figure most prominently identified with the immediate post-Dimitrov era, 1950 to 1956. He remained unchallenged leader for several years after Stalin's death in 1953, bending only slightly, and falling from power finally in 1956, after Khrushchev's denunciation of Stalin and Moscow's reconciliation with Tito.

9. Wladyslaw Gomulka (1905–1982) was secretary-general of the Polish Workers' Party from 1944 to 1948, when his criticism of the Soviet Union led to his demotion and imprisonment (1951–1954). After the 1956 riots in the industrial center of Poznan, which resulted in more independence for Poland from Moscow, Gomulka became first secretary of the Party. In 1970 he resigned following demonstrations over price increases.

10. Jakub Berman (c. 1901–1984) was a Polish politician of Jewish origin, who was a member of Poland's small prewar Communist Party. Berman spent the war in Moscow and returned to Poland with the Soviet army. Closely associated with Stalin's policies, he rose to deputy prime minister between 1954 and 1956, but was expelled from the Party in 1957 in connection with Khrushchev's campaign of de-Stalinization.

11. Kranj is a small city in Slovenia to the north of Ljubljana, Slovenia's capital.

12. Blagoje Nešković (1907–1984) was a Serbian Communist who fought in the Spanish Civil War and joined Tito's Partisans in 1941. In 1945 he was premier of Serbia. A member of the Central Committee of the Yugoslav Communist Party, Nešković was accused of deviation in 1952 and stripped of his posts.

13. See pages 201ff. in *Rise and Fall* for this central incident in the dramatic events and for all subsequent evaluation of the "confrontation" (*sukob*) with Stalin. Some material from the earlier book is quoted verbatim, but it will be found only scattered (though sequentially) through the published text.

14. Topčider is a wooded park in the south of Belgrade off Marshal Tito Street and to the west of Dedinje, the hilltop residential section.

15. Draža Mihailović (1893–1946) was a colonel in the prewar Royal Army who organized the Chetnik resistance to the German occupation in 1941. He was promoted to general and named minister of war by the royal government-in-exile. Mihailović was eventually tracked down by the Partisans in 1946, captured, condemned as a traitor, and executed.

16. All these pages on the Fifth Congress, which represented a kind of postlude to the face-off between Tito and Stalin, follow roughly pages 198–212 in *Rise and Fall*.

6

1. László Rajk (1909–1949) was Hungary's foreign minister. As minister of the interior he had liquidated the middle-class Smallholders party in 1947. Rajk

was yet another of Eastern Europe's home-grown Communists who were purged in favor of Moscow-trained Communists who had spent the war years in Russia. Rajk's show trial was particularly infamous for his avid confession to all possible crimes, starting with being a secret Titoist, plotting the assassination of all the top-ranking Hungarian Communists, and turning his country into a vassal state of Yugoslavia with himself as premier.

2. Markos Vafiadis (1906–1992), commander of the KKE (Democratic Army of Greece) forces during the second Greek Communist uprising (1946–1949). His small guerrilla army had its main strength in the villages as opposed to the urban centers, where the Marxist leader Zachiaridis overruled Markos and his tactics in favor of conventional warfare. Markos was relieved of his command in 1948.

3. See pp. 234–35 in *Rise and Fall.*

4. The White Guards were counterrevolutionary military units in the 1917 Revolution and the civil war that followed. Guards units generally were descended from the elite regiments founded by Peter the Great in the early eighteenth century (Izmailovsky, Semyonov, Preobrazhensky). Color symbolism goes back to the French Revolution, red being the color of blood and always after 1789 being identified with revolution. "White" as a political term originated as the color of the fleur-de-lys, which was identified with the aristocracy. In the Russian Revolution, first there were the Red Guards, then White Guards as their opposite.

5. Alexander S. Suvorov (1729–1800) was a Russian field marshal, born in Finland of Swedish descent, who served in the Seven Years' War (1756–1763), the Russo-Turkish War (1773–1774), and again commanded the Russian army against the Turks (1787–1792). Created a field marshal in 1794, he defeated the French in a number of battles (1799), and was commander in chief of all the Russian armies by 1800, the year of his death.

6. Dean Acheson (1893–1971), by training a lawyer, served as secretary of state in Truman's cabinet from 1949 to 1953. Acheson's foreign policy, in accordance with the recommendations of George Kennan, aimed at the containment of the Soviet Union. Acheson played a leading role in developing the Truman Doctrine, the Marshall Plan, and NATO.

7. Hector McNeil (1907–1955) was minister of state in the British cabinet in the postwar Labour government of Clement Attlee and British representative to the United Nations, 1946–1948. In the latter position, where McNeil had occasion frequently to defend NATO, his chief opponents were Molotov and Vyshinsky.

8. Andrei Januariyevich Vyshinsky (1883–1954) was a Soviet diplomat and lawyer and chief prosecutor in Stalin's show trials (1934–1938). He became foreign minister in 1949 and remained in office until Stalin's death, when he was demoted to deputy foreign minister and permanent delegate to the United Nations.

9. Nikolai Vasilevich Gogol (1809–1852) was a short-story writer, novelist, and dramatist and Russia's first outstanding prose writer. He is known above all for his superb sense of comic hyperbole and grotesque detail.

10. Ernest Bevin (1881–1951) was a British politician and labor leader who devoted his life to union organization. He formed and was general secretary (1921–1940) of the Transport and General Workers' Union, in 1937 becoming its chairman. In 1940 Bevin became minister of labor and national service,

serving in Churchill's war cabinet. As foreign secretary (1945–1951) in the post-war Labour government, Bevin contributed to the formation of NATO.

11. Material in the foregoing paragraphs also appeared in *Rise and Fall,* pp. 263–65.
12. Cf. *Rise and Fall,* pp. 265–66.
13. Branko Ćopić (b. 1915) is a Bosnian writer in the realistic vein, mainly of the 1950s and 1960s, who began publishing his work before the war and has distinguished himself since as both a novelist and a children's poet.

7

1. Brioni (*Brijuni*) is an Adriatic island very close to the tourist center of Pula at the tip of the Istrian peninsula.
2. Senj is a small town opposite the island of Krk on the Croatian section of the Adriatic coast.
3. Aneurin Bevan (1897–1960) was a British politician from Wales. A brilliant orator, he clashed with the Labour Party in 1939 over its ambivalent attitude toward Hitler. As minister of health from 1945 to 1951 he was the architect of the National Health Service.
4. Leskovac is a small Serbian city south of Niš on the road to Macedonia.
5. Skoplje (in Macedonian, Skopje) is the capital of Macedonia and the fourth-largest city in the former Yugoslavia.
6. The original name of this story was "Anatomy of a Moral." It was first published in *Nova Misao* in January 1954, shortly before its author was expelled from the Central Committee. An English-language version of the story, much abridged, appeared that April in *Life* magazine, under the title "A Romance That Rocked Yugoslavia." (Djilas's earnest anatomizing of caste and class, or, perhaps better, of the women and trophy wives of the "new class," was left out of the *Life* version.) Later this same *conte à clef,* now back under its original title, served as the title piece for a collection of eighteen of the author's political essays published in translation by Praeger in 1959 (*Anatomy of a Moral: The Political Essays of Milovan Djilas,* edited by Abraham Rothberg with an introduction by Paul Willen). For the hero and heroine, read Peko Dapčević, the army chief of staff and Djilas's close friend, and Milena Vrajak, his twenty-one-year-old movie actress wife. The haughty lady at the stadium entrance who later encounters "our bride" in the box was said to be Milica S. Vukmanović-Tempo.
7. Throughout this exchange the two women use the formal form of "you," as two people of roughly equal standing who do not know one another. Under the circumstances, however, this "polite plural" is distinctly standoffish, with icy overtones.

8

1. See note 13 to Chapter 1. To the Yugoslav ear, *Land Without Justice* implies that there was no tradition of reprisal, which, of course, was not true. To my ear, the title in English carries a connotation both of general lawlessness and of a rough, frontier kind of "justice." The title in Serbian (*Besudna zemlya*), again, implies rather *Land Without Courts* or *Land Lacking Codified Law.*

2. The sequence of paragraphs is virtually identical to that of the Praeger edition's chapter bearing the title "The New Class." At this point a paragraph apparently was omitted in the original edition of 1957.

3. The essay from which Djilas quoted forms a part of Chapter 7 ("Administrative Systems—Bureaucracy") in Dubin's book, is by Robert Merton, and is titled "The Nature and Sources of Pathological Bureaucratic Behavior." Merton used the term "functionary," easily transferred into Serbian by Djilas. The term is French by origin, a borrowing pure and simple. In all his writings I have seen, Djilas referred to "functionaries," the standard term, ignoring the Russian-derived *činovnik* (clerk) and *službenik* (employee). To my mind, there is little to choose between them—the one occupies a function, the other an office. However, it must be said that the word "functionary" smells of Marxist-Leninist jargon and so conveys the "truth" of a Milovan Djilas freighted by his past.

4. Called "Orlov," another Russian name, in the Praeger edition. I have not checked this apparent discrepancy. The English title would be *Stalin in Power.*

5. Stalin's Thermidor is an allusion to the French Republican calendar of 1793–1806, which for a time replaced the Gregorian one. The date "9 Thermidor" (the word means "heat"), corresponding to July 27, was the date in 1794 when Robespierre was arrested, and the Reign of Terror gave way to a period of reaction that led eventually to Napoleon's *coup d'état* in 1799, bringing the Revolution to an end. "Stalin's Thermidor" will therefore signify "reaction."

6. In succinct Russian, most likely кто кого (kto kavo), literally "who whom," all the rest being supplied by context.

1. Mikhail Aleksandrovich Bakunin (1814–1876) was a Russian radical political leader who worked in exile and had many followers in Italy, Spain, Russia, and elsewhere. In his later years Bakunin was closely associated with the doctrine of anarchy: Russia should be organized on the basis of voluntary association and cooperative production free from state dictates. To this end he advocated the violent destruction of the existing regime by a few leaders who would organize the peasants. It was Bakunin who first formulated the doctrine that a good revolutionary end justifies any means to achieve it.

2. Louis Auguste Blanqui (1805–1881) was a French revolutionary more interested in the practice of revolution than in abstract ideas. He introduced the notion, later taken up by Marx, that revolutions must begin with the temporary dictatorship of an elite devoted to the socialist cause.

3. Pierre Joseph Proudhon (1809–1865) was a French socialist and political theorist. In his treatises *Qu'est-ce que la propriété* (1840) and *Système des contradictions économiques ou philosophie de la misère* (1846) he argued that all property was theft and that in a just society orderly anarchy would replace oppressive government.

4. Georgi Valentinovich Plekhanov (1857–1918) was a political philosopher and chief exponent in Russia of philosophical Marxism. Plekhanov spent about forty years in exile (from 1880), mainly in Geneva, becoming the intellectual leader of the Russian Social Democratic movement. He laid much emphasis on

moving through capitalism to socialism and affected the thought and philosophy of Lenin. Plekhanov opposed the Bolshevik Revolution but is credited with deeply influencing the development of socialist thought and policy in Russia.

5. Yuli Osipovich Martov (1873–1923) was a leader of the Menshevik wing of the Russian Social Democratic Labor Party, both before and after 1917, and as such was an opponent of Lenin, who tried to thwart his bid for personal domination of the Party. Martov believed that social democrats should abstain from power while bourgeois governments prepared the way for a socialist takeover. Martov was ambivalent toward Bolshevik power, opposing White restoration and foreign intervention but at the same time defending the concept of an opposition party (meaning his Mensheviks) within the Soviet system. Having failed in this effort, in 1920 Martov went into exile in Europe, where he continued to oppose the institutionalization of the Bolshevik minority dictatorship.

6. Georg Wilhelm Friedrich Hegel (1770–1831), German philosopher whose system, commonly known as Hegelianism, was the leading philosophy of metaphysics during the second quarter of the nineteenth century.

7. Enrico Berlinguer (1922–1984) was a protégé of Togliatti's who rose to be general secretary of the Italian Communist Party in 1972. From the late 1960s on, Berlinguer consistently made headlines, first by questioning the ouster of Khrushchev and later by defying the Soviet Party line generally. Berlinguer was a champion of compromise with the Christian Democrats, and with every election his Party gained more votes and more seats in the Chamber of Deputies.

8. "Eurocommunism," a term coined in the mid-1970s, meant the trend among the various nonruling European Communist Parties toward independence from Moscow. As a trend it was given a great boost by Tito's defection in 1948, followed by the repression of Hungary's rebellion in 1956 and the invasion of Prague in 1968, not to mention the revelations of Stalin's excesses. As a term, "Eurocommunism" received wide publicity after the publication in Spanish of Santiago Carillo's book, *Eurocomunismo y estado* (1977). However, by the late 1980s, with Gorbachev's encouragement, all Communist Parties were taking independent courses in any case. Eurocommunism was by now the norm.

9. Karl von Clausewitz (1780–1831) was a Prussian army officer who served with the Russian army in 1812. Clausewitz is best remembered for his books on the "science" of war, especially his *Vom Kriege* (3 vols., 1833).

10. Friedrich Engels (1820–1895) was a German socialist. In 1847 he collaborated with Karl Marx on the *Communist Manifesto*. Engels then fled to England, where for almost a decade he was a manufacturer at Manchester (1850–1859). From 1860 to his death he lived in London. Engels was associated with Marx in spreading socialist propaganda, and edited and published Marx's works.

11. Lev Borisovich Kamenev (1883–1936) was a Soviet politician who failed to win a favorable position in the power struggle after Lenin's death in 1924. Kamenev was arrested on charges of being implicated in Kirov's assassination (1934), tried in the first public purge trial (August 1936), and shot.

12. Grigori Yevseyevich Zinoviev (1883–1936) was a Russian Communist leader who joined the Social Democratic Party in 1901 and became associated with Lenin in forming the Bolshevik Party (1903). He was with Lenin in Switzerland during the early years of World War I, returning to Russia in 1917. After Lenin's death in 1924, Zinoviev became allied with Kamenev and Stalin in a

ruling triumvirate, but soon conspired with Kamenev and Trotsky *against* Stalin and was expelled from his various offices (1926–1927). Zinoviev abjectly recanted his opposition in 1928 and was readmitted to the Party, but later was accused of complicity in Kirov's murder, confessed, and was executed along with Kamenev in 1936.

13. Georgi L. Pyatakov (1890–1937) was a Bolshevik leader active in the Civil War and was an early head of the Soviet government in Ukraine (January 1919). Pyatakov was accused of conspiracy in the second purge trial ("trial of the seventeen," January 1937) and shot.

14. Louis Fischer (1896–1970) was an American journalist who from 1922 was the European correspondent of *The Nation* magazine, serving chiefly in Russia. Author of more than twenty books, including *The Life of Lenin,* for which he won a National Book Award in 1964, Fischer spent some fourteen years in Moscow and was fluent in Russian. Besides his works on Lenin and Stalin, he produced a life of Gandhi (1950), wrote on Spain during that country's civil war, and during World War II interviewed all the heads of major governments.

15. Rudolf Slanský (1901–1952) was a Czechoslovak statesman who was the victim of an anti-Semitic purge. Slanský, secretary-general of the Communist Party in Czechoslovakia's postwar government, was among the nine Jews executed for espionage there during Stalin's last years. He was posthumously absolved.

16. An allusion to Dostoyevsky's "percentage" argument, voiced first and most elaborately in *The Possessed* by one of his minor socialist atheists, Shigalyov, and later by his most infamous but also most influential atheist, the Grand Inquisitor in *The Brothers Karamazov.*

17. *Kriti kao zmija noge* (to guard in utmost secrecy)—to conceal as the snake conceals its legs.

18. Lenin's Testament was also dealt with above in the second portion of the section titled "Stalin, Lenin's Heir."

19. Zhu De (or Chu Teh, 1886–1976) was a Chinese soldier, later a marshal, who became a Communist while a student in Germany and who after his return helped organize the Communist uprising against the Guomindang Nationalists in Nanjing (1927). Zhu De joined Mao in 1928 and was made commander of what would later be the People's Liberation Army, a post he retained until 1954.

20. Jiang Gaishek (1886–1975) was a Chinese general and statesman. He joined the revolutionary party of Sun Yat-sen in 1911, worked with him in Canton, and was sent by him to Russia in 1923. Jiang developed the Guomindang army between 1923 and 1925. He broke with Communist extremists and transferred the seat of government to Nanjing in 1927. Jiang first followed a policy of civil war against the Communists between 1927 and 1936 but later, in alliance with them, changed his policy of appeasement toward Japan to one of opposition. As generalissimo he conducted war against Japan from 1937 to 1941. He was president of the National government from October 1943 onward, but was forced to relocate it to Taiwan in 1949.

21. The *zagorje* (land beyond the mountains) is a hilly, very picturesque district outside of Zagreb. It is a region of wooded heights covered with vines, inter-

spersed with parklands through which wind fast-running trout streams. The district is dotted with villages, utterly remote from the world of today, where ancient ways and customs still thrive in their place of origin, villages presided over by the crumbling walls of an ancient castle. Tito was born in the little village of Kumrovec, where his birth house has been converted into a museum. In the courtyard there still stands a monument to him by Antun Avgustinčić.

10

1. Kronstadt is on a fortified island in the Gulf of Finland about twenty miles from today's St. Petersburg, a major fortress and naval base, a training and repair center for the Baltic fleet, and a large mercantile port. It was the site of a revolt in February 1921 by disaffected sailors of the garrison against the new Bolshevik regime, the first big example of left-wing protest from below against Communist domination. The Kronstadt rebellion was suppressed with great brutality by the Communists, specifically Trotsky and Zinoviev, against whom the rebels' demands were levied.

2. Andrei Dmitrievich Sakharov (1921–1989), trained as a physicist, played a key role in developing the Soviet hydrogen bomb in the late 1940s and 1950s and was the youngest person ever to be elected a full member of the Soviet Academy of Sciences. As a human rights activist and therefore a dissident, however, he gave up his emoluments and privileged position in the 1960s. A "repentant scientist" in the manner of Einstein, Sakharov gradually turned his energies against the nuclear danger and spoke out against Soviet repression. His "manifesto," translated into English as *Progress, Coexistence, and Intellectual Freedom* (1968), took the Westernizing, liberal view of worldwide problems to which Djilas makes reference here. Sakharov was awarded the Nobel Peace Prize in 1975. After denouncing the Soviet invasion of Afghanistan, he was exiled by Brezhnev to the closed city of Gorky (1980–1986), where he and his wife were subjected to KGB harassment. After being brought back to Moscow by Gorbachev, Sakharov was elected (April 1989) to the Congress of People's Deputies, where he led a small reform movement and was a very active speaker from the floor.

3. Andrei Alekseyevich Amalrik (1938–1980), trained as a historian, became one of the most honored Soviet dissidents of the younger generation. He was repeatedly exiled in the 1960s and 1970s. His book *Involuntary Journey to Siberia* (1966) was based on the first of these. Amalrik was best known for his pessimistic essay *Will the Soviet Union Survive Until 1984?* (1970), whose ironic title was an allusion to Orwell. (The author mistakenly expected war to break out before that date between China and the USSR.)

4. Alexander Isayevich Solzhenitsyn (b. 1918) is the Russian dissident novelist, memoirist, and historian who first came to literary prominence with the novella *One Day in the Life of Ivan Denisovich* (1962) and then went on to chronicle the underside of Soviet society in several very long and very important works, both fiction and nonfiction: *The First Circle, The Gulag Archipelago,* etc. In 1970, he was awarded the Nobel Prize in Literature. After his expulsion from Russia in 1974, Solzhenitsyn lived in exile in Vermont for many years. He

returned to Russia in 1995, settling into a private home he built for himself outside Moscow.

5. Roy Aleksandrovich Medvedev (b. 1925) is a Russian neo-Marxist historian who has published frequently in the West. His first and best-known work was *Let History Judge* (1973), a massive indictment of Stalinism as historical aberration, an accident that developed into a form of religious psychology referred to by Medvedev as "pseudosocialism."

6. Charter 77 was an organization formed in Prague in 1977 to monitor the Czechoslovak government's adherence to the Helsinki Accord (the U.N. Declaration of Human Rights). The group's initial manifesto was signed by 242 members, including the country's leading dissidents, Václav Havel (now president of the Czech Republic) among them.

7. Nikolai Aleksandrovich Berdyaev (1874–1948) was a Russian philosopher and theologian who flirted briefly with Marxism in his youth but parted from Marxism's materialist viewpoint after the turn of the century in favor of a spiritual emphasis on the power of faith to transform human lives. His major works in English translation are *Spirit and Reality* (1939) and *Slavery and Freedom* (1948).

8. György (Georg) Lukacs (1885–1971) was a Hungarian philosopher and literary critic, writing chiefly in German. Today he is classed as a neo-Marxist, known for his creation of a Marxist aesthetics and his apology for communism, but also for his thoughtful advocacy of literary realists such as Balzac. Lukacs was an admirer of Kafka and one of Thomas Mann's most perceptive early critics. He was in sympathy with the Hungarian uprising of 1956 and even had an official position in the Imre Nagy government. Lukacs was punished briefly by exile in Romania after the revolt was suppressed by the Soviet army, but returned to Hungary after a few months to become an ornament of the Kadar regime.

9. Herbert Marcuse (1898–1979) was a German-born political philosopher and social critic who published in English after emigrating to New York in 1934. He was associated first with the Institute for Social Research attached to Columbia, and later with Brandeis University, where he held a permanent professorship. The works for which he is most famous are *Reason and Revolution* (1941), *Eros and Civilization* (1955), and *One-Dimensional Man* (1964).

10. Roger Garaudy (b. 1913) is a French philosopher who was active politically in the French Communist Party (1966–1970), in the National Assembly (1956–1958), and in the National Senate (1959–1962). He also directed the Center for Marxist Research and Study (1960–1970), and was editorial head of the radical French journal *Alternatives socialistes.* Garaudy advocates a pluralistic Marxism that assimilates such worldviews as existentialism, structuralism, Christianity, and empiricism. His major book has been *Marxism in the Twentieth Century* (1970).

11. Rudi Dutschke (1940–1979) was a German radical student leader and Marxist scholar who was at the forefront of the student revolt in the late 1960s. His one major theoretical publication (1974) was *Versuch, Lenin auf die Füsse zu stellen* (An Attempt to Stand Lenin on His Feet).

12. Daniel Cohn-Bendit (b. 1945), a student of sociology at the University of Nanterre in France, who exemplifies the spirit of the student demonstrations in Paris in May 1968. Believing that peaceful demonstrations were as outmoded as

parliamentary politics, Cohn-Bendit advocated the occupation of university campuses and their conversion into "anti-universities" to debate problems of capitalism and imperialism. Cohn-Bendit's book cited by Djilas called into question the very role of a vanguard party and exalted spontaneity in the revolutionary process. He later became active in the (ecologist) Green Party in Germany.

13. Both these words, with appended articles ("the labor," "the work"), appear in English in Djilas's manuscript. Arendt quotes from Locke's *Second Treatise of Civil Government,* "The labour of our body and the work of our hands" (p. 79 of *The Human Condition*) at the start of her critical chapter on Marx. Djilas may have chosen his words from this citation.

14. William D. Haywood (1869–1928) was a labor activist at about the turn of the century in the leadership of the Western Federation of Miners and the Industrial Workers of the World.

15. *Bodalsya telyonok s dubom* (The oak and the calf went head to head, butted each other), a Russian saying employed by Solzhenitsyn as title for his 1975 memoir, alluding, of course, to his own position vis-à-vis the government apparatus. It was translated by Harry Willets as *The Oak and the Calf* (New York: Harper & Row, 1979, 1980) and has been referred to ever since by that curtailed rendering.

16. Vladimir Emelyanovich Maksimov (pseud., b. 1932) is a poet, story writer, and novelist who emigrated to Paris in 1974 after his second novel, *Quarantine,* began circulating in *samizdat* and he was expelled from the Writers' Union. (Since then he has completed a third novel, *Farewell from Nowhere.*) Maksimov, who was much respected by Solzhenitsyn, agreed to be the editor of *Kontinent.* This is a quarterly journal published in Russian and German whose first issue appeared in late 1974 in Frankfurt-am-Main, with contributions by Solzhenitsyn, Sinyavsky, Ionesco, Brodsky, and Sakharov. *Kontinent,* true to its main sponsor (Solzhenitsyn), adopted a neo-Slavophile political line.

17. Andrei Donatovich Sinyavsky (b. 1925) writes what he himself has called "phantasmagoric" stories. These were smuggled abroad and published in the West under the pseudonym Abram Tertz. One of the best known of his tales in English was called "The Makepeace Experiment" (in Russian, *Lyubimov*—the word derives from "beloved"), whose principal character vainly attempts to create an ideal life for his fellow townsmen. The satire lies in an analogy to the history of Russia whose rulers were in truth often preoccupied with doing good for their subjects. Together with another writer who had published satires abroad under a pseudonym (Yuli Daniel, a.k.a. Nikolay Arzhak), Sinyavsky/Tertz was brought to trial in early 1966 and sentenced to seven years' imprisonment for "anti-Soviet propaganda."

18. Vladimir Nikolaevich Voinovich (b. 1932) is a comic, satirical writer of short novels arising from the inauthenticity of Soviet reality. His finest work, *The Life and Extraordinary Adventures of Private Ivan Chonkin* (tr. 1977), exemplifies his style. Voinovich is yet another writer whose work circulated in *samizdat* and had to be published abroad in translation before it ever appeared in Russian. ("Chonkin" was printed in Russian in Paris in 1979.) He and his family were forced to emigrate to West Germany late in 1980.

19. Nikolay Alekseyevich Nekrasov (1821–1878) was a poet of the mid-nineteenth century who became the leading exponent of the realist and "civic" tendency in Russian poetry. He was best known for his narrative poems about peasant life that took advantage of the devices of folk song (*The Pedlars,* 1861; *Frost the Red-Nosed,* 1863). A lengthy satirical poem in unrhymed verse, *Who Can Be Happy in Russia?* (1873–1876), exemplifies the civic tendency in Nekrasov's verse.

20. Ivan Alekseyevich Bunin (1870–1953) was a leading author of the late nineteenth and twentieth centuries, a lyric poet and prose writer who emigrated in 1918. Settling in France, he continued to publish and was the first Russian man of letters (before Solzhenitsyn in 1970) to be awarded and to accept the Nobel Prize for Literature (1933). Bunin is known as an émigré writer, even though he published important work long before the Revolution of 1917, including his much-anthologized masterpiece *The Gentleman from San Francisco* (1915).

21. Boka Kotorska (Bay of Kotor; Spanish *boca,* "mouth") is a large estuary and natural harbor in the Adriatic on the border with Albania, prized for its dramatic beauty and the site of resorts.

22. This last section in the present chapter was included as a newspaper clipping and bears the dateline "end of August 1991."

11

1. The author is perhaps referring here to the period immediately following NEP, which came to an end in 1929 with the first five-year plan. These plans, of course, set goals for industrialization, among other line items such as agricultural output, real wages, etc.

2. The text has "Atlantic Pact." I have substituted NATO.

3. Robert Owen (1771–1858) was a British philanthropist and manufacturer responsible for the betterment of working conditions and housing. He established model communities in Indiana (New Harmony, 1825) and elsewhere (Scotland, 1826, Ireland, 1831, England, 1839).

4. Claude Henri de Rouvroy, Compte de Saint-Simon (1760–1825), was the founder of French socialism. His book *Du système industriel* (1821) advocated an industrial state in which poverty is eliminated and in which science replaces religion as the spiritual authority.

5. Charles Fourier (1772–1837) was a French socialist who advocated the organization of society on cooperative principles. Fourier sought the abolition of all restrictions, including marriage, and set out his plan of an ideal society in *Le Nouveau Monde industriel* (1829–1830).

6. The writer is referring to the controversy between Slavophiles and Westerners, or Westernizers, in nineteenth-century intellectual history. In our own history books Panslavism is more narrowly identified with the 1870s official policy that Russia should protect the Serbs, Bulgarians, and other coreligionists in the Balkans against the Ottoman Turks. I am not sure why he calls Slavophilism, a broad social and cultural movement, "Panslavism." That Solzhenitsyn falls into the Slavophile camp may be true, but to say he is Panslavist seems anachronistic.

7. Canossa, the name of a castle in North Italy, has come to mean any forced compromise by a lay authority with an ecclesiastical one—in effect, submission. Djilas seems to use the term loosely, symbolically. If his analogy were carried out to the letter, Moscow would = the Holy Roman Empire submitting to Belgrade = the Papistry, which in turn would imply that the spiritual center of communism had shifted to Yugoslavia. The original event in question occurred in 1077 and involved rights of churchly investiture of laypersons.

8. This is a sensitive passage. The Serbian word *natsija* (nation) is often used to refer not to national states or homogeneous peoples in the West European sense but to communities bonded by a common religion or cultural practices. "Ethnic" doesn't apply either. The Muslims, Catholic Croats, and Orthodox Serbs of Bosnia are "ethnically" of the same origin and all speak the same language. For lack of better, I have had recourse to the awkward phrase "cultural and religious communities."

A BIOGRAPHICAL NOTE
ON THE AUTHOR

1. Regarding Djilas's imprisonments, he was sentenced to fifteen years and served nine all told, as his son correctly states. A reader may be confused by the discrepancy between years indicated as a sentence and years in fact served. Djilas was subjected to four trials in all. The first of these took place in January 1954 and ended in a verdict of up to one and a half years of conditional imprisonment, a term he did not actually serve. After his arrest in November 1956 for his statement the previous month on the Hungarian intervention and a subsequent article in *The New Leader,* Djilas was again tried and sentenced to three years in prison. While still there he was tried and sentenced to seven years more for *The New Class.* Released conditionally early in 1961, Djilas was rearrested in April 1962 (for *Conversations with Stalin*), and after still another trial, held in secret, received still another sentence, this time for five years. In July 1962 he entered Sremska Mitrovica prison for the second and last time (in the "new" Yugoslavia he had done so much to create), and was finally set free "unconditionally" on the last day of 1966.

   In sum, Djilas was sentenced to a total of fifteen years (plus the one and a half "conditional" years) but actually served a total of nine, in two stretches, 1956–61 and 1962–66. To this total one may add the three years spent in prison (the selfsame prison, ironically, Sremska Mitrovica) in the "old," prewar Yugoslavia, as described in Chapter One. See his final book of memoirs, *Rise and Fall,* pp. 377–404, for details.

IN LIEU OF AN
EPILOGUE

1. Dobrica Ćosić (b. 1921) is a Serbian writer known for his three novels, *Distant Is the Sun* (Daleko je sunce, 1951), *Roots* (Koreni, 1954), and *Divisions* (Deobe, 1962).

2. The statement by Milovan Djilas read as follows:

> The replacement of President Ćosić is especially significant in the way it was carried out, which was conspiratorial. Much may have changed, but settling accounts with one's political opponents has essentially remained the same. This legacy of settling scores is venemously confirmed by accusing people with different opinions of having committed mortal, political sins. No one of intelligence and honor, even without knowing Ćosić personally, can believe that it so much as crossed the mind of a man with such a biography and such views to prepare a *coup d'état*. It is sad and tragic for our political situation that he has been replaced at the initiative of the far right and with the blessing and approval of a party that boasts of being Eurosocialist.
>
> In any case, when it comes to basic political issues, especially recently, Ćosić did not fundamentally differ from official policy. He stood apart in his personal style, his personal initiatives, his refusal to be merely a decorative figurehead, to take a posture that is painful, wicked, destructive. For our prevailing relationships this was simply too much to bear, that such figureheads cannot, will not, be politically useful.

3. Matija Bećković (b. 1939) is a Serbian poet considered representative of the younger generation of Belgrade poets.
4. Živojin Pavlović (b. 1933) is a Serbian prose writer and film director.
5. Borislav-Mihiz Mihajlović (b. 1922) is a Serbian poet, literary critic, and dramatist considered (in the 1960s) to be one of the liveliest critics of Serbian literature. He has enjoyed a particularly wide popular response to his dramatizations and dramas.
6. Jovan Skerlić (1877–1914) was a Serb who was an influential professor at the University of Belgrade and one of the greatest literary critics and historians of the early twentieth century.
7. Ivo Andrić (1892–1975) was a professional diplomat, short story writer, novelist, and general man of letters from Bosnia who was awarded the Nobel Prize in Literature for 1961. Though he was cited for one of his novels, *Bridge on the Drina* (Na Drini ćuprija, 1945), Andrić wrote other, equally distinguished fiction. He and Miroslav Krleža, both prolific writers and much translated, both considered for the Nobel Prize, also had much that set them apart and have frequently been juxtaposed in Yugoslav critical thought.

REMARKS
BY THE EDITOR

1. Several of the essays mentioned here have been dropped, as having appeared before in English translation.

INDEX

A NOTE ON THE TYPE

This book was set in ITC Esprit, a typeface designed by Jovica Veljović and issued by the International Typeface Corporation in 1985. This lively type is built on a transitional roman structure and is characterized by large x-height, small aperture, and exaggerated serifs, spurs, and ball terminals. Jovica Veljović received his master's degree in calligraphy and lettering at the Academy of Applied Arts in Belgrade. He now lives in Germany and teaches type design and calligraphy at the Fachhochschule Hamburg. Among the other faces he has designed are Adobe Ex Ponto, ITC Veljovic, and ITC Gamma.

COMPOSED BY STRATFORD PUBLISHING SERVICES, INC., BRATTLEBORO, VERMONT

PRINTED AND BOUND BY BERRYVILLE GRAPHICS, BERRYVILLE, VIRGINIA

DESIGNED BY MISHA BELETSKY